Alfresco Developer Guide

Customizing Alfresco with actions, web scripts, web forms, workflows, and more

Jeff Potts

PUBLISHING

BIRMINGHAM - MUMBAI

Alfresco Developer Guide

First published: October 2008

Production Reference: 3041208

Published by Packt Publishing Ltd.
32 Lincoln Road
Olton
Birmingham, B27 6PA, UK.

ISBN 978-1-847193-11-7

www.packtpub.com

Cover Image by Karl Moore (karl.moore@ukonline.co.uk)

Credits

Author

Jeff Potts

Reviewers

Alan Fehr

James Urquhart

Jean Barmash

Jens Schuetter

Michael Ruflin

Xavier Naud

Senior Acquisition Editor

David Barnes

Development Editor

Nikhil Bangera

Technical Editors

Aditi Srivastava

John Antony

Copy Editor

Sneha Kulkarni

Editorial Team Leader

Mithil Kulkarni

Project Manager

Abhijeet Deobhakta

Project Coordinator

Rajashree Hamine

Indexer

Rekha Nair

Proofreader

Chris Smith

Production Coordinator

Aparna Bhagat

Cover Work

Aparna Bhagat

About the Author

Jeff Potts leads the industry's largest group of certified Alfresco consultants as the Director of the Enterprise Content Management Practice at Optaros, a global consulting firm focused on assembling Next Generation Internet solutions featuring open source components. Jeff has over 10 years of ECM practice leadership and over 16 years of IT and technology implementation experience in IT departments and professional services organizations.

Jeff began working with and blogging about Alfresco in November of 2005. In 2006 and 2007, Jeff published a series of Alfresco tutorials and published them on his blog, `ecmarchitect.com`. That work, together with other Community activity in Alfresco's forum, Wiki site, and Jira earned him Alfresco's 2007 Community Contributor of the Year Award. The same year, Optaros earned Alfresco's Global Partner of the Year and Implementation of the Year awards.

Jeff's areas of business expertise include document management, content management, workflow, collaboration, portals, and search. Throughout his consulting career he has worked on a number of projects for Fortune 500 clients across the Media and Entertainment, Airline, Consumer Packaged Goods, and Retail sectors using technology such as Alfresco, Documentum, Java, XSLT, IBM WebSphere, and Lotus Domino.

Prior to Optaros, Jeff was a Vice President at Hitachi Consulting (formerly Navigator Systems, Inc.) where he founded and grew the ECM practice around legacy knowledge management, document management, Web Content Management (WCM), and collaboration solutions, in addition to custom development.

Jeff is a frequent speaker at Alfresco and Content Management industry events and has written articles for technical journals. This is his first book.

This book would not have been possible without Optaros. What an awesome place to work and what a stellar team to work with. Thanks to Bob Gett, Mavis Chin, and Marc Osofsky for providing an incredible level of senior leadership support. Dave Gynn, John Eckman, and Seth Gottlieb (we miss you, Seth!) also provided early inspiration and counsel. Noreen Vincent helped with marketing and promo. Optaros colleagues from around the world rolled up their sleeves and dug in with code and technical editing: Olivier Pépin, Brian Doyal, Xavier Naud, Jens Scheutter, Alan Fehr, and Michael Ruflin all gave incredible amounts of thorough and thoughtful feedback. The book is significantly better than it would have been because of your involvement.

Alfresco has been tremendously supportive of and excited about this project. Thanks to John Powell, John Newton, Matt Asay, Dr. Ian Howells, Paul Holmes-Higgin, Luis Sala, Phil Robinson, Michael Uzquiano, and Nancy Garrity for providing information and support and for building such a cool platform. Alfresco team members also pitched in with technical reviews: David Caruana, James Urquhart, Jean Barmash, and Peter Monks spent time reading chapters and providing feedback when they probably should have been cranking out 3.0 code.

David Barnes at Packt Publishing deserves thanks for suggesting the project and getting it on track. Rajashree Hamine and Nikhil Bangera have done a great job holding me to task and handling everything on the Packt side.

My ecmarchitect.com readers deserve a big thanks. Your helpful feedback and encouragement motivated me to keep posting. I look forward to continuing the conversation.

Finally, to Christy, Justin, and Caroline: Thank you for putting up with the late nights and lost weekends, providing so much encouragement, and being so understanding.

About the Reviewers

Alan Fehr is a Senior Consultant at Optaros. He has worked on a number of Alfresco projects and was responsible for the client project that eventually turned into DoCASU (Optaros' open source, custom user interface for Alfresco). Alan holds an M. Sc. in Computer Science from the Swiss Federal Institute of Technology in Zurich.

Jean Barmash is the Director of Technical Services at Alfresco, the Open Source Enterprise Content Management Company. In that role, he helps Alfresco customers and partners to design and architect content-centric solutions based on the Alfresco platform. Additionally, he frequently conducts training sessions and works with the Alfresco community to share his expertise.

Jean brings a wealth of experience in different areas of technology creation, including architecture, management, development, and training. Most recently, he consulted to several Wall Street firms and ran the technology training program for one of the leading investment banks.

Jean is a frequent speaker at industry events such as the Enterprise 2.0 Conference, Open Source Business Conference, and IT Architect Regional Conference in New York, and is active in the NY Tech community.

I'd like to thank Peter Monks for being a great mentor, as I learned a tremendous amount from working with him.

Jens Schuetter has 10 years of experience in building and designing J2EE solutions with a focus on content aggregation and travel portals.

In the beginning of his career, Jens worked as an e-business consultant in the south of France for clients such as Amadeus and IBM. He later joined Amadeus, where he developed and designed market-leading products for the travel industry. In 2006 he co-founded Travenues where he helped to launch launch `ixigo.com`, today India's foremost travel infomediary. Recently, he worked as Technical Lead for Optaros on several large-scale implementations of the Alfresco ECM. He holds a Master in Computer Science from Bielefeld University.

Michael Ruflin is a Senior Consultant at Optaros, Inc. with several years experience in designing and developing Java, J2EE and PHP software applications. Michael has worked on several Alfresco projects including a document management and collaborative workspace solution based on Alfresco, JSF, and OpenOffice and, most recently, as a member of the Alfresco 3.0 Share development team. Michael Ruflin holds a Master's Degree in Computer Science from the Swiss Federal Institute of Technology in Lausanne (EFPL).

Table of Contents

Preface

Alfresco is the leading open source platform for Enterprise Content Management. The progress the Alfresco Engineering team has made since that first production release in June of 2005 has simply been amazing. The platform is well on its way to fulfilling its vision of becoming a viable alternative to those from legacy vendors who simply cannot keep up with the pace of innovation inherent in a solution assembled from open source components.

This book takes you through the process of customizing and extending the Alfresco platform. It uses a fictitious professional services company called "SomeCo" as an example. SomeCo has decided to roll out Alfresco across the enterprise. Your job is to take advantage of Alfresco's extension mechanism, workflow engine, and various APIs to meet the requirements from SomeCo's various departments.

Although many customizations can be made by editing XML and properties files, this book is focused on developers. That might mean writing Java code against the foundation API to implement an action or a behavior, maybe creating some server-side JavaScript to use as the controller of a RESTful web script, or perhaps implementing custom business logic in an advanced workflow. The point is that all but the most basic implementations of any ECM platform require code to be written. The goal of this book is to help you identify patterns, techniques, and specific steps that you can use to become productive on the platform more quickly.

By the end of this book, you will have stepped through every aspect of the Alfresco platform. You will have performed the same types of customizations and extensions found in typical Alfresco implementations. Most importantly, when someone comes to you and asks, "How would you do this in Alfresco?", you'll have at least one answer and maybe even some source code to go with it.

What This Book Covers

Chapter 1 is for people new to the Alfresco platform. It walks you through the capabilities of Alfresco and gives some examples of the types of solutions that can be built on the platform. You'll also learn what tools and skills are required to implement Alfresco-based solutions.

Chapter 2 is about getting your development environment set up. Like preparing for a home improvement project, this is the trip to the hardware store to get the tools and supplies you'll need to get the job done. Throughout the book, you will be building and deploying changes. So just as in any software development project, it pays to get that process working up front. You'll also learn about the debugging tools that are available to you. The chapter includes a short and simple customization example to test out your setup.

Chapter 3 starts where all Alfresco projects should begin: defining the content model. You'll learn how to define the content model as well as how to expose the model to the Alfresco web client. Once you've got it in place, you'll write some Java code that utilizes the Web Services API to test out the model. This will also be your first taste of the JavaScript API. The exercises set up the initial content model for SomeCo.

Chapter 4 begins to show you the power of the repository by exposing you to some of the mechanisms or hooks that can be used to perform "hands off" operations on content. You'll learn about actions, behaviors, transformers, and metadata extractors. The exercises include implementing a rule action for SomeCo's Human Resources department to help manage HR policies, writing a custom behavior to calculate user ratings, and writing a custom metadata extractor to make Microsoft Project files indexable by the Lucene search engine.

Chapter 5 takes you through web client customizations. First, it establishes whether or not you should be customizing the web client at all. Once that's out of the way, you learn how to add new menu items, how to create your own custom component renderers, and how to define new dialogs and wizards. Examples in this chapter include writing a new "Execute Script" UI Action to make it easier to run server-side JavaScript, creating a "Stoplight" component to graphically show project status, and creating a multi-step wizard SomeCo's HR department can use to set up job interviews.

Chapter 6 focuses on the web script framework. Web scripts are an important part of the platform because they allow you to expose the repository through a RESTful API. They are also core to the Surf framework that is in the 3.0 release. The exercises in this chapter are about creating a set of URLs that can be called from the frontend web site to retrieve and persist user ratings of objects in the repository.

Chapter 7 is about advanced workflows. You'll learn how the embedded JBoss jBPM workflow engine works and how to define your own workflows, including how to implement your own business logic. The chapter includes a comparison between the capabilities of Alfresco's simple workflow and advanced workflow so that you can decide which one is appropriate for your needs. By the end of the chapter, you will have built a workflow that SomeCo will use to review and approve Whitepapers for external publication. The process includes an asynchronous step, which leverages the web script knowledge you gained in the previous chapter.

Chapter 8 takes you through the key developer-related aspects of Alfresco's Web Content Management functionality. The chapter is not an exhaustive WCM how-to. Rather, the chapter starts with a simple web form and then quickly moves to using the API to work with WCM assets. You'll also leverage advanced workflow and web script techniques you learned in previous chapters to work with WCM sites and assets. You'll create a "no approval" workflow that SomeCo will use for Job Postings and web scripts developers can use to deploy web sites to test servers and to commit changes to staging.

Chapter 9 covers a variety of security-related topics. You'll learn how to define your own custom roles, and how to create users and groups with the API. Although not strictly developer-centric, you'll also learn how to configure Alfresco to authenticate and synchronize with an LDAP directory and how to implement Single Sign-On (SSO) between Alfresco and other web resources.

A set of Appendices is included at the end of the book. There you'll find reference information such as the JavaScript API, a set of diagrams showing the out-of-the-box content model, and a list of the out-of-the-box public spring beans.

Appendix C is available for download from the book's page on `Packtpub.com`. You can visit `http://www.packtpub.com/files/3117_AppendixC.pdf` to directly download it. It includes a section on packaging and deploying AMPs, and an overview of the new Surf framework.

What You Need for This Book

To work through the examples in this book, you will need:

- Alfresco. Either Enterprise or Labs will work. The examples have been tested on 2.2 Enterprise and 3.0 Labs. Chapter 2 provides further details on obtaining Alfresco.
- Alfresco SDK.
- Apache Ant.
- Apache Tomcat.
- Eclipse, although other IDEs (or even a text editor) will work.

There are other tools or libraries that you will need for certain exercises, which will be mentioned as necessary.

Who This Book is For

This book will be most useful to developers who are writing code to customize Alfresco for their organization or who are creating custom applications that sit on top of Alfresco.

This book is for Java developers, and you will get most from the book if you already work with Java, but you need not have prior experience on Alfresco. Although Alfresco makes heavy use of open source frameworks such as Spring, Hibernate, JavaServer Faces, and Lucene, no prior experience using these is assumed or necessary.

Conventions

In this book, you will find a number of styles of text that distinguish between different kinds of information. Here are some examples of these styles, and an explanation of their meaning.

Code words in text are shown as follows: "The question mark in the user value placeholder declares the argument as optional."

A block of code will be set as follows:

```
{"rating" :
  {
     "average" : "1.923",
     "count" : "13",
  }
}
```

When we wish to draw your attention to a particular part of a code block, the relevant lines or items will be made bold:

```
enableLookups="false" disableUploadTimeout="true"
acceptCount="100" scheme="https" secure="true"
clientAuth="false" sslProtocol="TLS"
keystoreFile="/root/.keystore"
keystorePass="changeit"
```

Any command-line input and output is written as follows:

```
<process-definition xmlns="urn:jbpm.org:jpdl-3.1" name="scwf:
publishWhitepaper">
```

New terms and **important words** are introduced in a bold-type font. Words that you see on the screen, in menus or dialog boxes for example, appear in our text like this: "Click the **Browse Website** link in the **Staging Sandbox** ."

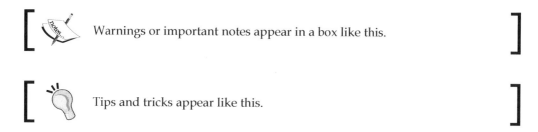

Warnings or important notes appear in a box like this.

Tips and tricks appear like this.

Reader Feedback

Feedback from our readers is always welcome. Let us know what you think about this book, what you liked or may have disliked. Reader feedback is important for us to develop titles that you really get the most out of.

To send us general feedback, simply drop an email to feedback@packtpub.com, making sure to mention the book title in the subject of your message.

If there is a book that you need and would like to see us publish, please send us a note in the **SUGGEST A TITLE** form on www.packtpub.com or email suggest@packtpub.com.

If there is a topic that you have expertise in and you are interested in either writing or contributing to a book, see our author guide on www.packtpub.com/authors.

Customer Support

Now that you are the proud owner of a Packt book, we have a number of things to help you to get the most from your purchase.

Downloading the Example Code for the Book

Visit http://www.packtpub.com/files/code/3117_Code.zip to directly download the example code.

The downloadable files contain instructions on how to use them.

Errata

Although we have taken every care to ensure the accuracy of our contents, mistakes do happen. If you find a mistake in one of our books—maybe a mistake in text or code—we would be grateful if you would report this to us. By doing this you can save other readers from frustration, and help to improve subsequent versions of this book. If you find any errata, report them by visiting http://www.packtpub.com/support, selecting your book, clicking on the **let us know** link, and entering the details of your errata. Once your errata are verified, your submission will be accepted and the errata added to the list of existing errata. The existing errata can be viewed by selecting your title from http://www.packtpub.com/support.

Piracy

Piracy of copyright material on the Internet is an ongoing problem across all media. At Packt, we take the protection of our copyright and licenses very seriously. If you come across any illegal copies of our works in any form on the Internet, please provide the location address or website name immediately so we can pursue a remedy.

Please contact us at copyright@packtpub.com with a link to the suspected pirated material.

We appreciate your help in protecting our authors, and our ability to bring you valuable content.

Questions

You can contact us at questions@packtpub.com if you are having a problem with some aspect of the book, and we will do our best to address it.

1
The Alfresco Platform

This chapter introduces the Alfresco platform and answers the question, "What can I do with this thing?" A few examples will be provided to help answer this question from the "solving business problems" perspective. The chapter then skims over basic configuration and customization before introducing the advanced customization concepts covered throughout the book. The chapter concludes with a brief discussion on the different Alfresco editions that are available.

In this chapter, we will go through the following points:

- Examples of practical solutions built on Alfresco
- High-level components of the Alfresco platform
- Examples of the types of customizations that you will likely perform as a part of your implementation
- Technologies you will use to extend the platform

Alfresco in the Real World

Alfresco will tell you that the product is a platform for **Enterprise Content Management (ECM)**. But ECM is a somewhat nebulous and nefarious term. What does it really mean? It depends on who is saying it. ECM vendors usually use it as an umbrella term to describe a collection of content-centric technologies that includes:

- **Document Management (DM)**: Capturing, organizing, and sharing binary files. These files are typically produced from office productivity software, but the scope of the files being managed is unlimited.
- **Web Content Management (WCM)**: Managing files and content specifically intended to be delivered to the Web. The key theme of WCM is to reduce the "web developer" bottleneck and empower non-technical content owners to publish their own content.

- **Digital Asset Management (DAM)**: Managing graphics, video, and audio. You can think of this as DM with added functionality specific to the needs of working with rich media such as thumbnailing, transcoding, and editing. Like WCM, the intent is to streamline the production process.

- **Records Management (RM)**: Managing content as a legal record. Like DAM, RM starts with DM and adds functionality specific to the world of RM such as retention policies, records plans, and audit trails.

- **Imaging**: This includes capturing, tagging, and routing images of documents from scanners.

Most people will also include Collaboration, Search, and occasionally, Portals as well.

Practitioners have a different perspective. They will say that ECM is less about the technology and more about how you capture, organize, and share information across the entire enterprise. For them, the "how" is more important than the "what".

What's important to know from an Alfresco perspective is that Alfresco is a platform for doing all these things.

So rather than worrying about a concise definition of ECM, let's look at a few examples to illustrate how clients are using Alfresco today, particularly in Alfresco's sweet spots such as Document Management and Web Content Management.

Basic Document Management

Alfresco started its life as a document management repository with some basic services for document management. Alfresco focused on this smart area initially for two reasons. First, it allowed Alfresco to establish a strong foundation and then build upon that foundation by expanding into other areas of ECM, with WCM being the prime example. Second, there is a huge market for systems that can manage unstructured content (aka "documents"). The market is so big because document management is a problem for everyone. All companies generate files that benefit from the kind of features document management provides such as check-in/check-out, versioning, metadata, security, full-text search, and workflow.

Examples of classic document management are often found in manufacturing, packaged goods, or other companies with large research and development divisions. As you can imagine, companies such as these deal with thousands of documents every day. The documents are in a variety of formats and languages, and are created and leveraged by many different types of stakeholders from various parts of the company.

The critical functionality required for basic document management includes things such as:

- **Easy integration with authoring tools**: If users can't get documents into and out of the repository easily, user adoption will suffer. This means users must be able to open and save documents to the repository from applications such as Microsoft Office, Microsoft Windows Explorer, and email.

- **Security**: Many documents, particularly legal documents and anything around new product development, are very sensitive. Employees must be able to log in with their normal username and password, and see only the documents they have access to.

- **Library services**: This is a grouping of foundational document management functionality that includes check-in/check-out, versioning, metadata, and search. The ability to offer these library services is one of the things that sets a document repository apart from a plain file system.

- **Workflow**: Quite literally, workflow describes the "flow of work" or business process related to a document. Requirements vary widely in this area and not everyone will leverage workflows right away. Workflows can be used to streamline and automate manual business processes by letting the document management system keep track of who needs to do what to a document at any particular time.

- **Scalability/Reliability**: The system needs to scale in order to support several hundred or more users and hundreds of thousands or even millions of documents with some percentage of growth each year. Because the repository holds content that's critical to the business, it needs to be highly available.

- **Customizable user interface**: The out of the box Alfresco web client is made for generic document management, which may be appropriate in many cases. Most clients will want to make at least some customizations to the web client to help increase productivity and improve user adoption.

The following diagram shows an example of high-level architecture to understand how basic document management might be implemented:

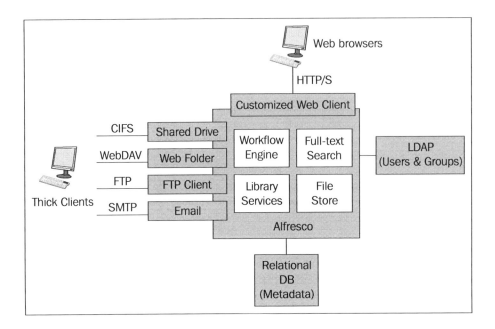

The diagram shows a single instance of Alfresco authenticating against **LDAP**. Some content managers are using the web client via **HTTP/S**, while others are using Windows Explorer, Microsoft Office, and other **Thick Clients** to work with content via one or more protocols such as **CIFS**, **WebDAV**, **FTP**, or **SMTP**. As noted in the diagram, Alfresco stores metadata in a **Relational DB** and the actual content files on the file system.

Most of the techniques for customizing Alfresco for DM solutions apply to other ECM solutions such as WCM, RM, Imaging, and DAM. Of course, there are business concepts and technical implementation details specific to each that make them unique, but the details provided in this book apply to all because the specialized solutions are built as extensions to the core Alfresco repository. WCM is built on the core repository as well, but the functionality it adds is significant enough to warrant a closer look.

Web Content Management

On the surface, WCM is very similar to document management. In both cases, content owners store files in a repository. Often, the content is assigned metadata, is secured, is indexed for search, and is routed through a workflow. The most obvious difference between DM and WCM is that the content being managed is meant specifically to be published on a web site or as part of a web application. Beyond that high-level distinction, there are several other differences that make WCM worthy of separate discussion. These include:

- Content authoring tools used to create content
- Separation of presentation from content
- Systematic publication or deployment of content

Let's briefly look at each of these.

Content Authoring Tools

The majority of document management solutions deal with files generated by an office suite. Of course, there are exceptions such as various types of graphics files, CAD/CAM drawing formats, and other specialized tools. But mostly, the files are generated by a small number of different tools and an even smaller number of different software vendors.

In the case of WCM, there is a wide variety of tools involved from text editors to **Integrated Development Environments** (**IDEs**) to graphics programs with multiple vendors in each category. This means the WCM solution needs to be very flexible in the way it integrates with authoring tools. The alternative, which is forcing authors to give up their favorite tools in favor of a standard, can be a management nightmare.

Separation of Presentation from Content

WCM does not require the separation between content's appearance on the web site and its storage. But many implementations take advantage of this principle because it makes redesigning the site easier, facilitates multi-channel publishing, and enables people to author content without web skills.

To understand why this is so, think about a web site that has its content and presentation of that content merged together. When it is time to redesign the site, you have to touch every single web page because every page contains presentation markup. Similarly, content authoring is limited to people with technical skills. Otherwise, there is a risk that the content owner (for example, the person writing a press release or a job posting) will inadvertently clobber the page design.

One way to address this is to separate the content (the press release copy) from the presentation of that content. A common way to do that is to store the content as presentation-independent XML. The XML can then be transformed into any presentation that's needed. A redesign is as simple as changing the presentation in a single place, and then regenerating all of the pages.

The impact of separating content from presentation is three-fold. First, assuming the content consumers aren't interested in reading raw XML, something has to be responsible for transforming the content. Depending on the implementation, it may be up to the WCM system or a frontend web application.

Second, in the case of static content, any change in the underlying content has to trigger a transformation so that the presentation will be up-to-date, keeping in mind that there may be more than one file affected by the change. For example, data from a job posting appears in the job posting detail as well as the list of job postings. If the posting and the job posting index are both static, the list has to be regenerated whenever the job posting changes.

Third, content authors lose the benefit of **WYSIWYG (What You See Is What You Get)** content authoring because the content doesn't immediately look the way it will as soon as it is published to the web site. The WCM system, then, has to be able to let content authors "preview" the content as they author it, preferably in the context of the entire site.

Systematic Publication or Deployment

A Document Management system is a lot like a relational database in the sense that it is typically an authoritative, centralized repository. There are exceptions, but for the most part, content resides in the repository and is retrieved by the systems and applications that need it. On the other hand, a WCM system often faces a publication or deployment challenge. Files go into the repository, but must be delivered somewhere to be consumed. This might happen on a schedule, at the request of a user, as part of a workflow, or all of the above. Granted, some web sites retrieve their content dynamically; but most sites have at least a subset of content that should be statically delivered to a web server.

Alfresco WCM Example

Let's look at an example of a basic corporate web site. Most companies have a mix of "About Us" content that probably doesn't change very often, press releases or "News" that might get updated daily, and maybe some document-based content such as marketing slicks, product information sheets, technical specifications, and so on. There's also some content that is used to build the site such as HTML, XML, JavaScript, Flash, CSS, and image files.

It is likely that there are several different teams with several different skill sets, all collaborating to produce the site. In this example, suppose the "About Us" and "News pages" come from the marketing team, the site is built by the web team and the document-based content can come from many organizations within the company.

Alfresco WCM sits on top of the core Alfresco product to provide additional WCM-specific functionality. An important distinction between Alfresco WCM and other open source Content Management Systems is that Alfresco is a "de-coupled" CMS while something such as Drupal is a "coupled" CMS. This means that Alfresco manages the web site but does not concern itself with presentation unlike Drupal, which is both a repository and a presentation framework. This doesn't mean that Alfresco can only manage static sites. You can easily query the repository in any number of ways. It just means it is up to you to provide the frontend from the ground up.

Using Alfresco, the WCM implementation for this example might look like this:

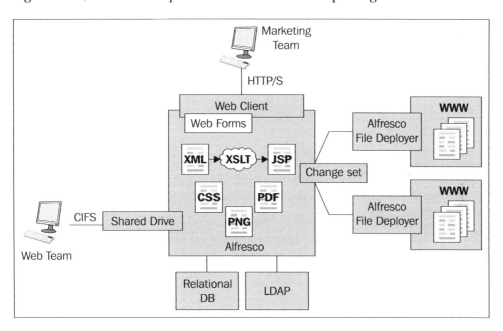

Note that in the diagram there is a mix of structured content (**XML**) and unstructured content (**CSS**, **PNG**, and **PDF**). The structured content gets created through Alfresco web forms and is transformed to one or more formats (in this case, **JSP**) using **XSLT** or FreeMarker. The unstructured content is simply uploaded via either the web client or **CIFS**.

Regardless of whether it is created with a web form or uploaded to the repository directly, the content has to make it to a web server at some point. In this example, the content is being deployed to the frontend web server using Alfresco's file deployment mechanism. In Chapter 8, other content deployment patterns will be explored.

Custom Content-Centric Applications

Content-centric applications are those in which the primary purpose of the application is to process, produce, collaborate on, or manage unstructured or semi-structured content.

The Alfresco web client is an example of a content-centric application, although it is meant for a very general, all-purpose use case. When solutions are very close to basic document management, the web client can be customized as previously discussed. At some point, it makes more sense to build a separate custom application with Alfresco as the backend repository for that application.

Consider the sales process within a company, for example. Sales people create proposals. Those proposals are usually routed internally for review and approval, and then are delivered to the client. If the client accepts the proposal, a contract is drawn up and the product is delivered. The out of the box web client could be used to manage these documents, assign metadata, manage the review process through workflows, and make it all searchable. But the sales team might be even more productive if it used a purpose-built user interface. For this solution, a frontend built with a scripting language such as PHP, a Java framework such as Seam, or even a **Rich Internet Application (RIA)** technology such as Flex might be a good option. Alfresco would provide the document management services. The frontend would talk to Alfresco via SOAP or RESTful services.

Another example is a "community" site. With so much buzz around Web 2.0, companies are looking for ways to add community features to their online presence such as forums, blogs, and personalized content as well as user-generated content such as comments, ratings, and rich media.

As discussed previously in the WCM section, Alfresco is very good at publishing static files to one or more web servers or application servers. What it lacks, at least in the current release, is a presentation framework. Many clients appreciate this separation because it gives them complete freedom with regard to how they build the frontend. But in the case of a community site, it would be a good thing to be spared of building the frontend from scratch.

One way to implement this kind of solution is to use an open source portal such as Liferay or JBoss Portal for the frontend. Alfresco can manage the content and also the business process used to approve that content for publication in the community site. **Portlets** can be written that use either **SOAP**-based or **REST**-based web services calls, to query for and display content stored in the repository.

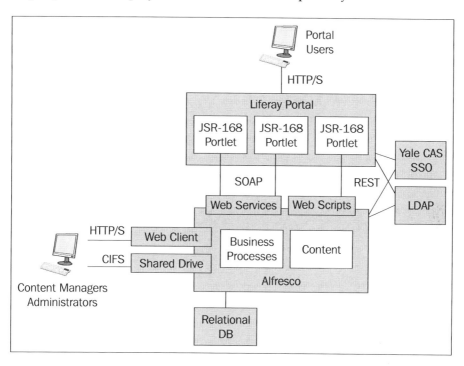

Note that the diagram also shows a **Single Sign-On** (SSO) solution so that users have to log in only once when moving back-and-forth between the portal and Alfresco. This isn't strictly required, but it is worth considering, particularly with freely available open source SSO solutions such as **Yale CAS**.

The openness of the Alfresco repository, particularly its ability to be easily exposed as a set of services, makes Alfresco an ideal platform for content-centric applications. As the examples have shown, custom content-centric web applications use Alfresco as the backend. As a result, they have complete flexibility in frontend technology choices from portals to lower-level frameworks to no framework at all.

Example Used throughout This Book

In this book, we'll assume we are rolling out Alfresco throughout a consulting firm. Professional services firms make great examples because they tend to generate a variety of different documents. The other reason is that document and content management is usually a big challenge, which is the core to the business. But the examples should be applicable to any business that generates a significant amount of documents.

The example firm, SomeCo, wants to leverage document and content management throughout the organization to make it easier to find important information, streamline certain business processes, and secure sensitive documents.

SomeCo's company organization is pretty standard. It consists of Operations, Sales, Human Resources, Marketing, and Finance/Legal. Examples of the different types of content each department is concerned with are shown in the following table:

Department	Example document types	Format and Process Notes
Finance/Legal	Client Proposals for Project Work	• Microsoft Word and Adobe PDF.
	Statements of Work	• Several iterations between the firm and the client before a "final" version is completed.
	Master Services Agreements	• Some documents may require internal review and approval.
	Non-Disclosure Agreements (NDAs)	
Marketing	Case studies	• Microsoft Word, Microsoft PowerPoint, Adobe PDF, and Adobe Flash.
	Whitepapers	• Mostly single-author content.
	Marketing plans	• Some content may come from third parties.
	Marketing slicks/Promotional material	• Some content may need to be published on the web site.

Department	Example document types	Format and Process Notes
Human Resources	Job postings Resumes Interview feedback Offer letters Employee Profiles /Biographies Project reviews Annual reviews	• Microsoft Word, Adobe PDF, and HTML. • Single-author content with consumers being spread throughout the company. • Some content formats are unpredictable (such as resumes). Some are very standard and could be templatized (such as offer letters). • With the exception of job postings, none of this content should go near the Web. • Some content needs strict internal permissions.
Sales	Forecast Presentations Proformas	• Microsoft Excel and Microsoft Powerpoint. • Some business process and automated document-handling possibilities such as Forecast. • Searchability of presentations is important.
Operations	Methodology Utilization reports Status reports	• All Microsoft Office formats. • Some opportunity for integration into enterprise systems such as time tracking and project management.

Examples throughout the rest of the book will show how Alfresco can be implemented and customized to meet the needs of the various organizations within SomeCo. During a real implementation, time would be spent gathering requirements, selecting the appropriate open source components to integrate with the solution, finalizing architecture, and structuring the project. There are plenty of other books and resources that discuss how to roll out content management across an enterprise and others that cover project methodologies. So none of that will be covered here.

Alfresco Architecture

Many of Alfresco's competitors (particularly in the closed-source space) have sprawling footprints composed of multiple, sometimes competing, technologies that have been acquired and integrated over time. Some have undergone massive infrastructure overhauls over the years, resulting in bizarre vestigial tails of sorts. Luckily, Alfresco doesn't suffer from these traits (at least not yet!). On the contrary, Alfresco's architecture:

- Is relatively straightforward
- Is built with state-of-the-art frameworks and open source components
- Supports several important content management and related standards

Let's look at each of these characteristics, starting with a high-level look at the Alfresco architecture.

High-Level Architecture

The following diagram shows Alfresco's high-level architecture. By the time you finish this book, you'll be intimately familiar with just about every box in the diagram:

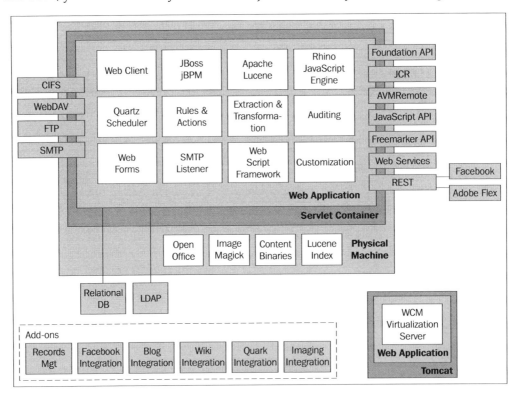

The important takeaways at this point are as follows:

- There are many ways to get content into or out of the repository, whether that's via the protocols on the left side of the diagram or the APIs on the right.

- Alfresco runs as a web application within a servlet container. In the current release, the web client runs in the same process as the content repository.

- Customizations and extensions run as part of the Alfresco web application. An extension mechanism separates customizations from the core product to keep the path clear for future upgrades.

- Metadata resides in a **Relational DB** while content files and **Lucene index** reside on the file system. The diagram shows the content residing on the same physical file system as Alfresco, but other types of file storage could be used as well.

- The **WCM Virtualization Server** is an instance of **Tomcat** with Alfresco configuration and JAR files. The Virtualization Server is used to serve up live previews of the web site as the site is being worked on. It can run on the same physical machine as Alfresco or can be split out to a separate node.

Add-Ons

The "Add-ons" are pieces of functionality not found in the core Alfresco distribution. If you are working with the binary distribution, it means you'll have additional files to download and install on top of the base Alfresco installation.

Add-ons are provided by Alfresco, third-party software vendors, and members of the Alfresco community such as partners and customers. Alfresco makes several add-on modules available such as Records Management and Facebook integration. Software vendor Kofax provides add-on software that integrates Alfresco with the Kofax imaging solution. Members of the Alfresco community create and share add-on modules via the Alfresco Forge, a web site set up by Alfresco for that purpose. But the majority of what is available is language packs used to localize the Alfresco web client.

Open Source Components

One of the reasons Alfresco has been able to create a viable offering so quickly is because it didn't start from scratch. The Alfresco engineers assembled the product from many finer-grained open source components. Why does this matter? First, instead of reinventing the wheel, they used proven components. This saved them time, but it also resulted in a more robust, more standard-based product. Second, it eases the transition for people new to the platform. If a developer already knows

JavaServer Faces (JSF) or Spring, for example, many of the customization concepts are going to be familiar. (And besides, as a developer, wouldn't you rather invest your time and effort in learning standard development frameworks rather than proprietary "development kits"?)

The following table lists some of the major open source components used to build Alfresco:

Open Source Component	Use in Alfresco
Apache Lucene (`http://lucene.apache.org/`)	Full-text and metadata search
Hibernate (`http://www.hibernate.org/`)	Database persistence
Apache MyFaces (`http://myfaces.apache.org/`)	JSF components in the web client
FreeMarker (`http://freemarker.org/`)	Web script framework views, custom views in the web client, web client dashlets, email templates
Mozilla Rhino JavaScript Engine (`http://www.mozilla.org/rhino/`)	Web script framework controllers, Server-side JavaScript, Actions
OpenSymphony Quartz (`http://www.opensymphony.com/quartz/`)	Scheduling of asynchronous processes
Spring ACEGI (`http://www.acegisecurity.org/`)	Security (authorization), roles, and permissions
Apache Axis (`http://ws.apache.org/axis/`)	Web services
OpenOffice.org (`http://www.openoffice.org/`)	Conversion of office documents into PDF
Apache FOP (`http://xmlgraphics.apache.org/fop/`)	Transformation of XSL:FO into PDF
Apache POI (`http://poi.apache.org/`)	Metadata extraction from Microsoft Office files
JBoss jBPM (`http://www.jboss.com/products/jbpm`)	Advanced workflow
ImageMagick (`http://www.imagemagick.org`)	Image file manipulation
Chiba (`http://chiba.sourceforge.net/`)	Web form generation based on XForms

Does this mean you have to be an expert in all open source components used to build Alfresco to successfully implement and customize the product? Not at all! Developers looking to contribute significant product enhancements to Alfresco or those making major, deep customizations to the product may require experience with a particular component, depending on exactly what they are trying to do. Everyone else will be able to customize and extend Alfresco using basic Java and web application development skills.

Major Standards and Protocols Supported

Software vendors love buzz words. As new acronyms climb the hype cycle, vendors scramble to figure out how they can at least appear to support the standard or protocol so that the prospective clients can check that box on the **Request for proposal (RFP)** (don't even get me started on RFPs). Commercial open source vendors are still software vendors and thus are no less guilty of this practice. But because open source software is developed in the open by a community of developers, its compliance to standards tends to be more genuine. It makes more sense for an open source project to implement a standard than to go off in some new direction because it saves time. It promotes interoperability with other open source projects, and stays true to what open source is all about: freedom and choice.

Here, are the significant standards and protocols Alfresco supports:

Standard/Protocol	Comment
FTP	Content can be contributed to the repository via FTP. Secure FTP is not yet supported.
WebDAV	WebDAV is an HTTP-based protocol commonly supported by content management vendors. It is one way to make the repository look like a file system.
CIFS	CIFS allows the repository to be mounted as a shared drive by other machines. As opposed to WebDAV, systems (and people) can't tell the difference between an Alfresco repository mounted as a shared drive through CIFS and a traditional file server.
JCR API (JSR-170)	JCR is a Java API for working with content repositories such as Alfresco. Alfresco is a JCR-compliant repository. There are two levels of JCR compliance. Alfresco is Level 1 compliant and is near to Level 2 compliant.
Portlet API (JSR-168)	The Web Script Framework lets you define a RESTful API to the repository. Web Scripts can return XML, HTML, JSON, and JSR-168 portlets. In the current release, this requires the portal and Alfresco to be running in the same JVM, but this restriction may go away in the near future.
SOAP	The Alfresco Web Services API uses SOAP-based web services.
OpenSearch (http://www.opensearch.org)	Alfresco repositories can be configured as an OpenSearch data source, which allows Alfresco to participate in federated search queries. OpenSearch queries can be executed from the web client as well. This means if your organization has several repositories that are OpenSearch-compliant (including non-Alfresco repositories), they can be searched from within the web client.

Standard/Protocol	Comment
XForms, XML Schema	Web forms are defined using XML Schema. Not all XForms widgets are supported.
XSLT, XSL:FO	Web form data can be transformed using XSL 1.0.
LDAP	Alfresco can authenticate against an LDAP directory or a Microsoft Active Directory server.

Customizing Alfresco

Alfresco offers a significant amount of functionality out of the box, but most clients will customize it in some way. At a high level, the types of customizations typically done during an implementation can be divided into basic customizations and advanced customizations.

Basic Customization

Many Alfresco customizations can be done without writing a single line of code. Some may be done even by end users through the web client. Others might require editing a properties file or an XML file. These basic configuration and customization tasks are described in-depth in *Alfresco Enterprise Content Management Implementation* by Munwar Shariff, Packt Publishing. Let's look at them briefly here so that you can get an idea of what you don't have to code.

Dashlets

When users log in to Alfresco, the first thing that is usually displayed is the **My Alfresco Dashboard**. The dashboard is a user-configurable layout that contains dashlets. (If you are familiar with portals, think "portal page" and "portlet"). Users choose the layout of the dashboard (number of columns) as well as the specific dashlets they want displayed in each column.

There are a number of dashlets available out of the box, or you can develop your own and add them to the user-selectable list. Examples of out of the box dashlets include workflow-related dashlets such as **My Tasks To Do** and **My Completed Tasks** as well as content-related dashlets such as **My Documents** and **My Spaces**:

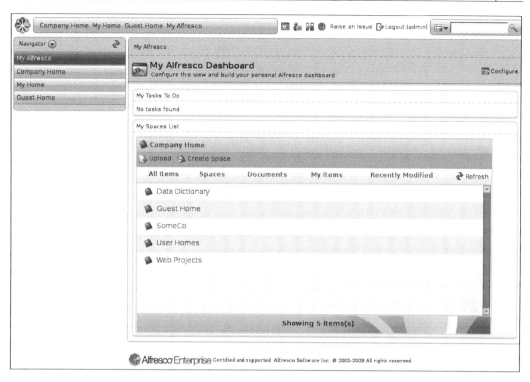

A dashlet is implemented as a JSP page. The JSP page can contain JSF components and make calls to JSF-managed beans. If FreeMarker is more your style, the JSP page can easily delegate its rendition to a FreeMarker template. Obviously, developing custom dashlets is probably not something you'd let your business users do; but it is still considered a basic customization.

Custom Views

Alfresco's web client uses a hierarchical folder metaphor for navigating the repository. Alfresco calls folders "spaces" because in Alfresco, folders can do more than just contain documents. They can also have metadata, rules, and permissions associated with them. I will use "folders" and "spaces" interchangeably throughout the book. The default behavior when a folder is opened is to display the contents of the folder. A common requirement is to display metadata or other information that's not available in the standard content list. One way to do this is to implement a custom view using FreeMarker templates. The custom view can then be applied to the folder by a business user to display it as needed, without changing the underlying folder list functionality.

There are several out of the box FreeMarker templates that can be used as custom views such as "My Documents" and "Recent Documents". Most likely, you'll want to create your own using one of the out of the box templates as an example.

Rules and Rule Actions

A rule is something that says, "When a piece of content is created, updated, or deleted, check these conditions. If these conditions are met, take these actions". Conditions may check whether a piece of content is a particular mime type, or a specific content type. They may also check whether a piece of content has a specific aspect applied, or whether the content's name property matches a particular pattern. Rules can be defined on any folder in the repository. Child folders can inherit rules from their parent.

Rule actions are repeatable operations that enable us to do things similar to those that can be done using JavaScript or Java. Out of the box actions include things such as check-in content, check-out content, move an item to another folder, specialize the type of the content, add an aspect to the content, transform content from one format to another, and so on.

Configuring folders to run rule actions is something non-technical users can do through the web client. In Chapter 4, you'll learn how to write your own custom rule actions using the Alfresco API.

Simple Workflow

Alfresco has two options for implementing workflow: simple workflow or advanced workflow. The good thing about simple workflows is that end users can configure them as needed without any technical skills or developer support.

Here's how it works. A web client user creates a rule to "add a simple workflow" to a document when it is placed in the folder. When a document has a simple workflow, it means it has a "forward step" and a "backward step". A user configuring the simple workflow decides whether to use one or both steps, and assigns appropriate names for steps such as "Approve" and "Reject". When the step is invoked, the content can be copied or moved to another folder. Users create serial processes by setting up multiple folders, each with rules to add the appropriately configured simple workflow to the incoming content. For example, there might be folders called "Draft"," In Review", and "Approved". The state of a document is determined by the folder in which it resides.

Simple workflows have obvious limitations:

- Workflows are limited to serial processes. Content can only move forward or backward, one step at a time.

- Content can only be in one process at a given time.

- Content must change physical locations to reflect a change in state.

- There is no opportunity for capturing (and acting on) process-related metadata.

- Tasks can't be assigned to individuals or groups. (Of course, you could limit folders to specific individuals or groups through permissions, which would have a similar effect to a task assignment. But you wouldn't be able to easily pull a list of tasks for a specific user across all simple workflows).

- Other than creating additional rules and rule actions for the folders used in a simple workflow, there is no way to add logic for decisions or other more complex constructs.

Advanced Customization

The basic configuration and customizations show that there is quite a lot of tweaking and tailoring that can happen before a developer gets involved. This is a good thing. It means a good chunk of the customization requirements can be dealt with quickly. In the case of simple workflows, they can be delegated to the end users altogether! Hopefully, this leaves more time for the more advanced (and more interesting) customizations required for a successful implementation.

Examples of Advanced Customizations

The advanced customizations are the customizations that are likely to require code. They are the focus of the book. To give you an idea of what's possible (and in an effort to provide an appetizer before the main meal is served), let's go over some of the areas of advanced customization.

Extend the Content Model

Alfresco's out of the box content model can be extended to define your own content types, content aspects, content metadata (properties), and relationships (associations). The out of the box model is very generic, and defines only a minimal subset of the metadata that will probably need to be captured with the content.

For example, SomeCo might want to capture different metadata for its Marketing documents than for its HR documents. Or maybe there is a set of metadata that doesn't belong to any one content type in particular, but should rather be grouped together in an aspect and attached to objects as needed. These and other content modeling concepts will be covered in Chapter 3.

Perform Automatic Operations on Content

There are several "hooks" or places where you can insert logic or take action to handle content automatically. These include rule actions, behaviors, content transformers, and metadata extractors. Rule actions have already been discussed. Behaviors are like actions but instead of being something that an end user can invoke on any piece of content, behaviors are tightly bound to their content type. Content transformers, as the name suggests, transform content from one format to another. Metadata extractors inspect content as it is added to the repository, and pull out data to store in the content object's properties. These tools for handling content automatically will all be covered in Chapter 4.

Customize the Web Client

Chapter 5 covers web client customization. Just about everything in the web client can be tweaked. Menu items can be rearranged or new menus and items can be created. If a JSP doesn't work quite the way it needs to, you can override it with your own custom version of the page. Don't like the out of the box date picker? Component renderers for out of the box data types can be overridden or completely new renderers for custom types can be created. If you need to guide users through a multi-step process, you can create custom dialogs and wizards.

In the current release, the web client is built with JSF. In the near future, Alfresco may be moving toward a lighter-weight framework based on web scripts. Regardless of what happens with the new and improved web client, the "classic" web client will be around for a while, so it is a good idea to know how to make it fit your requirements.

Create a RESTful API

Web scripts are one of the more exciting additions to the Alfresco architecture. The **Next Generation Internet (NGI)** or Web 2.0 (or 3.0 or whatever you want to call it) is built on RESTful services. The reason is that RESTful services are typically much easier to work with using scripting languages and AJAX toolkits than SOAP-based services, because they are invoked through plain old URLs. When a repository has a RESTful interface, it is much easier to incorporate as part of an NGI solution.

The web script framework, based on the **Model-View-Control** (**MVC**) pattern, allows you to build your own RESTful API to the repository. It will be covered in detail in Chapter 6, but the high-level summary is that URLs get mapped to a controller implemented as JavaScript or Java. The controller performs whatever logic is needed, then forwards the request to the view. The view is implemented as a FreeMarker template. The template could return anything from markup to XML to JSON. The framework is so powerful and flexible that Alfresco refactors several pieces of the web client to leverage web scripts. RESTful services via web scripts are well on their way to becoming the preferred way to integrate with the Alfresco repository.

Streamline Complex Business Processes with Advanced Workflows

Advanced workflows provide a way to automate complex business processes. Alfresco's advanced workflows are executed by the embedded JBoss jBPM engine, which is a very powerful and popular open source workflow engine.

Rather than basic workflows, which are end-user configurable and limited to serial processes, advanced workflows offer the power of parallel flows, the ability to add logic to the process via JavaScript and Java, and much more.

A handful of advanced workflows are available out of the box. These are most useful as starting points for your own custom advanced workflows. Exactly how it has to be done will be covered in Chapter 7.

Get Your Web sites under Control

Alfresco WCM uses the same web client user interface as everything else in Alfresco, so customization techniques covered in other chapters will apply here. Chapter 8 focuses on specific WCM implementation details such as creating web forms with XML Schema and presentation template development using XSLT and FreeMarker.

Integrate with Other Systems

Most of the coding and configuration discussed so far can be divided into two parts: (1) Customizations made to the core repository and (2) Customizations made to the web client. There is a third bucket to be considered, which is coding and configuration related to integrating Alfresco with other solutions. Maybe Alfresco needs to authenticate against an LDAP directory. Maybe a portal will get its content from Alfresco, or perhaps some other third-party application needs to share content with Alfresco. Chapter 9 discusses how to handle security and integration.

Dusting Off Your Toolbox

Looking across both the basic and advanced customizations provides some idea about the extensibility of the platform. A commonly asked question at this point in the architecture discussion is, "Does Alfresco have an API?". Actually, it has several. Let's look at what APIs are available and where they are used. This should also give you some idea as to the tools and skills you'll need to have in your toolbox as you embark on your own projects.

The following table shows the APIs available and where they are used:

Alfresco API	Where Used	Comments
Foundation API	Rule actions, behaviors, Java-based web scripts, web client customizations, jBPM, standalone applications that embed the Alfresco repository.	As the name suggests, this is the core Alfresco API. Most of the work with this API involves writing Java in Plain Old Java Objects (POJOs) that are "wired in" to Alfresco via Spring- or JSF-managed beans.
Web Services API	Web and non-web applications that need remote access to the repository.	Alfresco ships client-side classes for Java and PHP, but any language that can use SOAP-based web services can use this API to do almost everything the Foundation API can do.
JCR API	Web and non-web applications. Can be used remotely via the JCR-RMI bridge.	JCR is a standard (JSR-170) Java API for interacting with content repositories. The JCR API does not have the full functionality of the Foundation API.
FreeMarker API	Custom views, mail templates, web script view logic, WCM presentation transformations.	FreeMarker is an open source templating engine.
AVMRemote API	WCM presentation transformations, web applications.	This API is specific to working with content stored in Alfresco WCM web projects.
Web Script Framework	Web and non-web applications that need to use REST to interact with the repository.	More of a framework than an API, web scripts implement a Model-View-Controller (MVC) pattern that relies on the JavaScript, FreeMarker, and Foundation APIs.
Flex API	Web scripts, Flash components.	Built on the web script framework, the Flex API is really a set of hooks that make it easier to use Adobe's Flex tools to build Rich Internet Applications (RIAs) on top of Alfresco.
Facebook API	Web scripts, social networking applications.	Similar to the Flex API, the Facebook API is a set of web scripts that make it easier for Alfresco-based web scripts to make calls to the Facebook API.

As the list of APIs shows, knowing Java will be the key to just about any successful customization effort. FreeMarker and JavaScript are important, but are easily picked up using Alfresco's code and online resources as references.

What about Adobe Flex?

Alfresco has a vision for a web client with a much richer interface. At one point, the plan was to build the web client entirely with Adobe Flex. Alfresco has since backed off that approach. It is more likely that Flash components will be added where it makes sense.

From a skills standpoint, it is still uncertain how deep Flex skills will need to be to customize Alfresco as it evolves into a richer interface. Hopefully, Alfresco will abstract the configuration and customization of the Flex-based components such that clients can get it without Flex skills. If that doesn't happen, it should be fairly easy for anyone with knowledge of JavaScript and XML to pick up Flex skills.

Understanding Alfresco's Editions

Alfresco has two editions of its products (sometimes called "networks"): Labs and Enterprise. It also offers a "Small Business Network" package through the Red Hat Exchange, but this is essentially a user-limited Enterprise version licensed on a "per seat" rather than a "per CPU" basis.

Those familiar with the difference between Fedora Linux and Red Hat Enterprise Linux, or JBoss.org and JBoss.com will immediately understand the distinction between the Alfresco Labs and Alfresco Enterprise editions. Both editions are open source and are available without up-front license fees. However, the Labs edition is completely unsupported while Alfresco provides commercial support for the Enterprise edition. In fact, you can't get access to the Enterprise edition without purchasing a support subscription from Alfresco.

The Labs edition is essentially the developers' playground. It may contain experimental features and community contributions. In source code terms, it can be thought of as the "daily build" or the "unstable build". Therefore, it should not be used in critical applications because it changes quite often. From time to time, functionality will be taken from Labs and placed in the Enterprise code line where it will be integrated with the rest of the product, tested, and officially released as a new supported version.

Initially, the Enterprise edition incorporated every feature available in Labs because the two were parts of the same code line. However, this has changed. The two are now separate code lines. There is no guarantee that a feature in Labs will ever make it to Enterprise. But if there is a good reaction to the functionality among Labs users, if the functionality is being demanded by Enterprise customers, and if the code plays well with the Enterprise code base, it is likely to be made part of the Enterprise release at some point. This means you should be very careful if you choose to put solutions based on Labs in front of your users. If they fall in love with a feature unique to the Labs edition and then demand commercial support from Alfresco, you might find yourself in a very tough position.

Significant Feature Differences

At the time of this writing, the latest supported release from Alfresco is Alfresco Enterprise 2.2. The latest community release is Alfresco Labs 3.0 Preview. Of course, there are many feature differences between the two. The most significant difference is that the Labs edition includes the Flex and Facebook APIs as well as the new Surf web framework, and the new 3.0 web client called Share.

What's Used in This Book

The vast majority of examples used in this book will work on both the Enterprise and Labs editions (2.2 and 3.0, respectively). Where a specific release is required, it will be noted wherever possible.

Summary

Hopefully, this chapter has given you several ideas about how Alfresco can be used to implement Document Management, Web Content Management, and custom content-centric applications by walking through examples of each. The details may still be fuzzy, but the goal was to introduce the major components and capabilities of the Alfresco platform.

The key points covered in this chapter were:

- Alfresco can be used to solve a variety of content-related business problems from document management to web content management to workflow and collaboration.
- Throughout the rest of the book you'll customize and extend Alfresco to meet the needs of SomeCo, a fictitious consulting firm.

- Alfresco is assembled with open source components, runs as a web application within an application server, and exposes the repository through many different protocols and APIs.

- Alfresco can be customized. Some types of customization are very basic (more configuration than customization) and can be performed by end users through the web client. Others are more advanced and require coding. The advanced customizations are the subject of this book.

- The most common tools used to extend the platform are Java, JavaScript, FreeMarker, and XML.

- The two flavors or editions of Alfresco—Labs and Enterprise—are somewhat analogous to Fedora and Red Hat Enterprise Linux. Labs is "daily build", primarily for developers and experimentation while Enterprise is for production systems.

2
Getting Started with Alfresco

Before you can customize Alfresco, you need to get your development environment in order. In this chapter, you'll learn how to get the **Software Development Kit (SDK)** set up in Eclipse, how to build and deploy customizations, helpful debugging tips, and the cleanest and quickest way to "reset" your Alfresco sandbox. The chapter includes an example that shows how to package and deploy some extremely basic customizations just to get your feet wet. Specifically, you are going to learn:

- Where to get the Alfresco SDK, how to build it, and how to set it up in Eclipse
- How to extend Alfresco without modifying the Alfresco source code or configuration
- How to package and deploy your customizations
- How to use the Eclipse debugger and log4j to troubleshoot problems
- How to start clean for testing or debugging purposes

This book assumes you already have Alfresco installed and running on Tomcat, and are also using MySQL as the backend database; but that's up to you. If you need help getting your basic installation up and running, refer to the Appendix.

It may seem odd to talk about deployment before you've learned how to create something worth deploying, but these techniques will be used in all subsequent chapters. So you might as well get everything set up and tested now so that you don't have to deal with it later.

Obtaining the SDK

If you are running the Enterprise network, it is likely that the SDK has been provided to you as a binary. Alternatively, you can check out the Enterprise source code and build it yourself. In the Enterprise SVN repository, specific releases are tagged. So if you wanted 2.2.0, for example, you'd check out V2.2.0-ENTERPRISE-FINAL. The Enterprise SVN repository for the Enterprise network is password-protected. Consult your Alfresco representative for the URL, port, and credentials that are needed to obtain the Enterprise source code.

Labs network users can either download the SDK as a binary from SourceForge (`https://sourceforge.net/project/showfiles.php?group_id=143373&package_id=189441`) or check out the Labs source code and build it. The SVN URL for the Labs source code is `svn://svn.alfresco.com`. In the Labs repository, nothing is tagged. You must check out HEAD.

Step-by-Step: Building Alfresco from Source

Regardless of whether you are using Enterprise or Labs, if you've decided to build from the source it is very easy to do it. At a high level, you simply check out the source and then run `Ant`. If you've opted to use the pre-compiled binaries, skip to the next section. Otherwise, let's use Ant to create the same ZIP/TAR file that is available on the download page. To do that, follow these steps:

1. Check out the source from the appropriate SVN repository, as mentioned earlier.

2. Set the TOMCAT_HOME environment variable to the root of your Apache Tomcat install directory.

3. Navigate to the root of the source directory, then run the default `Ant` target:

   ```
   ant build.xml
   ```

4. It will take a few minutes to build everything. When it is done, run the distribute task like this:

   ```
   ant -f continuous.xml distribute
   ```

5. Again, it may take several minutes for this to run. When it is done, you should see several archives in the **build | dist** directory. For example, running this Ant task for Alfresco 3.0 Labs produces several archives. The subset relevant to the book includes:

   - `alfresco-labs-sdk-*.tar.gz`
   - `alfresco-labs-sdk-*.zip`
   - `alfresco-labs-tomcat-*.tar.gz`

- ° `alfresco-labs-tomcat-*.zip`
- ° `alfresco-labs-war-*.tar.gz`
- ° `alfresco-labs-war-*.zip`
- ° `alfresco-labs-wcm-*.tar.gz`
- ° `alfresco-labs-wcm-*.zip`

6. You should extract the SDK archive somewhere handy. The next step will be to import the SDK into Eclipse.

Setting up the SDK in Eclipse

Nothing about Alfresco requires you to use Eclipse or any other IDE. But Eclipse is very widely used and the Alfresco SDK distribution includes Eclipse projects that can easily be imported into Eclipse, so that's what these instructions will cover.

In addition to the Alfresco JARs, dependent JARs, Javadocs, and source code, the SDK bundle has several Eclipse projects. Most of the Eclipse projects are sample projects showing how to write code for a particular area of Alfresco. Two are special, however. The **SDK AlfrescoEmbedded** project and the **SDK AlfrescoRemote** project reference all of the JARs needed for the Java API and the Web Services API respectively. The easiest way to make sure your own Eclipse project has everything it needs to compile is to import the projects bundled with the SDK into your Eclipse workspace, and then add the appropriate SDK projects to your project's build path.

Step-by-Step: Importing the SDK into Eclipse

Every developer has his or her own favorite way of configuring tools. If you are going to work with multiple versions of Alfresco, you should use version-specific Eclipse workspaces. For example, you might want to have a `workspace-alfresco-2.2` workspace as well as a `workspace-alfresco-3.0` workspace, each with the corresponding Alfresco SDK projects imported. Then, if you need to test customizations against a different version of the Alfresco SDK, all you have to do is switch your workspace, import your customization project if it isn't in the workspace already, and build it. Let's go ahead and set this up. Follow these steps:

1. In Eclipse, select **File | Switch Workspace** or specify a new workspace location. This will be your workspace for a specific version of the Alfresco SDK so use a name such as `workspace-alfresco-3.0`. Eclipse will restart with an empty workspace.

2. Make sure the Java compiler compliance level preference is set to 5.0 (**Window | Preferences | Java | Compiler**). If you forget to do that, Eclipse won't be able to build the projects after they are imported.

3. Select **File | Import | Existing Projects into Workspace**. For the root directory, specify the directory where the SDK was uncompressed.

 You want the root SDK directory, not the **Samples** directory.

4. Select all of the projects that are listed and click **Import**.

After the import, Eclipse should be able to build all projects cleanly. If not, double-check the compiler compliance level. If that is set but there are still errors, make sure you imported all SDK projects including **SDK AlfrescoEmbedded** and **SDK AlfrescoRemote**.

Now that the files are in the workspace, take a look at the Embedded project. That's quite a list of dependent JAR files! The Alfresco-specific JARs all start with `alfresco-`. It depends on what you are doing, of course, but the JAR that is referenced most often is likely to be `alfresco-repository.jar` because that's where the bulk of the API resides.

The SDK comes with zipped source code and Javadocs, which are both useful references (although the Javadocs are pretty sparse). It's a good idea to tell Eclipse where those files are, so you can drill in to the Alfresco source when debugging. To do that, right-click on the Alfresco JAR, and then select **Properties**. You'll see panels for **Java Source Attachment** and **Javadoc Location** that you can use to associate the JAR with the appropriate source and Javadoc archives.

The following image shows the **Java Source Attachment** for `alfresco-repository.jar`:

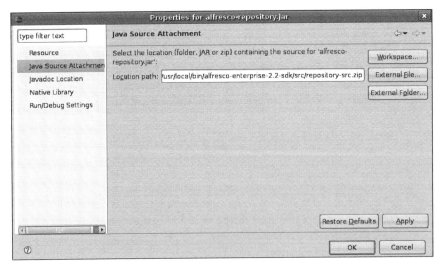

The following image shows the **Javadoc Location** panel for
`alfresco-repository.jar`.

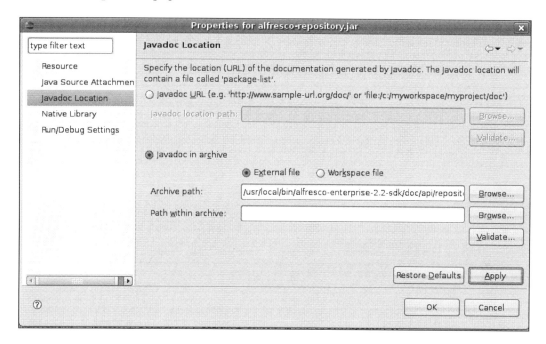

Source and **Javadoc** are provided for each of the Alfresco JARs, as shown in the
following table. Note that source and Javadoc for everything is available. This is
open source software after all, not just all bundled with the SDK:

Alfresco JAR	Source archive	Javadoc archive
`alfresco-core.jar`	`Src|core-src.zip`	`Doc|api|core-doc.zip`
`alfresco-remote-api.jar`	`Src|remote-api-src.zip`	`Doc|api|remote-api-doc.zip`
`alfresco-web-client.jar`	`src|web-client-src.zip`	`doc|api|web-client-doc.zip`
`alfresco-repository.jar`	`src|repository-src.zip`	`doc|api|repository-doc.zip`

Extending Alfresco

Alfresco provides an extension mechanism that keeps customizations separate from
the files that are a part of the Alfresco distribution. It is important to keep your
customizations separate from Alfresco's in order to help streamline future upgrades
and to simplify troubleshooting.

Understanding the Extension Mechanism

When you implement Alfresco, you will inevitably identify things you want to tweak and potentially define an entirely new functionality that you would like to add to the platform. The approach you will use to extend Alfresco with your own customizations is the same you use when extending other Spring or JSF-based web applications. You will extend the existing or write new Spring beans, JSF-managed beans, Java classes, JSPs, tag libraries, and other files. The custom files are deployed as a part of the Alfresco web application. The trick is to override or extend Alfresco with your own code, while keeping those extensions and customizations separate from the Alfresco core. This means you have to know what goes where and the answer to that depends on what's being extended.

When implementing your solution, you are likely to create or customize one or more of the following types of files:

- Standard Java web application files (JSP pages, tag libraries, resource bundles, and Java classes)
- Framework files (Spring beans, JSF-managed beans, and their associated configuration files)
- Alfresco configuration files (properties files and XML files)
- Solution-specific files (content models, business process definitions, web scripts, JavaScript, and Freemarker templates)

Let's look at how each of these areas is extended.

Standard Java Web Application Files

Given that you probably have experience developing Java web applications, there is not much need to go into detail here. The Java classes you develop as a part of your customization will go into a JAR file. The JAR file will reside in the WEB-INF|lib of the Alfresco web application. Therefore, you should name it such that it is easy to spot among the hundred or so JAR files distributed as part of Alfresco. Similarly, any tag libraries that you develop will reside in WEB-INF alongside Alfresco's taglibs.

Custom JSP pages should be kept separate from Alfresco's to make them easier to identify. One way to do this is to create an **extension** directory under **jsp**, but it is completely up to you. The same goes for scripts, images, and CSS.

Framework Files

Alfresco makes heavy use of the Spring Framework for **Inversion of Control (IoC)** and the MyFaces implementation of the **JavaServer Faces (JSF)** standard for web client user interface components and navigation. Each of these frameworks can be extended.

Spring Configuration Files

Spring configuration files always end in `-context.xml`. That's how Spring knows to read them when the application starts up. Alfresco's Spring configuration files reside in **WEB-INF | classes | alfresco**.

You can override Alfresco's Spring bean configurations with your own by creating custom Spring configuration files. Custom Spring configuration files must follow the `*-context.xml` naming convention. They need to reside in a directory called `alfresco | extension`, but that directory can be anywhere on the Classpath. The convention is to use either the `shared | classes` directory in `$TOMCAT_HOME` or `WEB-INF | classes`.

 If you are curious, Alfresco (or more specifically, Spring) knows to load custom context files in the `alfresco | extension` directory because that's what is configured in `WEB-INF | classes | alfresco | applicat ion-context.xml`. You can find other interesting Spring configuration files by searching `web.xml` for `context.xml`.

Let's look at an example. Here's the out of the box Alfresco Spring bean that's used to tell Alfresco about the default custom content model file:

```
<bean id="extension.dictionaryBootstrap" parent="dictionaryModelBootst
rap" depends-on="dictionaryBootstrap">
    <property name="models">
        <list>
            <value>alfresco/model/defaultCustomModel.xml</value>
        </list>
    </property>
</bean>
```

This Spring bean happens to reside in a file called `core-services-context.xml`, but that's not important. Suppose you want to configure Alfresco with an additional custom content model, don't worry that you haven't yet learned what a content model XML file is; the point is that there is a bean defined as part of the out of the box configuration with a property ("models", in this case) we might want to set. To do that, you'd create a new file following the `*-context.xml` naming convention. In that file, you would place a bean configuration that sets the model's property the way you want it. The question you have to ask is: Do you want to completely override the exact same bean that Alfresco has configured out of the box, or do you want to create a new instance of a bean that would co-exist with Alfresco's?

In this example, you could override Alfresco's `extension.dictionaryBootstrap` bean by adding your own bean to your context file with the matching bean ID, and then set the model's property as needed like this:

```xml
<?xml version='1.0' encoding='UTF-8'?>
<!DOCTYPE beans PUBLIC '-//SPRING//DTD BEAN//EN' 'http://www.
springframework.org/dtd/spring-beans.dtd'>
<beans>
<!-- Registration of new models -->
<bean id="extension.dictionaryBootstrap" parent="dictionaryModelBootst
rap" depends-on="dictionaryBootstrap">
        <property name="models">
            <list>
                <value>alfresco/extension/model/scModel.xml
                </value>
                <value>alfresco/extension/model/scWorkflowModel.xml
                </value>
            </list>
        </property>
</bean>
</beans>
```

The custom Spring configuration file could be named anything you want as long as it ends with `-context.xml`. In this example, the `models` property points to two custom model XML files called `scModel.xml` and `scWorkflowModel.xml`. Your custom bean would override Alfresco's `extension.dictionaryBootstrap` bean because it loads the custom context files last.

For this particular bean, the problem with overriding `extension.dictionaryBootstrap` is that someone else might develop an add-on module for Alfresco that overrides the same bean. The one that gets loaded last will win, which may not be what you want. So instead, in this case, the better approach is to create a unique bean ID such as this:

```xml
<?xml version='1.0' encoding='UTF-8'?>
<!DOCTYPE beans PUBLIC '-//SPRING//DTD BEAN//EN' 'http://www.
springframework.org/dtd/spring-beans.dtd'>

<beans>
    <!-- Registration of new models -->
    <bean id="someco.dictionaryBootstrap" parent="dictionaryModelBoots
     trap" depends-on="dictionaryBootstrap">
        <property name="models">
```

```
            <list>
                <value>alfresco/extension/model/scModel.xml</value>
                <value>alfresco/extension/model/scWorkflowModel.xml
                </value>
            </list>
        </property>
    </bean>
</beans>
```

When adding new beans to your context files, make sure you are making a conscious decision regarding whether you are deliberately overriding a bean with your own definition, or are simply creating a new instance of a bean instead. Neither one is always right; it just depends on what you are trying to do.

> If you aren't familiar with Spring, you might be wondering about the "parent" and "depends-on" attributes. A parent bean is like a template: The child inherits the parent bean's configuration and can override the parent settings. The depends-on attribute is used to make sure that Spring instantiates the dependent bean first. Learn more about the Spring Framework at http://www.springframework.org.

There are many Spring beans configured in Alfresco out of the box. The Appendix includes a list of the beans that are considered "public services". In addition to the Appendix, you can also use the files distributed with Alfresco. The out of the box Spring bean configuration files are named `*-context.xml`, and reside in **WEB-INF | classes | alfresco**. Within the Alfresco distribution, the `extensions | extension` directory contains a set of sample files. If you wanted to set up some scheduled actions, for example, you could copy `scheduled-actions-services-context.xml.sample` from the distribution to your extension directory, rename it to `scheduled-actions-services-context.xml`, and then modify it as needed.

JavaServer Faces Configuration Files

Alfresco uses **JavaServer Faces (JSF)** for its UI component model. Alfresco uses the MyFaces implementation of the JSF specification. Note that for the rest of the book, it will be referred to simply as "JSF" even though, technically, JSF is a specification and MyFaces is the implementation of that spec.

Like Spring, JSF relies on XML files to configure the framework. Alfresco's JSF files reside in the WEB-INF directory, and all begin with "faces". Custom JSF components and navigation rules are declared in a faces configuration file. Unfortunately, there is not as much flexibility in the location of your JSF configuration files as there is with Spring. For JSF, it comes down to two choices: `WEB-INF | faces-config-custom.xml` or `faces-config.xml` in META-INF within a JAR file that resides in Alfresco's

WEB-INF | lib directory. Which one you use depends on what you are trying to do. If you are overriding Alfresco's existing JSF navigation rules, you have to go the META-INF route. If you are overriding Alfresco's existing JSF component declarations, you have to go the WEB-INF route. If you aren't overriding anything, you can pick either.

For example, let's suppose you want to override the `login.jsp` page with a custom version. As previously discussed, the new JSP should go into `jsp|extension` to keep it separate from Alfresco's JSPs. Alfresco uses JSF to configure navigation rules related to login. If you search the files within the WEB-INF directory for the string `login.jsp`, you'll see that the JSF file that defines the navigation rules related to login is `faces-config-navigation.xml`. In this example, the goal is to use a custom login page. That means, the existing navigation rules pointing to the out of the box `login.jsp` page have to be overridden. To change the navigation to use the `custom` `login.jsp` page, copy the appropriate navigation-rule elements (there are two) into a new file called `faces-config.xml` and change the `from-view-id` and `to-view-id` elements to reference the custom JSP as follows:

```xml
<?xml version='1.0' encoding='UTF-8'?>
<!DOCTYPE faces-config PUBLIC "-//Sun Microsystems, Inc.//DTD
JavaServer Faces Config 1.1//EN" "http://java.sun.com/dtd/
web-facesconfig_1_1.dtd">
<faces-config>

    <navigation-rule>
      <description>
         The decision rule used by the NavigationHandler to
         determine which view must be displayed after the
         current view, login.jsp is processed.
      </description>
      <from-view-id>/jsp/extension/login.jsp</from-view-id>
      <navigation-case>
         <description>
            Indicates to the NavigationHandler that the browse.jsp
            view must be displayed if the Action referenced by a
            UICommand component on the login.jsp view returns
            the outcome "success".
         </description>
         <from-outcome>success</from-outcome>
         <to-view-id>/jsp/browse/browse.jsp</to-view-id>
      </navigation-case>
    </navigation-rule>

    <!-- rule to get back to the login page from anywhere -->
    <navigation-rule>
```

```
        <from-view-id>/jsp/*</from-view-id>
        <navigation-case>
            <from-outcome>logout</from-outcome>
            <to-view-id>/jsp/extension/login.jsp</to-view-id>
        </navigation-case>
        <navigation-case>
            <from-outcome>relogin</from-outcome>
            <to-view-id>/jsp/extension/relogin.jsp</to-view-id>
        </navigation-case>
    </navigation-rule>
</faces-config>
```

Because this Faces configuration overrides existing navigation rules, the file has to be called `faces-config.xml` and it has to reside in the META-INF directory of a JAR file placed in Alfresco's `WEB-INF|lib` directory.

Note that this isn't a complete example for customizing the login page. There's another step involving an Alfresco configuration file. Alfresco configuration files are covered in the next section.

Alfresco Configuration Files

Not all configurations are handled through standard frameworks such as Spring and JSF. Some configuration changes are made using properties files or Alfresco configuration XML. For example, the most commonly customized properties file is `custom-repository.properties`. In it, you can find things such as the username and password used to connect to the underlying relational database, the database driver, and the data directory file path. Like the Spring files, there are sample properties files in the **extensions|extension** directory of the Alfresco distribution.

The full out of the box `repository.properties` file resides in `WEB-INF|classes|alfresco`. To override any of the properties in that file, add custom values to a file called `custom-repository.properties` in the `alfresco|extension` directory. This file is specifically named in the repository-properties Spring bean so if, for some reason, you have more than one or you want to change the name, you must specify the updated properties file location in the configuration for the repository-properties bean. By default, that bean is configured in `custom-repository-context.xml`.

When you browse the `WEB-INF|classes|alfresco directory`, you'll see several XML files that are not Spring configuration files (they don't end in `context.xml`). These are configuration files that use Alfresco's configuration mechanism. The list of these files can be found in the configuration for the **webClientConfigSource** bean that resides in **WEB-INF|classes|alfresco|web-client-application-context.xml**.

The best example of a file of this type is `web-client-config.xml`. An earlier section discussed overriding the default login page by creating a new `login.jsp` and modifying the JSF navigation rule. In addition to the navigation rules, Alfresco has a setting that tells it what the initial login page should be. That setting is in `web-client-config.xml`. A portion of the relevant section of that file is shown here:

```
<config>
    <admin>
        <initial-password>admin</initial-password>
    </admin>
    <client>
        <!-- the error page the client will use -->
        <error-page>/jsp/error.jsp</error-page>

        <!-- the login page the client will use -->
        <login-page>/jsp/login.jsp</login-page>
```

To complete the custom login example, the login-page element needs to be updated to point to the custom login JSP. The override has to happen in a file named `web-client-config-custom.xml` residing in `alfresco|extension`. It can't be named anything else because the webClientConfigSource bean names it explicitly. In this case, the `web-client-config-custom.xml` file would contain the following:

```
<config>
    <client>
        <!-- the login page the client will use -->
        <login-page>/jsp/extension/login.jsp</login-page>
```

Note that only the settings that need to be overridden are repeated in `web-client-config-custom.xml`. In this case, that's just the **login-page** element.

If you look at `web-client-config.xml`, you'll notice a few different types of elements. Depending on what's being configured, Alfresco configuration XML might use elements with specific names (`admin`, `client`, and `login-page` in the previous example). In other cases, an element named `config` is used with `evaluator` and `condition` attributes to define exactly what's being configured. Consider the configuration that specifies what languages should be shown in the drop-down box on the login page. The language configuration in the out of the box `web-client-config.xml` file looks like this:

```
<config evaluator="string-compare" condition="Languages">
    <!-- the list of available language files -->
    <languages>
        <language locale="en_US">English</language>
    </languages>
</config>
```

To override or extend this list, the `config` element can be copied to `web-client-config-custom.xml` and updated as needed:

```
<config evaluator="string-compare" condition="Languages">
    <languages>
            <language locale="ca_ES">Catalan</language>
            <language locale="hr_HR">Croatian</language>
            <language locale="cs_CZ">Czech</language>
            <language locale="da_DK">Danish</language>
    </languages>
</config>
```

In this case, four new languages would be added to the dropdown for a total of five languages. If, instead, you wanted to replace English with only these four choices, you would add the `replace` attribute to the `config` element like this:

```
<config evaluator="string-compare" condition="Languages"
replace="true">
    <languages>
    <language locale="ca_ES">Catalan</language>
    <language locale="hr_HR">Croatian</language>
    <language locale="cs_CZ">Czech</language>
<language locale="da_DK">Danish</language>
</languages>
</config>
```

Solution-Specific Files

There are several types of files that, conceptually, sit on top of the Alfresco platform as a part of the solution you are implementing with Alfresco. These include files such as content models, business process definitions, web scripts, server-side JavaScript, and FreeMarker templates. Alfresco ships several of these with the product. Some are purely meant to be used as examples, while others are functional pieces of the platform. With the exception of content models that can import and extend Alfresco's out of the box content models, there is no need to extend these files directly. Instead, your custom versions of these types of files will sit alongside Alfresco's.

These files can live on the file system or in the repository. When they reside on the file system, they need to be on the classpath. So they should be placed in the **alfresco|extension** directory. When stored in the repository, each type of file has a designated folder within the **|Company Home|Data Dictionary** folder.

For example, suppose you write a JavaScript file to implement the business logic for an action. Ignoring the details on actions for the moment, you can choose to store that JavaScript file either on the file system, perhaps in a directory called **scripts** in the `alfresco|extension` directory, or in the repository within the Scripts folder under **Data Dictionary**.

Business process definitions can live on the file system and in the repository, but they can also be deployed directly to the JBoss jBPM engine. This will be discussed in the Advanced Workflow chapter.

Avoid Modifying Alfresco Code and Configuration

Now that you've got the full source code for Alfresco, it may be tempting to make changes directly to the Alfresco web application. Avoid this temptation at all costs. As soon as you recompile an Alfresco class, tag library, JSP page, or even a configuration file, you've complicated your life unnecessarily.

"But this is open source," you may say, "Why can't I change it if I want to?". Yes, it is open source and, yes, you can change it to your heart's content. But when you do so, be prepared to effectively take ownership of that code going forward. It will be up to you to figure out whether a problem is in your code or Alfresco's. You will also have to devote more time to upgrades than you would have, had you kept your customizations separate from Alfresco's code. In the U.S., a phenomenon that seems to be peculiar to antique shop owners is the posting of a sign that reads, "You break it, you bought it". That certainly applies to modifying the Alfresco source code directly.

There are three situations when, try as you might, you may have to touch Alfresco's files. First, you may identify a bug in the Alfresco source as well as a fix. In this situation, the best thing to do is to put the fix in place as a temporary measure, file a JIRA ticket, and attach the fix to the ticket. Alfresco will confirm the bug and implement the fix (sometimes using your code unchanged and sometimes with its own). Enterprise customers can usually get a patch right away. Labs users may have to run on their own fix until the problem is resolved in a future build.

The second situation is that sometimes (and this is increasingly rare) there may be a configuration change or customization that cannot be implemented through the standard extension mechanism. This is really no different than the previous scenario. If this happens, treat it like a bug. Make the change then file a ticket. Alfresco's intent is for the product to be extensible without the need to change the core installation, so anything less than that is a bug.

The third situation is that you might identify a product enhancement that cannot be implemented without modifying the source. In this case, it is a very good idea to talk to Alfresco (either your representative or via the forums) before you start coding, particularly if it is a big change. They might already be working on the same enhancement. Or, they might be able to gauge demand for the enhancement as well as provide implementation advice. If this enhancement is critical to your solution but no one else is interested in it, you'll have a hard decision to make because it may be a long time before the enhancement gets incorporated into the product. Moving forward without Alfresco's commitment to incorporate the enhancement into the product could mean supporting your own fork of the Alfresco source for the foreseeable future.

Packaging and Deploying Customizations

Now you know how to extend Alfresco without getting your files tangled up with the core distribution. But what is the best way to package them up and deploy them to the server? Most people choose Ant to build and package their customizations. Once they are packaged, you have three options for deploying them as part of the Alfresco web application:

- Copy your files on top of an exploded Alfresco web application.
- Integrate your files with the Alfresco WAR, which you then deploy.
- Package your changes as an **Alfresco Module Package (AMP)** file. The AMP is then installed in—merged into—an Alfresco WAR, which is then deployed to the application server.

The first two approaches are self-explanatory. Copying custom files into an exploded Alfresco web application is the least trouble of the three. It is fast, and makes for a very efficient development cycle. A common approach is to use an `Ant build` file to zip everything into an archive, and then unzip the archive on top of the exploded Alfresco web application. This is the approach you'll use as you work through the examples in this book.

Some application servers, such as JBoss, have a deployment process that deploys WAR files automatically. In this case, it might be useful to integrate the custom files with the Alfresco WAR and then copy the WAR to the deployment directory. Again, using one or more Ant tasks is a common approach in this situation.

The third approach is to use an AMP. Conceptually, the AMP approach is no different than the "integrate with the Alfresco WAR" option: An AMP file is really just a ZIP of your customizations, which are then merged with an Alfresco WAR. The difference is that when you "install" an AMP into the Alfresco WAR, the AMP tools can do things such as check for specific versions of Alfresco, make a backup of the Alfresco WAR, and notify you if the AMP has already been installed to the WAR. More details on working with AMPs can be found in the Appendix.

The following table summarizes the three approaches:

Deployment Approach	Considerations
Copy customizations over the top of an expanded Alfresco web application.	Fastest development cycle.
	Easy to point to a definitive set of changes.
	Some Change Management organizations like to deal only with WAR files.
Merge customizations with the Alfresco WAR.	Change Management likes it—Leverages standard "I deploy the WAR you give me" procedures.
	When developing locally, merging with the WAR seems unnecessary.
Package customizations as an AMP, which is then "installed" into the Alfresco WAR and deployed.	Facilitates version and dependency checking.
	Easier to share with others, particularly when the set of customizations may need to coexist with customizations provided by others.
	Same development overhead as "merge with WAR" option.
	Uses nonstandard, Alfresco-only tool.

Separating Server-Specific Customizations

In every implementation, there is usually a set of customizations that is server-specific and a set that is not server-specific. A good practice is to keep server or environment-specific customizations separate from customizations that do not depend on a specific server or environment. For example, suppose in your shop you have three environments—one each for **Development**, **Test**, and **Production**. Let's assume that you want to configure Alfresco to authenticate against an LDAP directory. You ought to be able to take your Alfresco WAR and deploy it, unchanged, to Development, Test, and Production. If each environment has its own LDAP server, and you include the LDAP configuration as a part of the WAR, you won't be able to do that.

The way to address this is to make sure that only customizations that are independent of server or environment get packaged together. Server-specific customizations should be packaged separately. You might even want to use two different Eclipse projects. One might be called **server extensions** and the other **client extensions**, for example. In this case, the LDAP configuration is a **server extension**.

Using this approach, when you package your client customizations, you should be able to deploy the same package to Development, Test, or Production without modification.

Step-by-Step: Packaging and Deploying a Simple Customization

Let's run through an end-to-end example for a simple customization to validate what you've learned so far. In this example you're going to do two things. First, you're going to modify the login page to display the proud SomeCo logo and the Alfresco version. Second, you're going to extend the content model with a few simple types. To do this, follow these steps:

1. If you haven't already, create a new Java project in Eclipse called `client-extensions` and update its build path to be dependent on **SDK AlfrescoEmbedded**, which is one of the projects included with the Alfresco SDK that references all of the dependent JARs.

2. How you set up the directory structure in your Java project is mostly a personal preference. The source code that accompanies the book will follow Alfresco's project structure fairly close, thus making it easier to follow.

3. Given that, create the following directory structure in the client-extensions project:

   ```
   |config|alfresco|extension|model
   |src|java
   |src|web|jsp|extension
   |src|web|META-INF
   |src|web|someco|images
   ```

4. The examples in this book use Apache Ant to package and deploy the customizations to your local Alfresco web application. The `build.xml` file refers to a `build.properties` file. The `build.properties` file should be used to specify variables specific to your setup. If you set up your Eclipse project folder structure as described earlier, you shouldn't have to edit the `build.xml` file; the `build.properties` file should be all you need to touch. The source code that accompanies this chapter includes a `build.properties.sample` file. Rename it to `build.properties`, and then edit it to point to the expanded Alfresco SDK and the exploded Alfresco webapp directory in Tomcat. Here is an example:

   ```
   alfresco.sdk.remote.dir=|usr|local|bin|alfresco-labs-3.0-sdk|lib|
                                                                remote
   alfresco.sdk.server.dir=|usr|local|bin|alfresco-labs-3.0-sdk|lib|
                                                                server
   alfresco.web.dir=|usr|local|bin|apache|apache-tomcat-5.5.17|
                                                    webapps|alfresco
   ```

Now you are ready to populate the project with Alfresco customizations. The exact details aren't important right now: The point of the exercise is to learn what goes where. So rather than building each file from scratch, use the following table to figure out what files need to be copied from the source code included with the chapter into your Eclipse project. The "Where it came from" column shows where I got the file, in case you are curious. You'll learn how to build these files in the subsequent chapters:

File (Path relative to the root of the Eclipse project)	File description	Where it came from

`|src|web|jsp|extension| login.jsp`
 	
`|src|web|jsp|extension| relogin.jsp`
	Modified `login.jsp` and `relogin.jsp`	Copied from Alfresco's web application and modified

`|src|web|someco|images| someco-logo.png`	SomeCo corporate logo	High-dollar branding consultants, focus groups, hours of graphics design work
`|src|web|META- INF|faces-config.xml`	Custom `faces-config. xml` file to override Alfresco's navigation rules related to login	Copied from Alfresco's web application and modified
`|config|alfresco| extension|web-client- config-custom.xml`	Custom web client configuration to override login page path with the path to the custom page	Copied from Alfresco's web application and modified

5. That's all that is required to customize the login page. To make the example slightly more interesting, let's make a very small extension to Alfresco's content model. A full chapter is devoted to extending the content model, so, again, don't sweat the details at this point. For now, just copy each of the files shown in the following table from the source code that accompanies this chapter into your Eclipse project:

File (Path relative to the root of the Eclipse project)	File description	Where it came from
`|config|alfresco| extension|someco- model-context.xml`	Model context file (Spring bean configuration)	Copied from `custom-model- context.xml.sample` in `[dis tribution]|extensions| extension` and modified
`|config|alfresco| extension|model| scModel.xml`	Model XML file	Copied from `customModel. xml.sample` in `[distributi on]|extensions|extension` and modified
`|config|alfresco| extension|web-client- config-custom.xml`	Custom web client configuration to expose custom types to the web client user interface	Modified the same `web- client-config-custom. xml` file as the one used for the custom login page

6. Now deploy the customizations. If it is running, shut down Tomcat. Then use Ant to package and deploy the files. You can use Eclipse to invoke the `deploy` target or use the command line as follows:

```
ant deploy
```

After successfully running the Ant target, your changes will be sitting in the Alfresco web application directory you specified in `build.properties`. To test this out, start Tomcat back up and see if the customizations made it.

The login page should look like this:

Log in, navigate to a folder, and create some content. You should see **Someco Document** and **Someco Whitepaper** as available content types.

Taking a Look at the Build File

The sample code in this book uses Ant to package and deploy the customizations. The initial `build.xml` file is very straightforward. The list of Ant targets and what they do is probably more important than the actual contents of the `build.xml` file. The Ant targets are shown in the following table:

Ant Target	What it does
clean	Removes all generated files
compile	Compiles `src` to `${bin.dir}`
deploy	Unzips the `${package.file.zip}` into `${alfresco.web.dir}`
package-extension	Creates a ZIP called `${package.file.zip}` that can be unzipped on top of an exploded Alfresco web application
package-jar	Jars up the compiled classes and `${web.dir}/META-INF` into `${package.file.jar}`
setup	Creates the `${build.dir}` and `${bin.dir}` directories
zip-project	Zips the entire Eclipse project as is into `${project.file.zip}`

You can recreate the table output by asking Ant for project help on the command line:

```
ant -p
```

Troubleshooting

There are three primary troubleshooting tools you will become intimately familiar with: Log4j, your favorite Java debugger, and the Alfresco Node Browser. There are other, less-frequently used tools and techniques that will be discussed when the time is right.

Log4j

Most of you are already familiar with this common logging tool, so not a lot of discussion is needed. For everyone else, here are the basics. The verbosity of the log output, the specific classes being logged, and other logging settings are controlled by the `log4j.properties` file located in **WEB-INF|classes**. This is one file distributed with Alfresco that is OK to touch. For example, if you are testing out some server-side JavaScript, you might want to change the JavaScript-related logger from error to debug like this:

```
log4j.logger.org.alfresco.repo.jscript=DEBUG
```

If you want to add your own logger for one of your own Java classes, add a new logger to the end of the file like this:

```
log4j.logger.com.someco=DEBUG
```

Then, within your class, call the logger's methods like this:

```
public class SetWebFlag extends ActionExecuterAbstractBase {
private static Logger logger = Logger.getLogger(SetWebFlag.class);
@Override
protected void executeImpl(Action action, NodeRef actionedUponNodeRef)
{
if (logger.isDebugEnabled()) logger.debug("Inside executeImpl");
```

The call to `DebugEnabled()` isn't required, but it may help a bit with performance.

Step-by-Step: Debugging from within Eclipse

Like Log4j, stepping through the source code of a web application with a remote debugger will be familiar to many readers. Just in case it is new to you, this section walks you through the setup when using Eclipse as your IDE and Alfresco running in a standalone Tomcat instance.

At a high level, what you are going to do is tell Tomcat to send debug information to a specific port. Then, you will tell Eclipse to listen for that information using the same port. This setup will let you set breakpoints in the source code (both yours and Alfresco's), which will get tripped when the JVM processes a statement that has a breakpoint set.

Follow these steps to set this up:

1. Set the **JPDA_TRANSPORT** environment variable to **dt_socket**.

2. Set the **JPDA_ADDRESS** environment variable to 8000.

3. In Tomcat's startup script, change the line that invokes Catalina to include jpda. On Linux, this looks like:

    ```
    exec "$PRGDIR"/"$EXECUTABLE" jpda start "$@"
    ```

4. Start Tomcat. You should see a message like "**Listening for transport dt_socket at address: 8000**".

5. In Eclipse, go to the **Debug Configuration** dialog and create a new **Remote Java Application.** Browse to the project you want to debug. Take the defaults for everything else:

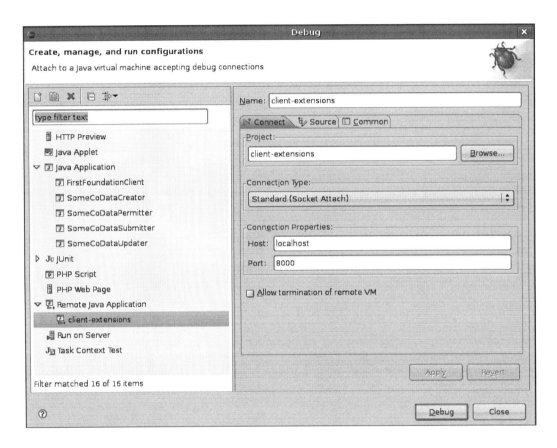

6. Click **Debug.**

You are now ready to debug. If you want to try this out on your own, try setting a breakpoint on something you will hit quickly such as the getUsername method in the LoginBean. You can navigate to it in Eclipse by going to the **SDK AlfrescoEmbedded** project, Referenced Libraries, alfresco-web-client.jar, in the org.alfresco.web.bean package. Once you've found the getUsername method in the LoginBean Java source, double-click the left margin to set a breakpoint. The checkmark that appears as part of the breakpoint indicates that this breakpoint is enabled and the class is loaded:

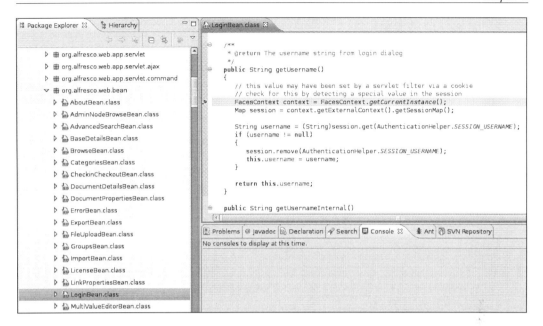

Now open the Alfresco web application in your browser and click the **Login** link. Eclipse will launch the Debugger perspective. You can then step through the source line by line using the **bouncing arrow** icons or click the **green arrow** to continue to the next breakpoint:

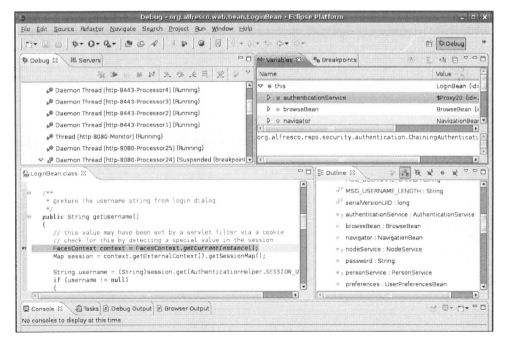

Node Browser

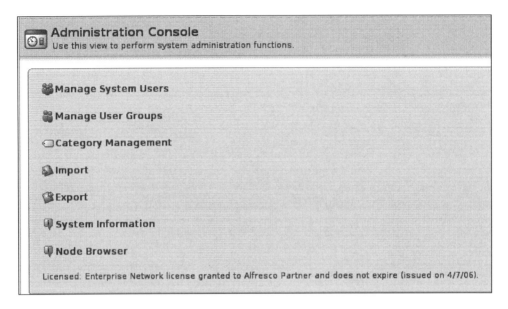

The Alfresco Node Browser, accessible through a link on the **Administration Console,** lets you navigate through the low-level representation of the repository. As you drill into each store and navigate the hierarchy of nodes stored within it, the **Node Browser** displays useful information about each node such as its path, unique ID, node reference, and type. Every property on the node is displayed as well as the aspects that have been applied, the permissions that have been set, and the relationships that have been established with other objects.

Besides being able to navigate the hierarchy, the Node Browser also provides a search box. If you know a node's reference, you can go right to it using the Node Browser's search tool. The search box is also handy for testing out Lucene and Xpath queries.

Starting Over

During development, it is quite common to have to start with a fresh repository. Usually this is because you've made a significant change to the model, and you'd rather blow everything away than clean up inconsistencies. The Alfresco repository is made up of two parts: the metadata stored in the relational database and the binary files stored on the file system. To clear out the repository, you have to clear out both. If you delete the data directory but not the database, you will see a bunch of data integrity problems because the binary files that the database knows about are no longer there.

The **extras** directory in your Alfresco distribution has scripts you can use to quickly drop and recreate the database. Some people find it convenient to create a script that executes the remove database script, then create database script, and then purges the data directory.

Summary

This chapter was about getting your development environment ready to go, providing an overview of how the platform is extended, and understanding the debugging tools that are available. Specifically, you learned:

- Where to get the Alfresco SDK, how to build it, and how to get it set up in Eclipse.

- How to extend Alfresco without modifying Alfresco's source code or configuration. You learned the specific extension technique to use depending on the type of file being customized.

- The three ways to deploy customizations:
  1. Copy the customizations into an exploded Alfresco web application directory.
  2. Copy the customizations into the Alfresco WAR, then deploy it.
  3. Package the customizations as an AMP and use the Module Management Tool to install the module into the Alfresco WAR, which is subsequently deployed.

- What to do when things inevitably go wrong. Familiar techniques such as log4j and remote debugging are available, just as they would be with any web application. In addition, the Node Browser can be a useful tool for inspecting the underlying data structure or testing out search queries.

- How to start clean for testing or debugging purposes. You learned that dropping and recreating the database as well as clearing out the data directory followed by a Tomcat restart will always give you a sparkling new repository to work with.

3

Working with Content Models

From setting up the initial content model to programmatically creating, searching for, and deleting content, how you work with the content in a content management system is a foundational concept upon which the rest of the solution is built. In this chapter, you'll learn:

- What a repository is and how it is structured
- How to make the underlying content model relevant to your business problem by extending Alfresco's out of the box model with your own content types
- What practices are the best for creating your own content models
- How to configure the web client to expose your custom content model via the user interface
- How to interact with the repository via the Web Services and JavaScript APIs

Defining SomeCo's Content Model

Recall from Chapter 1 that SomeCo is rolling out Alfresco across the organization. Each department has its own type of content to work with and different requirements for how it works with that content. SomeCo could just start uploading content into Alfresco. That would be better than nothing, but it relegates Alfresco to lowly file server status, doesn't take advantage of the full power of the platform, and makes for a really boring (and short) book. SomeCo would be better off formalizing the different types of content it works with by extending the Alfresco content model to make it SomeCo-specific.

Step-by-Step: Starting the Custom Content Model with Custom Types

Let's start small and build the model up over successive examples. First, let's create a custom content type for Whitepapers, which are a type of marketing document. This is going to involve creating a content model file, which is expressed as XML, and then telling Alfresco where to find it using a Spring bean configuration file.

To start the content model, follow these steps:

1. Create an extension directory. In the Eclipse client-extensions project, under `|config|alfresco`, create a new folder called `extension` if you do not already have one. As discussed in Chapter 2, the extension directory keeps your customizations separate from Alfresco's code.

2. Create a custom model context file. A custom model context file is a Spring bean configuration file. Spring bean configuration files were also discussed in Chapter 2. Create the file in the extension directory and call it `someco-model-context.xml`. Add the following:

    ```
    <?xml version='1.0' encoding='UTF-8'?>
    <!DOCTYPE beans PUBLIC '-//SPRING//DTD BEAN//EN'          '
    http://www.springframework.org/dtd/spring-beans.dtd'>
        <beans>
         <!-- Registration of new models -->
         <bean id="someco.dictionaryBootstrap"
         parent="dictionaryModelBootstrap" depends-on="dictionaryBoots
         trap">
            <property name="models">
                <list>
                    <value>alfresco/extension/model/scModel.xml
                    </value>
                </list>
            </property>
         </bean>
    </beans>
    ```

3. Create a model file that implements the custom content model. The extension directory is going to fill up over time, so create a new directory under extension called `model`. Create a new XML file in the model directory called `scModel.xml` (this name matches the value specified in the `someco-model-context.xml` file).

4. Add the following XML that is used to describe the model, import other models that this model extends, and declare the model's namespace:

```
<?xml version="1.0" encoding="UTF-8"?>
<!-- Definition of new Model -->
<model name="sc:somecomodel" xmlns="http://www.alfresco.org/model/
dictionary/1.0">
 <!-- Optional meta-data about the model -->
 <description>Someco Model</description>
 <author>Optaros</author>
 <version>1.0</version>
 <!-- Imports are required to allow references to definitions in
   other models -->
 <imports>
  <!-- Import Alfresco Dictionary Definitions -->
  <import uri="http://www.alfresco.org/model/dictionary/1.0"
  prefix="d" />
  <!-- Import Alfresco Content Domain Model Definitions -->
  <import uri="http://www.alfresco.org/model/content/1.0"
    prefix="cm" />
 </imports>
 <!-- Introduction of new namespaces defined by this model -->
 <namespaces>
  <namespace uri="http://www.someco.com/model/content/1.0"
   prefix="sc" />
 </namespaces>
```

5. Next, add the types. A **Whitepaper** is a type of marketing document that, in turn, is only one of several types of content SomeCo deals with. It's a hierarchy. That hierarchy will be reflected in the model. Add this XML to the model file below the "namespaces" element:

```
<types>
 <!-- Enterprise-wide generic document type -->
 <type name="sc:doc">
  <title>Someco Document</title>
  <parent>cm:content</parent>
 </type>
 <type name="sc:marketingDoc">
  <title>Someco Marketing Document</title>
  <parent>sc:doc</parent>
 </type>
 <type name="sc:whitepaper">
 <title>Someco Whitepaper</title>
 <parent>sc:marketingDoc</parent>
 </type>
</types>
```

6. Be sure to close the model tag so the XML is valid.

   ```
   </model>
   ```

7. The final step is to deploy the changes and then restart Tomcat so that Alfresco will load the custom model. Copy the `build.xml` file from the source code that accompanies this chapter into the root of your Eclipse project, replacing the `build.xml` file you used in the exercises for the previous chapter.

8. Run `ant deploy`.

9. Restart Tomcat.

Watch the log during the restart. You should see no errors related to loading the custom model. If there is a problem, the message usually looks something like "Could not import bootstrap model".

With this change in place, the repository is now capable of telling the difference between a generic piece of content and SomeCo-specific pieces of content such as marketing documents and Whitepapers.

Types

Types are like types or classes in the object-oriented world. They can be used to model business objects, they have properties, and they can inherit from a parent type. "Content", "Person", and "Folder" are three important types defined out of the box. Custom types are limited only by your imagination and business requirements. Examples include things such as "Expense Report", "Medical Record", "Movie", "Song", and "Comment".

Did you notice the names of the types you created in the example? Names are made unique across the repository by using a namespace specific to the model. The namespace has an abbreviation. The model you created for SomeCo defines a custom model, which declares a namespace with the URI of `http://www.someco.com/model/content/1.0` and a prefix of "sc". Any type defined as a part of the model will have a name prefixed with "sc:". Using namespaces in this way helps to prevent name collisions when content models are shared across repositories.

Step-by-Step: Adding Properties to Types

The Marketing department thinks in terms of marketing campaigns. In fact, they want to be able to search by a specific campaign and find all of the content tied to a particular campaign. Not to hurt the Marketing team's feelings, but the HR, Sales, and Operations teams couldn't care less about campaigns.

You are going to address this by adding a property to the `sc:marketingDoc` type to capture the marketing campaigns the document is related to. You could make this property a text field. But letting users enter a campaign as free-form text is a recipe for disaster if you care about getting valid search results later because of the potential for misspelling the campaign name. Plus, SomeCo wants to let each document be associated with multiple campaigns, which compounds the free-form text entry problem. So, for this particular property it makes sense to constrain its values to a list of valid campaigns.

To allow the Marketing team to "tag" a piece of content with one or more campaigns selected from a list of valid campaign names, update the model by following these steps:

1. Edit the `scModel.xml` file in **config | alfresco | extension**. Replace the `sc:marketingDoc` type definition with the following:

```
<type name="sc:marketingDoc">
    <title>Someco Marketing Document</title>
    <parent>sc:doc</parent>
    <properties>
      <property name="sc:campaign">
        <type>d:text</type>
        <multiple>true</multiple>
        <constraints>
          <constraint ref="sc:campaignList" />
        </constraints>
      </property>
    </properties>
</type>
```

2. Now, define the campaign list constraint. Between the "namespaces" and "types" elements, add a new "constraints" element as follows:

```
<constraints>
  <constraint name="sc:campaignList" type="LIST">
          <parameter name="allowedValues">
              <list>
                  <value>Application Syndication</value>
          <value>Private Event Retailing</value>
                  <value>Social Shopping</value>
              </list>
          </parameter>
      </constraint>
</constraints>
```

3. Save the `model` file.

4. Run `ant deploy`.

5. Restart Tomcat.

Again, Tomcat should start cleanly with no complaints about the content model.

Properties and Property Types

Properties are pieces of metadata associated with a particular type. In the previous example, the property was the marketing campaign. The properties of a SomeCo Expense Report might include things such as "Employee Name", "Date submitted", "Project", "Client", "Expense Report Number", "Total amount", and "Currency". The Expense Report might also include a "content" property to hold the actual expense report file (maybe it is a PDF or an Excel spreadsheet, for example).

You may be wondering about the `sc:whitepaper` type. Does anything special need to happen to make sure whitepapers can be tied to campaigns as well? Nope! In Alfresco, content types inherit the properties of their parent. The `sc:whitepaper` type will automatically have an `sc:campaign` property. In fact, it will have all sorts of properties inherited from its ancestor types. The file name, content property, and creation date are three important examples.

Property types (or data types) describe the fundamental types of data the repository will use to store properties. The data type of the `sc:campaign` property is `d:text`. Other examples include things such as dates, floats, Booleans, and content that is the property type of the property used to store content in a node. Because these data types literally are fundamental, they are pretty much the same for everyone. So they are defined for you out of the box. Even though these data types are defined out of the box, if you wanted to change the Alfresco data type "text" so that it maps to your own custom class rather than `java.lang.String`, you could.

Constraints

Constraints can optionally be used to restrict the values that Alfresco will store in a property. In the following example, the `sc:campaign` property used a LIST constraint. There are three other types of constraints available: REGEX, MINMAX, and LENGTH. REGEX is used to make sure that a property value matches a regular expression pattern. MINMAX provides a numeric range for a property value. LENGTH sets a restriction on the length of a string.

Constraints can be defined once and reused across a model. For example, out of the box, Alfresco makes available a constraint named `cm:filename` that defines a regular expression constraint for file names. If a property in a custom type needs to restrict values to those matching the filename pattern, the custom model doesn't have to define the constraint again. It simply refers to the `cm:filename` constraint.

Step-by-Step: Relating Types with Associations

SomeCo has a generic need to be able to identify documents that relate to each other for any reason. A Whitepaper might be tied to a solution offering data sheet, for example. Or maybe a project proposal the Legal department has should be related to the project plan the Operations team is managing. These relationships are called **associations**.

Let's update the model file to include a related-documents association in the `sc:doc` type so that any SomeCo document can be related to any other.

To add assocations to the model, follow these steps:

1. Edit the `scModel.xml` file.

2. Add the following associations element to the `sc:doc` type. Notice that the target of the association must be an `sc:doc` or one of its child types. The association is not mandatory, and there may be more than one related document:

```
<type name="sc:doc">
  <title>Someco Document</title>
  <parent>cm:content</parent>
  <associations>
   <association name="sc:relatedDocuments">
   <title>Related Documents</title>
   <source>
    <mandatory>false</mandatory>
    <many>true</many>
   </source>
   <target>
    <class>sc:doc</class>
    <mandatory>false</mandatory>
    <many>true</many>
   </target>
   </association>
  </associations>
</type>
```

3. Save the `model` file.

4. Deploy your changes using `ant deploy` and restart Tomcat.

When you restart, watch the log for errors related to the content model. If everything is clean, keep going.

Associations

Associations define relationships between types. Without associations, models would be full of types with properties that store "pointers" to other pieces of content. Going back to the expense report example, suppose each expense is stored as an individual object. In addition to an Expense Report type, there would also be an Expense type. In this example, associations can be used to tell Alfresco about the relationship between an Expense Report and one or more Expenses.

Here's an important note about the content model schema that may save you some time: Order matters. For example, if a type has both properties and associations, properties go first. If you get the order wrong, Alfresco won't be able to parse your model. There is an XML Schema file that declares the syntax for a content model XML file. It is called `modelSchema.xsd`, and it resides in the Alfresco web application under **WEB-INF | classes | alfresco | model**.

In the `sc:relatedDocuments` association you just defined, note that both the source and target class of the association is `sc:doc`. That's because SomeCo wants to associate documents with each other regardless of content type. Defining the association at the `sc:doc` level allows any instance of `sc:doc` or its children to be associated with zero or more instances of `sc:doc` or its children. It also assumes that SomeCo is using `sc:doc` or children of that type for all of its content. Content stored as the more generic `cm:content` type would not be able to be the target of an `sc:relatedDocuments` association.

Associations come in two flavors: Peer Associations and Child Associations. (Note that Alfresco refers to Peer Associations simply as "Associations", but that's confusing. So the book will use the "Peer" distinction.) Peer Associations are just that—they define a relationship between two objects, but neither is subordinate to the other. Child Associations, on the other hand, are used when the target of the association (or child) should not exist when the source (or parent) goes away. This works like a cascaded delete in a relational database: Delete the parent and the child goes away.

An out of the box association that's easy to relate to is `cm:contains`. The `cm:contains` association defines a Child Association between folders (`cm:folder`) and all other objects (instances of `sys:base` or its child types). So, for example, a folder named `Human Resources` (an instance of `cm:folder`) would have a `cm:contains` association between itself and all of its immediate children. The children could be instances of custom types like Resume, Policy, or Performance Review. If you delete a folder, the folder's children are also deleted.

Another example might be a "Whitepaper" and its "Related Documents". Suppose that SomeCo publishes Whitepapers on its web site. The Whitepaper might be related to other documents such as product marketing materials or other research. If the relationship between the Whitepaper and its related documents is formalized, it can be shown in the user interface. To implement this, as part of the Whitepaper content type, you'd define a Peer Association. You could use `sys:base` as the target type to allow any piece of content in the repository to be associated with a Whitepaper, or you could restrict the association to a specific type. In this case, because it uses a Peer association, related documents don't get deleted when the Whitepaper gets deleted. You can imagine the headaches that would cause if that weren't the case!

Step-by-Step: Adding Aspects to the Content Model

SomeCo wants to track the client name and, optionally, the project name for pieces of client-related content. But any piece of content in the repository might be client-related. Proposals and Status Reports are both project-related, but the two will be in different parts of the model (one is a type of legal document while the other is a type of operations document). Whether a piece of content is client-related or not, it transcends department—almost anything can be client-related. The grouping of properties that need to be tracked for content that is client-related is called an **aspect**.

Here's another example. SomeCo would like to selectively pull content from the repository to show on its web site. Again, any piece of content could be published on the site. So an indication of whether or not a piece of content is "webable" should be captured in an aspect. Specifically, content that needs to be shown on the web site needs to have a flag that indicates the content is "active" and a date when the content was set to active. These will be the aspect's properties.

Let's modify the content model to include these two aspects. To add the client-related and webable aspects to the content model, follow these steps:

1. Edit the `scModel.xml` file.

2. Add a new `aspects` element below the `types` element to contain the new aspects. Add one `aspect` element to define the client-related aspect and another to define the web-related aspect. You'll notice that the syntax for the `aspect` element is identical to the `type` element:

```xml
<aspects>
  <aspect name="sc:webable">
   <title>Someco Webable</title>
   <properties>
    <property name="sc:published">
     <type>d:date</type>
    </property>
    <property name="sc:isActive">
     <type>d:boolean</type>
     <default>false</default>
    </property>
   </properties>
  </aspect>
  <aspect name="sc:clientRelated">
   <title>Someco Client Metadata</title>
   <properties>
    <property name="sc:clientName">
     <type>d:text</type>
     <mandatory>true</mandatory>
    </property>
    <property name="sc:projectName">
     <type>d:text</type>
     <mandatory>false</mandatory>
    </property>
   </properties>
  </aspect>
</aspects>
```

3. Save the `model` file.

4. Run `ant deploy` and restart Tomcat.

Alfresco should start cleanly without making any model-related complaints.

Aspects

To appreciate aspects, first consider how inheritance works and its implications on the content model. Suppose that SomeCo only wants to display a subset of the repository's content on the web site. (In fact, this is the case. The SomeCo write-up in Chapter 1 said that, except for job postings, HR content shouldn't go near the public web.) In the recent example, webable content needs to have a flag that indicates whether or not it is "active", and a date that indicates when it became active.

Without aspects, there would only be two options to model these properties. The first option would be to put the properties on `sc:doc`, the root object. All child content types would inherit from this root type, thus making the properties available everywhere. The second option would be to individually define the two properties only in the content types that will be published to the portal.

Neither of these is a great option. In the first option, there would be properties in each and every piece of content in the repository that may or may not ultimately be used. This can lead to performance and maintenance problems. The second option too isn't much better for several reasons. First, it assumes that the content types to be published to the portal are known when you design the model. Second, it opens up the possibility that the same type of metadata might get defined differently across content types. Third, it doesn't provide an easy way to encapsulate behavior or business logic that might be tied to the published date. Finally, property names must be unique across the model. So you'd have to modify the names of the properties in every type in which they were used, otherwise it would be a serious pain later when you try to run queries across types.

As you already know, the best option is to use aspects. Aspects allow "cross-cutting" of the content model with properties and associations by attaching them to content types (or even specific instances of content at runtime rather than design time) when and where they are needed.

In this case, SomeCo's webable aspect will be added to any piece of content that needs to be displayed on the web site, regardless of type.

Another nice thing about aspects is that they give you a way to have multiple inheritances. As you saw in the model, types can only inherit from a single parent. But you can add as many aspects to a type or object instance as you need.

Step-by-Step: Finishing up the Model

Let's finish up the model by doing two things: First, the remaining departments need content types added to them. Second, there is an out of the box aspect that needs to be applied to all the content. It's called `generalclassifiable`. It allows content to be categorized. SomeCo wants all of its content to be classifiable as soon as it hits the repository. To make that happen, you need to define the aspect as mandatory. Because SomeCo wants it across the board, you can do it on the root type `sc:doc`, and have it trickle down to all of SomeCo's types.

To add the remaining departmental content types as well as make the `generalclassifiable` aspect mandatory, follow these steps:

1. Edit the `scModel.xml` file.

2. Add the the following types:

    ```
    <type name="sc:hrDoc">
     <title>Someco HR Document</title>
     <parent>sc:doc</parent>
    </type>

    <type name="sc:salesDoc">
     <title>Someco Sales Document</title>
     <parent>sc:doc</parent>
    </type>

    <type name="sc:opsDoc">
     <title>Someco Operations Document</title>
     <parent>sc:doc</parent>
    </type>

    <type name="sc:legalDoc">
     <title>Someco Legal Document</title>
     <parent>sc:doc</parent>
    </type>
    ```

3. Modify the `sc:doc` type to include `cm:generalclassifiable` as a mandatory aspect. Note that you can add as many mandatory aspects as you need:

    ```
    <type name="sc:doc">
     <title>Someco Document</title>
     <parent>cm:content</parent>
     <associations>

     </associations>
     <mandatory-aspects>
     <aspect>cm:generalclassifiable</aspect>
     </mandatory-aspects>
    </type>
    ```

4. Save the `model` file.

5. Run `ant deploy` and restart Tomcat.

Watch the log for content model-related errors. If everything starts up cleanly, you are ready to move on. In the next set of examples, you'll configure the web client so that you can work with your new model.

Modeling Summary

A content model describes the data being stored in the repository. The content model is critical. Without it, Alfresco would be little more than a file system. Here is a list of key information that the content model provides Alfresco:

- Fundamental data types and how those data types should persist to the database. For example, without a content model, Alfresco wouldn't know the difference between a string and a date.

- Higher order data types such as "content" and "folder" as well as custom content types such as "SomeCo Standard Operating Procedure" or "SomeCo Sales Contract".

- Out of the box aspects such as "auditable" and "classifiable" as well as SomeCo-specific aspects such as "rateable", "commentable", or "client-related".

- Properties (or metadata) specific to each content type.

- Constraints placed on properties (such as property values that must match a certain pattern or property values that must come from a specific list of possible values).

- Relationships or "associations" between content types.

Alfresco content models are built using a small set of building blocks: Types, Properties, Property Types, Constraints, Associations, and Aspects. When planning your Alfresco implementation, it may make sense to diagram the proposed content model just as you would a data model in a traditional web application.

The content model implemented in the examples could be diagrammed as follows:

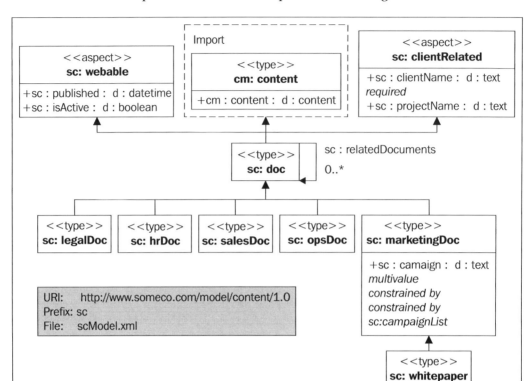

The Appendix contains similar diagrams for the out of the box content models for your reference.

Custom Behavior

You may find that your custom aspect or custom type needs to have behavior or business logic associated with it. For example, every time an Expense Report is checked in, you might want to recalculate the total by iterating through the associated Expenses. One option would be to incorporate this logic into rules or actions in the Alfresco web client or your custom web application. But some behaviors are so fundamental to the aspect or type that they should really be "bound" to the aspect or type, and invoked any time Alfresco works with those objects. Behavior really gets out of the realm of modeling and into "handling content automatically", which is the subject of Chapter 4. For now, just realize that associating business logic with your custom aspects and types (or overriding out of the box behavior) is possible.

Modeling Best Practices

Now that you know the building blocks of a content model, it makes sense to consider some best practices. Here are the top ten:

1. **Don't change Alfresco's out of the box content model.** If you can possibly avoid it, do not change Alfresco's out of the box content model. Instead, extend it with your own custom content model. If requirements call for several different types of content to be stored in the repository, create a content type for each one that extends from `cm:content` or from an enterprise-wide root content type.

2. **Consider implementing an enterprise-wide root type.** Although the need for a common ancestor type is lessened through the use of aspects, it still might be a good idea to define an enterprise-wide root content type such as `sc:doc` from which all other content types in the repository inherit, if for no other reason, than it gives content managers a "catch-all" type to use when no other type will do.

3. **Be conservative early on by adding only what you know you need.** A corollary to that is to be prepared to blow away the repository multiple times, until the content model stabilizes. Once you get content in the repository (that implements the types in your model), making model additions is easy, but subtractions aren't. Alfresco will complain about "integrity errors" and may make content inaccessible when the content's type or properties don't match the content model definition. When this happens to you (and it will happen), you can choose one of these options:

   ○ Leave the old model in place
   ○ Attempt to export the content, modify the exported data (see "ACP Files" in the Appendix), and re-import
   ○ Drop the Alfresco tables, clear the data directory, and start fresh

   As long as everyone in the team is aware of this, option three is not a big deal in development. But make sure expectations are set appropriately and have a plan for handling model changes once you get to production. This might be an area where Alfresco will improve in future releases, but for now it is something you have to watch out for.

4. **Avoid unnecessary content model depth.** There don't seem to be any Alfresco Content Modeling Commandments that say, "Thou shall not exceed X levels of depth in thine content model, lest thou suffer the wrath of poor performance". But it seems logical that degradation would occur at some point. If your model has several levels of depth beyond `cm:content`, you should at least do a proof-of-concept with a realistic amount of data, software, and hardware to make sure you aren't creating a problem for yourself that might be very difficult to reverse down the road.

5. **Take advantage of aspects.** In addition to the potential performance and overhead savings through the use of aspects, aspects promote reuse across the model, the business logic, and the presentation layer. When working on your model, you may find that two or more content types have properties in common such as `sc:webable` and `sc:clientRelated`. Ask yourself if those properties are being used to describe some higher-level characteristic common across the types that might be modeled better as an aspect.

6. **It may make sense to define types that have no properties or associations.** You may find yourself defining a type that gets everything it needs through either inheritance from a parent type or from an aspect (or both). In the SomeCo model `sc:marketingDoc` is the only type with a property. You might ask yourself if the empty type is really necessary. It should at least be considered. It might be worth it, just to distinguish the content from other types of content for search purposes, for example. Or, while you might not have any specialized properties or associations for the content type, you could have specialized behavior that's only applicable to instances of the content type.

7. **Remember that folders are types too.** Like everything else in the repository, folders are instances of types, which means they can be extended. Content that "contains" other content is common. In the earlier expense report example, one way to keep track of the expenses associated with an expense report would be to model the expense report as a sub-type of `cm:folder`.

8. **Don't be afraid to have more than one content model XML file.** When it is time to implement your model, keep this in mind: It might make sense to segment your models into multiple namespaces and multiple XML files. Names should be descriptive. Don't deploy a model file called `customModel.xml` or `myModel.xml`.

9. **Implement a Java interface that corresponds to each custom content model you define.** Within each content model Java class, define constants that correspond to model namespaces, type names, property names, aspect names, and so on. You'll find yourself referring to the qualified name (`Qname`, for short) of types, properties, and aspects quite often; so it helps to have constants defined in an intuitive way. The constants should be `QName` objects except in cases where the Web Services API needs to leverage them. The Web Services API doesn't have the `QName` class, so there will need to be a string representation of the names as well in that case.

10. **Use the source!** The out of the box content model is a great example of what's possible. The `forumModel` and `recordsModel` have some particularly useful examples. In the next section you'll learn where the model files live and what's in each. So you'll know where to look later when you say to yourself, "Surely, the folks at Alfresco have done this before".

This last point is important enough to spend a little more time on. The next section discusses the out of the box models in additional detail.

Out of the Box Models

The Alfresco source code is an indispensable reference tool that you should always have ready along with the documentation, wiki, forums, and Jira. With that said, if you are following along with this chapter but have not yet downloaded the source, you are in luck. The out of the box content model files are written in XML and get deployed with the web client. They can be found in the `alfresco.war` file in **|WEB-INF|classes|alfresco|model**. The following table describes several of the model files that can be found in the directory:

File	Namespaces*	Prefix	Imports	Description
`dictionaryModel.xml`	`model|dictionary|1.0`	d	None	Fundamental data types used in all other models like text, int, Boolean, datetime, and content.
`systemModel.xml`	`model|system|1.0`	sys	d	System-level objects like base, store root, and reference.
	`system|registry|1.0`	reg		
	`system|modules|1.0`	module		
`contentModel.xml`	`model|content|1.0`	cm	d sys	Types and aspects extended most often by your models like Content, Folder, Versionable, and Auditable.
`bpmModel.xml`	`model|bpm|1.0`	bpm	d sys cm	Advanced workflow types like task and startTask. Extend these when writing your own custom advanced workflows.
`forumModel.xml`	`model|forum|1.0`	fm	d cm	Types and aspects related to adding discussion threads to objects like forum, topic, and post.

The table lists the most often referenced models. Alfresco also includes two WCM-related model files, the JCR model and the web client application model, which may also be worth looking at, depending on what you are trying to do with your model.

In addition to the model files, the `modelSchema.xsd` file can be a good reference. As the name suggests, it defines the XML vocabulary Alfresco content model XML files must adhere to.

Configuring the UI

Now that the model is defined, you could begin using it right away by writing code against one of Alfresco's APIs that creates instances of your custom types, adds aspects, and so on. In practice, it is usually a good idea to do just that to make sure the model behaves as you expect. But you'd probably like to log in to the web client to see the fruits of your labor from the last section, so let's discuss what it takes to make that happen. By the end of this discussion, you will be able to use the web client to work with the SomeCo-specific content model to do things such as these:

- Display and update custom properties and associations
- Create instances of SomeCo-specific content types
- Configure actions that involve SomeCo types and aspects
- Use Advanced Search to query with SomeCo-specific parameters

Configuring the UI to expose the custom content model involves overriding and extending Alfresco's out of the box web client configuration. To do this, you'll create your own SomeCo-specific version of the web client configuration XML that overrides Alfresco's. For more details on how the out of the box web client configuration is structured and what is available to be extended, refer to the Appendix.

Step-by-Step: Adding Properties to the Property Sheet

When a user looks at a property sheet for a piece of content stored as one of the custom types or with one of the custom aspects attached, the property sheet should show the custom properties. If there are associations, those should be shown as well:

In order to configure the properties sheet to show custom properties and associations, follow these steps:

1. In the `client-extensions` Eclipse project, create a new XML file called `web-client-config-custom.xml` in the extension directory if it isn't there already. If you are creating it from scratch, populate it with an empty `alfresco-config` element. You'll add child elements to it in the subsequent steps.

2. To add properties to property sheets, use the `aspect-name` evaluator for aspects and the `node-type` evaluator for content types. SomeCo has two aspects that need to be added to the properties sheet: `sc:webable` and `sc:clientRelated`. For `sc:webable`, add the following `config` element to `web-client-config-custom.xml` as a child of `alfresco-config`:

```
<!-- add webable aspect properties to property sheet -->
 <config evaluator="aspect-name" condition="sc:webable">
  <property-sheet>
   <show-property name="sc:published" display-label-id=
                                             "published" />
   <show-property name="sc:isActive" display-label-id="isActive"
                                             read-only="true" />
  </property-sheet>
 </config>
```

3. Add the `config` element to show the properties for the `clientRelated` aspect on your own.

4. Add the following to display the `relatedDocuments` association for SomeCo documents and Whitepapers:

```
<config evaluator="node-type" condition="sc:doc">
 <property-sheet>
  <show-association name="sc:relatedDocuments" />
 </property-sheet>
</config>
<config evaluator="node-type" condition="sc:whitepaper">
 <property-sheet>
  <show-association name="sc:relatedDocuments" />
 </property-sheet>
</config>
```

5. Add the following to display the campaign property for SomeCo Marketing Documents:

```
<!-- show campaign on maraketingDoc property sheet -->
<config evaluator="node-type" condition="sc:marketingDoc">
 <property-sheet>
  <show-property name="sc:campaign" display-label-id="campaign" />
 </property-sheet>
</config
```

6. Save the file.

7. Deploy the customizations (`ant deploy`), restart Tomcat, and test.

In Chapter 2, you deployed a small set of customizations to validate your development environment. With the web client configuration modifications you just made, you should be able to log in to Alfresco and create instances of Marketing and Whitepaper documents. When you look at the properties for an instance of a Whitepaper, you should see a component that lets you pick **Related Documents**:

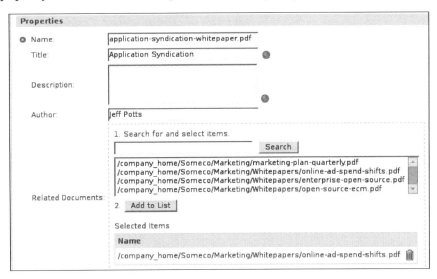

When you look at the properties for an instance of a marketing document, you should see a component that lets you choose the associated campaign:

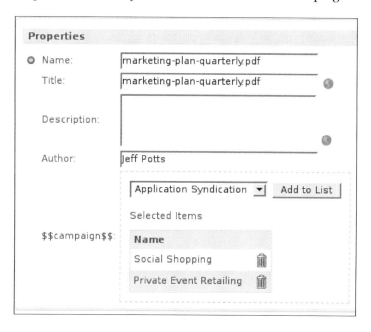

Note that you may see some placeholder text for the **Campaign** label (and corresponding warnings in the log) because you haven't externalized that label yet. We'll fix that shortly.

Externalizing Display Labels

Note the `display-label-id` attribute of the `show-property` element in the previous code. An alternative is to specify the label explicitly in this file using the `label` attribute. But a better practice is to externalize the string so that the interface can be localized if needed, so this example uses `display-label-id`. The actual label value is defined elsewhere in a resource bundle.

Making Properties Read-Only

In the previous code, the read-only attribute on the show-property element for `sc:isActive` prevents web client users from editing the property. It does not, however, prevent the property from being set through scripts or API calls. In this case, SomeCo wants it to be "read-only", so that it can be set through other means such as by actions or during an approval step in a workflow.

Step-by-Step: Adding Types and Aspects to WebClient Dropdowns

When a user clicks **Create** or **Add Content**, the custom types should be a choice in the list of content types. And when a user configures a rule on a space and uses content types or aspects as a criterion or action parameter, the custom types and aspects should be included in the dropdowns.

When you tested your last change you probably noticed that the types you created in Chapter 2 were shown, but not the types you added in this chapter for Legal, HR, Sales, and so on. Similarly, if you tried to add the client-related or webable aspects to an object, you weren't able to select either aspect from the list.

Just as you did for custom properties and associations in the previous example, you have to override Alfresco's web client configuration to get custom types and aspects to show up in the web client.

To add custom types and aspects to the appropriate dropdowns, follow these steps:

1. Edit `web-client-config-custom.xml`.

2. To add content types to the list of available types in the **create content** and **add content** dialogs, use the `string-compare` evaluator and the `Content Wizards` condition. Add the following to `web-client-config-custom.xml` beneath the previous `config` element:

    ```xml
    <!-- add someco types to add content list -->
    config evaluator="string-compare" condition="Content Wizards">
     <content-types>
      <type name="sc:doc" />
      <type name="sc:whitepaper" />
      <type name="sc:legalDoc" />
      <type name="sc:marketingDoc" />++
      <type name="sc:hrDoc" />
      <type name="sc:salesDoc" />
      <type name="sc:opsDoc" />
     </content-types>
    </config>
    ```

3. The list of types and aspects used when rule actions are configured are all part of the same `config` element. The `Action Wizards` config has several child elements that can be used. The aspects element defines the list of aspects shown when the `add aspect` action is configured. The `subtypes` element lists types that show up in the dropdown when configuring the

content type criteria for a rule. The `specialise-types` element (note the UK spelling) lists the types available to the `specialize type` action. Add the following to `web-client-config-custom.xml` below the previously added `config` element:

```xml
<config evaluator="string-compare" condition="Action Wizards">
 <!-- The list of aspects to show in the add/remove features
                                                  action -->
     <!-- and the has-aspect condition -->
  <aspects>
   <aspect name="sc:webable"/>
   <aspect name="sc:clientRelated"/>
  </aspects>

  <!-- The list of types shown in the is-subtype condition -->
  <subtypes>
   <type name="sc:doc" />
   <type name="sc:whitepaper" />
   <type name="sc:legalDoc" />
   <type name="sc:marketingDoc" />
   <type name="sc:hrDoc" />
   <type name="sc:salesDoc" />
   <type name="sc:opsDoc" />
  </subtypes>

   <!-- The list of content and/or folder types shown in the
                                    specialise-type action -->
  <specialise-types>
   <type name="sc:doc" />
   <type name="sc:whitepaper" />
   <type name="sc:legalDoc" />
   <type name="sc:marketingDoc" />
   <type name="sc:hrDoc" />
   <type name="sc:salesDoc" />
   <type name="sc:opsDoc" />
  </specialise-types>
 </config>
```

4. Save the `web-client-config-custom.xml` file.

5. Deploy your changes using `ant deploy`, restart Tomcat, and test.

To test these changes out, log in to the web client. Now when you create new content, all of the SomeCo types should be in the content type dropdown:

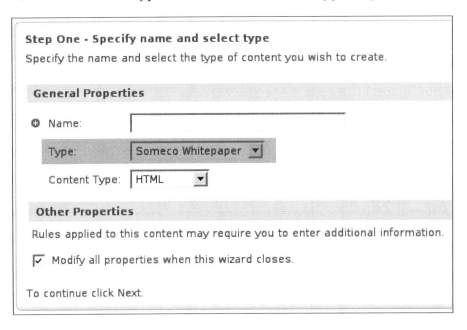

To test the aspect-related changes, configure a new rule on a space. The first step when defining a rule action is to identify the criteria for running the action. If you select either **Items that have a specific aspect applied** or **Items of a specified type or its sub-types**, you should see the SomeCo custom types when you click **Set Values and Add:**

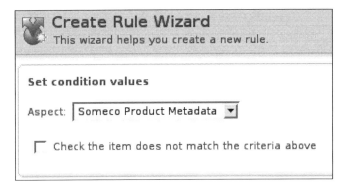

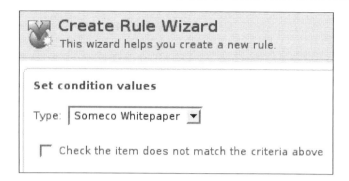

The SomeCo custom types should also be listed as content type choices for the **specialize type** action, and custom aspects should be listed as choices for the **add aspect** action. To test this, view the details for a folder or a piece of content and then click **Run Action** to launch the rule action wizard. When choosing either the **specialize type** or **add aspect** actions, the list that gets displayed when you click **Set Values** and **Add** should include items from the custom model.

Step-by-Step: Adding Properties and Types to Advanced Search

When a user runs an advanced search, he or she should be able to restrict search results to instances of custom types and/or content with specific values for the properties of custom types. As before, this involves modifying `web-client-config-custom.xml`.

To add custom properties and types to the advanced search dialog, follow these steps:

1. The `Advanced Search config` specifies which content types and properties can be used to refine an advanced search result set. Add the following to `web-client-config-custom.xml` below the previously-added `config` element.

```
<config evaluator="string-compare" condition="Advanced Search">
  <advanced-search>
   <content-types>
    <type name="sc:doc" />
    <type name="sc:whitepaper" />
    <type name="sc:legalDoc" />
    <type name="sc:marketingDoc" />
    <type name="sc:hrDoc" />
    <type name="sc:salesDoc" />
    <type name="sc:opsDoc" />
   </content-types>
```

```
<custom-properties>
 <meta-data aspect="sc:webable" property="sc:published" display-
   label-id="published" />
 <meta-data aspect="sc:webable" property="sc:isActive" display-
   label-id="isActive" />
 <meta-data aspect="sc:clientRelated" property="sc:clientName"
   display-label-id="client" />
 <meta-data aspect="sc:clientRelated" property="sc:projectName"
   display-label-id="project" />
 </custom-properties>
 </advanced-search>
</config>
```

2. Deploy the changes by running ant deploy, restart Tomcat, and test.

3. To test out this change, log in to the web client and go to **Advanced Search**. The SomeCo types should be listed in the **Content Type** dropdown. The custom properties should be listed under **Additional Options:**

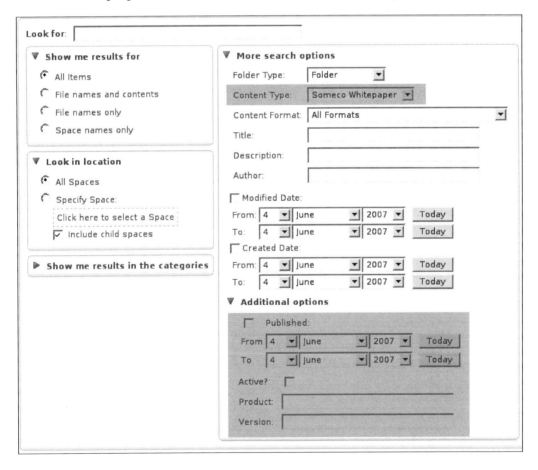

Step-by-Step: Setting Externalized Label Values

You probably noticed when you were testing the web client changes that all of the labels were showing unresolved label IDs. You need to create a new properties file to fix that. The file will hold name-value pairs that match the `display-label-id` attributes in `web-client-config-custom.xml`.

To configure the label IDs, follow these steps:

1. Create a file called `webclient.properties` in the same directory as `web-client-config-custom.xml`.

2. In this example, there are five properties that need labels. Populate `webclient.properties` as follows.

    ```
    #sc:webable
    published=Published
    isActive=Active?
    #sc:clientRelated
    client=Client
    project=Project
    #sc:marketingDoc
    campaign=Campaign
    ```

3. Deploy your changes by running `ant deploy`, restart Tomcat, and test.

4. Log in to the web client and open the properties for a document. Now the label IDs should be resolving to the externalized string values.

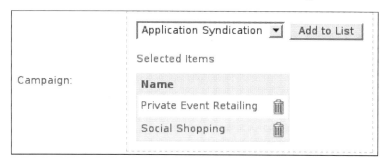

 At the time of this writing, there was a bug related to web client configuration property files and AMPs (AWC-1149). If you want to deploy the project as an AMP, your `webclient.properties` file will need to go into **alfresco | extension** instead of your module-specific directory. Until this issue is resolved, this means there is the possibility of an overwrite if the directory already contains a `webclient.properties` file. For more information on deploying AMPs, see the Appendix.

Setting up Additional Locales

The whole point in externalizing the labels is that the client can be localized to multiple languages. If you want to create a set of labels for a specific locale, you would create a file in the extension directory called `webclient_[locale].properties` with the same keys and their localized values.

Working with Content Programmatically

Now the repository has a custom model and that model has been exposed to the Alfresco web client. For simple document management solutions, this may be enough. But often, code will also be required as a part of your implementation. It might be code in a web application that needs to work with the repository, code that implements custom behavior for custom content types, code that implements Alfresco web client customizations, or code that implements a controller for a web script.

As mentioned in Chapter 1, there are several APIs available depending on what you want to do. Let's learn how to use code to create content, create associations between content, search for content, and delete content. You'll see a JavaScript example, several examples using the Web Services API with Java, and one example showing the API with PHP. Additional API examples can be found in the Appendix.

Step-by-Step: Creating Content with JavaScript

The first example shows how to create some content and add aspects to that content using JavaScript.

To create content, add aspects, and set properties using JavaScript, follow these steps:

1. Create a new file in **src | scripts** called `createContent.js`.

2. Set up some variables you'll use later in the script.

   ```
   var contentType = "whitepaper";
   var contentName = "sample-a";
   var timestamp = new Date().getTime();
   ```

3. Write code that will create the new node as a child of the current space. The "space" variable is a root object that is available when the script is executed against a folder. Notice the `contentName` and `timestamp` variables are being concatenated to make sure the name is unique on successive runs.

   ```
   var whitepaperNode = space.createNode(contentName + timestamp,
                                         "sc:" + contentType);
   ```

4. Add a statement that uses the ScriptNode API to add the `sc:webable` aspect.

```
whitepaperNode.addAspect(sc:webable);
```

5. Add code to set some properties. These properties include out of the box properties such as `cm:name` as well as SomeCo-specific properties.

```
whitepaperNode.properties["cm:name"] = contentName + " (" +
                                       timestamp + ")";
whitepaperNode.properties["sc:isActive"] = true;
whitepaperNode.properties["sc:published"] = new Date("04/01/2007");
```

6. The ScriptNode API can work with the content property directly. Add a statement to store some content on the node, and then call save to persist the changes.

```
whitepaperNode.content = "This is a sample " + contentType + "
                         document called " + contentName;
whitepaperNode.save();
```

7. Test the script by uploading it to the repository and then running it against a folder. Using the Web Client, add the file to the Data `Dictionary/Scripts` folder.

8. Navigate to the Whitepapers folder. Then do **View Details**, **Run Action**, **Execute Script** to initiate the Run Action Wizard.

9. Use **Set Values and Add** to select `createContent.js` from the available scripts.

10. Click **OK,** and then **Finish** to execute the script.

A new Whitepaper should now be sitting in the folder. Later in the book, you'll add a new UI action that makes executing scripts even easier.

Leveraging Root Objects

In this example, you used `space` to refer to the space the script was executed against. There is also a `document` root object that can be used when running the script against a document. Refer to the Appendix for the full list of root objects.

Knowing When to Save Documents

Method calls that affect a node's properties require `save` to persist the changes. If in this example we were only adding an aspect, we wouldn't have to save the document because the change is persisted immediately.

Using JavaScript for Batch Manipulation

During projects you will often find that you need to perform batch operations on nodes in the repository. You might want to execute an action against all documents in all subfolders starting at a given path, for example. JavaScript is a quick way to perform such mass operations and doesn't require code to be compiled and packaged.

Writing Content to the Content Property

Properties store data about a node. The terms "metadata" and "attributes" are synonymous with "properties".

Content refers to the main unit of data being managed by the system: a file. A PDF file, for example, is a piece of content. Plain-text data such as XML, HTML, or JavaScript are also examples of content.

Content is stored as a property on the node. In Alfresco, the content is really stored on the file system, but as developers using the API, we don't care about where the content is physically stored. In this example, we created plain-text content simply by writing a string to the content property. This means it is really easy to create content in the repository, especially if it is plain text.

Creating Content with Java Web Services

JavaScript is fast to develop and very succinct, but it must run on the Alfresco server. Alfresco's Web Services API is one option to consider when you want to run code on a different machine than the Alfresco server.

Let's look at the same task that was in the previous example (creating a SomeCo Whitepaper, adding the `sc:webable` aspect, and setting some properties), but this time using the Java Web Services API. The code used for creating content is almost exactly the same code that comes with the Alfresco SDK Samples, but it is helpful to break it down to see what's going on.

An overview of the steps involved is:

Authenticate to start a session.

1. Get a reference to the folder where the content will be created.
2. Create an array of `NamedValue` objects. Each `NamedValue` object corresponds to a property that will be set on the new object.
3. Create a series of **Content Manipulation Language (CML)** objects that encapsulate the operations to be executed.

4. Execute the CML and dump the results.

5. Update the new node with content.

Rather than creating this class yourself, follow along by looking at the class called `com.someco.examples.SomeCoDataCreator` in **src|java** in the source code included with the chapter. Then, you can follow the steps for running this class on your local machine.

`SomeCoDataCreator` is a runnable Java class that accepts arguments for the username, password, and folder in which to create the content, type of content to create, and a name for the new content.

The first thing the code does is to start a session by authenticating with the server:

```
AuthenticationUtils.startSession(getUser(), getPassword());
```

Next, a `timeStamp` is saved. The timestamp will be used to make the content name unique. Then, the code gets a reference to the folder where the content will be created:

```
String timeStamp = new Long(System.currentTimeMillis()).toString();
Store storeRef = new Store(Constants.WORKSPACE_STORE, "SpacesStore");
ParentReference docParent = new ParentReference(
  storeRef,
  null,
  getFolderPath(),
  Constants.ASSOC_CONTAINS,
  Constants.createQNameString(
    SomeCoModel.NAMESPACE_SOMECO_CONTENT_MODEL,
    getContentName() + timeStamp));
```

Refer to the highlighted code. What is a Store? An Alfresco repository is a collection of stores. In JCR parlance, the stores are called **workspaces**. But in this book, unless the example is dealing with the JCR specifically, they will be referred to as **stores.** A given Alfresco instance has one repository with multiple stores. When you are working with the API, you sometimes have to specify which store you are working with.

Notice that in addition to the folder path, the `ParentReference` constructor used to create the folder reference expects the type of association being created (contains) as well as the name of the child object.

Next, the code creates a `NamedValue` for each property that's going to be set on the new object and then creates an array of all `NamedValue` objects:

```
NamedValue nameValue = Utils.createNamedValue(Constants.PROP_NAME,
getContentName() + " (" + timeStamp + ")");

NamedValue activeValue = Utils.createNamedValue
(Constants.createQNameString(SomeCoModel.NAMESPACE_SOMECO_CONTENT_
MODEL, SomeCoModel.PROP_IS_ACTIVE_STRING), "true");

NamedValue publishDateValue = Utils.createNamedValue(
 Constants.createQNameString(SomeCoModel.NAMESPACE_SOMECO_CONTENT_
MODEL, SomeCoModel.PROP_PUBLISHED_STRING),
 "2007-04-01T00:00:00.000-05:00");

NamedValue[] contentProps = new NamedValue[] {nameValue, activeValue,
publishDateValue};
```

Take a look at the date string (for the curious, it's the ISO 8601 format). That `-05:00` is the GMT timezone offset.

Now CML comes into play. The web services API uses CML objects to encapsulate various content operations. In this case, the example code needs to create a node and add aspects to the node so it uses `CMLCreate` and `CMLAddAspect`.

Note the `ref1` string. That's an arbitrary reference that Alfresco uses to relate the CML statements. Without it, Alfresco wouldn't know which content object to add the aspects to. So if you were creating multiple objects in one shot, for example, you would use unique reference strings for each object. The value isn't persisted anywhere. It is discarded after the CML is executed.

First, the `CMLCreate` object gets created. The `CMLCreate` constructor needs to know the parent reference (`docParent`), the type of content being created, and an array of property values to set:

```
CMLCreate createDoc = new CMLCreate(
 "ref1",
 docParent,
 null,
 null,
 null,
 Constants.createQNameString(SomeCoModel.NAMESPACE_SOMECO_CONTENT_
MODEL, SomeCoModel.TYPE_SC_DOC_STRING),
 contentProps);
```

Then, one `CMLAddAspect` object gets created for each aspect to be added:

```
CMLAddAspect addWebableAspectToDoc = new CMLAddAspect
(Constants.createQNameString(SomeCoModel.NAMESPACE_SOMECO_CONTENT_
MODEL, SomeCoModel.ASPECT_SC_WEBABLE_STRING),
```

```
  null,
  null,
  "ref1");

CMLAddAspect addClientRelatedAspectToDoc = new CMLAddAspect(
  Constants.createQNameString(SomeCoModel.NAMESPACE_SOMECO_CONTENT_
MODEL, SomeCoModel.ASPECT_SC_CLIENT_RELATED_STRING),
  null,
  null,
  "ref1");
```

To execute the CML, the code instantiates a new CML object. Setters on the CML object specify the operations to perform, in this case one document creation and two aspect additions. The code then uses the `RepositoryService` to run the update, which passes back an array of `UpdateResults`. The `dumpUpdateResults` method just iterates through the `UpdateResult` array and writes some information to sysout:

```
// Construct CML Block
CML cml = new CML();
cml.setCreate(new CMLCreate[] {createDoc});
cml.setAddAspect(new CMLAddAspect[] {addWebableAspectToDoc,
addClientRelatedAspectToDoc});

// Execute CML Block
UpdateResult[] results = WebServiceFactory.getRepositoryService().
update(cml);
Reference docRef = results[0].getDestination();
dumpUpdateResults(results);
```

Now the node exists, but it doesn't have any content. The last chunk of code writes some text content to the newly created node. This example uses a string for the content, but it could just as easily write the bytes from a file on the local file system:

```
// Nodes are created, now write some content
ContentServiceSoapBindingStub contentService = WebServiceFactory.
getContentService();
ContentFormat contentFormat = new ContentFormat("text/plain", "UTF-
8");
String docText = "This is a sample " + getContentType() + " document
called " + getContentName();
Content docContentRef = contentService.write(docRef, Constants.PROP_
CONTENT, docText.getBytes(), contentFormat);
System.out.println("Content Length: " + docContentRef.getLength());
```

As you can see, this code accomplishes exactly the same end result as the JavaScript example; but it is a bit more verbose.

Step-by-Step: Run SomeCoDataCreator Class to Create Content

To run the SomeCoDataCreator class to create some content, follow these steps:

1. Copy the `com.someco.examples.SomeCoDataCreator.java` file into **src|java** within your client-extensions project in Eclipse.

2. The Web Services API needs to know the hostname of the Alfresco server that the remote classes are communicating with. Create a file called `webserviceclient.properties` in the client-extensions project's **config|alfresco|extension** directory. Assuming both your Alfresco server and your code reside on the same machine, the file should look like this:

   ```
   # Set the following property to reference the Alfresco server
   that you would like the web service client to communicate with

   repository.location=http://localhost:8080/alfresco/api
   ```

3. If you haven't already, log in to Alfresco and create the following folder structure in your repository: **Someco|Marketing|Whitepapers**.

4. Execute the class by running `ant data-creator`. The `Ant` target will compile and execute the class.

If everything is successful, the result should be something like:

```
Command = create; Source = none; Destination = b901941e-12d3-11dc-
9bf3-e998e07a8da1
Command = addAspect; Source = b901941e-12d3-11dc-9bf3-e998e07a8da1;
Destination = b901941e-12d3-11dc-9bf3-e998e07a8da1
Command = addAspect; Source = b901941e-12d3-11dc-9bf3-e998e07a8da1;
Destination = b901941e-12d3-11dc-9bf3-e998e07a8da1
Content Length: 26
```

If you decide to use Eclipse or command-line Java to run the class rather than the `Ant` target, make sure you have the `webserviceclient.properties` file on your classpath or the Web Services API will not be able to locate the Alfresco server.

Creating Content with PHP Web Services

Java is not a requirement for SOAP-based web services. Alfresco also delivers PHP classes that use the Web Services API. Here's how the "create content and add aspects" example would look like in PHP:

```php
<?php
  require_once "Alfresco/Service/Session.php";
  require_once "Alfresco/Service/SpacesStore.php";
```

```
require_once "Alfresco/Service/Node.php";

...snip...

  function createContent($username, $password, $folderPath,
$contentType, $contentName) {

 // Start and create the session
 $repository = new Repository("http://localhost:8080/alfresco/api");
 $ticket = $repository->authenticate($username, $password);
$session = $repository->createSession($ticket);

 $store = new Store($session, "SpacesStore");

 // Grab a reference to the SomeCo folder
 $results = $session->query($store, 'PATH:"' . $folderPath . '"');
 $rootFolderNode = $results[0];

 if ($rootFolderNode == null) {
  echo "Root folder node (" . $folderPath . ") is null<br>";
  exit;
 }

 $timestamp = time();

 $newNode = $rootFolderNode>createChild
("{http://www.someco.com/model/content/1.0}" . $contentType, "cm_
contains", "{http://www.someco.com/model/content/1.0}" . $contentType
. "_" . $timestamp );

 if ($newNode == null) {
  echo "New node is null<br>";
  exit;
 }

 // Add the two aspects
 $newNode->addAspect("{http://www.someco.com/model/content/
1.0}webable");
 $newNode->addAspect("{http://www.someco.com/model/content/
1.0}clientRelated");

 echo "Aspects added<br>";

 // Set the properties
 $properties = $newNode->getProperties();

 $properties["{http://www.alfresco.org/model/content/1.0}name"] =
$contentName . " (" . $timestamp . ")";
 $properties["{http://www.someco.com/model/content/1.0}isActive"] =
"true";
 $properties["{http://www.someco.com/model/content/1.0}published"] =
"2007-04-01T00:00:00.000-05:00";

 $newNode->setProperties($properties);
```

```
echo "Props set<br>";

$newNode->setContent("cm_content", "text/plain", "UTF-8", "This is a
sample " . $contentType . " document named " . $contentName);

echo "Content set<br>";

$session->save();

echo "Saved changes to " . $newNode->getId() . "<br>";
    }
?>

Running the PHP script in a web browser produces:
Aspects added
Props set
Content set
Saved changes to 5a8dac5e-1314-11dc-ab93-3b56af79ba48
```

The PHP file lives in the `src/php` folder in the `client-extensions` Eclipse project included with the source. See the Appendix for instructions on how to set up your environment to run this PHP example.

The rest of the chapter includes Java Web Services API examples. Refer to the source code that will be provided in Chapter 6 and the Appendix for additional JavaScript examples.

Creating Associations

Now let's switch back to the Java Web Services API and look at a class that creates a related-documents association between two documents.

The high-level steps are essentially the same as in the earlier Java example:

1. Create the references and objects the CML needs.

2. Set up the CML objects.

3. Execute the CML and dump the results.

This class is called `com.someco.examples.SomeCoDataRelater`. The class is runnable and accepts a source UUID and a target UUID as arguments. You can get them from the output of the `SomeCoDataCreator` class.

After logging in, the code creates references to the source and target using the UUIDs passed in as arguments:

```
Reference docRefSource = new Reference(storeRef, getSourceUuid(),
null);
Reference docRefTarget = new Reference(storeRef, getTargetUuid(),
null);
```

Then, the code creates a CMLCreateAssociation object. The constructor accepts predicate objects, which are easily created using the reference objects, and the type of association being created:

```
CMLCreateAssociation relatedDocAssoc = new CMLCreateAssociation(new
Predicate(new Reference[]{docRefSource}, null, null),
  null,
  new Predicate(new Reference[] {docRefTarget}, null, null),
  null,   Constants.createQNameString(SomeCoModel.NAMESPACE_SOMECO_
CONTENT_MODEL,
    SomeCoModel.ASSN_RELATED_DOCUMENTS_STRING));
```

The rest should look very familiar. A new CML object is instantiated and its setCreateAssociation method is called with an array of CMLCreateAssociation objects. In this case, there is only one association being created:

```
// Setup CML block
CML cml = new CML();
cml.setCreateAssociation(new CMLCreateAssociation[]
{relatedDocAssoc});
```

Then, the Repository Service executes the CML and returns the array of UpdateResults, which get passed to the dumpUpdateResults method:

```
// Execute CML Block
UpdateResult[] results = WebServiceFactory.getRepositoryService().
update(cml);
dumpUpdateResults(results);
```

Just to confirm everything worked out as expected, the code calls a method to dump the associations of the source object:

```
System.out.println("Associations of sourceUuid:" + getSourceUuid());

dumpAssociations(docRefSource, Constants.createQNameString
(SomeCoModel.NAMESPACE_SOMECO_CONTENT_MODEL, SomeCoModel.ASSN_RELATED_
DOCUMENTS_STRING));
```

Step-by-Step: Run SomeCoDataRelater Class to Create Association

To run the SomeCoDataRelater class to create an association between two objects, follow these steps:

1. Copy the com.someco.examples.SomeCoDataRelater.java file from the chapter source code to your client-extension project.

2. If you haven't already done so, make sure you have created at least two instances of sc:doc in your repository. A fast way to do that is to run ant data-creator a couple of times. Make sure you note the source UUID from the console output.

3. Run the class using the `Ant` task called `data-relater`. The `Ant` task accepts two arguments, `${sourceId}` and `${targetId}` for the source and target UUIDs. For example,

```
ant data-relater -DsourceId=1355e60e-160b-11dc-a66f-bb03ffd77ac6
-DtargetId=bd0bd57d-160c-11dc-a66f-bb03ffd77ac6
```

Running the `SomeCoDataRelater` Java class produces:

```
Command = createAssociation; Source = 1355e60e-160b-11dc-a66f-
bb03ffd77ac6; Destination = bd0bd57d-160c-11dc-a66f-bb03ffd77ac6
Associations of sourceUuid:1355e60e-160b-11dc-a66f-bb03ffd77ac6
bd0bd57d-160c-11dc-a66f-bb03ffd77ac6
{http://www.alfresco.org/model/content/1.0}name:Test Document 2
(1181340487582)
```

Now you can use the Alfresco Web Client to view the associations. Remember the `web-client-config-custom.xml` file? It specified that the property sheet for `sc:doc` or `sc:whitepaper` objects should show the `sc:relatedDocuments` associations. Alternatively, the Node Browser that is available in the Administration Console is a handy way to view associations.

Searching for Content

Now that you have some content in the repository, you can test out Alfresco's full-text search engine, **Lucene**. Content in the repository is synchronously indexed by Lucene when it is created. Query strings use the Lucene query syntax to find content based on full-text content, property values, path, and content type.

Let's review some code that will show several different examples of Alfresco queries using Lucene. The code will:

1. Authenticate to start a session.
2. Get a reference to the node where the search should start.
3. Establish a query object using the Lucene query string.
4. Execute the query and dump the results.

The class is called `com.someco.examples.SomeCoDataQueries`. Just like the content creation code, the class will be a runnable Java application that accepts the username, password, and folder name as arguments.

There are two methods of interest in this class: `getQueryResults()` and `doExamples()`. The `getQueryResults()` method is a generic method that executes a specified query string and returns a list of `ContentResult` objects. (`ContentResult` is an inner class that is used as a helper to manage the query result properties). The `doExamples()` method calls `getQueryResults()` repeatedly to show different search string examples.

Let's take a look at `getQueryResults()`. First, the code sets up the query object and executes the query using the `query()` method of the `RepositoryService`:

```
public List<ContentResult> getQueryResults(String queryString) throws
Exception {
  List<ContentResult> results = new ArrayList<ContentResult>();
  Query query = new Query(Constants.QUERY_LANG_LUCENE, queryString );
  // Execute the query
  QueryResult queryResult = getRepositoryService().query(getStoreRef(),
query, false);
  // Display the results
  ResultSet resultSet = queryResult.getResultSet();
  ResultSetRow[] rows = resultSet.getRows();
```

Next, the code iterates through the results, extracting property values from the search results and storing them in a helper object called `contentResult`.

```
if (rows != null) {
 // Get the infomation from the result set
 for(ResultSetRow row : rows) {
  String nodeId = row.getNode().getId();
  ContentResult contentResult = new ContentResult(nodeId);
  // iterate through the columns of the result set to extract
  // specific named values
  for (NamedValue namedValue : row.getColumns()) {
    if (namedValue.getName().endsWith(Constants.PROP_CREATED) == true)
{
  contentResult.setCreateDate(namedValue.getValue());
      } else if (namedValue.getName().endsWith(Constants.PROP_NAME) ==
true) {
     contentResult.setName(namedValue.getValue());
    }
   }
  results.add(contentResult);
 } //next row
} // end if
return results;
}
```

The `doExamples()` method sets up query strings and calls `getQueryResults()`. One such call is shown here:

```
System.out.println("Finding content of type:" +
 SomeCoModel.TYPE_SC_DOC_STRING);
queryString = "+TYPE:\"" +
 Constants.createQNameString(SomeCoModel.NAMESPACE_SOMECO_CONTENT_
MODEL,
  SomeCoModel.TYPE_SC_DOC_STRING) + "\"";
dumpQueryResults(getQueryResults(queryString));
```

Step-by-Step: Run SomeCoDataQueries Class to See Lucene Example

Running the `SomeCoDataQueries` class is a good way to see some example Lucene search strings and the resulting output:

1. Copy the `com.someco.examples.SomeCoDataQueries.java` file from the source code to the client-extensions project.

2. Create one or more instances of `sc:doc` in the repository by running `SomeCoDataCreator` or by adding content to the repository manually (remember to choose a SomeCo content type).

3. Execute the `data-queries` Ant task.

Your results will vary based on how much content you've created and the values you've set in the content properties. The output should look something like:

```
======================
Finding content of type:doc
----------------------
Result 1:
id=1355e60e-160b-11dc-a66f-bb03ffd77ac6
name=Test Whitepaper (1181339773331)
created=2007-06-08T16:56:13.932-05:00
----------------------
Result 2:
id=bd0bd57d-160c-11dc-a66f-bb03ffd77ac6
name=Test Document 2 (1181340487582)
created=2007-06-08T17:08:08.150-05:00
----------------------
Result 3:
id=1fe9cf04-160b-11dc-a66f-bb03ffd77ac6
name=Test Document (1181339794431)
created=2007-06-08T16:56:35.028-05:00
======================
Find content in the root folder with text like 'sample'
----------------------
Result 1:
id=bd0bd57d-160c-11dc-a66f-bb03ffd77ac6
name=Test Document 2 (1181340487582)
created=2007-06-08T17:08:08.150-05:00
----------------------
Result 2:
id=1fe9cf04-160b-11dc-a66f-bb03ffd77ac6
name=Test Document (1181339794431)
```

```
created=2007-06-08T16:56:35.028-05:00
---------------------
Result 3:
id=1355e60e-160b-11dc-a66f-bb03ffd77ac6
name=Test Whitepaper (1181339773331)
created=2007-06-08T16:56:13.932-05:00
======================
Find active content
---------------------
Result 1:
id=bd0bd57d-160c-11dc-a66f-bb03ffd77ac6
name=Test Document 2 (1181340487582)
created=2007-06-08T17:08:08.150-05:00
---------------------
Result 2:
id=1fe9cf04-160b-11dc-a66f-bb03ffd77ac6
name=Test Document (1181339794431)
created=2007-06-08T16:56:35.028-05:00
---------------------
Result 3:
id=1355e60e-160b-11dc-a66f-bb03ffd77ac6
name=Test Whitepaper (1181339773331)
created=2007-06-08T16:56:13.932-05:00
======================
Find active content with a client property containing 'Lebowski'
======================
Find content of type sc:whitepaper published between 1/1/2006 and
6/1/2007
---------------------
Result 1:
id=1355e60e-160b-11dc-a66f-bb03ffd77ac6
name=Test Whitepaper (1181339773331)
created=2007-06-08T16:56:13.932-05:00
```

There are a couple of other useful tidbits in this class that have been omitted here such as how to use the `ContentService` to get the URL for the content and how the UUID for the root folder is retrieved. Explore the code that accompanies this chapter to see the class in its entirety.

See the Appendix for more information on the Lucene search syntax.

Deleting Content

Now it is time to clean up after yourself by deleting content from the repository. Deleting follows the same pattern as searching except that instead of dumping the results, the class will create CMLDelete objects for each result and then will execute the CML to perform the delete.

Let's review the com.someco.examples.SomeCoDataCleaner class. This runnable class optionally accepts a content type and a folder path to narrow down the scope of what's being deleted.

First, the code sets up the query object:

```
// Create a query object, looking for all items of a particular type
String queryString = "TYPE:\"" + Constants.createQNameString(SomeCoMod
el.NAMESPACE_SOMECO_CONTENT_MODEL, getContentType()) + "\"";
            if (getFolderPath() != null) queryString =
queryString + " AND PATH:\"" + getFolderPath() + "/*\"";
            Query query = new Query(Constants.QUERY_LANG_LUCENE,
queryString);
```

Then, the RepositoryService executes the query:

```
// Execute the query
QueryResult queryResult = repositoryService.query(storeRef, query,
false);

// Get the resultset
ResultSet resultSet = queryResult.getResultSet();
ResultSetRow[] rows = resultSet.getRows();
```

A CMLDelete object is created for each row returned and added to an array:

```
// if we found some rows, create an array of DeleteCML objects
if (rows != null) {
    System.out.println("Found " + rows.length + " objects to
delete.");

 CMLDelete[] deleteCMLArray = new CMLDelete[rows.length];
 for (int index = 0; index < rows.length; index++) {
  ResultSetRow row = rows[index];
  deleteCMLArray[index] = new CMLDelete(new Predicate(new Reference[]
{new Reference(storeRef, row.getNode().getId(), null)}, null, null));
 }
```

As in prior examples, the final step is to set up the CML object, execute the CML using the RepositoryService, and dump the results:

```
// Construct CML Block
CML cml = new CML();
cml.setDelete(deleteCMLArray);

// Execute CML Block
UpdateResult[] results =
  WebServiceFactory.getRepositoryService().update(cml);
dumpUpdateResults(results);

} //end if
```

 Note that this code deletes every matching object in the repository (or the specified folder path) of type sc:doc (or the specified content type) and its children. You would definitely want to "think twice and cut once" if you were running this code on a production repository!

Step-by-Step: Running SomeCoDataCleaner Class to Delete Content

To execute the SomeCoDataCleaner class to delete content from your repository, follow these steps:

1. Copy the com.someco.examples.SomeCoDataCleaner.java file from the source code for the chapter to your client-extensions project.

2. Running this class isn't too exciting if there isn't any content in the repository. Create some if you don't have any. The Ant task assumes you will create one or more sc:whitepaper objects.

3. Run the data-cleaner Ant task.

Again, your results will vary based on the content you've created. The output should look similar to the following:

```
Found 2 objects to delete.
Command = delete; Source = b6c3f8b0-12fb-11dc-ab93-3b56af79ba48;
Destination = none
Command = delete; Source = d932365a-12fb-11dc-ab93-3b56af79ba48;
Destination = none
```

Summary

This chapter was about customizing Alfresco's content model, configuring the web client to allow end users to work with the custom content model via the web client, and using the Web Services API and JavaScript API to create, search, update, and delete objects in the repository. Specifically, you learned:

- The Alfresco repository is a hierarchical collection of stores and nodes.
- The Alfresco content model defines the data types of nodes and properties, and the relationships between nodes.
- Extending the content model to make it relevant to your business problem involves creating an XML file to describe the model, then telling Alfresco about it through a Spring bean configuration file.
- The fundamental building blocks used to define the content model include: Types, Aspects, Properties, and Associations.
- Best practices for creating your own content models include using aspects as much as possible, considering the use of a root content type, and leveraging the out of the box content model as a reference.
- Configuring the web client to expose your custom content model via the user interface involves overriding configuration elements in Alfresco's out of the box web client configuration.

There are several options for interacting with the repository with code. Examples in this chapter included the Web Services API (both PHP and Java) and the JavaScript API.

4
Handling Content Automatically with Actions, Behaviors, Transformers, and Extractors

Alfresco provides several types of hooks that can be used to perform interesting operations on content. Whether an operation is triggered by an end user as is the case with Actions (sometimes called "**Rule Actions**") or it is handled automatically with Behaviors, Transformers, or Extractors, this chapter is about leveraging what is already available out of the box and, more importantly, how to develop your own when what is available doesn't meet your needs.

By the end of this chapter, you will know how to:

- Create your own actions using Java
- Bind Java- and JavaScript-based behavior to types and aspects
- Configure and extend metadata extractors
- Write custom content transformers

Encapsulating Content Operations in Actions

As you might suspect, an action or a rule action is something a user can do to a piece of content. Actions are discrete units of work and can optionally be configured at runtime by the user. Some of the out of the box actions are Check-out, Check-in, Update, Cut, Copy, Edit, and Delete.

In the last chapter, SomeCo created some metadata related to publishing Whitepapers on the Web. The **sc:webable** aspect included a flag to identify whether or not a piece of content should show up on the Web as well as a published date that captures when the flag was set.

The **sc:isActive** flag was configured to be read-only, so SomeCo needs a way to set that flag. They might want to do it automatically when content is added to a folder, they might want to set it during a step in a workflow, or through a link in one of the web client menus. By using an action, you can write the code once and call it from all of those places.

Step-by-Step: Creating a Basic Action

At its most basic, a custom rule action requires three things:

1. An action executer class.
2. A Spring bean configuration file.
3. A properties file to externalize action-related strings.

Let's create an action to add the **sc:webable** aspect to a document, and set its **isActive** flag and publish date. By the end of these steps you will have an action that can be executed by an end user, a step in a workflow (and anywhere else Alfresco JavaScript can run), or a link in the user interface. Follow these steps:

1. Create a new class in your **java | src** directory called `com.`
   `someco.web.action.executer.SetWebFlag`. The class extends
   `ActionExecuterAbstractBase`, which means there are two methods that
   need to be implemented: `executeImpl` and `addParameterDefinitions`.

   ```
   public class SetWebFlag extends ActionExecuterAbstractBase {
   ```

2. Start implementing the `executeImpl` method. This code expects a parameter
   containing the flag indicating how the `isActive` property should be set. For
   now, the parameter is optional. So if it is null, default it to true.

   ```
   protected void executeImpl(Action action, NodeRef
                                       actionedUponNodeRef) {
   boolean activeFlag = (Boolean)action.getParameterValue
                                       (PARAM_ACTIVE);

   if (activeFlag == null) activeFlag = true;
   ```

3. Setting the properties appropriately is a two-step process. First, grab the current properties from the node. (The `nodeService` is a dependency that will get set through a Spring bean configuration.)

```
Map<QName, Serializable> properties = nodeService.getProperties
                                            (actionedUponNodeRef);
```

4. Then add the new property value to the properties map.

```
properties.put( SomeCoModel.PROP_IS_ACTIVE, activeFlag);
```

5. If the `activeFlag` is being set to true, set the published date property to the current date.

```
if (activeFlag) {
        properties.put( SomeCoModel.PROP_PUBLISHED, new Date());
}
```

6. Next, check for the aspect. If the aspect has already been added, just set the properties. Otherwise, it needs to be added. The aspect can be added and the properties can be set in one step.

```
Node node = new Node(actionedUponNodeRef);
// if the aspect has already been added, set the properties
if (node.hasAspect( SomeCoModel.ASPECT_SC_WEBABLE)) {
nodeService.setProperties(actionedUponNodeRef, properties);
} else {
// otherwise, add the aspect and set the properties
nodeService.addAspect(actionedUponNodeRef,   SomeCoModel.ASPECT_SC_
                                        WEBABLE, properties);

}
}
```

7. Save the class.

8. Now implement the `addParameterDefinitions` method. This method defines the parameters our action uses. The method is implemented as follows.

```
protected void addParameterDefinitions(List<ParameterDefinition>
                                            paramList) {
paramList.add(
new ParameterDefinitionImpl(// Create a new parameter defintion to
                                            add to the list
        PARAM_ACTIVE, // The name used to identify the parameter
DataTypeDefinition.BOOLEAN, // The parameter value type
        false, // Indicates whether the parameter is mandatory
        getParamDisplayLabel(PARAM_ACTIVE))); // The parameters
display label
}
```

9. The last step is to create the local variable for the `nodeService` and the associated setter method. The fastest way to do this is to simply add the local variable and then use Eclipse to generate the setter methods. The class also has a couple of constants, shown below, to make it easier for others to work with the action class.

```
protected NodeService nodeService;
public final static String NAME = "set-web-flag";
public final static String PARAM_ACTIVE = "active";
```

10. To save you time, the imports you'll need are shown here:

```
import java.io.Serializable;
import java.util.Date;
import java.util.List;
import java.util.Map;
import org.alfresco.repo.action.ParameterDefinitionImpl;
import org.alfresco.repo.action.executer.
                                ActionExecuterAbstractBase;
import org.alfresco.service.cmr.action.Action;
import org.alfresco.service.cmr.action.ParameterDefinition;
import org.alfresco.service.cmr.dictionary.DataTypeDefinition;
import org.alfresco.service.cmr.repository.NodeRef;
import org.alfresco.service.cmr.repository.NodeService;
import org.alfresco.service.namespace.QName;
import org.alfresco.web.bean.repository.Node;
import org.apache.log4j.Logger;
import com.someco.model.SomeCoModel;
```

11. Save the class.

12. Now write a Spring bean configuration file. It can be named anything as long as it ends in `context.xml`. Call it `someco-actions-context.xml`. The contents of the config file are shown below. Note the bean ID needs to match the NAME constant in the action executer. Also note the second bean that points to a properties file. You'll create the properties file it refers to in the next step.

```
<?xml version='1.0' encoding='UTF-8'?>
<!DOCTYPE beans PUBLIC '-//SPRING//DTD BEAN//EN' 'http://www.
springframework.org/dtd/spring-beans.dtd'>
<beans>
    <bean id="set-web-flag" class="com.someco.web.action.executer.
    SetWebFlag" parent="action-executer">
        <property name="nodeService">
            <ref bean="NodeService" />
        </property>
        <property name="publicAction">
            <value>true</value>
        </property>
    </bean>
```

```
<bean id="extension.actionResourceBundles" parent="
actionResourceBundles">
        <property name="resourceBundles">
                list>
        <value>alfresco.extension.somecoactions</value>
    </list>
    </property>
        </bean>
</beans>
```

13. Create a file called somecoactions.properties. It contains externalized strings for the action.

```
set-web-flag.title=Sets the SC Web Flag
set-web-flag.description=This will add the sc:webable aspect and
                                    set the isActive flag.
```

14. Deploy the new action by running ant deploy, then restart Tomcat.

15. Log in to Alfresco. Create a test Whitepaper document in **SomeCo | Marketing | Whitepapers**.

16. To run your new action, open the details for the document, and then click **Run Action**:

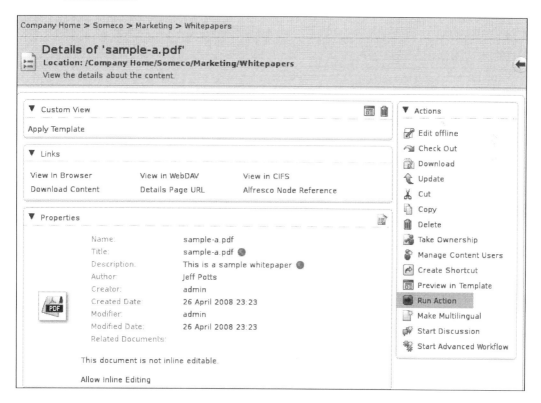

You should see your action in the list. Select it, then click **Set Values and Add**. Click **Finish** to run the action:

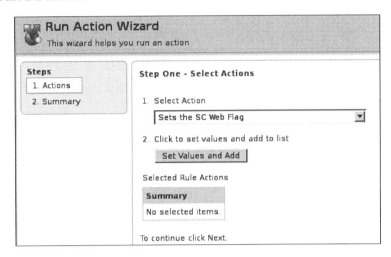

The document you just ran the action against should now have the sc:webable aspect. The isActive property should be set to true, and the published property should be set to the current date:

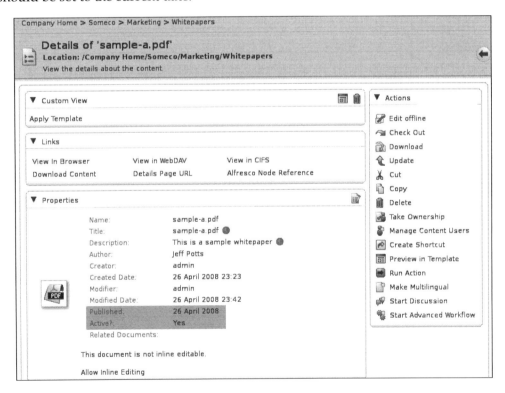

Hiding the Action from End Users

The publicAction parameter in the actions Spring bean configuration (someco-actions-context.xml) tells Alfresco whether or not to include the action in the **Run Action** wizard action list. For now, the flag is set to true. In the next chapter, you'll learn how to trigger the action from a UI action link. You will be able to make the UI Action Link hide or disappear based on logic (such as whether or not the current user is a member of a particular group). At that point, you'll set the flag to false to keep end users from running the action via the Run Action wizard.

Creating Actions that Require User-Specified Parameters

In the previous example, an end user does not need to specify any parameters for the action to run successfully. But some actions can be reused much more broadly if they are set up to allow an end user to specify parameters.

For example, imagine that SomeCo's Human Resources department wants to store HR policies in the repository. Suppose they have a three-folder system for keeping track of **Draft**, **Active**, and **Archive** policies. Policies often replace or supersede existing policies. The HR department would like to tag a draft policy with the policy it replaces (a policy sitting in the **Active** folder). The HR Department will cut and paste policies from the **Draft** folder to the **Active** folder. When the draft policy is pasted into the **Active** folder, the policy it replaces should automatically move from the **Active** folder to the **Archive** folder:

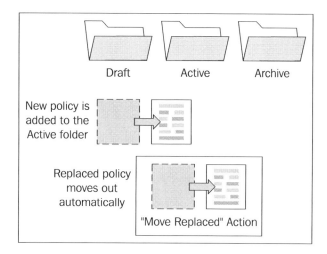

The code that moves the old policy from the **Active** folder into the **Archive** folder can be implemented as an action. The action can be called by a rule that fires when a document is added to a folder. The action's job is to figure out whether or not the incoming document is replacing another document in the same folder. If it is, the action needs to move the replaced document to a target folder. In this case, the target folder is the **Archive** folder. Without letting the user set the parameter, the target folder would have to be hardcoded. Instead, you'll create this action with a parameter so that if the target folder ever changes (from **Archive** to **Old Policies**, for example), or if someone else wants to use the action with their own set of folders, it won't require a code change.

Step-by-Step: Creating an Action that Accepts Parameters

Before starting, think about similar code that might already exist within Alfresco that you could leverage for the new action. Alfresco is open source. So it would be a shame to ignore the source and end up recreating a functionality that already exists. Plus, following the same pattern to implement our customization will make it easier for someone to support and share our code with others.

It turns out that there is already an out of the box **Move** action. The out of the box Move action moves the node against which the action is running to a target folder specified as a parameter. The difference between Alfresco's Move action and the new custom action is that the node that needs to be moved isn't the node the action is running against; it's the node containing the old policy. The action can get to the old policy because the new policy document has a "replaces" relationship with the old policy document. So the action will look to see if the newly arrived document has a "replaces" relationship. If it does, it will grab the target of that relationship (the document being replaced) and move it to the target folder.

The previous example consisted of an Action Executer class, its Spring bean configuration file, and a properties file. To create an action that accepts parameters, you will be creating a UI to set the destination folder, which requires the same ingredients as a basic action plus a JSP page and a bean handler.

To create a new action that accesses parameters, follow these steps:

1. There isn't anything in the SomeCo model related to HR policies. So update **config | alfresco | extension | model | scModel.xml** with a new type called `sc:hrPolicy` that is a child of `sc:hrDoc`:

```
<type name="sc:hrPolicy">
        <title>Someco HR Policy</title>
                <parent>sc:hrDoc</parent>
</type>
```

2. Alfresco has a `cm:replaceable` aspect available out of the box that will work perfectly for this. All HR policies are replaceable. So make the aspect a mandatory aspect of the new type by adding the following immediately after the parent element of the `sc:hrPolicy` type:

```
<mandatory-aspects>
       <aspect>cm:replaceable</aspect>
</mandatory-aspects>
```

3. Although the aspect is available out of the box, it isn't configured to show in the UI by default. So add the following to `web-client-config-custom.xml`:

```
<!-- show replaces association on docs with cm:replaceable -->
       <config evaluator="aspect-name" condition="cm:replaceable">
              <property-sheet>
                     <show-association name="cm:replaces" />
              </property-sheet>
       </config>
```

4. That's all for the model-related changes. Now let's work on the action executer class. Alfresco's executer class for the Move action is called `org.alfresco.repo.action.executer.MoveActionExecuter`. You can find it in the source code for the Alfresco Repository project. Copy it into **src | java** and call it `com.someco.action.executer.MoveReplacedActionExecuter`. Just as in the previous example, the heavy lifting is done in the `executeImpl` method. The out of the box code looks like this:

```
public void executeImpl(Action ruleAction, NodeRef
 actionedUponNodeRef) {
if (this.nodeService.exists(actionedUponNodeRef) == true) {
 NodeRef destinationParent = (NodeRef)ruleAction.
 getParameterValue(PARAM_DESTINATION_FOLDER);
 QName destinationAssocTypeQName = (Qname)ruleAction.
 getParameterValue(PARAM_ASSOC_TYPE_QNAME)   QName
 destinationAssocQName = (Qname)ruleAction.
 getParameterValue(PARAM_ASSOC_QNAME);
this.nodeService.moveNode( actionedUponNodeRef,
 destinationParent, destinationAssocTypeQName,
 destinationAssocQName);
}
}
```

5. The code simply grabs some parameter values and then calls the NodeService to do the move. All you need to do is modify it to find the nodes related to the current node by a "replaces" association, and then for each result set up and perform a move:

```
public void executeImpl(Action ruleAction, NodeRef
actionedUponNodeRef) {
// get the replaces associations for this node
List assocRefs = nodeService.getTargetAssocs(actionedUponNodeRe
f, ((QNamePattern) QName.createQName(NamespaceService.CONTENT_
MODEL_1_0_URI, "replaces")) );
        // if there are none, return
        if (assocRefs.isEmpty()) {
            // no work to do, return
            return;
        } else {
            for (AssociationRef assocNode : assocRefs) {
// create a noderef for the replaces association NodeRef
assocRef = assocNode.getTargetRef();
// if the node exists
                if (this.nodeService.exists(assocRef) ==
true) {
NodeRef destinationParent = (NodeRef)ruleAction.
getParameterValue(PARAM_DESTINATION_FOLDER);
QName destinationAssocTypeQName = (Qname)ruleAction.
getParameterValue(PARAM_ASSOC_TYPE_QNAME);
String currentNameString = (String) this.nodeService.
getProperty(assocRef, ContentModel.PROP_NAME);
this.nodeService.moveNode(assocRef,destinationParent,destinat
ionAssocTypeQName,QName.createQName(NamespaceService.CONTENT_
MODEL_1_0_URI, currentNameString));
                }
            } // next assocNode
        } // end if isEmpty
}
```

6. The only other change needed is to change the value of the constant NAME from move to move-replaced:

```
public static final String NAME = "move-replaced";
```

7. That's it for the Action executer class. Now for the bean handler. Alfresco's bean handler class for the Move action is called `org.alfresco.web.bean.actions.handlers.MoveHandler` and it resides in the source code for the Alfresco Web Client project. The bean handler class handles the view for the action configuration. Since both the "Move" action and the new "Move Replaced" action have a destination folder and no other configurable properties, only minor modifications are needed. Copy the out of the box bean handler class into your `src|java` folder. Name the class `com.someco.action.handler.MoveReplacedHandler`.

8. You'll be using your own JSP for the presentation so change the `getJSPPath()` method to this:

    ```
    public final static String CUSTOM_ACTION_JSP = "/jsp/extension/
    actions/" + MoveReplacedActionExecuter.NAME + ".jsp";
    public String getJSPPath() {
    return CUSTOM_ACTION_JSP;
    }
    ```

9. Next, change the `generateSummary()` method. It is responsible for printing a message that summarizes what the action will do. The actual text will be in a resource bundle, so just change the property name from `action_move` to `action_move_replaced`.

10. The JSP page that handles the move configuration for the class is identical to the out of the box move. Both the out of the box action and the new custom action accept the destination folder as a parameter. But the titles are different, so you'll need a copy of Alfresco's page. Plus, in the future you might want to add additional parameters. Copy **|source|web|jsp|actions|move.jsp** from either the Alfresco web application or the Alfresco Web Client project source code into your custom project. The JSP should reside in **src|web|jsp| extension|actions|move-replaced.jsp**.

11. The customized JSPs will be deployed to the same **web|jsp** directory as the out of the box JSPs. So any existing relative links that need to point to out of the box JSPs need an extra "../" prepended to them. In this case, there are three includes that need to be updated to look like this:

    ```
    <%@ include file="../../parts/titlebar.jsp" %>
    <%@ include file="../../parts/shelf.jsp" %>
    <%@ include file="../../parts/breadcrumb.jsp" %>
    ```

12. To point to the custom title property in the resource bundle, change the `titleId` attribute of the `r:page` tag from `title_action_move` to `title_action_move_replaced`:

    ```
    <r:page titleId="title_action_move_replaced">
    ```

13. That's it for the Java and JSP code. Now it is time to tie it all together with the appropriate Spring bean configuration and properties files. Declare the action executer class and point to the resource bundle. Edit **config | alfresco | extension | someco-action-context.xml.** Add the following:

```
<!-- Move Replaced Action Bean -->
<bean id="move-replaced" class="com.optaros.alfresco.repo.action.
executer.MoveReplacedActionExecuter" parent="action-executer">
        <property name="nodeService">
                <ref bean="NodeService" />
        </property>
</bean>
```

14. Update `somcoactions.properties` with:

```
move-replaced.title=Move replaced document to space
move-replaced.description=This will move the target node of a
replaces association to a specified space.
```

15. The summary text and the JSP title get pulled from **alfresco | extension | webclient.properties**. Add the following entries to the file:

```
action_move_replaced=Move replaced to ''{0}''
title_action_move_replaced=Move Replaced Action
```

16. Finally, the web client has to be told which handler to use when the **Set Values and Add** button is clicked. Edit the `web-client-config-custom.xml` file and add:

```
<config evaluator="string-compare" condition="Action Wizards">
    <!-- add custom action handler for "Move Replaced" action -->
    <action-handlers>
        <handler name="move-replaced" class="com.someco.action.
        handler.MoveReplacedHandler" />
    </action-handlers>
</config>
```

17. Deploy and restart Tomcat.

You have just created a new type, `sc:hrPolicy`, which has a mandatory `cm:replaces` aspect. That means that HR policies can point to other policies in the repository that they will replace once approved. You can also now run the custom Move Replaced action against an HR policy. When setting up the action, the web client UI will present the custom JSP to allow the user to specify a target folder for the replaced document.

To set up a test, follow these steps:

1. Log in to Alfresco.

2. Create a new folder called **Human Resources** under SomeCo. Under that, create a folder called **Policies**.

3. Within **Policies**, create folders for **Draft**, **Approved**, and **Archived**.

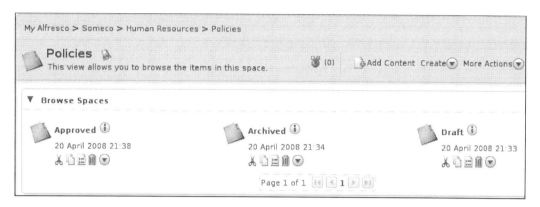

4. Create an HR policy in the **Approved** folder called **Existing Policy**.

5. Create an HR Policy in the **Draft** folder called **New Policy**. Edit the **replaces** property to point to the **Existing Policy** document.

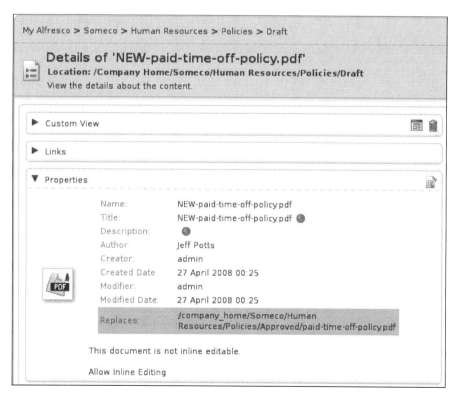

6. Create an inbound rule in the **Approved** folder that runs the **Move Replaced** action:

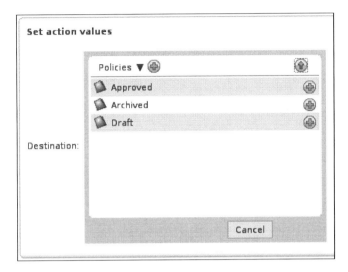

7. Clicking **Set Values and Add** should execute the handler for the custom action, allowing you to specify the **Archived** folder as the destination folder. Complete the rule wizard until the rule is successfully saved:

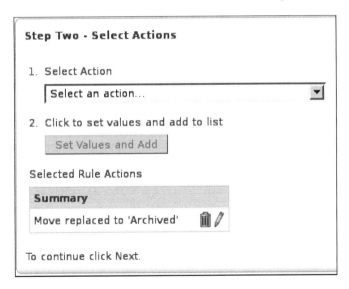

8. Now cut and paste the **New Policy** document into the **Approved** folder. The action should automatically trigger, moving the **Existing Policy** into the **Archived** folder.

Incorporating Parameter Values in the Action Description

Did you notice that the `action_move_replaced` string in `webclient.properties` included a replacement string?

```
action_move_replaced=Move replaced to ''{0}''
```

Alfresco will replace the placeholders with their parameter values. If there were additional parameters, the placeholder would be numbered sequentially.

Specifying Parameters when Code Executes an Action

In this example, the end user is specifying the destination folder when the action is configured through the web client. Parameters can also be specified when executing actions from Java and JavaScript. For example, here is a JavaScript snippet that invokes the `add features` action to add an aspect. The `add features` action takes one parameter, which is the name of the aspect to add:

```
var aspectName = "sc:clientRelated";
var addAspectAction = actions.create("add-features");
addAspectAction.parameters["aspect-name"] = aspectName;
addAspectAction.execute(document);
```

Executing actions from code is very common, especially when you need to run an action against a number of documents at once. Suppose SomeCo's HR department was already using Alfresco and you are just coming up with this "Move Replaced" idea. You would need to add the `cm:replaces` aspect to all existing HR policies. You could write JavaScript similar to the snippet above that would execute the `add features` action against all of the results in a search query to save you the trouble of doing it manually for each existing document.

Binding Logic to Custom Types with Behaviors

So far, you've seen how to write code that works with custom content types, properties, aspects, and associations. But the code wasn't tightly coupled to the objects on which it operated. With an action, the business logic is triggered by something—an item in the user interface, a schedule, or a workflow—rather than being bound to the content type or aspect.

Actions are very useful when the business logic the action carries out is generic enough to be applied to many types of objects. The out of the box "add aspect" or SomeCo's custom "move replaced" actions are obvious examples of actions that work regardless of the underlying content type.

But there are times when you want code to be tightly coupled to a content type because you need to be sure it gets executed, rather than leaving it up to a rule on a space that triggers an action or a workflow that does the same. Fortunately, Alfresco provides just such a mechanism; it's called **behaviors**.

Step-by-Step: Writing a Simple Behavior in Java

Suppose you want to execute some code every time something happens to a particular type of node. You could write a rule action to do this and then configure a folder to execute the action. But what if the content you want to hook this code to is scattered across the repository? What you need is a behavior. Let us create a simple behavior that binds itself to a few different policies so you can see when a behavior is triggered based on what's happening to the content. To create this simple behavior, you'll need:

- A Java class to implement the behavior
- A Spring bean configuration file to configure the behavior
- A type to bind the behavior to
- A modified `log4j.properties` file to see debug messages

By the end of these steps, you'll be able to see the policies that get fired when you create, read, update, and delete content.

To create the policy logger behavior, follow these steps:

1. Create a new Java class in **src|java** called `com.someco.behavior.PolicyLogger`.

2. You're going to bind your behavior to the `OnCreateNode`, `OnContentRead`, `OnContentUpdate`, `OnUpdateNode`, and `OnDeleteNode` policies. So the class needs to implement the appropriate interfaces as follows:

```
public class PolicyLogger
        implements ContentServicePolicies.OnContentUpdatePolicy,
                   ContentServicePolicies.OnContentReadPolicy,
                   NodeServicePolicies.OnCreateNodePolicy,
                   NodeServicePolicies.OnUpdateNodePolicy,
                   NodeServicePolicies.OnDeleteNodePolicy {
```

3. Next, set up some local variables. You'll need a logger to log messages when the policies are fired, Behavior objects (note the British spelling in the code), and a `PolicyComponent` bean:

```
private Logger logger = Logger.getLogger(PolicyLogger.class);
// Behaviours
private Behaviour onContentRead;
private Behaviour onContentUpdate;
private Behaviour onCreateNode;
private Behaviour onUpdateNode;
private Behaviour onDeleteNode;
// Dependencies
private PolicyComponent policyComponent;
```

4. Create an `init` method that creates the behaviors:

```
if (logger.isDebugEnabled()) logger.debug("Initializing policy
logger behaviour");
    // Create behaviours
this.onContentRead = new JavaBehaviour(this, "onContentRead",
NotificationFrequency.EVERY_EVENT);
this.onContentUpdate = new JavaBehaviour(this, "onContentUpdate",
NotificationFrequency.EVERY_EVENT);
this.onCreateNode = new JavaBehaviour(this, "onCreateNode",
NotificationFrequency.EVERY_EVENT);
this.onUpdateNode = new JavaBehaviour(this, "onUpdateNode",
NotificationFrequency.EVERY_EVENT);
this.onDeleteNode = new JavaBehaviour(this, "onDeleteNode",
NotificationFrequency.EVERY_EVENT);
```

5. Then, bind the behaviors to Alfresco's policies for the SomeCo Operations Document type (it could be any type, but use this one for this example):

```
// Bind behaviours to node policies
this.policyComponent.bindClassBehaviour(QName.createQName
(NamespaceService.ALFRESCO_URI, "onContentRead"), SomeCoModel.
TYPE_SC_OPS_DOC, this.onContentRead);
this.policyComponent.bindClassBehaviour(QName.createQName
(NamespaceService.ALFRESCO_URI, "onContentUpdate"), SomeCoModel.
TYPE_SC_OPS_DOC, this.onContentUpdate);
this.policyComponent.bindClassBehaviour(QName.createQName(
NamespaceService.ALFRESCO_URI, "onCreateNode"), SomeCoModel.
TYPE_SC_OPS_DOC, this.onCreateNode);
this.policyComponent.bindClassBehaviour(QName.createQName(
NamespaceService.ALFRESCO_URI, "onUpdateNode"), SomeCoModel.
TYPE_SC_OPS_DOC, this.onUpdateNode);
this.policyComponent.bindClassBehaviour(QName.createQName
(NamespaceService.ALFRESCO_URI, "onDeleteNode"), SomeCoModel.
TYPE_SC_OPS_DOC, this.onDeleteNode);
```

6. Now implement the behaviors. In this case, you're just going to log a message:

```
public void onContentUpdate(NodeRef nodeRef, boolean flag) {
        if (logger.isDebugEnabled()) logger.debug("Content update
policy fired");
        }
        public void onContentRead(NodeRef nodeRef) {
        if (logger.isDebugEnabled()) logger.debug("Content read
policy fired");
        }
        public void onUpdateNode(NodeRef nodeRef) {
        if (logger.isDebugEnabled()) logger.debug("Node update
policy fired");
        }
        public void onCreateNode(ChildAssociationRef childAssocRef)
{
if (logger.isDebugEnabled()) logger.debug("Node create policy
fired");
        }
        public void onDeleteNode(ChildAssociationRef childAssocRef,
boolean isNodeArchived) {
if (logger.isDebugEnabled()) logger.debug("Node delete policy
fired");
        }
```

7. Create a setter method for the `PolicyComponent` dependency:

```
public void setPolicyComponent(PolicyComponent policyComponent) {
        this.policyComponent = policyComponent;
}
```

8. That's all for the Java class. Create a new Spring bean configuration file in **config | alfresco | extension** called `someco-behavior-context.xml`. Add the following to register the new bean:

```
<?xml version='1.0' encoding='UTF-8'?>
<!DOCTYPE beans PUBLIC '-//SPRING//DTD BEAN//EN' 'http://www.
springframework.org/dtd/spring-beans.dtd'>
<beans>
        <bean id="policyLogger" class="com.someco.behaviour.
                                PolicyLogger" init-method="init">
                <property name="policyComponent">
                <ref bean="policyComponent" />
                </property>
        </bean>
</beans>
```

9. Confirm that your `log4j.properties` file has:

   ```
   log4j.logger.com.someco=DEBUG
   ```

10. Now deploy, restart, and test. When the server starts up, you should see:

    ```
    DEBUG [someco.behaviour.PolicyLogger] Initializing policy logger
    behaviour
    ```

Notice that you've bound the behavior to the Operations Document type. That means the behavior code will get executed any time Alfresco takes an action against an instance of the type that matches one of the policies you've bound to. To see this in action, log in to Alfresco and create, update, and delete a couple of Operations Documents. Watch the Tomcat log as you do so. You'll see that those policies get fired multiple times during a typical transaction.

Binding to Multiple Types/Aspects

In this example, we bound only to the Operations Document type. But there is nothing specific to any particular type in the class you just wrote. If you had behavior logic that was common to multiple content types or aspects, you could bind them to this behavior as well. For example, add the following to the `init` method:

```
this.policyComponent.bindClassBehaviour(QName.createQName(NamespaceS
ervice.ALFRESCO_URI, "onContentRead"),SomeCoModel.ASPECT_SC_CLIENT_
RELATED, this.onContentRead);
```

Now in addition to Operations Document instances, the `onContentRead` behavior code will fire when reading any content of any type that has SomeCo's client-related aspect.

As a best practice, you should only do this when the behavior is truly common. If you had behavior unique to Operations Documents and the client-related aspect, those should be broken into two different classes.

Frequency

Notice that the constructor included a frequency argument. This declares how often your behavior should be triggered. In the `PolicyLogger` example, you specified **EVERY_EVENT**. The other two choices are **FIRST_EVENT** and **TRANSACTION_COMMIT**.

Figuring Out to Which Policies to Bind

There are many out of the box policies to which your behavior can be bound. To find out what's available, you need to look only as far as the source code (or Javadocs). If you grep the repository project in the Alfresco source code for classes that end in "`*Policies.java`", you'll find four interfaces. Each of those interfaces contains inner interfaces that represent the policies you can hook into. Check the Javadocs or source code for specifics. The following table shows the breadth of what's available.

To make it easier to read the table, the inner interface that follows the pattern of `<method-name>Policy` is omitted. For example, the `onContentUpdate` method is a method of the inner interface `OnContentUpdatePolicy`:

Interface	Method
org.alfresco.repo.content.ContentServicePolicies	onContentUpdate
	onContentRead
org.alfresco.repo.copy.CopyServicePolicies	onCopyNode
	onCopyComplete
org.alfresco.repo.node.NodeServicePolicies	beforeCreateStore
	onCreateStore
	beforeCreateNode
	onCreateNode
	onMoveNode
	beforeUpdateNode
	onUpdateNode
	onUpdateProperties
	beforeDeleteNode
	onDeleteNode
	beforeAddAspect
	onAddAspect
	beforeRemoveAspect
	onRemoveAspect
	beforeCreateNodeAssociation
	onCreateNodeAssociation
	beforeCreateChildAssociation
	onCreateChildAssociation
	beforeDeleteChildAssociation
	onDeleteChildAssociation
	onCreateAssociation
	onDeleteAssociation

Interface	Method
org.alfresco.repo.version.VersionServicePolicies	beforeCreateVersion
	afterCreateVersion
	onCreateVersion
	calculateVersionLabel

Step-by-Step: Writing a Simple Behavior in JavaScript

You've seen how to implement a simple behavior in Java. But what if you wanted to implement the behavior using JavaScript instead? Behaviors can be implemented in JavaScript and bound to policies through Spring. Let's re-implement the PolicyLogger bean using JavaScript; but this time we'll bind to a different type.

The ingredients are the same as in the Java example, except that we'll be creating a JavaScript file instead of a Java class. This involves:

1. Creating a server-side JavaScript file that implements the behavior.
2. Creating a Spring bean to bind the JavaScript-based behavior to the appropriate policies.
3. Modifying log4j.properties to set the server-side JavaScript log level to DEBUG.

To create a JavaScript version of the PolicyLogger, do the following:

1. In your Eclipse project, create a "**scripts**" directory under the **config | alfresco | extension** folder, and add a file called **onUpdateNode.js** with the following content:

```
var scriptFailed = false;
// Check the arguments
if (behaviour.args == null) {
        logger.log("The args have not been set.");
        scriptFailed = true;
} else {
        if (behaviour.args.length == 1) {
                var actedOnNode = behaviour.args[0];
                logger.log("You just updated:" + actedOnNode.name);
        } else {
        logger.log("The number of arguments is incorrect.");
        scriptFailed = true;
}
}
}
```

2. Edit the `someco-behavior-context.xml` file in **config | alfresco | extension**. Java behaviors bind themselves to policies. JavaScript behaviors, on the other hand, use the Spring bean configuration to bind to policies. Add the following bean to the file:

```
<bean id="onUpdateHrDoc" class="org.alfresco.repo.policy.
registration.ClassPolicyRegistration" parent="policyRegistration">
    <property name="policyName">
        <value>{http://www.alfresco.org}onUpdateNode</value>
    </property>
    <property name="className">
        <value>{http://www.someco.com/model/content/
                                    1.0}hrDoc</value>
    </property>
    <property name="behaviour">
        <bean class="org.alfresco.repo.jscript.ScriptBehaviour"
                                    parent="scriptBehaviour">
            <property name="location">
                <bean class="org.alfresco.repo.jscript.
                                    ClasspathScriptLocation">
                    <constructor-arg>
                    <value>alfresco/extension/scripts/
                                    onUpdateNode.js</value>
                    </constructor-arg>
                </bean>
            </property>
        </bean>
    </property>
</bean>
```

3. Edit `log4j.properties`. Set `log4j.logger.org.alfresco.repo.jscript` to DEBUG.

4. Now deploy and test.

To test the JavaScript behavior, create a new HR Doc and watch the log. You should see multiple JavaScript logger messages.

Binding Behavior to Child Types

In this example, you bound the `onContentRead.js` to the `onContentRead` policy of the SomeCo HR Doc type. Remember that HR policy is a child of HR Doc. So what will happen when you read an HR Policy? Children inherit the behaviors of their parents, so when you read an HR Policy, the behavior logic in the script should fire.

Step-by-Step: Writing a User Ratings Calculator

So far, the behaviors you've written have just written log messages, which isn't terribly exciting. SomeCo's Marketing department has a requirement to consider, though. Marketing wants to let website users rate Whitepapers on a scale of one to five. They then want to show the average rating for a given Whitepaper. Once this is in place, they'll be able to call their website 2.0, which will be a big win for everybody.

You're reading an Alfresco book, so let's assume the decision has been made to persist those ratings to Alfresco, though in real life that may or may not be the best thing to do (it might make more sense to store ratings and other user-generated content in a relational database).

A new type, `sc:rating`, will be created to store an individual rating. A new aspect, `sc:rateable`, will be created to attach to Whitepapers to identify them as something that can be rated and to store the summary statistics for the Whitepaper. Ratings will be associated with Whitepapers through child associations. That way, if the Whitepaper goes away, so will the ratings, which is what we want.

A Whitepaper's rating needs to be recalculated either when a new rating is created or when a rating is deleted. One possibility would be to bind the behavior to the `NodeService` policy's `onCreateChildAssociation` and `onDeleteChildAssociation` methods for the Whitepaper node. But that would mean the behavior would constantly be inspecting the association type to see if it needs to take any action because there could be other child associations besides ratings. Instead, the behavior will be bound to the rating node's `onCreateNode` and `onDeleteNode` policies. Any time a ratings node is created, the behavior will re-calculate the Whitepaper's summary statistics.

Here is what you're going to need to do:

1. Extend the SomeCo model with a rateable aspect and a rating type (and perform all of the UI configuration steps that go with it).

2. Write the custom behavior class and bind it to the appropriate policies.

3. Configure a Spring bean to initialize the behavior class and pass in any dependencies.

4. Build, deploy, restart, and test. In a later chapter, you'll work on the frontend that will create ratings via web scripts. In this example, you'll create some server-side JavaScript to create a few ratings to test out the behavior.

Let's get started. To create a behavior class that calculates the average rating across child rating objects, follow these steps:

1. Edit the `scModel.xml` in **config | alfresco | extension | model**. Add the new rating type:

```
<type name="sc:rating">
<title>Someco Rating</title>
<parent>sys:base</parent>
<properties>
        <property name="sc:rating">
                <type>d:int</type>
                <mandatory>true</mandatory>
        </property>
        <property name="sc:rater">
                <type>d:text</type>
                <mandatory>true</mandatory>
        </property>
</properties>
</type>
```

 Note that `sc:rating` inherits from `sys:base`. That's because there won't be any content stored in a rating object; it only has properties. This is sometimes called a "content-less object". One side effect of this decision is that rating objects won't show up in the user interface.

2. Now add the `sc:rateable` aspect. The rateable aspect has one property to store the average rating, one to store the number of ratings, and one to store the sum of the ratings. The aspect also defines the child association that keeps track of the content's related ratings:

```
<aspect name="sc:rateable">
            <title>Someco Rateable</title>
            <properties>
                <property name="sc:averageRating">
                    <type>d:double</type>
                    <mandatory>false</mandatory>
                </property>
                <property name="sc:totalRating">
                    <type>d:int</type>
                    <mandatory>false</mandatory>
                </property>
                <property name="sc:ratingCount">
                    <type>d:int</type>
                    <mandatory>false</mandatory>
```

```
                        </property>
                   </properties>
                   <associations>
                        <child-association name="sc:ratings">
                              <title>Rating</title>
                              <source>
                                    <mandatory>false</mandatory>
                                    <many>true</many>
                              </source>
                              <target>
                                    <class>sc:rating</class>
                                    <mandatory>false</mandatory>
                                    <many>true</many>
                              </target>
                        </child-association>
                   </associations>
              </aspect>
```

3. Save and close the `scModel.xml` file.

4. Edit `web-client-config-custom.xml` in **config | alfresco | extension**. The rateable properties and associations need to show up on property sheets for objects with the aspect. So add the following:

```
<!-- add rateable aspect properties to property sheet -->
<config evaluator="aspect-name" condition="sc:rateable">
     <property-sheet>
<show-property name="sc:averageRating" display-label-id="average"
read-only="true" />
<show-child-association name="sc:ratings" display-label-
id="ratings" read-only="false" />
     </property-sheet>
</config>
```

5. The rateable aspect needs to show up on the **add aspect** list. So add the rateable aspect to the existing list of SomeCo custom aspects in `web-client-config-custom.xml`. Note that this snippet only shows the `<aspects>` element of the "Action Wizards" config element. The rest is unchanged from previous chapters:

```
<config evaluator="string-compare" condition="Action Wizards">
<!-- The list of aspects to show in the add/remove features
action -->
     <!-- and the has-aspect condition -->
     <aspects>
          <aspect name="sc:webable"/>
          <aspect name="sc:clientRelated"/>
          <aspect name="sc:rateable"/>
     </aspects>
```

6. The label IDs need values in the `webclient.properties` file:

```
#sc:rateable
average=Avg Rating
ratings=Ratings
```

7. Modify `com.someco.model.SomeCoModel.java` to include new constants for the type, aspect, properties, and association that we just added to the model:

```
public static final QName TYPE_SC_RATING = QName.
createQName(SomeCoModel.NAMESPACE_SOMECO_CONTENT_MODEL, "rating");
public static final QName ASPECT_SC_RATEABLE = QName.
createQName(SomeCoModel.NAMESPACE_SOMECO_CONTENT_MODEL,
"rateable");
public static final QName PROP_RATING = QName.
createQName(SomeCoModel.NAMESPACE_SOMECO_CONTENT_MODEL, "rating");
public static final QName PROP_AVERAGE_RATING= QName.
createQName(SomeCoModel.NAMESPACE_SOMECO_CONTENT_MODEL,
"averageRating");
public static final QName PROP_TOTAL_RATING= QName.
createQName(SomeCoModel.NAMESPACE_SOMECO_CONTENT_MODEL,
"totalRating");
public static final QName PROP_RATING_COUNT= QName.
createQName(SomeCoModel.NAMESPACE_SOMECO_CONTENT_MODEL,
"ratingCount");
public static final QName ASSN_SC_RATINGS = QName.
createQName(SomeCoModel.NAMESPACE_SOMECO_CONTENT_MODEL,
"ratings");
```

8. Create a new class called `com.someco.behavior.Rating`. Let's worry about how to handle new ratings first and deletions later. Given that, the class declaration is:

```
public class Rating
implements NodeServicePolicies.OnCreateNodePolicy {
```

9. The class has two dependencies that Spring will take care of. One is the `NodeService`, which will be used to produce the summary statistics, and the other is the `PolicyComponent`, which is used to bind the behavior to the policies. Add the two local class variables for the dependencies as well as one for the `onCreateNode` behavior:

```
// Dependencies
private NodeService nodeService;
private PolicyComponent policyComponent;
// Behaviours
private Behaviour onCreateNode;
```

10. Add the `init` method to create and bind the behaviors:

```
public void init() {
    // Create behaviours
    this.onCreateNode = new JavaBehaviour(
    this,
    "onCreateNode",
    NotificationFrequency.TRANSACTION_COMMIT);
    // Bind behaviours to node policies
    this.policyComponent.bindClassBehaviour(
    Qname.createQName(NamespaceService.ALFRESCO_URI,
                                        "onCreateNode"),
    SomeCoModel.TYPE_SC_RATING,
    this.onCreateNode);
```

11. In the `onCreateNode` behavior method, call a method that knows what to do when ratings are added:

```
public void onCreateNode(ChildAssociationRef childAssocRef) {
addRating(childAssocRef);
}
```

12. Add the `addRating` method. It grabs the running total and rating count from the parent, adds the rating to the total, increments the count, and computes the new average:

```
public void addRating(ChildAssociationRef childAssocRef) {
    // get the parent node
    NodeRef parentRef = childAssocRef.getParentRef();
    NodeRef childRef = childAssocRef.getChildRef();
Integer total = (Integer)nodeService.getProperty(parentRef,
                            SomeCoModel.PROP_TOTAL_RATING);
    if (total == null) total = 0;
    Integer count = (Integer)nodeService.getProperty(parentRef,
                            SomeCoModel.PROP_RATING_COUNT);
    if (count == null) count = 0;
    Integer rating = (Integer)nodeService.getProperty(childRef,
                            SomeCoModel.PROP_RATING);
    if (rating == null) rating = 0;
    Double average = 0d;
    total = total + rating;
    count = count + 1;
    average = total / new Double(count);
    // store the average on the parent node
nodeService.setProperty(parentRef,
                    SomeCoModel.PROP_AVERAGE_RATING, average);
nodeService.setProperty(parentRef,
                        SomeCoModel.PROP_TOTAL_RATING, total);
```

```
                    nodeService.setProperty(parentRef,
                              SomeCoModel.PROP_RATING_COUNT, count);
        return;
        }
```

13. Add the setters for the NodeService and PolicyComponents:

```
public void setNodeService(NodeService nodeService) {
        this.nodeService = nodeService;
}
public void setPolicyComponent(PolicyComponent policyComponent) {
        this.policyComponent = policyComponent;
}
```

14. Configure the behavior class as a Spring bean. Edit `someco-behavior-context.xml` in **config|alfresco**. Add the following bean:

```
<bean id="ratingBehaviour" class="com.someco.behaviour.Rating"
                                            init-method="init">
        <property name="nodeService">
                <ref bean="nodeService" />
        </property>
        <property name="policyComponent">
                <ref bean="policyComponent" />
        </property>
</bean>
```

15. Deploy, restart, and test.

Step-by-Step: Testing the New Rating Behavior

In the previous chapter, you used Java to test out the model by writing code against the Alfresco Web Services API. This time, create server-side JavaScript you can use any time you need to create some test rating nodes for a piece of content. To do that, follow these steps:

1. Log in to the Alfresco Web Client and navigate to the Company's **Home|Data Dictionary|Scripts**.

2. Next, create a new piece of content named `addTestRating.js` with the following content:

```
// add the aspect to this document if it needs it
if (document.hasAspect("sc:rateable"))
{
    logger.log("Document already as aspect");
} else
{
```

```
        logger.log("Adding rateable aspect");
        document.addAspect("sc:rateable");
    }
    // randomly pick a num b/w 1 and 5 inclusive
    var ratingValue = Math.floor(Math.random()*5) + 1;
    var props = new Array(2);
    props["sc:rating"] = ratingValue;
    props["sc:rater"] = person.properties.userName;
    // create a new ratings node and set its properties
    var ratingsNode = document.createNode("rating" + new Date().
                    getTime(), "sc:rating", props, "sc:ratings");
    ratingsNode.save();
    logger.log("Ratings node saved.");
```

3. Now create a Whitepaper under **SomeCo|Marketing|Whitepapers**.

4. On the new Whitepaper's detail page, click **Run Action** and select the **Execute Script** action. Click **Set Values and Add** to choose the addTestRating.js script. Click **Finish** to run the script.

Every time you run addTestRating.js against a piece of content, a new rating (with a random value) will be created as a child node of that content. If you look at the properties of the Whitepaper, you should see the average rating and a list of the ratings objects:

The default out of the box display for associations is simply a list of paths to the associated content. That's not helpful, in this case, if you want to see an individual rating value. You can either use the node browser to see the rating value, or use the dumpRatings.js script in **src | scripts** to write the rating values to the log.

Handling Deleted Ratings

If you edit the properties of a Whitepaper, you'll notice that each rating has a trashcan icon. If you delete a rating, the rating will go away. But you didn't bind onDeleteNode to a behavior, so the average will not get recalculated. Let's see how we can fix that.

To handle deleted ratings, you're going to edit com.someco.behavior.Rating to add a new behavior for onDeleteNode that will call a method to recalculate the rating stats. Follow these steps:

1. First, the class now needs to implement the OnDeleteNodePolicy, so update the class declaration:

    ```
    public class Rating
            implements NodeServicePolicies.OnDeleteNodePolicy,
                        NodeServicePolicies.OnCreateNodePolicy {
    ```

2. Update the init method with the appropriate logic to instantiate and bind the onDeleteNode behavior:

    ```
    this.onDeleteNode = new JavaBehaviour(this, "onDeleteNode",
                        NotificationFrequency.TRANSACTION_COMMIT);
    this.policyComponent.bindClassBehaviour(QName.createQName
                (NamespaceService.ALFRESCO_URI, "onDeleteNode"),
                SomeCoModel.TYPE_SC_RATING, this.onDeleteNode);
    ```

3. Add the onDeleteNode method. The method calls a method used to recalculate the rating statistics:

    ```
    public void onDeleteNode(ChildAssociationRef childAssocRef,
    boolean isNodeArchived) {
            recalculateAverage(childAssocRef.getParentRef());
    }
    ```

4. Finally, implement the recalculateAverage method. The method knows how to iterate over a node's children to calculate the total rating, rating count, and average. The reason why it can't use a running total approach like addRating is that by this point, the rating has already been deleted:

    ```
    public void recalculateAverage(NodeRef parentRef)
    {
    if (logger.isDebugEnabled())
     logger.debug("Inside computeAverage");
    ```

```
// check the parent to make sure it has the right aspect
if (nodeService.hasAspect(parentRef,
                          SomeCoModel.ASPECT_SC_RATEABLE))
{
    // continue, this is what we want
} else
{
if (logger.isDebugEnabled())
logger.debug("Rating's parent ref did not have rateable aspect.");
return;
}
// get the parent node's children
List<ChildAssociationRef> children = nodeService.getChildAssocs
                                          (parentRef);
Double average = 0d;
int total = 0;
// This actually happens when the last rating is deleted
if (children.size() == 0)
{
    // No children so no work to do
        if (logger.isDebugEnabled())
        logger.debug("No children found");
} else
{
    // iterate through the children to compute the total
    for (ChildAssociationRef child : children)
    {
        int rating = (Integer)nodeService.getProperty(
                    child.getChildRef(),SomeCoModel.PROP_RATING);
        total += rating;
    }
    // compute the average
    average = total / (children.size() / 1.0d);
    if (logger.isDebugEnabled())
    logger.debug("Computed average:" + average);
}
// store the average on the parent node
nodeService.setProperty(parentRef,
                        SomeCoModel.PROP_AVERAGE_RATING, average);
nodeService.setProperty(parentRef,
                        SomeCoModel.PROP_TOTAL_RATING, total);
nodeService.setProperty(parentRef,
                    SomeCoModel.PROP_RATING_COUNT, children.size());
if (logger.isDebugEnabled())
logger.debug("Property set");
return;
}
```

5. Now save, deploy, restart, and test.

You should be able to use the `addTestRating.js` JavaScript you created earlier to add one or more test ratings to a Whitepaper. Then, edit the details of the Whitepaper and delete one or more of the ratings. When you click **OK,** the transaction will commit, the listener will be notified, and the Whitepaper's average rating will recalculate. You may have to close and open the details before you see the updated average.

Extracting Metadata from Files

Many authoring tools provide a mechanism for capturing metadata within the authoring tool user interface. If certain pieces of metadata are already stored as part of the file, why force content contributors to re-key the metadata when they add the content to the repository? Alfresco can use metadata extractors to inspect the file, extract the metadata, and save the metadata in the node's properties.

A metadata extractor is a Java class configured as a Spring bean that either gets called when content is created in the repository, or when the extractor is invoked by a rule action. Alfresco knows which extractor to use for a given piece of content because metadata extractors declare the MIME types they support.

Metadata extractors have a default mapping that identifies which pieces of file metadata should be stored in which node properties. The property mapping can be overridden by pointing to a custom mapping in the Spring bean configuration.

Customizing Metadata Extractors

SomeCo would like to set the `sc:clientName` property with the value of the keywords property in Word and PDF files. Alfresco already provides extractors for Word and PDF. The Word extractor knows how to retrieve the keywords from a Word file, but it isn't mapped to a property by default. The PDF extractor, on the other hand, does not pull the keywords out of the box, so the extractor class will have to be extended. Each of these will be tackled, in two separate examples.

Step-by-step: Customizing the Metadata Mapping

Let's customize the metadata mapping for the Office extractor so that when SomeCo adds Office documents to the repository, the keywords property gets stored in the `sc:clientName` property. This is just a matter of overriding the default mapping file. To do that, follow these steps:

1. Create a new Spring context file in **alfresco | extension** called `someco-extractor-context.xml`.

2. Then, add a bean to the `someco-extractor-context.xml` file that overrides the out of the box `extracter.Office` bean, and points to a custom mapping file:

```
<bean id="extracter.Office" class="org.alfresco.repo.content.
metadata.OfficeMetadataExtracter" parent="baseMetadataExtracter" >
    <property name="inheritDefaultMapping">
        <value>true</value>
    </property>
    <property name="mappingProperties">
        <bean class="org.springframework.beans.factory.
                                config.PropertiesFactoryBean">
            <property name="location">
                <value>classpath:alfresco/extension/someco-office-
                    document-extractor-mappings.properties</value>
            </property>
        </bean>
    </property>
</bean>
```

3. Create a new file in the same directory called `someco-office-document-extractor-mappings.properties`. (Hey, at least it is descriptive.) The custom mapping just needs to specify what to do with the keywords. The namespace for the property's content model also has to be declared. The entire contents of the properties file looks like this:

```
namespace.prefix.sc=http://www.someco.com/model/content/1.0
keywords=sc:clientName
```

4. Deploy the change using `ant deploy`, and restart Tomcat.

Now set up a test. When a document is added to SomeCo's Sales folder, three things need to happen: The document needs to be specialized to `sc:salesDoc`, the `sc:clientRelated` aspect needs to be added, and the metadata needs to get extracted. One way to make sure that happens is to set up an inbound rule on the Sales folder. Let's do it:

1. Log in to the web client.

2. Navigate to the **Someco|Sales** folder. (Create it if it does not exist.)

3. Use "More Actions, Manage Rules" to create an inbound rule that operates on all documents. The three actions it needs to perform, in order, are (1) specialize the type, (2) add an aspect, and (3) extract metadata.

4. Save the rule.

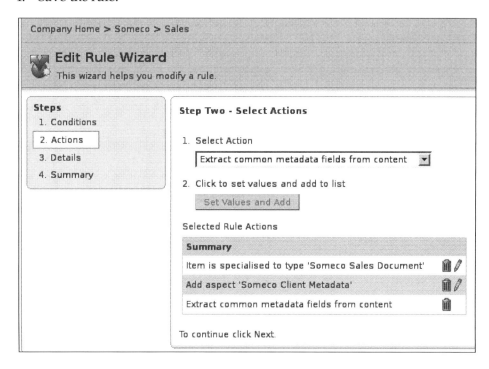

5. Create a test Microsoft Office document. (You can use OpenOffice. Just save the file as one of the Microsoft Office formats). Use **File**, **Properties** to set the Keywords with a client name. Save the file.

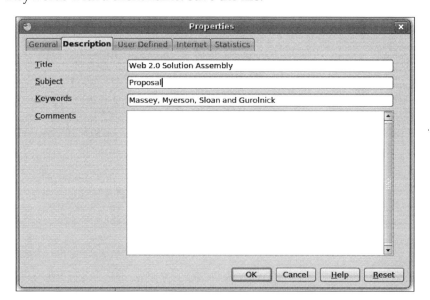

6. Add the file to the Sales folder. When the properties sheet is displayed, the **Client Name** property should default to the value you set using Office:

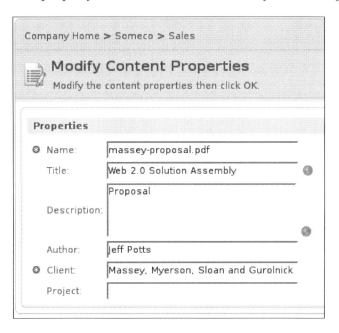

If metadata extraction is automatic, you may be wondering why we explicitly invoked it as part of the rule. It's a workaround for a little timing problem. Without the rule to explicitly invoke metadata extraction, Alfresco will perform the metadata extraction on its own because it recognizes the MIME type and it knows it has a metadata extractor configured for that MIME type. The problem is that it performs the metadata extraction before it has added the aspect. So in the web client, the clientName property doesn't default to the extracted metadata as you've specified. Using a rule to explicitly invoke the extraction forces Alfresco to add the aspect, then set the property. A side effect to this workaround is that the extractor gets invoked twice—once by Alfresco when the document is initially created, and a second time when the rule is fired.

Overriding the Default Mapping

Note that in this case, in the extractor Office Spring bean, inheritDefaultMapping, is set to true. This means the extractor will continue to extract the author, title, subject, created date, and modified date, in addition to the keywords. If you want to override instead of extend the default mapping, (extracting only keywords, in this example), set this to false.

Leveraging Out of the box Metadata Extractors

There are several metadata extractors configured out of the box. These include:

- Microsoft Office, OpenOffice.org, and Adobe PDF: These extract summary information such as author, title, subject, and created date
- HTML: This extracts author, title, and description from META tags
- MP3: This extracts song, album, artist, year, track number, and several other fields from ID3 tags
- XML: This extracts Strings from XML using XPath expressions

When you add a piece of content matching any of these types to the repository, Alfresco invokes the metadata extractor and populates the node's properties as specified in the extractor's default mapping file.

A complete list of the out of the box metadata extractors, their class names, bean IDs, and the out of the box properties they extract is provided in the Appendix.

Digging into an Extractor Class

Let's take a peek at the Office extractor to get a feel for how it works. Metadata extractors reside in the Alfresco source for the "repository" project within the `org.alfresco.repo.content.metadata` package. Metadata extractors extend `AbstractMappingMetadataExtracter` (don't let the misspelling trip you up), which in turn implements the `MetadataExtracter` class. Each extractor is responsible for implementing the `extractRaw()` method. The `extractRaw()` method pulls all of the properties anyone might want, and writes them to a Map using `putRawValue()`. It is important to note that extractors are doing this work, regardless of whether or not you've configured the extractor mapping to pull a specific property.

Exactly how the properties are extracted from a file is up to the person implementing the extractor. Hopefully, an enterprise-ready, open-source library will already exist for working with the particular file type you need to work with.

Step-by-Step: Customizing a Metadata Extractor Class

For extracting the keywords property from Office documents, a simple mapping file override was all that was needed. But SomeCo also commonly deals with PDF. Adobe PDF files also have a keyword property, but the out of the box metadata extractor for PDF doesn't extract the keywords. That means the existing class has to be extended. Luckily, the existing extractor can be reused with only a trivial enhancement needed to meet the requirements.

To modify the out of the box PDF extractor to extract keywords from PDF files, follow these steps:

1. Take a look at the source for the `org.alfresco.repo.content.metadata.PdfBoxMetadataExtracter` class. It's in the source code for the repository project. The relevant code is shown here:

   ```
   PDDocumentInformation docInfo = pdf.getDocumentInformation();

   putRawValue(KEY_AUTHOR, docInfo.getAuthor(), rawProperties);
   putRawValue(KEY_TITLE, docInfo.getTitle(), rawProperties);
   putRawValue(KEY_SUBJECT, docInfo.getSubject(), rawProperties);

   Calendar created = docInfo.getCreationDate();
   if (created != null) {
       putRawValue(KEY_CREATED, created.getTime(), rawProperties);
   }
   ```

2. The extractor uses a library called `PdfBox` to interrogate the PDF. Fortunately, `PDDocumentInformation` has a `getKeywords()` method. All that needs to be done, then, is to create a new extractor class based on the `PdfBoxMetadataExtracter` with an extra call to `putRawValue()` that passes in the results of the `getKeywords()` method. Copy the Alfresco extractor class into your Eclipse project under **src | java**. Call the new class `com.someco.extracter.EnhancedPdfExtracter`. (Keep the misspelling to stay consistent with the Alfresco extractor package and class names.)

3. Now modify the `extractRaw` method. Add a new call to `putRawValue` after the similar call that grabs the subject:

   ```
   putRawValue(KEY_KEYWORDS, docInfo.getKeywords(), rawProperties);
   ```

4. By default, the extractor classes look for a default file mapping using the extractor class name. Copy the `PdfBoxMetadataExtracter.properties` file into the same folder as the class, and name it `EnhancedPdfExtracter.properties`.

5. The entry mapping keywords to `sc:clientName` can go in the default properties file. But it feels cleaner and more consistent with the prior example to create a `someco-pdf-document-extractor-mappings.properties` file in **alfresco | extension** and add it there:

   ```
   namespace.prefix.sc=http://www.someco.com/model/content/1.0
   keywords=sc:clientName
   ```

6. The final step, then, is to add a new Spring bean to `someco-extractor-context.xml` to override the `extracter.PDFBox` bean with the new class and custom properties file:

```
<bean id="extracter.PDFBox" class="com.someco.extracter.
EnhancedPdfExtracter" parent="baseMetadataExtracter" >
    <property name="inheritDefaultMapping">
        <value>true</value>
    </property>
    <property name="mappingProperties">
        <bean class="org.springframework.beans.factory.config.
        PropertiesFactoryBean">
            <property name="location">
                <value>classpath:alfresco/extension/someco-pdf-
                document-extractor-mappings.properties</value>
            </property>
        </bean>
    </property>
</bean>
```

7. Deploy, restart, and test.

You can test this by setting the keywords property on a PDF, then dropping it into the Sales folder. The keywords property should get extracted properly.

 The log4j logger related to out of the box metadata extractors is called `log4j.logger.org.alfresco.repo.content.metadata`.

Now regardless of whether an Office document or a PDF is added to the repository, the value of the file's keywords property will be extracted and stored in the `sc:clientName` property.

Transforming Content from One Format to Another

A content transformer is used to transform content from one format to another. Content transformers are implemented as a Java class configured as a Spring bean. Alfresco finds the appropriate transformer based on source and target MIME type. There are two important use cases for transformers. The first is when an end user triggers a transformation, usually through an action. The most well-known out of the box example is converting Microsoft Office documents to PDF. Other out of the box transformers include:

- HTML-to-Text (`HtmlParserContentTransformer`)

- Microsoft Excel-to-CSV (`PoiHssfContentTransformer`)
- Microsoft Word-to-Text (`TextMiningContentTransformer`)
- PDF-to-Text (`PdfBoxContentTransformer`)

See the Appendix for further details on the out of the box transformers.

The second key transformer use case involves the Lucene full-text search engine. Lucene indexes content when it is added to the repository. But it only understands plain text. When a binary file is added to the repository, Alfresco looks for a transformer that can convert the file to plain text. The plain text is then fed to Lucene. If there is a content type that Alfresco doesn't know how to full-text index out of the box, the trick is to write a content transformer for it and you're in business.

Step-by-Step: Writing a Custom Transformer

SomeCo works a lot with Microsoft Project files. The project files have task and resource information that would be useful to search against. But Alfresco doesn't have a content transformer that deals with Microsoft Project files, so out of the box Microsoft Project files aren't full-text indexed. In order to rectify that situation, you're going to have to write a custom transformer that converts Microsoft Project files to plain text.

Content transformers extend `AbstractContentTransformer`, which implements the `ContentTransformer` interface. At a minimum, all that is required for a custom content transformer is to implement two methods. The `getReliability()` method is used to declare the MIME types that are supported. The `transformInternal()` method is used to actually perform the transformation. Obviously, you'll also need an API that knows how to read the source format.

 What does reliability mean? You can file this under "Seemed like a good idea at the time". The original intent was to declare how reliable your transformation was for a given set of MIME types. In reality, people only used a reliability factor of 1.0 for the MIME types the transformation supported rather than adding lesser scores for MIME types that the transformer *might* support. So, effectively, you are declaring exactly which MIME types your transformer supports by implementing the method with a reliability factor of "1.0". As of Alfresco 3.0, the original `AbstractContentTransformer` class has been deprecated and the `ContentTransformer` interface has been updated with a more obvious method called `isTransformable`. It returns true if the transformer can transform the content from the source to the target MIME type.

As luck would have it, the SourceForge project, MPXJ, provides a Java API for working with Microsoft Project files. Luckier still, it relies on the same version of Apache POI as Alfresco does.

So, to do this task you'll need to:

1. Write a custom class that extends `AbstractContentTransformer`.

2. Configure a Spring bean to declare the new transformer.

3. Tell Alfresco about the Microsoft Project MIME type.

To write a custom content transformer that uses MPXJ to convert Microsoft Project files to plain text, follow these steps:

1. Create a new class in **src | java** called `com.someco.transformer.`
   `ProjectToPlainText` that extends `AbstractContentTransformer`.

2. The first method to implement is `getReliability()`. This method should return a value of 1.0 for supported source and target MIME types, and a 0.0 for everything else. The following code tells Alfresco that for a source MIME type matching Microsoft Project and a target MIME type of plain text, this transformer is up to the task:

```
public double getReliability(String sourceMimetype, String
                                            targetMimetype) {

        // only support MPP -> TEXT
        if (sourceMimetype.equals(ProjectToPlainText.MIMETYPE_
                                            PROJECT) &&
            targetMimetype.equals(MimetypeMap.MIMETYPE_TEXT_
                                            PLAIN)) {

                return 1.0;
        } else {
            return 0.0;
        }
    }
```

3. Next is the `transformInternal()` method. It does the bulk of the work, although the MPXJ library does the heavy lifting. The method uses the MPXJ library to iterate through the tasks and writes out the task information:

```
protected void transformInternal(ContentReader reader,
                                        ContentWriter writer,
            Map<String, Object> options) throws Exception {

        Writer out = new BufferedWriter(new OutputStreamWriter
                            (writer.getContentOutputStream()));

        ProjectFile mpp = new MPPReader().read (reader.
                                getContentInputStream());
```

```
ProjectHeader projectHeader = mpp.getProjectHeader();
List<Task> listAllTasks = mpp.getAllTasks();
List<Resource> listAllResources = mpp.getAllResources();

out.write(projectHeader.getProjectTitle());
for (Task task : listAllTasks) {
        out.write("ID:" + task.getID());
        out.write(" TASK:" + task.getName());
        if (task.getNotes() != null) out.write(" NOTES:"
                                     + task.getNotes());
        if (task.getContact() != null) out.write("
                        CONTACT:" + task.getContact());
        out.write("\r\n");
}
for (Resource resource : listAllResources) {
        out.write("RESOURCE:" + resource.getName());
        if (resource.getEmailAddress() != null) out.
           write(" EMAIL:" + resource.getEmailAddress());
        if (resource.getNotes() != null) out.write("
                        NOTES:" + resource.getNotes());
        out.write("\r\n");
}
out.flush();
if (out != null) {
        out.close();
}
}
```

The labels that get output in all caps ("NOTES", "CONTACT", and so on) don't do anything special. In fact, they add unnecessarily to the index. But if you actually want to try to read this output, it helps to have some markers in there. In a production implementation, it is probably best to leave them out.

4. That's all for the class. Now create a file in alfresco|extension called someco-transformer-context.xml with the following (two new beans will be added in subsequent steps):

```
<?xml version='1.0' encoding='UTF-8'?>
<!DOCTYPE beans PUBLIC '-//SPRING//DTD BEAN//EN' 'http://www.
                    springframework.org/dtd/spring-beans.dtd'>

<beans>
</beans>
```

5. The first bean to add declares the new transformer. The ID isn't important. It just follows the Alfresco convention of starting with "`transformer.`":

```
<bean id="transformer.Project"
      class="com.someco.transformer.ProjectToPlainText"
      parent="baseContentTransformer" />
```

6. The second bean tells Alfresco about a new MIME type map. The SomeCo MIME type map is needed to add Microsoft Project to the list of MIME types Alfresco knows about:

```
<bean id="mimetypeConfigService" class="org.alfresco.config.xml.
                        XMLConfigService" init-method="init">
    <constructor-arg>
        <bean class="org.alfresco.config.source.UrlConfigSource">
            <constructor-arg>
                <list>
                    <value>classpath:alfresco/mimetype/mimetype-
                                        map.xml</value>
                    <value>classpath:alfresco/mimetype/mimetype-
                                        map-openoffice.xml</value>
                    <value>classpath:alfresco/extension/someco-
                                        mimetype-map.xml</value>
                </list>
            </constructor-arg>
        </bean>
    </constructor-arg>
 </bean>
</beans>
```

7. Create a new custom MIME type map in **config | alfresco | extension** called `someco-mimetype-map.xml`, which matches the file path specified in the bean. The MIME type map is an Alfresco configuration file that contains:

```
<alfresco-config area="mimetype-map">
    <config evaluator="string-compare" condition="Mimetype Map">
        <mimetypes>
            <mimetype mimetype="application/vnd.ms-project"
                                    display="Microsoft Project">
                <extension>mpp</extension>
            </mimetype>
        </mimetypes>
    </config>
</alfresco-config>
```

8. Deploy, restart, and test.

To see what's going on with the out of the box content transformers, set `log4j.logger.org.alfresco.repo.content.transform` equal to `DEBUG`.

To test the new content transformer, add a Microsoft Project file anywhere in the repository, then do a search for a piece of text contained within the file, but not in the file name. The test should return the Microsoft Project file. This would not have been possible prior to deploying the custom Microsoft Project-to-Plain Text content transformer.

Summary

This chapter covered four different ways in which you can automatically process content as it is created, read, updated, and deleted. Specifically, you learned how to:

- Write custom actions both with and without action parameters, as well as how to invoke actions from JavaScript

- Bind logic to custom types using behaviors, including the logic that has a deal with the fact that it may have to wait until an existing transaction completes

- Extract metadata from binary files to reduce the amount of re-keying content contributors have to do when adding content to the repository

- Transform content from one format to another to facilitate full-text searching, or to simply provide a way for users to generate additional output formats from the same piece of content

When planning your own Alfresco implementations and Alfresco-based solutions, it is important to keep these hooks in mind. This is because the more code that can be moved into these areas, the more flexible and end-user configurable your solution will be.

5
Customizing the Web Client User Interface

The Alfresco Web Client is an all-purpose user interface for general document management. As such, it may not be specific enough for the solution you are trying to implement. Or, you may have the opposite problem—too many choices can confuse the users. The good news is that Alfresco's Web Client is easily configurable and can be extended.

By the end of this chapter, you will know how to:

- Add new menu items to the web client
- Show/hide menu items based on things such as permissions or arbitrary logic
- Create custom renderers to change how the web client shows repository data
- Create custom dialogs and wizards to gather information from a user
- Assess whether the solution you are building should be based on a custom version of Alfresco's Web Client or would be more appropriate as a custom application

It is important to note that with the 3.0 release, Alfresco introduced a new web framework called **Surf**, and a new client for team collaboration called **Share** that is built on the Surf framework. At some point, it is likely that Alfresco will write a new client for document management as well that leverages the new framework. The current web client is likely to be relegated to more of an administrative client before it is ultimately retired. This chapter is about customizing the "classic" JSF-based web client. Surf is discussed in the Appendix.

Knowing When to Customize Alfresco's Web Client and When to Write Your Own

Before you set off on that big Alfresco web client customization project you've been dreaming of, it is important to ask yourself if the Alfresco Web Client is the right place for your customizations. The key consideration is how closely does your solution resemble the generic "document management" use case? If the answer is that it is quite close such that the list of substantial customizations is fairly small, then proceed. SomeCo's internal rollout is a good example of this. So far, everything SomeCo is looking to do with Alfresco has been about managing documents. The customizations have been small tweaks aimed at streamlining certain tasks for the end users.

However, if your solution is radically different from document management or is composed of several significant customizations, you should think twice about customizing the web client. Instead, consider building a custom application loosely coupled to the repository through services. Here's why:

- At some point, it takes longer to customize the web client to meet the requirements than it would have to build a custom solution on top of the repository. Solutions that stray too far from the "document management" use case end up wasting a lot of development effort removing or hiding Alfresco's out of the box features.

- Numerous and/or significant customizations present a heavy maintenance and upgrade burden, even when you stick to Alfresco's extension mechanism. As the number and complexity of the customizations increase, make sure what's left of the web client after you've customized it still adds enough value to compensate for the costs and overhead.

- If your solution could work without the Alfresco Web Client, why lock yourself in? An n-tier solution leveraging Alfresco to provide "content as a service" will be much more flexible in the long run.

- Alfresco controls the future direction of the web client. You can certainly influence Alfresco's product road map to a much greater extent than you can with proprietary vendors. But Alfresco, the commercial software company, still has ultimate control over Alfresco, the product. If you make significant investments in a solution based on a customized web client, you are risking future migration costs if and when Alfresco decides to change how the web client is built. The recent move away from JSF to Surf in the 3.0 Share client is a good example of the significant shifts that can occur in relatively short time horizons.

All of this can be summarized with the old adage, "Use the right tool for the right job". If the customizations you are making seem natural and in line with how the web client is "supposed" to be used, you are using the right tool for the right job. If, however, you are constantly "fighting" with the web client features or metaphors, you may be pushing the web client beyond what it was originally intended for. This may cause issues for you down the line.

Adding New Menu Items with UI Actions

Probably the simplest form of web client customization is adding to or changing the existing links in the various menus throughout the client. Somewhat confusingly, these links are called UI Actions.

Step-by-Step: Adding a Simple UI Action

Suppose SomeCo wanted to add a link to the corporate website within the Alfresco user interface. To illustrate a few of the options available, let's add the link to three different places within the UI:

1. The **document browse menu**, which is the menu shown for each document in a list of documents.

2. The **document browse actions menu**, which is the menu shown when you click **More Actions** for a specific document in a list of documents.

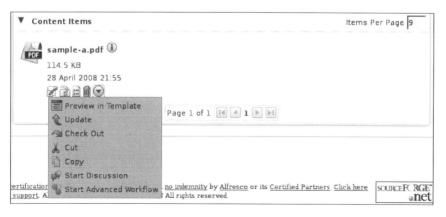

3. The **document details actions menu**, which is the list of actions shown when viewing the document details.

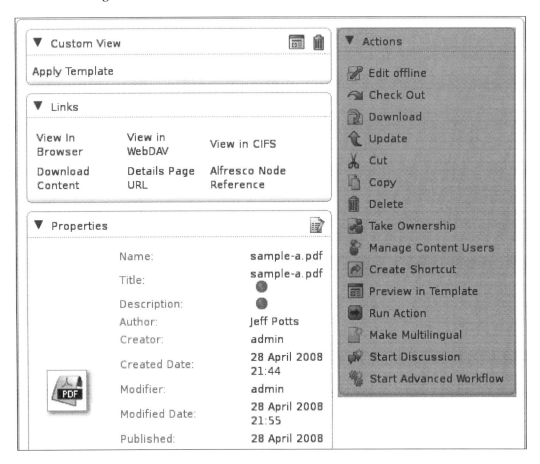

Adding the UI action to these menus (called action groups) is a simple matter of configuration. It involves finding an icon to represent the UI action, and then updating `web-client-config-custom.xml` to specify in which action groups the UI action should appear.

To add a UI action that invokes a URL to the menus specified above, do the following:

1. First, you need a 16x16 icon to go with your menu item. In the case of the document browse actions menu, the icon is all that is shown. So, an icon is pretty important. Unless one of your graphically-talented friends is sitting next to you anxiously waiting to generate some compelling iconography for

you, grab the globe icon Alfresco uses as a part of its WCM product out of **alfresco | images | icons | website.gif** and copy it into **| src | web | someco | images | icons | website.gif.** (You could just reference Alfresco's GIF where it resides, but what if they change or rename it in the next point release? Grab a copy now and you won't have to worry about it.)

2. Next, edit `web-client-config-custom.xml` in **config | alfresco | extension**. Add a new `config` element and an `actions` element under that. You're about to add several children to the `actions` element.

```
<config>
   <actions>
```

3. Now add an `action` element. This defines the UI action.

```
<!--  Link to SomeCo's Web Site -->
<action id="web_site">
   <label>SomeCo</label>
   <href>http://www.optaros.com</href>
   <image>/someco/images/icons/website.gif</image>
   <target>new</target>
</action>
```

4. Now you have a UI action definition that can be referenced in any number of action groups by referring to its ID. Adding a UI action to an action group is a matter of extending the action group definition in the out of the box `web-client-config-actions.xml` file (or any other Alfresco configuration file that defines actions). Add the `action-group` elements for the menus you want to add the UI action to; in this case that's `document_browse`, `document_browse_menu`, and `doc_details_actions`.

```
<action-group id="document_browse">
   <action idref="web_site" />
</action-group>
<action-group id="document_browse_menu">
   <action idref="web_site" />
</action-group>
<action-group id="doc_details_actions">
   <action idref="web_site" />
</action-group>
```

5. Close out the `action` and `config` elements, then save and close the `web-client-config-custom.xml` file.

```
   </actions>
</config>
```

6. Deploy, restart, and test.

You should now be able to log in and see a link to the SomeCo website in the **browse document menu**:

in the **browse document actions menu**:

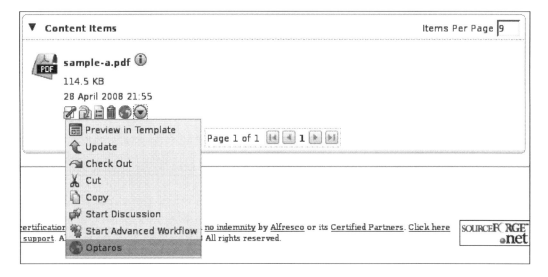

and in the **document details** menu:

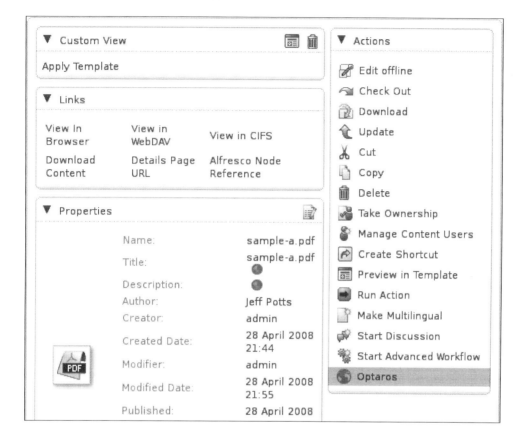

Showing/Hiding the Label

Did you notice the difference between the **document browse** menu and the other two menus? In the **document browse** menu, only the icon is shown. Where is that configured? The action-group element in `web-client-config-custom.xml` is extending the out of the box definition for the `document_browse` action group. Action groups can set options that affect all of the actions defined in the group. In this case, the action group sets `show-link` to `false`, which hides the text and shows only the icon:

```
<!-- Actions for a document in the Browse screen -->
<action-group id="document_browse">
    <show-link>false</show-link>
...
```

Leveraging Out of the Box Examples

You can see the full syntax of the `action-group` and `action` elements by looking at Alfresco's web client configuration files. These reside in **WEB-INF | classes | alfresco**. Search the directory for files containing the string `action-group`. See the Appendix for more information on the available action groups.

Using Other Types of UI Actions

If you looked at the source, you noticed that simple HREFs are not the only kind of targets that UI actions can invoke. You can call local JavaScript functions, server-side JavaScript, JSF actions (yet another use of the term "actions"), JSF-managed bean methods, and action listeners.

For example, the simplest UI action you can possibly create involves a UI action definition in `web-client-config-custom.xml`, a navigation rule, and a JSP page. Let's look at a `hello world` example.

Here's a portion of a `config` section from `web-client-config-custom`. Notice that unlike the previous example, in this snippet, the UI action is defined "in-line" rather than using `idrefs`. At a minimum, you need a label and an action:

```
<!-- Actions Menu for Document Details screen -->
<action-group id="doc_details_actions">
    <action idref="web_site" />
    <action id="hello_world">
    <label>Hello World</label>
        <action>hello</action>
    </action>
</action-group>
```

In this case, the action is a JSF action that maps to a JSF navigation rule:

```
<navigation-rule>
    <from-view-id>/jsp/*</from-view-id>
    <navigation-case>
        <from-outcome>hello</from-outcome>
        <to-view-id>/jsp/extension/hello.jsp</to-view-id>
    </navigation-case>
</navigation-rule>
```

The `hello.jsp` needs nothing more than the minimum set of required JSF tags:

```
<%@ taglib uri="http://java.sun.com/jsf/html" prefix="h" %>
<%@ taglib uri="http://java.sun.com/jsf/core" prefix="f" %>
<f:view>
```

```
<h:form acceptcharset="UTF-8">
    <h:outputText value="Hello, World!" />
</h:form>
</f:view>
```

Most UI actions in Alfresco's Web Client that invoke JSF actions call dialogs and wizards. They look like this:

```
<action>dialog:checkinFile</action>
```

You'll learn about dialogs and wizards shortly. Before getting to that, let's work through a UI action example that uses action listeners.

Step-by-Step: Adding a UI Action to Set the Web Flag

The previous example was pretty basic. You added a link that called a web page. But what if you wanted to perform an operation within the context of Alfresco? In Chapter 4 you learned that actions (not to be confused with "UI actions") encapsulate content operations. You also learned that many of the links you see in the web client user interface are implemented as actions. It shouldn't be a surprise to you that custom actions, such as the `set-web-flag` action you created in Chapter 4, can be wired into the web client user interface through UI actions.

Recall that a subset of SomeCo's Whitepapers will be available on the Web. Whitepapers that need to be published to the Web are identified by the `sc:webable` aspect, which contains an `isActive` flag. SomeCo employees can add or remove a Whitepaper to or from the Web by setting the flag to true or false. But SomeCo doesn't want just anybody to be able to set that flag. Alfresco doesn't have field-level security out of the box. So how can this be implemented?

One way to do this is to configure the property to be read-only in the interface and then use a UI action, available only to the people who need it, to set the flag appropriately.

Let's do just that. Like the simple web link example, it is going to involve bugging our creative pal to generate us a couple of icons, updating `web-client-config-custom.xml` to identify the UI action, and associating it with an action group. But it will also require a small Java class—an action listener—that will enable us to write a `success` message to the web client after the flag has been set. In this example, you'll also externalize the UI action label by updating `webclient.properties`.

To create a UI action that calls the set web flag action to modify the `isActive` flag, do the following:

1. There are a couple of out of the box icons that will do quite nicely for the enable/disable UI action. Copy `create_website.gif` and `delete_website.gif` from **alfresco|images|icons to |src|web|someco|images|icons**.

2. Edit **|config|alfresco|extension|web-client-config-custom.xml**. Add new `action` elements for the enable and disable UI actions to the existing `config|action` element. First, add the UI action to enable the document for the Web:

```
<!-- set sc:isActive to true -->
<action id="web_enable">
   <permissions>
      <!-- each permission can be an Allow or Deny check -->
      <permission allow="true">Write</permission>
   </permissions>
   <label-id>enableWeb</label-id>
   <image>/someco/images/icons/create_website.gif</image>
   <action-listener>#{WebSettingsBean.setActive}
   </action-listener>
   <params>
      <param name="id">#{actionContext.id}</param>
      <param name="active">true</param>
   </params>
</action>
```

3. Recall that the custom action you built in Chapter 4 used a parameter to specify whether to set the `isActive` flag to true or false. To add a `disable` UI action, all you have to do is repeat the UI action definition created in the prior step and modify the label, icon, and `active` parameter:

```
<!-- set sc:isActive to false -->
<action id="web_disable">
   <permissions>
      <!-- each permission can be an Allow or Deny check -->
      <permission allow="true">Write</permission>
   </permissions>
   <label-id>disableWeb</label-id>
      <image>/someco/images/icons/delete_website.gif</image>
   <action-listener>#{WebSettingsBean.setActive}
   </action-listener>
   <params>
      <param name="id">#{actionContext.id}</param>
      <param name="active">false</param>
   </params>
</action>
```

4. The new UI actions will appear on the document details menu, so add the references to the appropriate `action-group` element:

    ```xml
    <!-- Actions Menu for Document Details screen -->
    <action-group id="doc_details_actions">
            <action idref="web_enable" />
            <action idref="web_disable" />
            <action idref="web_site" />
    </action-group>
    ```

5. While you are in `web-client-config-custom.xml`, set the read-only flag on the `isActive` property to true to force users to use the UI Action link, instead of modifying the property directly:

    ```xml
    <!-- add webable aspect properties to property sheet -->
    <config evaluator="aspect-name" condition="sc:webable">
        <property-sheet>
           <show-property name=
            "sc:published" display-label- id="published" />
           <show-property name="sc:isActive"
           display-label-id="isActive" read-only="true" />
        </property-sheet>
    </config>
    ```

6. Externalize the strings by updating **|config|alfresco|webclient.properties**. Add key-value pairs for the enable or disable labels as well as a `success` message your listener will print after the action runs:

    ```
    # Web Enable/Disable UI actions
    enableWeb=SC Enable Web
    disableWeb=SC Disable Web
    success_web_set_active=Successfully updated the active flag.
    ```

7. Now write the action listener as a JSF-managed bean. Create a new class in **src|java** called `com.someco.web.bean.WebSettingsBean`. Declare the class, and specify the constants and class variables as follows:

    ```java
    public class WebSettingsBean {
       private static final String PARAM_ID = "id";
       private static final String PARAM_ACTIVE = "active";
       private static final String MSG_SUCCESS_WEB_SET_ACTIVE =
                                    "success_web_set_active";
       private static final String PANEL_ID_SPACE_PROPS =
                                                "space-props";

       /** The BrowseBean to be used by the bean */
       protected BrowseBean browseBean;

       public WebSettingsBean() {
       }
    ```

8. Implement the `setActive` method. It gets called when the UI Action is invoked. It is passed as an `ActionEvent` through which you can get the parameters:

```
/**
 * Action handler called when the enable or disable action is
                                                   clicked.
 * @param event
 */
public void setActive(ActionEvent event) {
    UIActionLink link = (UIActionLink)event.getComponent();
    Map<String, String> params = link.getParameterMap();
    String id = params.get(PARAM_ID);
    String active = params.get(PARAM_ACTIVE);
        Boolean activeFlag = Boolean.parseBoolean(active);
```

9. Complete the method by starting a transaction, running the action, setting an informational message in the UI, and then completing the transaction:

```
FacesContext fc = FacesContext.getCurrentInstance();

if (id != null && id.length() != 0)
    try {
        NodeRef ref =
        new NodeRef(Repository.getStoreRef(),id);
        // start the transaction
        UserTransaction tx = null;
        try {
            tx = Repository.getUserTransaction(fc);
            tx.begin();

            ActionImpl action = new ActionImpl
            (ref, SetWebFlag.NAME, null);
            action.setParameterValue
            (SetWebFlag.PARAM_ACTIVE, activeFlag);
            SetWebFlag actionExecuter =
            (SetWebFlag)FacesContextUtils.
            getWebApplicationContext(fc).
            getBean(SetWebFlag.NAME);
            actionExecuter.execute(action, ref);

            String msg = Application.getMessage(fc,
            MSG_SUCCESS_WEB_SET_ACTIVE);
            FacesMessage facesMsg = new FacesMessage
            (FacesMessage.SEVERITY_INFO, msg, msg);
            String formId = Utils.getParentForm
            (fc, event.getComponent()).getClientId(fc);
```

```
                fc.addMessage(formId + ':' + PANEL_ID_SPACE_PROPS,
                         facesMsg);
                // commit the transaction
                tx.commit();

                this.browseBean.getDocument().reset();
                }
                catch (Throwable err)
                {
                  Utils.addErrorMessage(MessageFormat.format
                (Application.getMessage(fc, Repository.ERROR_GENERIC)
                     err.getMessage()), err);
                try { if (tx != null)
                  tx.rollback(); } catch (Exception tex) {}
                  }
      } catch (InvalidNodeRefException refErr)
          {
           Utils.addErrorMessage(MessageFormat.format
           (Application.getMessage(fc, Repository.ERROR_NODEREF)
           ,new Object[] {id}) );
          }
}
```

10. To close out the class, add the setter for the browse bean that will be injected by JSF:

```
public void setBrowseBean(BrowseBean browseBean) {
    this.browseBean = browseBean;
}
```

11. Finally, create a `faces-config-custom.xml` file for the JSF-managed listener bean. As you learned in Chapter 2, the file will ultimately reside in Alfresco's WEB-INF. So put it in the |**src**|**web**|**WEB-INF** directory in your Eclipse project:

```
<?xml version='1.0' encoding='UTF-8'?>
<!DOCTYPE faces-config PUBLIC "-//Sun Microsystems, Inc.//DTD
                             JavaServer Faces Config 1.1//EN"
                        "http://java.sun.com/dtd/web-
                                    facesconfig_1_1.dtd">
<faces-config>
    <managed-bean>
       <description>The bean that manages
         SC Web   settings.</description>
       <managed-bean-name>WebSettingsBean</managed-bean-name>
       <managed-bean- class>com.someco.web.bean.WebSettingsBean
       </managed-bean-class>
```

```
            <managed-bean-scope>session</managed-bean-scope>
            <managed-property>
                <property-name>browseBean</property-name>
                <value>#{BrowseBean}</value>
            </managed-property>
        </managed-bean>
    </faces-config>
```

12. Deploy, restart, and test.

To test this, log in to the web client as admin. If you don't have a Whitepaper in **Som eco|Marketing|Whitepapers**, go ahead and add one. When you open the details for the document, you should see both the **Enable** and **Disable** actions:

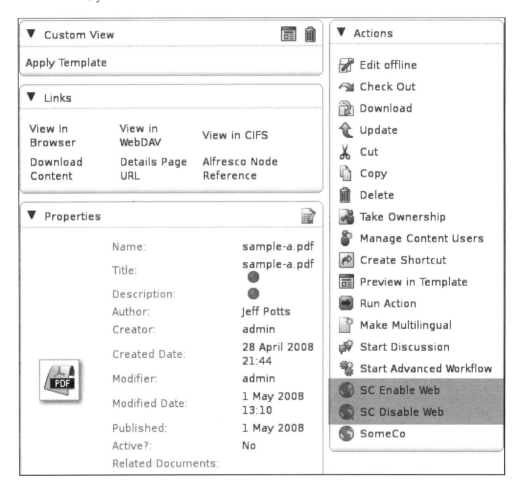

They are visible to you because admin has write permissions on this object. You should be able to click **Enable** and **Disable**, and see the **Active** property change from **No** to **Yes** and back again depending on which action you click.

Restricting the UI Action by Permission

If you haven't already done so, use the admin panel to create a test user. Don't add the user to any groups and don't change any settings for the Whitepapers folder or the test Whitepaper. If you log out as admin and log in again as the test user, you should not see the actions. They are missing because the new test user has not been granted at least "write" permission on the test Whitepaper.

If you grant your test user write access (Editor, Collaborator, or Coordinator) to the Whitepapers folder or directly to the test Whitepaper, they will be able to see the actions.

The permission elements that are part of the UI action's definition in `web-client-config-custom.xml` can use any of the permission groups Alfresco knows about. In this case you specified `Write`, which is a lower-level permission group. But you could also specify one of the higher-level groups such as `Coordinator` if it makes sense to do so for your solution. See the Appendix for information on the out of the box permission groups.

Writing Action Evaluators to Show/Hide UI Actions

In the previous example, you set up two UI actions to enable and disable the `isActive` flag for a webable piece of content. The actions only show up if a user has the appropriate permissions. But what if SomeCo wants to give several different people or groups `Write` permission, but only wants a subset of those folks to be able to publish documents to the Web? Not only that, but isn't it a bit sloppy to show the **Enable** link when the `isActive` flag is already set to **True** (and **Disable** when it is already set to **False**)?

Both of these issues are easily addressed by implementing an Action Evaluator. An Action Evaluator is a Java class that decides whether or not a UI Action should show up.

Step-by-Step: Evaluating Whether or Not to Show the Set Web Flag UI Actions

SomeCo wants to create a group called "Publisher" and populate it with the people and groups allowed to click the **Enable** and **Disable** UI Actions created in the previous example. Additionally, if the flag is set to **True**, the **Enable** UI Action should not be displayed. If the flag is set to **False**, the **Disable** UI Action should not be displayed.

To make this happen, you are going to implement an Action Evaluator. This involves writing a Java class that implements the `ActionEvaluator` interface, and then wiring it into your UI Action by updating the action configuration in `web-client-config-custom.xml`.

Follow these steps:

1. Create a new Java class in **src | java** called `com.someco.action.evaluator.WebEnableEvaluator`. The class implements `org.alfresco.web.action.ActionEvaluator`.

    ```
    public class WebEnableEvaluator implements ActionEvaluator {
    ```

2. The work is done in the `evaluate` method. You must return **True** to show the UI action or **False** to hide it. First, check the group. If the user isn't in the group, there's no need to go any further; the action should be hidden (the `GroupMembershipCheck` and the `Constants` classes will be implemented shortly):

    ```
    public boolean evaluate(Node node) {
        // check the group, if the current user is not in the group,
          hide the action
        FacesContext context = FacesContext.getCurrentInstance();
        // check the group
        if (!GroupMembershipCheck.isCurrentUserInGroup(context,
          Constants.GROUP_WEB_PUBLISHER))
        {
            return false;
        }
    ```

3. Then, check for an aspect. If there is no aspect, you know it isn't enabled. So there's no need to go further; the action should be shown:

    ```
    // otherwise, check the aspect, then check the active property
    NodeRef ref = new NodeRef(Repository.getStoreRef(),
      node.getId());
    // if the aspect hasn't yet been added, it can be enabled
    if (!node.hasAspect(SomeCoModel.ASPECT_SC_WEBABLE)) {
        return true;
    }
    ```

4. If it has the aspect, just return the opposite of whatever the flag is set to. (If the flag is set to true, you want to hide the action, so return false):

```
// check the active property
NodeService nodeSvc = Repository.getServiceRegistry(context).
                                          getNodeService();
  boolean active = (Boolean)nodeSvc.getProperty(ref,
                                SomeCoModel.PROP_IS_ACTIVE);

  return !active;
}
```

5. In Labs 3.0, there is a `BaseActionEvaluator` class that evaluators can extend, but it isn't available in Enterprise 2.2. To be compatible with both releases you are instead implementing the `ActionEvaluator` interface, which expects an overloaded evaluate method that accepts an object. Use the following method to simply downcast the `Object` to a `Node` and call the method you just implemented:

```
public boolean evaluate(Object obj) {
    if (obj instanceof Node) {
       return evaluate((Node)obj);
    } else {
       // if you don't give me a Node, I don't know how to evaluate
       return false;
    }
}
```

6. Now implement the evaluator for the **Disable** UI Action. You could probably code the evaluate method to work with both actions. But it is cleaner to go ahead and use a separate class called `com.someco.action.evaluator.WebDisableEvaluator`. The only difference between this class and the previous one is the `evaluate` method, which you should implement as follows:

```
public boolean evaluate(Node node) {
        // if the aspect hasn't been added, it cannot be disabled
        if (!node.hasAspect(SomeCoModel.ASPECT_SC_WEBABLE)) {
           return false;
        }
        // otherwise, check the group, then check the active
                                                      property
        FacesContext context = FacesContext.getCurrentInstance();
        // check the group
        if (!GroupMembershipCheck.isCurrentUserInGroup(context,
                          Constants.GROUP_WEB_PUBLISHER)) {
            return false;
        }
```

```
// check the active property
NodeRef ref = new NodeRef(Repository.getStoreRef(),
                          node.getId());
NodeService nodeSvc = Repository.getServiceRegistry(context)
                               .getNodeService();
boolean active = (Boolean)nodeSvc.getProperty(ref,
                          SomeCoModel.PROP_IS_ACTIVE);

return active;
}
```

7. Both evaluators check group membership. It's a small bit of logic, but repeating it across both classes may leave you with feelings of guilt. So create a new class called `com.someco.util.GroupMembershipCheck` with the following content:

```
public class GroupMembershipCheck {
    public static boolean isCurrentUserInGroup(FacesContext
                                    context, String groupName) {
    // The authority service returns authorities with their
                                        authority type
    // prefix prepended to the name, so we'll do that as well
    groupName = AuthorityType.GROUP.getPrefixString() +
                                        groupName;

    // get the current user
    String currentUserName = Repository.getServiceRegistry(
      context).getAuthenticationService().getCurrentUserName();

    // get the list of groups this user is a member of
    Set<String> authorityList = Repository.getServiceRegistry
      (context).getAuthorityService().getContainingAuthorities
      (AuthorityType.GROUP, currentUserName, false);

    // look in the list to see if groupName is in there. If so,
                                        return true;
    return authorityList.contains(groupName);
    }
}
```

8. Ideally, the name of the group we're checking would be passed in to the Evaluator as an argument; but that's not supported. Instead, create a class called `com.someco.util.Constants` and add the group name as a constant. As the SomeCo solution evolves, additional shared constants can be added to this class. For now it needs to contain:

```
public class Constants {
    // Groups
    public static final String GROUP_WEB_PUBLISHER = "Publisher";
}
```

9. Deploy, restart, and test.

To test the new evaluator classes, log in as either admin or test user, and confirm that you cannot see either action. That means the group check is working because admin doesn't yet belong to the "Publisher" group. Once you've confirmed that the group check is functional, you can create a group called "Publisher" and assign both admin and your test user to the group. Only one action should be available, depending on the presence of the webable aspect and the value of the isActive flag.

Now you have a relatively secure way to control who can make a document publishable on SomeCo's website. It's only relatively secure because anyone with write access can still change that flag through the API.

In addition to letting us secure the property, it gives publishers a quick way to set the publish status. They don't even have to edit the details. They can simply click on menu items.

From a support perspective, it is also pretty clean:

- If someone decides that they want to be able to set the flag from a different place in the UI, the existing UI action can be mapped to a different action group.

- If SomeCo wants to change who can set the flag, they can simply add or remove users and groups to and from the "Publisher" group.

- If the logic ever needs to change (suppose SomeCo wants to start tracking the date a piece of content was disabled for the Web instead of tracking only the publish date, for example), the code lives in one place: inside the rule action. The UI actions wouldn't have to be touched.

Changing How the Web Client Renders Data with Custom Component Renderers

Alfresco built the web client with Spring and JSF. The good news is that if you don't like how the web client components work, JSF makes it possible to configure, customize, and extend the components to fit your needs. The bad news is that the JSF component lifecycle is complicated and there are multiple approaches to implementing JSF components. Unfortunately, Alfresco's approach isn't consistent across all components. So unless you are already a JSF expert, it can be tough to follow the source code.

Let's look at a couple of basic examples that can at least get you pointed in the right direction. Suppose that SomeCo's Operations department wants to track status reports in Alfresco. Status reports will be written as documents and uploaded to the Operations space. Two properties will help the Operations team get a feel for the project's status: statusSummary will be a text property meant to capture a couple of sentences summarizing the status report, and statusIndicator will be a single-value select box consisting of color-coded statuses that are Red, Yellow, or Green.

Rather than create a "status report" type, you will model the two status-related properties as part of a "status-able" aspect so that any document in the repository could have status metadata associated with it.

You've done enough modeling and web client wiring by this point to know what to do if these were the only requirements. So let's make it interesting. First, the standard text field that Alfresco uses to edit text properties isn't going to be very usable for typing a two-sentence summary. Second, the head of the Operations team is a very visual person. He or she doesn't want to see the words Red, Yellow, or Green to know a project's status, but wants to see a traffic light icon with the appropriate light lit up.

Both of these can be addressed through JSF changes. In the case of the text area, Alfresco has provided a TextAreaGenerator that accepts row and column arguments. You just need to configure the web client to use it. To display a traffic light depending on a property value, you'll need to write a new generator and a custom renderer and then tell the web client to use it.

Step-by-Step: Making a Text Field a Specific Size

SomeCo wants to track a status summary and a status indicator for its project status reports. They want the statusSummary property to be edited with a text area that is 50-columns wide and 5-rows tall. This will involve:

1. Updating the model with a new status-able aspect that contains the status summary and status indicator properties

2. Updating web-client-config-custom.xml with configuration settings that show the new aspect in the appropriate menus and identifying a new generator to use for the summary property

3. Updating faces-config-custom.xml with a new JSF-managed bean that passes the row and column parameters to an out of the box text area generator class

To make this happen, follow these steps:

1. Edit | **config** | **alfresco** | **extension** | **model** | **scModel.xml**. Add a new aspect as follows.

```
<aspect name="sc:statusable">
   <title>Someco Status Tracking</title>
   <properties>
      <property name="sc:statusIndicator">
         <type>d:text</type>
         <mandatory>true</mandatory>
         <default>Green</default>
         <constraints>
            <constraint ref="sc:statusIndicatorList" />
         </constraints>
      </property>
      <property name="sc:statusSummary">
         <type>d:text</type>
         <mandatory>true</mandatory>
      </property>
   </properties>
</aspect>
```

2. The aspect refers to the LIST constraint that defines the possible values for the status indicator. Add the constraint definition at the top of the model file between the namespaces and types elements.

```
<constraints>
   <constraint name="sc:statusIndicatorList" type="LIST">
      <parameter name="allowedValues">
         <list>
            <value>Green</value>
            <value>Yellow</value>
            <value>Red</value>
         </list>
      </parameter>
   </constraint>
</constraints>
```

3. Save and close the model file.

4. Edit **|config|alfresco|extension|web-client-config-custom.xml**. The new aspect needs to be added to the `add features` list.

```
...
<config evaluator="string-compare" condition="Action Wizards">
    <!-- The list of aspects to show in the add/remove features
      action -->
    <!-- and the has-aspect condition -->
    <aspects>
      <aspect name="sc:webable"/>
      <aspect name="sc:clientRelated"/>
      <aspect name="sc:rateable"/>
      <aspect name="sc:statusable"/>
    </aspects>
  ...
```

5. In the property sheet configuration for the new aspect, specify the new generator for the component-generator attribute on the `sc:statusSummary` property.

```
<!--  add statusable properties to property sheet -->
<config evaluator="aspect-name" condition="sc:statusable">
    <property-sheet>
      <show-property name="sc:statusIndicator" display-label-
        id="statusIndicator" />
      <show-property name="sc:statusSummary" display-label-
        id="statusSummary" component-generator=
        "SummaryTextAreaGenerator" />
    </property-sheet>
</config>
```

6. Edit **|config|alfresco|extension|webclient.properties** to externalize the aspect's labels.

```
#sc:statusable
statusIndicator=Status
statusSummary=Summary
```

7. Edit **|src|web|WEB-INF|faces-config-custom.xml** to add the new generator as a JSF-managed bean.

```
<managed-bean>
    <description>
      The out-of-the-box textarea generator with specific rows and
      columns.
    </description>
    <managed-bean-name>SummaryTextAreaGenerator</managed-bean-name>
    <managed-bean-class>
```

```
    org.alfresco.web.bean.generator.TextAreaGenerator
</managed-bean-class>
<managed-bean-scope>request</managed-bean-scope>
<managed-property>
    <property-name>rows</property-name>
    <value>5</value>
</managed-property>
<managed-property>
    <property-name>columns</property-name>
    <value>50</value>
</managed-property>
</managed-bean>
```

8. Deploy, restart, and test.

To test this change, you need to add a document to the **Someco | Operations** folder and then add the new `SomeCo Status Tracking` aspect to it. When you edit the properties, you should see that a text area of the size you specified is used for the **Status** and **Summary**:

What Just Happened

A generator is a JSF-managed bean that is responsible for figuring out which JSF components need to be used for displaying and editing the property values. The out of the box generator beans are defined in `faces-config-beans.xml` in Alfresco's `WEB-INF` directory.

Properties have a default generator based on their type. You can override the default generator by specifying a new generator in the `component-generator` attribute of the `show-property` element of the property you want to override in `web-client-config-custom.xml`.

Overriding the Generator for All Properties

In this example, you created a new bean with the name `SummaryTextAreaGenerator` and pointed to the same class as the out of the box `TextAreaGenerator`. This allowed you to specify the row and column parameters for the text area used for the `Status Summary` field. If SomeCo had wanted to make all text areas of the same height and width, you could have overridden the existing `TextAreaGenerator` bean, specified the row and column parameters, and then specified `TextAreaGenerator` as the component generator.

Step-by-Step: Changing the Status Field on the Details Page to Display as a Stoplight Indicator

SomeCo wants to show a graphical representation of the status indicator. Alfresco is using the standard components for displaying and editing the status indicator property. The edit is fine the way it is, but the display needs to change to show a traffic light. This involves:

- Updating `web-client-config-custom.xml` to specify a component-generator for the status indicator field
- Writing a new JSF-managed bean to implement the component generator
- Writing a new renderer class
- Updating `faces-config-custom.xml` with the new managed bean and the renderer declaration
- Finding or creating some traffic light icons

Ready? Let's get started. Follow these steps:

1. Edit **|config|alfresco|extension|web-client-config-custom.xml** to specify a component-generator for the status indicator field as follows.

```
<!-- add statusable properties to property sheet -->
<config evaluator="aspect-name" condition="sc:statusable">
   <property-sheet>
      <show-property name="sc:statusIndicator"
       displaylabelid="statusIndicator"
        component-generator="StoplightGenerator" />
      <show-property name="sc:statusSummary"
       display-label-id="statusSummary" component-generator
       ="SummaryTextAreaGenerator" />
   </property-sheet>
</config>
```

2. Create a new class in **src|java** called `org.alfresco.web.bean.generator.StoplightGenerator`. The class needs to extend `org.alfresco.web.bean.generator.TextFieldGenerator` so that you can rely on Alfresco's editor component. Alfresco's class has protected methods in it, which is why we're putting our custom class in Alfresco's package.

```
public class StoplightGenerator extends TextFieldGenerator
```

3. There are two methods this class needs to override. First, implement the `createComponent` method. This method is responsible for figuring out whether the property sheet is being edited or just read, and then pulling in the appropriate components. If the property sheet is being read, the custom renderer should be used to show the traffic light. If it is being edited, Alfresco should use whatever it would have used had you not decided to extend the `TextFieldGenerator`. The first part of the method makes the call in the case of a read:

```
protected UIComponent createComponent(FacesContext context,
    UIPropertySheet propertySheet, PropertySheetItem item) {
    UIComponent component = null;

    if (item instanceof UIProperty) {
        if (!propertySheet.inEditMode()) {
            component = generate(context, item.getName());
```

4. The second part of the method can be implemented by copying and pasting code from the `createComponent` method of Alfresco's `TextFieldGenerator` with a minor tweak at the end. Instead of calling this class's `generate` method for a non-list-constrained property, you want to call super's generate method.

```
} else {
    // if the field has the list of values constraint
    // and it is editable a SelectOne component is
    // required otherwise create the standard edit component
    ListOfValuesConstraint constraint =
    getListOfValuesConstraint(context, propertySheet, item);

    PropertyDefinition propDef = this.getPropertyDefinition
    (context,propertySheet.getNode(), item.getName());

        if (constraint != null && item.isReadOnly() == false
        &&propDef != null && propDef.isProtected() == false)
        {component = context.getApplication().createComponent
          (UISelectOne.COMPONENT_TYPE);
          FacesHelper.setupComponentId(context, component,
          item.getName());
    // create the list of choices
        UISelectItems itemsComponent = (UISelectItems)
                context.getApplication().createComponent
                            ("javax.faces.SelectItems");

    List<SelectItem> items = new ArrayList<SelectItem>
                                                (3);

    List<String> values = constraint.getAllowedValues();
    for (String value : values) {
        Object obj = null;

        // we need to setup the list with objects of the
                                        correct type
        if(propDef.getDataType().getName().equals
                            (DataTypeDefinition.INT))
        {
            obj = Integer.valueOf(value);
        }
        else if (propDef.getDataType().getName().equals
            (DataTypeDefinition.LONG))
        {
            obj = Long.valueOf(value);
        } else if (propDef.getDataType().getName().equals
                        (DataTypeDefinition.DOUBLE))
        {
            obj = Double.valueOf(value);
        } else if (propDef.getDataType().getName().equals
                        (DataTypeDefinition.FLOAT))
```

```
            {
                obj = Float.valueOf(value);
            } else
            {
                obj = value;
            }
            items.add(new SelectItem(obj, value));
        }
        itemsComponent.setValue(items);
        // add the items as a child component
        component.getChildren().add(itemsComponent);
      } else {
        // use the standard component in edit mode
        component = super.generate(context, item.getName());
      }
    }
  }
  return component;
}
```

5. Now implement the generate method. This method creates the component that gets used to render the output for the property. The method first grabs a simple "output" component and then tells it to use the custom stoplight renderer:

```
public UIComponent generate(FacesContext context, String id)
{
    UIComponent component =     context.getApplication().createComp
onent(ComponentConstants.JAVAX_FACES_OUTPUT);
    component.setRendererType(Constants.STOPLIGHT_DISPLAY_RENDERER);
    FacesHelper.setupComponentId(context, component, id);
    return component;
}
```

6. Next, implement the renderer. The renderer is responsible for writing the image tag that points to the stoplight image depending on the value of the property. Create a new Java class in src/java called org.alfresco. web.ui.extension.renderer.StoplightDisplayRenderer. Unlike the generator class, the renderer doesn't need to be in an Alfresco package, but it seems like a good idea to keep it close to the generator. The class extends org.alfresco.web.ui.common.renderer.BaseRenderer.

```
public class StoplightDisplayRenderer extends BaseRenderer
```

7. Most of the work is done in the `encodeEnd` method, which is to inspect the value of the property and map it to an appropriate image.

```java
public void encodeEnd(FacesContext context, UIComponent component)
                                        throws IOException {
    if (component.isRendered() == false) return;

    ResponseWriter out = context.getResponseWriter();

    // render the field
    if(isMultiple(component)) {
        out.write(Utils.encode("Multiple value property fields
                                are not supported."));
    } else {
        String value = (String)((ValueHolder)component)
                                        .getValue();
        String stoplightImageRef = null;
          if(value == null) {
          stoplightImageRef = "/alfresco/someco/images/icons/
                                        stoplight-disable.png";
            value = "";
        } else if (value.toLowerCase().equals("red")){
         stoplightImageRef = "/alfresco/someco/images/icons/
                                        stoplight-red.png";
        } else if (value.toLowerCase().equals("yellow")) {
            stoplightImageRef = "/alfresco/someco/images/icons/
                                        stoplight-yellow.png";
        } else if (value.toLowerCase().equals("green")) {
            stoplightImageRef = "/alfresco/someco/images/icons/
                                        stoplight-green.png";
        } else {
            stoplightImageRef = "/alfresco/someco/images/icons/
                                        stoplight-disable.png";
            value = "";
        }
        // display stoplight image tag
         out.write("<div>");
         out.write("<img src=\"" + stoplightImageRef + "\"
                                    alt=\"" + value + "\"/>");
          out.write("</div>");
    }
}
```

8. The remaining methods in the class either support the `encodeEnd` method or override methods in the `Faces Renderer` class:

```
public boolean isMultiple(UIComponent component) {
   return false;
}

public boolean getRendersChildren() {
   return false;
}

public void decode(FacesContext context, UIComponent component) {
   if (Utils.isComponentDisabledOrReadOnly(component)) {
     return;
    }
}
```

9. There are two updates that you need to make to the **|src|web|WEBINF|faces-config-custom.xml** file. The first is the JSF-managed bean for the `StoplightGenerator`.

```
<managed-bean>
      <description>Bean that generates a stoplight control to
                                   display status</description>
      <managed-bean-name>StoplightGenerator</managed-bean-name>
      <managed-bean-class>
      org.alfresco.web.bean.generator.StoplightGenerator
      </managed-bean-class>
      <managed-bean-scope>request</managed-bean-scope>
   </managed-bean>
```

10. The second is that you have to declare the renderer.

```
<render-kit>
   <renderer>
      <component-family>javax.faces.Output</component-family>
      <renderer-type>org.alfresco.faces.StoplightDisplayRenderer
       </renderer-type>
       <renderer-class>
          org.alfresco.web.ui.extension.
          renderer.StoplightDisplayRenderer
        </renderer-class>
   </renderer>
</render-kit>
```

11. Look back at the generator class you wrote and you'll notice that it refers to a constant called STOPLIGHT_DISPLAY_RENDERER. The value of the constant needs to match the renderer type you just specified in faces-config-custom.xml. Edit com.someco.util.Constants. Add the constant with the value of the renderer type.

```
// Custom renderers
public static final String STOPLIGHT_DISPLAY_RENDERER = "org.
                    alfresco.faces.StoplightDisplayRenderer";
```

12. The last step is to copy the traffic light images from the source code provided with this chapter into your Eclipse project under **|src|web|someco|images |icons**. There are four and they all start with stoplight.

13. Deploy, restart, and test.

To test this, go take a look at the properties of the document you used to test the **Status** and **Summary** in the previous example. Now, instead of a boring text string, the status is shown using a visually striking traffic light metaphor:

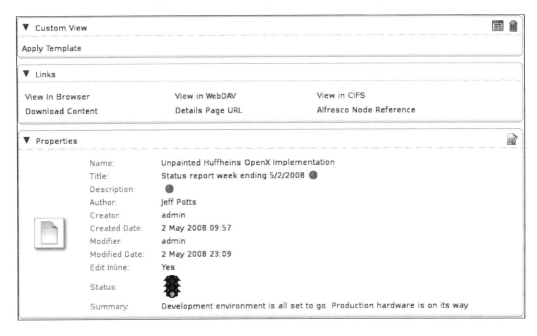

If you edit the properties, Alfresco should use its default list-constrained, single-value text field component, which is a drop-down selection list:

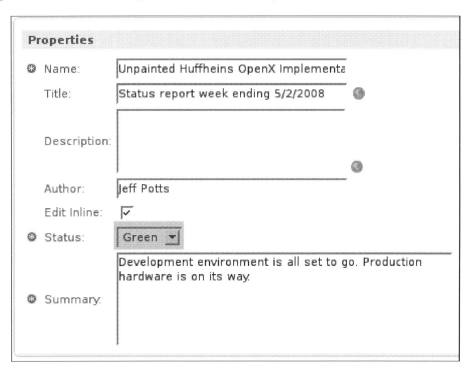

It is important to note that if you go back and remove the constraints from your model and try your test again, the component will still work. Of course, if the string you set for your status doesn't match any of the three colors, you'll end up with a burned-out traffic light.

Overriding and Customizing Components

You should now have a basic idea of how you can tweak generators and renderers. If you wanted to do something more complex—say for example you don't like the out of the box multi-value select behavior—you can override or develop new component classes. The steps are similar to what you've seen so far. Have a look at the Alfresco source in the `org.alfresco.web.ui.common.component` packages for examples.

Creating Custom Dialogs

You've seen that UI actions can launch actions and invoke other targets, like client-side and server-side JavaScript, but what if you need to accept user input prior to executing the backend code? In the previous chapter you created a custom Action Handler, which used a JSF-managed bean and a JSP page to accept action parameters. A **dialog** is a lot like an Action Handler. It uses a JSF-managed bean and a JSP page, but it is not specific to actions. You can use UI actions to invoke a dialog anywhere in the web client.

Let's walk through an example to see how this works.

Step-by-Step: Creating a Dialog to Execute Scripts

So far you've addressed several requirements from departments throughout SomeCo, but what about making your own life a little better? Running server-side JavaScript against folders and content is something you and SomeCo's Alfresco administrators will do on a regular basis. But executing scripts on folders and content using the out of the box web client takes way too many steps. It doesn't take long to grow tired of the whole "View Details, Run Action, Execute a Script, Set Values and Add, Select a Script, Finish" routine. Wouldn't it be nice to streamline this a bit?

In this example, you'll take out a few of the extra clicks by creating a new UI action that launches a custom dialog. The custom dialog lets the user pick from a list of scripts. When the user clicks **OK**, the script executes against the folder or document the user was sitting on when they clicked the UI action link. Implementing this requires:

1. Creating a JSF-managed bean to handle the dialog interaction and execute the chosen script

2. Configuring the bean in `faces-config.xml`

3. Creating a JSP page to present the user with a list of scripts

4. Updating `web-client-config-custom.xml` with the new UI action and dialog declarations

When you're done, you'll be able to run a script against any folder or file in the repository in about half the clicks it takes out of the box.

To develop the custom dialog, follow these steps:

1. Let's develop the backing bean first and then do the work to wire it in to the UI. Create a new Java class in **src|java** called `com.someco.web.bean.ExecuteScriptDialog`. The class needs to extend `org.alfresco.web.bean.dialog.BaseDialogBean`.

   ```
   public class ExecuteScriptDialog extends BaseDialogBean {
   ```

2. The dialog you are implementing is simple: It lets the user select a script to execute from a list, just like the out of the box action handler used when you run the `Execute Script` action. So you'll need two local variables. The first is a `String` to hold the selected script. The second is the `ActionService`, which will be injected by JSF and used to execute the action.

   ```
   protected String script;
   private ActionService actionService;
   ```

3. Most of the work is done in the `finishImpl()` method. This method is called when the user clicks **OK**. There are two node references you are going to need: the node reference of the space or content the UI action is being run against and the script the user wants to run against the space or content. The `BrowseBean` has one, and your dialog's getter has the other.

   ```
   protected String finishImpl(FacesContext context, String outcome)
   throws Exception {
           // get the space the action will apply to
           NodeRef nodeRef = this.browseBean.getActionSpace()
                                               .getNodeRef();

           // get the script the user selected in the dialog
            NodeRef scriptRef = new NodeRef(Repository.getStoreRef(),
                                                getScript());
   ```

4. You could copy and paste the same code the Script Action Executer uses when it executes a script. But it is a lot easier to just invoke the `Script action`. Add code that uses the Action Service to run the action.

   ```
           // use an action to execute the script
           Action action = this.actionService.createAction
                                       (ScriptActionExecuter.NAME);
           action.setParameterValue(ScriptActionExecuter.PARAM_
                                       SCRIPTREF, scriptRef);
           this.actionService.executeAction(action, nodeRef);

           // return the default outcome
            return outcome;
   }
   ```

5. Complete the rest of the class by adding the getter and setter for the script variable as well as an override for `getFinishButtonDisabled`. The override is needed so that the **OK** button shows up.

```
public boolean getFinishButtonDisabled() {
      return false;
}

public String getScript() {
   return script;
}

public void setScript(String script) {
   this.script = script;
}

public void setActionService(ActionService actionService) {
   this.actionService = actionService;
}
}
```

6. The next step is to let JSF know about your new managed bean by updating **|src|web|WEB-INF|faces-config-custom.xml** with this.

```
<managed-bean>
    <managed-bean-name>ExecuteScriptDialog</managed-bean-name>
    <managed-bean-class>com.someco.web.bean.ExecuteScriptDialog</
                                             managed-bean-class>
    <managed-bean-scope>session</managed-bean-scope>
    <managed-property>
       <property-name>nodeService</property-name>
       <value>#{NodeService}</value>
    </managed-property>
    <managed-property>
       <property-name>browseBean</property-name>
       <value>#{BrowseBean}</value>
    </managed-property>
    <managed-property>
       <property-name>actionService</property-name>
       <value>#{ActionService}</value>
    </managed-property>
</managed-bean>
```

7. Now implement the JSP. Create a new JSP file under **|src|web|jsp| extension|dialogs|execute-script.jsp**. One of the nice things about dialogs is that you don't have to worry about the containing markup. You implement only what's needed for the dialog. In this case, that means using a single-select drop-down menu.

```
<%@ taglib uri="http://java.sun.com/jsf/html" prefix="h" %>
<%@ taglib uri="http://java.sun.com/jsf/core" prefix="f" %>
<%-- Scripts drop-down selector --%>
<h:outputText value="#{msg.select_a_script}: " />
<h:selectOneMenu value="#{DialogManager.bean.script}">
   <f:selectItems value="#{TemplateSupportBean.scriptFiles}" />
</h:selectOneMenu>
```

8. Now you need two new icons. One is a 16 x 16 pixel icon that goes with the
   UI action. The other is a 32 x 32 pixel icon that gets displayed next to the
   dialog title. Copy execute_script.gif and execute_script_large.gif
   from the source code that accompanies this chapter into your Eclipse project's
   |src|web|someco|images|icons directory.

9. The last step prior to testing is to update **|config|alfresco|extension|
   web-client-config-custom.xml**. First, add a new dialogs configuration
   below the actions configuration.

```
       ...
       </actions>
   </config>

   <!-- Dialogs -->
   <config>
       <dialogs>
           < page="/jsp/extension/dialogs/execute-script.jsp"dialog
             name="executeScript"managed-bean="ExecuteScriptDialog"
             icon="/someco/images/icons/execute_script_large.gif"
               title="Execute Script"
           description="Executes a script against the selected node" />
       </dialogs>
   </config>
```

10. Next, create a UI action definition and then add a reference to it in the action
    groups where you want the link to appear in the web client:

```
           <!-- Actions Menu for a document in the Browse screen -->
           <action-group id="document_browse_menu">
               <action idref="web_site" />
               <action idref="execute_script" />
           </action-group>

           <!-- Actions Menu for Document Details screen -->
           <action-group id="doc_details_actions">
               <action idref="web_enable" />
               <action idref="web_disable" />
               <action idref="web_site" />
               <action idref="execute_script" />
```

```
    </action-group>

    <!-- Add action to more actions menu for each space -->
    <action-group id="space_browse_menu">
        <action idref="execute_script" />
    </action-group>

    <!-- Actions Menu for Space Details screen -->
    <action-group id="space_details_actions">
        <action idref="execute_script" />
    </action-group>

    <!-- Execute Script Dialog -->
    <action id="execute_script">
        <label>Run Script</label>
        <image>/someco/images/icons/execute_script.gif</image>
        <action>dialog:executeScript</action>
        <action-listener>#{BrowseBean.setupSpaceAction}
        </action-listener>
        <params>
            <param name="id">#{actionContext.id}</param>
        </params>
    </action>
```

11. Deploy, restart, and test.

After a successful restart, you should see the new **Run Script** menu item on the **browse space actions** menu, the **space details** menu, the **browse document actions** menu, and the **document details** menu:

Clicking on the link should invoke the new dialog. The dialog should show a list of scripts. Selecting a script and clicking **OK** will execute the selected script against the current folder or content:

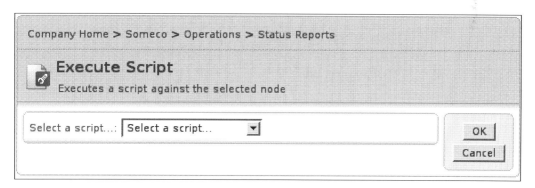

If you run a script that changes the node properties, you may have to close and re-open the details before you see the change.

Passing the Context to the Dialog

The action element for the **Execute Script** UI action in `web-client-config-custom.xml` has a child element (also called action) that invokes the dialog. But a few things need to be taken care of before showing the dialog, such as converting the ID of the current node to a Node object and letting the `NavigationBean` know where to return to when the dialog closes. You didn't have to worry about any of that because the out of the box `BrowseBean`, injected as a dependency into your class, has a method called `setupSpaceAction()` that does the worrying for you. This explains how your dialog knew which node to run the script against, and was able to get it from the following method call:

```
NodeRef nodeRef = this.browseBean.getActionSpace().getNodeRef();
```

Understanding the JSP

The JSP used to present the dropdown containing the available server-side JavaScript was extremely concise. But you may be wondering where those expressions were getting their values from. This expression:

`#{msg.select_a_script}`

outputs the **Select a Script** string. Alfresco already had this string externalized, so you don't have to create a new one. This keeps the user experience consistent between Alfresco out of the box and your customization.

The expression in the `selectOneMenu` tag binds the drop-down value to the script property of the custom dialog:

`#{DialogManager.bean.script}`

The `DialogManager` is a JSF-managed bean (`org.alfresco.web.bean.dialog.DialogManager`) responsible for building up and tearing down dialogs. The `DialogManager` keeps a reference to the current dialog in the bean property, in this case the `ExecuteScriptDialog` bean.

Where did the list of JavaScript files come from? This expression:

`#{TemplateSupportBean.scriptFiles}`

leverages an out of the box JSF-managed bean. The `getScriptFiles()` method knows how to determine where the scripts are stored, and then queries that location and sorts the results to produce the list of scripts. If you're curious, the bean's class is `org.alfresco.web.bean.TemplateSupportBean`, which is packaged in the `alfresco-web-client.jar` file.

Enabling and Disabling the OK Button

You hardcoded the return value for the `getFinishButtonDisabled()` method to false so that the **OK** button would always be enabled. You have probably noticed that some dialogs within Alfresco enable and disable buttons depending on whether or not certain requirements are met. It's a nice usability touch.

1. To make this enhancement to the Execute Script dialog, you need to first update the JSP with some client-side JavaScript that will check the value of the dropdown, and disable the **OK** button if a script hasn't been selected:

```
<script type="text/javascript">
function checkButtonState() {
      if (document.getElementById("dialog:dialog-body:script").
                                        value == "none" ) {
            document.getElementById("dialog:finish-button")
                                        .disabled = true;
      } else {
            document.getElementById("dialog:finish-button")
                                        .disabled = false;
      }
}
</script>
```

2. Then, update `selectOneMenu` to add an ID attribute and an `onChange` event:

```
<h:selectOneMenu id="script" value="#{DialogManager.bean.script}"
                              onchange="checkButtonState();">
      <f:selectItems value="#{TemplateSupportBean.scriptFiles}" />
</h:selectOneMenu>
```

 When hacking client-side Alfresco, a tool such as the Firebug Firefox plug-in can be invaluable. Get more information on Firebug at `http://www.getfirebug.com/`.

3. Finally, you have to take care of the case that occurs when the dialog is first displayed (prior to an `onChange` event). You can either call `checkButtonState()` from the document's `onLoad` event, or you can add logic to the `ExecuteScriptDialog` bean to handle it on the server side like this:

```
public boolean getFinishButtonDisabled() {
      if (getScript() != null && !getScript().equals("") &&
                              !getScript().equals("none")) {
            return false;
      } else {
            return true;
      }
}
```

With these small changes in place, the user is forced to make a script selection before clicking the **OK** button.

Creating Custom Wizards

Sometimes a single dialog isn't enough. There might be several logical steps that need to be used to gather information from a web client user, rather than presenting a huge form to gather everything at once. Or, steps might be conditional. There might be two different sets of data that need to be gathered based on choices made in prior steps. A wizard is very similar to a dialog, except that it spans multiple pages or steps. (In fact, both dialogs and wizards ultimately extend the same bean, `org.alfresco.web.bean.dialog.BaseDialogBean`.)

You're probably already used to the wizard concept from using the web client. Out of the box examples include the Add Content, Create Content, and Invite Space/ Content Users wizards.

SomeCo has a requirement that can be addressed with a custom wizard. SomeCo's Human Resources department wants to use Alfresco to help streamline their recruiting process. Beyond just storing resumes in the repository, SomeCo wants to make it easier to distribute resumes to people involved in the recruiting process and gather interview feedback. The process goes roughly like this:

Resumes are added to the **Someco|Human Resources|Resumes** folder.

1. An internal recruiter decides who will interview the candidate and sends a link to each interviewer.
2. Interviewers respond with feedback.
3. Feedback is assimilated and discussed before making a decision regarding the next step.

There are a couple of pain points in this process. First, the recruiters aren't consistent in how they send the resume to interviewers. Sometimes they send the file as an email attachment, or a link to the details page, or a link to download the resume directly. Recruiters don't want to have to think about the best way to send the resume. They just want to make it available. Interviewers don't want to be confused about how to get the resume; they want consistency in the process.

The second pain point is that the interviewers are slow to provide their feedback. Not only that, but they don't know what format to provide it in or what the process is. Sometimes interviewers send plain text, sometimes they send OpenOffice documents, and sometimes they leave voice mail. To make it worse, the interviewers don't always know who is interviewing a candidate, and whether or not they should copy the others on their feedback.

You're going to simplify things. You are going to implement a custom "Interview Setup" wizard the recruiters can invoke while they are looking at a candidate's resume. The wizard will let them select the interviewers, set up a discussion forum, and send a notification to the interviewers with a link to download the resume.

The wizard will consist of the following steps:

1. Assign interviewers: During this step, the recruiter will select users and/or groups to assign to the interviewer.

2. Set options: During this step, the recruiter will set options related to the interview. For this example, the only option will be whether or not to create a discussion thread attached to the resume to capture interview feedback.

3. Configure notification: During this step, the recruiter will decide whether or not to send a notification to the interviewers. If so, the recruiter will be able to modify the subject and body of the notification or specify a FreeMarker template to use to dynamically generate the notification.

4. Summary: During this step, the recruiter will be presented with a summary of the previous steps in case she or he wants to change any of the options prior to completing the wizard.

Implementing this wizard will involve:

- Creating a new SomeCo Resume content type.

- Writing a JSF-backed bean that persists the data gathered during each step, executes the necessary logic to set up the discussion thread, and sends the notification.

- Creating one JSP for each step in the wizard. In this example, we'll borrow heavily from Alfresco's `invite users` wizard for the interviewer selection, the notification configuration, and the summary page.

- Updating configuration files such as `faces-config.xml`, `web-client-config-custom.xml`, and `webclient.properties`.

The custom wizard bean has a fair amount of code. So this example will be broken into two parts. First, stub out the wizard to get a working foundation in place, and come back and add code to the wizard class to make it work.

Step-by-Step: Stubbing Out the Wizard

The first thing you're going to do is stub out the wizard. By the end of this example you should be able to launch the wizard and move through the steps, but it won't actually do anything.

To make a first pass at the custom wizard, follow these steps:

1. The first step isn't directly related to creating a custom wizard. You haven't yet created a type for SomeCo resumes, but we need one to capture resume-specific metadata.

2. Update |**config**|**alfresco**|**extension**|**model**|**scModel.xml** with the new type:

```
<type name="sc:resume">
    <title>Someco Resume</title>
    <parent>sc:hrDoc</parent>
    <properties>
        <property name="sc:candidateName">
            <type>d:text</type>
            <mandatory>true</mandatory>
        </property>
        <property name="sc:candidateRole">
            <type>d:text</type>
            <mandatory>true</mandatory>
            <constraints>
                <constraint ref="sc:roleList" />
            </constraints>
        </property>
    </properties>
</type>
```

3. Add the new `role list` constraint to the `constraints` element at the top of the model:

```
<constraint name="sc:roleList" type="LIST">
    <parameter name="allowedValues">
        <list>
            <value>Consultant</value>
            <value>Senior Consultant</value>
            <value>Technical Architect</value>
        </list>
    </parameter>
</constraint>
```

4. Save the model file.

5. Update |**src**|**java**|**com.someco.model.SomeCoModel.java** with constants for the new type and properties:

```
public static final String TYPE_SC_RESUME = "resume";
public static final String PROP_CANDIDATE_NAME = "candidateName";
public static final String PROP_CANDIDATE_ROLE = "candidateRole";
```

6. Create a new Java class in **|src|java** called `com.someco.web.bean.`
   `InterviewSetupWizard`. The class extends `org.alfresco.web.bean.`
   `wizard.BaseWizardBean`:

   ```
   public class InterviewSetupWizard extends BaseWizardBean {
   ```

7. Add the local variables and constants that will eventually be used when we finish out the class:

   ```
   // Constants
   private static final String MSG_USERS  = "users";
   private static final String MSG_GROUPS = "groups";
   private static final String MSG_ASSIGN = "assignment";
   private static final String MSG_OPTIONS = "options";
   private static final String MSG_NOTIFY = "notify";
   private static final String MSG_INTERVIEWER = "interviewer";
   private static final String MSG_CANDIDATE_ROLE = "candidate_role";
   private static final String MSG_RESUME_LINK = "resume_link";
   private static final String MSG_LABEL_DISCUSSION = "label_
                                              discussion";
   private static final String MSG_LABEL_NO_DISCUSSION = "label_no_
                                              discussion";
   private static final String MSG_LABEL_NOTIFY = "label_notify";
   private static final String MSG_LABEL_NO_NOTIFY = "label_no_
                                              notify";
   private static final String MSG_DEFAULT_DISCUSSION_TOPIC =
                                       "default_discussion_topic";

   private static final String STEP_NOTIFY = "notify";
   private static final String NOTIFY_YES = "yes";
   private static final String NOTIFY_NO = "no";

   // Dependencies
   private AuthorityService authorityService;
   private PersonService personService;
   private PermissionService permissionService;
   private ContentService contentService;

   /** datamodel for table of users */
   transient private DataModel userDataModel = null;

   /** list of user/group role wrapper objects */
   protected List<UserGroup> userGroups = null;

   /** tracks whether or not a discussion forum should be established
                                       for this resume */
   private boolean discussionFlag = true;

   /** tracks whether or not a notification should be sent to the
                                       interviewers */
   ```

```
private String notify = NOTIFY_NO;

/** gets the discussion topic to use in the forum */
private String discussionTopic = "Respond with your feedback on
                                            this candidate";

/** Helper providing template based mailing facilities */
protected TemplateMailHelperBean mailHelper;

/** JavaMailSender bean reference */
transient private JavaMailSender mailSender;
```

8. Add the `init` method:

```
@Override
public void init(Map<String, String> parameters) {
    super.init(parameters);

    notify = NOTIFY_NO;
    userDataModel = null;
    discussionFlag = true;
    discussionTopic = Application.getBundle(FacesContext.
      getCurrentInstance()).getString(MSG_DEFAULT_DISCUSSION_TOPIC);
    userGroups = new ArrayList<UserGroup>(5);
    mailHelper = new TemplateMailHelperBean();
    mailHelper.setMailSender(mailSender);
    mailHelper.setNodeService(getNodeService());

}
```

9. Add the `finishImpl` method. Just like a dialog, the `finishImpl` method gets called when the wizard is "finished". The logic you execute to set up the discussion and send the notification will go here eventually:

```
protected String finishImpl(FacesContext context, String outcome)
        throws Exception {

    // get the Space to apply changes too
    NodeRef nodeRef = this.getNode().getNodeRef();

    if (NOTIFY_YES.equals(this.notify)) {
        sendNotification(context, nodeRef);
    }

    // if the discussion flag is set, create a topic
    if (isDiscussionFlag()) {
        createDiscussion(nodeRef, getDiscussionTopic());
    }

    return outcome;
}
```

10. Add the `next` method. The `next` method gets called every time a step changes. In this case, we're going to use this method to build the default notification text:

```
public String next() {
        String stepName = Application.getWizardManager()
        .getCurrentStepName();
    if (STEP_NOTIFY.equals(stepName)) {
        buildDefaultNotification();
    }
    return null;
}
```

11. Implement a temporary `getSummary` method with a placeholder label and value. When the class is finished out, you'll add a more meaningful summary here:

```
public String getSummary()
    {
        List<String> labels = new ArrayList<String>();
        List<String> values = new ArrayList<String>();
        labels.add("foo");
        values.add("bar");
        String[] labelArray = new String[labels.size()];
         labels.toArray(labelArray);
        String[] valueArray = new String[values.size()];
        values.toArray(valueArray);
        return buildSummary(labelArray, valueArray);
    }
```

12. Implement the `getNode` method. This method grabs the node from the `BrowseBean` that was put there by the action listener, so the dialog will have the proper context:

```
protected Node getNode() {
    return this.browseBean.getActionSpace();
}
```

13. Implement stubs for `buildDefaultNotification()`, `sendNotification()`, and `createDiscussion()`:

```
public void buildDefaultNotification() {
    // TODO
}
public void sendNotification(FacesContext context, NodeRef
                                                    nodeRef) {
    // TODO
}
public void createDiscussion(NodeRef nodeRef, String topic) {
    // TODO
}
```

14. Implement the `UserGroup` inner class to use as a helper class for working with the list of users and groups that will be selected as interviewers:

```
public static class UserGroup implements Serializable {

    public UserGroup(String authority, String label) {
            this.authority = authority;
             this.label = label;
    }
    public String getAuthority() {
        return this.authority;
    }
    public String getLabel() {
        return this.label;
    }
    private String authority;
    private String label;
}
```

15. Generate the getters and setters. There are several of them. So rather than including them here, it is easier (and more reliable) for you to use Eclipse to generate the getters and setters for the local variables (Source, Generate Getters, and Setters.). If you aren't using Eclipse, use your IDE (or your raw typing prowess) to generate public getters and setters for the class variables you defined earlier.

16. Save the class.

17. Now you need to register the wizard bean with JSF. Update **|src|web| WEB-INF|faces-config-custom.xml** with the following:

```
<managed-bean>
    <managed-bean-name>InterviewSetupWizard</managed-bean-name>
    <managed-bean-class>com.someco.web.bean.InterviewSetupWizard
</managed-bean-class>
    <managed-bean-scope>session</managed-bean-scope>
    <managed-property>
        <property-name>nodeService</property-name>
        <value>#{NodeService}</value>
    </managed-property>
    <managed-property>
        <property-name>browseBean</property-name>
        <value>#{BrowseBean}</value>
    </managed-property>
    <managed-property>
        <property-name>personService</property-name>
        <value>#{PersonService}</value>
```

```
      </managed-property>
      <managed-property>
         <property-name>authorityService</property-name>
         <value>#{AuthorityService}</value>
      </managed-property>
      <managed-property>
         <property-name>permissionService</property-name>
         <value>#{PermissionService}</value>
      </managed-property>
      <managed-property>
         <property-name>contentService</property-name>
         <value>#{ContentService}</value>
      </managed-property>
   </managed-bean>
```

18. Save `faces-config-custom.xml`.

19. Create a stub JSP for the `assignment` step. Create a new file in **|src|web|jsp |extension|wizards|interview-setup-wizard** called `stub-assignment.jsp` with the following content:

    ```
    <%@ taglib uri="http://java.sun.com/jsf/html" prefix="h" %>
    <%@ taglib uri="http://java.sun.com/jsf/core" prefix="f" %>

    <h:outputText value="Replace this with the assignment step" />
    ```

20. Cut and paste the file you just created into the same directory with a new name of `stub-notify.jsp`. Search and replace `assignment` with `notify`.

21. Cut and paste again naming the new file `stub-options.jsp`. Make the same search and replace operation, this time with `options`.

22. Just like a dialog, wizards (and the actions that launch them) need icons. Copy `interview_setup_large.gif` and `interview_setup.gif` from the source code that accompanies this chapter into **|src|web|someco|images|icons|**.

23. Update **|config|alfresco|extension|web-client-config-custom.xml**. You've got several edits to make here. First, configure the new type. Note that in this example, you are trying something new—you are associating actions with a specific type. You could have used an Action Evaluator, but this is more efficient, and it gives you the added benefit of being able to hide actions that aren't appropriate for this type (such as the Web Enable/Disable UI actions):

    ```
    <!-- show props on resume property sheet, set type-specific
            action list -->
    <config evaluator="node-type" condition="sc:resume">
    <property-sheet>
       <show-property name="sc:candidateName" display-label-
                  id="candidateName" />
    ```

```
            <show-property name="sc:candidateRole" display-label-
                                               id="candidateRole" />
        </property-sheet>
        <actions>
            <!-- Override the actions menu for a document in the
                            Browse screen for this type -->
            <action-group id="document_browse_menu">
                <action idref="interview_setup" />
            </action-group>
            <!-- Override the actions menu for Document Details
                             screen for this type-->
            <action-group id="doc_details_actions">
                <action idref="web_enable" hide="true" />
                <action idref="web_disable" hide="true" />
                <action idref="interview_setup" />
            </action-group>
        </actions>
</config>
```

24. Next, add the resume type to the add content wizard. If you want the type to show up in other wizards as well, feel free to add it on your own. For the purposes of this example, the Content Wizard is the only place it is needed:

```
<!-- add someco types to add content list -->
<config evaluator="string-compare" condition="Content Wizards">
    <content-types>
        <type name="sc:doc" />
        <type name="sc:whitepaper" />
        <type name="sc:legalDoc" />
        <type name="sc:marketingDoc" />
        <type name="sc:hrDoc" />
        <type name="sc:hrPolicy" />
        <type name="sc:salesDoc" />
        <type name="sc:opsDoc" />
        <type name="sc:resume" />
    </content-types>
</config>
```

25. Now declare the UI action. The UI action was already added to the appropriate action groups in the type-specific configuration. So there is no need to associate it to any of the generic action groups:

```
<!-- Launch interview setup wizard -->
<action id="interview_setup">
    <label-id>interviewSetup</label-id>
    <image>/someco/images/icons/interview_setup.gif</image>
    <action>wizard:interviewSetup</action>
    <action-listener>#{BrowseBean.setupSpaceAction}</action-
                                               listener>
```

```
        <params>
                <param name="id">#{actionContext.id}</param>
        </params>
</action>
```

26. Now, declare the wizard by inserting the following after the closing `config` element of the `dialogs` declaration:

```
<!-- Wizards -->
    <config>
            <wizards>
                    <!-- Definition of the Interview Setup
                                                    wizard -->
                    <wizard name="interviewSetup" managed-bean=
                                            "InterviewSetupWizard"
                    title-id="interview_setup_title" description-
                                        id="interview_setup_desc"
                    icon="/someco/images/icons/interview_setup_large.
                    gif">
                <step name="assignment" title-id="assignment"
                description-id="interview_setup_step1_desc">
                <page path="/jsp/extension/wizards/interview-setup-
                wizard/stub-assignment.jsp"
                        title-id="interview_setup_step1_title"
                        description-id="interview_setup_step1_desc"
                        instruction-id="default_instruction" />
                </step>
                <step name="options" title-id="options"
                        description-id="interview_setup_step2_desc">
                <page path="/jsp/extension/wizards/interview-setup-
                  wizard/stub-options.jsp"
                        title-id="interview_setup_step2_title"
                        description-id="interview_setup_step2_desc"
                        instruction-id="default_instruction" />
                </step>
                <step name="notify" title-id="notify"
                        description-id="interview_setup_step3_desc">
                <page path="/jsp/extension/wizards/interview-setup-
                  wizard/stub-notify.jsp"
                        title-id="interview_setup_step3_title"
                        description-id="interview_setup_step3_desc"
                        instruction-id="default_instruction" />
                </step>
                <step name="summary" title-id="summary"description-
                id="summary_step_description">
                <page path="/jsp/wizard/summary.jsp"
                        title-id="summary"
                        description-id="summary_desc"
                        instruction-id="interview_setup_finish_
                        instruction" />
```

```
                        </step>
                </wizard>
            </wizards>
        </config>
```

27. Save `web-client-config-custom.xml`.

28. Deploy, restart, and test.

You now have a stubbed out wizard. You should be able to create a new SomeCo Resume document in the **Someco | Human Resources | Resumes** folder (create it if it doesn't exist).

Once you've created a resume and set its mandatory properties (candidate name and role), you should see the new UI action in the details and in the browse menu.

You should be able to click the UI action to launch the wizard and step back-and-forth through the wizard steps.

You'll notice a bunch of missing resource strings. Don't worry about those for now. You'll clean those up shortly. The point of the test is to make sure you can launch the wizard and click through the steps.

Step-by-Step: Finishing Out the Wizard

If everything is good so far, let's finish out the wizard class, externalize the strings, and watch the magic happen.

To implement the methods that make the wizard functional, follow these steps:

1. Let's put the JSP pages in place first. The summary JSP, as you may have noticed, is the out of the box summary used elsewhere in the web client. The `step` element in the wizard declaration points to where it resides as part of the web client. So no action is needed for the summary step in the wizard.

2. The notify JSP is also out of the box, but it changed locations between the Labs and Enterprise editions. So to make this example work for either edition, copy the `notify.jsp` JSP from Alfresco's web application to **|src|web|jsp|extension|wizards|interview-setup-wizard**. For Labs users, the JSP can be found in **alfresco|jsp|users|invite-users-wizard|notify.jsp**. For Enterprise users, the JSP is in **alfresco|jsp|wizard|invite-users|notify.jsp**.

3. The options JSP is simple. It requires a checkbox the user selects to indicate that a discussion area should be created, and a text field to let the user specify the discussion topic. Copy and paste the `stub-options.jsp` as `options.jsp` and insert the following content:

```
<h:panelGrid columns="2">
        <h:outputText value="Create discussion forum?" />
        <h:selectBooleanCheckbox title="discussionFlag"
                    value="#{WizardManager.bean.discussionFlag}" />
        <h:outputText value="Discussion topic:" />
        <h:inputText id="topic" value="#{WizardManager.bean.
                                        discussionTopic}" size="50"/>
</h:panelGrid>
```

4. The assignment JSP is a little more complex. It is essentially the out of the box `invite.jsp` with the role list stripped out. Copy and paste the `stub-assignment.jsp` as `assignment.jsp`, and insert the following content:

```
<%@ page buffer="32kb" contentType="text/html;charset=UTF-8" %>
<%@ page isELIgnored="false" %>

<h:panelGrid columns="1" cellpadding="2" style="padding-top:2px;
                            padding-bottom:2px;" width="100%">
<h:outputText styleClass="mainSubText" value="#{msg.specify_
                                        usersgroups}" />
<h:outputText styleClass="mainSubText" value="1. #{msg.select_
                                        usersgroups}" />
<a:genericPicker id="picker" showAddButton="false"
            filters="#{WizardManager.bean.filters}" queryCallback
                ="#{WizardManager.bean.pickerCallback}" />
<h:panelGroup styleClass="mainSubText">
<h:outputText value="2." /> <h:commandButton value="#{msg.add_to_
            list_button}" actionListener="#{WizardManager.bean.
            addSelection}" styleClass="wizardButton" />
```

```
    </h:panelGroup>
    <h:outputText styleClass="mainSubText" value="#{msg.selected_
                                          usersgroups}" />
    <h:panelGroup>
    <h:dataTable value="#{WizardManager.bean.userDataModel}" var="row"
    rowClasses="selectedItemsRow,selectedItemsRowAlt"
    styleClass="selectedItems" headerClass="selectedItemsHeader"
    cellspacing="0" cellpadding="4"
    rendered="#{WizardManager.bean.userDataModel.rowCount != 0}">
    <h:column>
    <f:facet name="header">
    <h:outputText value="#{msg.name}" />
    </f:facet>
    <h:outputText value="#{row.label}" />
    </h:column>
    <h:column>
    <a:actionLink actionListener="#{WizardManager.bean.
                  removeSelection}" image="/images/icons/delete.gif"
    value="#{msg.remove}" showLink="false" style="padding-left:6px" />
    </h:column>
    </h:dataTable>
    <a:panel id="no-items" rendered="#{WizardManager.bean.
                                  userDataModel.rowCount == 0}">
    <h:panelGrid columns="1" cellpadding="2" styleClass="selectedItems
              " rowClasses="selectedItemsHeader,selectedItemsRow">
    <h:outputText id="no-items-name" value="#{msg.name}" />
    <h:outputText styleClass="selectedItemsRow" id="no-items-msg"
                              value="#{msg.no_selected_items}" />
    </h:panelGrid>
    </a:panel>
    </h:panelGroup>
    </h:panelGrid>
```

5. With the real JSPs in place, you need to update the wizard declaration to change the JSPs referenced there from the stubs to the implemented JSPs. Edit **|config|alfresco|extension|web-client-config-custom.xml** as follows:

```
<step name="assignment" title-id="assignment" description-
 id="interview_setup_step1_desc">
        <page path="/jsp/extension/wizards/interview-setup-wizard/
        assignment.jsp"
            title-id="interview_setup_step1_title"
            description-id="interview_setup_step1_desc"
            instruction-id="default_instruction" />
</step>
```

```
<step name="options" title-id="options" description-id="interview_
   setup_step2_desc">
        <page path="/jsp/extension/wizards/interview-setup-wizard/
        options.jsp"
              title-id="interview_setup_step2_title"
              description-id="interview_setup_step2_desc"
              instruction-id="default_instruction" />
</step>
<step name="notify" title-id="notify" description-id="interview_
   setup_step3_desc">
        <page path="/jsp/extension/wizards/interview-setup-wizard/
        notify.jsp"
              title-id="interview_setup_step3_title"
              description-id="interview_setup_step3_desc"
              instruction-id="default_instruction" />
</step>
```

6. Now edit **src|java|com.someco.web.bean.InterviewSetupWizard.java**.
    Replace the temporary getSummary method with one that describes the
    choices the user has made throughout the wizard:

```
public String getSummary() {

        ResourceBundle bundle = Application.getBundle
                        (FacesContext.getCurrentInstance());

        List<String> labels = new ArrayList<String>();
        List<String> values = new ArrayList<String>();

        if (this.userGroups != null) {
              labels.add(bundle.getString(MSG_ASSIGN));
              StringBuffer buf = new StringBuffer();
              for (Iterator<UserGroup> userGroupsIter = this.
           userGroups.iterator(); userGroupsIter.hasNext();) {
                    buf.append(userGroupsIter.next()
                                              .getLabel());
                    if (userGroupsIter.hasNext()) buf.append
                                              (", ");
              }
              values.add(buf.toString());
        }
        labels.add(bundle.getString(MSG_OPTIONS));
        values.add(this.isDiscussionFlag() ? bundle.
      getString(MSG_LABEL_DISCUSSION) + this.getDiscussionTopic()
                 : bundle.getString(MSG_LABEL_NO_DISCUSSION));
        labels.add(bundle.getString(MSG_NOTIFY));
        values.add(this.notify.equals(NOTIFY_YES) ? bundle.
        getString(MSG_LABEL_NOTIFY) : bundle.getString(MSG_LABEL_
                                              NO_NOTIFY));
```

```
        String[] labelArray = new String[labels.size()];
        labels.toArray(labelArray);

        String[] valueArray = new String[values.size()];
        values.toArray(valueArray);

        return buildSummary(labelArray, valueArray);

    }
```

7. Implement the `buildDefaultNotification` method. The method retrieves metadata from the underlying `Resume` node, and then merges it with externalized strings to produce the subject and body of the notification:

```
public void buildDefaultNotification() {
        FacesContext context = FacesContext.getCurrentInstance();

        // prepare automatic text for email and display
        StringBuilder buf = new StringBuilder(256);
        String personName = Application.getCurrentUser(context).
                            getFullName(this.getNodeService());
        String msgInterviewer = Application.getMessage(context,
                                        MSG_INTERVIEWER);
        String msgRole = Application.getMessage(context,
                                        MSG_CANDIDATE_ROLE);
        String msgResumeLink = Application.getMessage(context,
                                        MSG_RESUME_LINK);

     String candidateName = (String) this.getNodeService().
                    getProperty(this.getNode().getNodeRef(),
                            SomeCoModel.PROP_CANDIDATE_NAME);
     String candidateRole = (String) this.getNodeService().
                    getProperty(this.getNode().getNodeRef(),
                            SomeCoModel.PROP_CANDIDATE_ROLE);
     String downloadURL = getDownloadURL();

     buf.append(MessageFormat.format(msgInterviewer, new Object[]
                            {personName, candidateName}));

        // default the subject line to an informative message
        this.mailHelper.setSubject(buf.toString());

        // add the role the candidate is interviewing for
        buf.append("\r\n\r\n");
        buf.append(MessageFormat.format(msgRole, new Object[]
                                        {candidateRole}));

        // provide a link to download the resume
        buf.append("\r\n\r\n");
        buf.append(MessageFormat.format(msgResumeLink, new Object[]
                                        {downloadURL}));

        // set the body content and default text to this text
```

```
this.mailHelper.setAutomaticText(buf.toString());
this.mailHelper.setBody(this.mailHelper.getAutomaticText());
}
```

8. Implement the `getDownloadURL` method, which is called by the `buildDefaultNotification` method in order to insert the full download URL for the resume into the notification body:

```
public String getDownloadURL() {
        String downloadURL = Utils.generateURL(FacesContext.
        getCurrentInstance(), this.getNode(), URLMode.HTTP_
        DOWNLOAD);
    String contextPath = FacesContext.getCurrentInstance().
    getExternalContext().getRequestContextPath();
    String servletUrl = ((HttpServletRequest)FacesCont
    ext.getCurrentInstance().getExternalContext().
    getRequest()).getRequestURL().toString();
    String hostname = servletUrl.substring(0, servletUrl.
                    indexOf('/', 8));

    StringBuffer buf = new StringBuffer();
    buf.append(hostname);
    buf.append(contextPath);
    buf.append(downloadURL);

        return buf.toString();
}
```

9. Implement the `sendNotification` method. This method gets called when it is time to send the notification. It is essentially the same code as that from the out of the box `BaseInviteUsersWizard` bean's `finishImpl` method:

```
public void sendNotification(FacesContext context,
NodeRef nodeRef) {
    User user = Application.getCurrentUser(context);
    String from = (String)this.getNodeService().
    getProperty(user.getPerson(), ContentModel.PROP_EMAIL);
    if (from == null || from.length() == 0) {
        // if the user does not have an email address get the
        default one from the config service
        from = Application.getClientConfig(context).
        getFromEmailAddress();
    }

    // for each user send an email
    for (int i=0; i<this.userGroups.size(); i++) {
        UserGroup userGroup = this.userGroups.get(i);
        String authority = userGroup.getAuthority();
        // if User, send email
```

```
                AuthorityType authType = AuthorityType.
                getAuthorityType(authority);
                if (authType.equals(AuthorityType.USER)) {
                    if (this.getPersonService().
                    personExists(authority) == true) {
                    this.mailHelper.notifyUser(this.
                    getPersonService().getPerson(authority),
                    nodeRef, from, "");
                    }
                } else if (authType.equals(AuthorityType.GROUP)) {
                    // else notify all members of the group
                    Set<String> users = this.
                    getAuthorityService().getContainedAuthorities
                    (AuthorityType.USER, authority, false);
                    for (String userAuth : users) {
                        if (this.getPersonService().
                        personExists(userAuth) == true) {
                            this.mailHelper.notifyUser(this.
                            getPersonService().getPerson
                            (userAuth), nodeRef, from, "");
                        }
                    } // next userAuth
                } // end if

        } // next i
    }
```

10. Implement the `createDiscussion` method. This method creates the nodes necessary to provide a discussion thread attached to the resume:

```
public void createDiscussion(NodeRef nodeRef, String topic) {
    // if the discussable aspect is already there
    if (this.getNodeService().hasAspect(nodeRef, ForumModel.
    ASPECT_DISCUSSABLE)) {
        // do nothing
    } else {
    // otherwise, add the discussable aspect
    this.getNodeService().addAspect(nodeRef, ForumModel.ASPECT_
    DISCUSSABLE, null);
    }

    // check for an existing discussion child node
    List<ChildAssociationRef> childRefs = this.getNodeService().
    getChildAssocs(nodeRef, ForumModel.ASSOC_DISCUSSION, QName.
    createQName(NamespaceService.FORUMS_MODEL_1_0_URI,
    "discussion"));
    ChildAssociationRef childRef;

    // if there isn't one
```

```
NodeRef forumNodeRef;
  if (childRefs.size() == 0) {
   // add the association
   String name = (String)this.getNodeService().
   getProperty(nodeRef, ContentModel.PROP_NAME);
   String msg = Application.getMessage(FacesContext.
   getCurrentInstance(), "discussion_for");
   String forumName = MessageFormat.format(msg, new Object[]
   {name});

   // create forum
   Map<QName, Serializable> forumProps = new HashMap<QName,
   Serializable>(1);
   forumProps.put(ContentModel.PROP_NAME, forumName);
   childRef = this.getNodeService().createNode(nodeRef,
        ForumModel.ASSOC_DISCUSSION,
        QName.createQName(NamespaceService.FORUMS_MODEL_1_0_
        URI, "discussion"),
        ForumModel.TYPE_FORUM, forumProps);

   forumNodeRef = childRef.getChildRef();

   // apply the uifacets aspect
   Map<QName, Serializable> uiFacetsProps = new
   HashMap<QName, Serializable>(5);
   uiFacetsProps.put(ApplicationModel.PROP_ICON, "forum");
   this.getNodeService().addAspect(forumNodeRef,
    ApplicationModel.ASPECT_UIFACETS, uiFacetsProps);
  } else {
        // otherwise, grab the first one
        childRef = childRefs.get(0);
        forumNodeRef = childRef.getChildRef();
  }

// check to see if this topic has already been added
if (this.getNodeService().getChildByName(forumNodeRef,
ContentModel.ASSOC_CONTAINS, topic) == null) {
  // create topic
   Map<QName, Serializable> topicProps = new HashMap<QName,
   Serializable>(1);
   topicProps.put(ContentModel.PROP_NAME, topic);
   ChildAssociationRef topicChildRef = this.getNodeService().
    createNode(forumNodeRef,
        ContentModel.ASSOC_CONTAINS,
        QName.createQName(NamespaceService.FORUMS_MODEL_1_0_
        URI, "topic"),
        ForumModel.TYPE_TOPIC, topicProps);

   NodeRef topicNodeRef = topicChildRef.getChildRef();
```

```
            // apply the uifacets aspect
            Map<QName, Serializable> uiFacetsProps =
              newHashMap<QName, Serializable>(5);
            uiFacetsProps.put(ApplicationModel.PROP_ICON, "topic");
            this.getNodeService().addAspect(topicNodeRef,
            ApplicationModel.ASPECT_UIFACETS, uiFacetsProps);
        } else {
          // do nothing, the topic is already there
        }
      }
    }
```

11. Implement the borrowed methods from the `BaseInviteUsersBean`. This is about 250 lines of code. For the most part, they come straight from `org.alfresco.web.bean.wizard.BaseInviteUsersWizard` with modifications to remove references to user roles. Rather than including them here, copy and paste the code from the source code that's included with the chapter. The methods are clearly marked with the banner that is shown as follows. Copy everything from the banner to the `UserGroup` inner class declaration:

```
/********************************************************
 * Methods borrowed from BaseInviteUsersWizard and modified for
                                               our needs
 ********************************************************/
```

12. Save the class.

13. Update |**config**|**alfresco**|**webclient.properties** to externalize the missing strings. Add the strings related to the Resume type:

```
#sc:resume
candidateName=Candidate
candidateRole=Role
Add the strings related to the new wizard:
# Interview Setup Wizard
interviewSetup=Interview Setup
assignment=Assign Interviewers
notify=Notify Interviewers
interview_setup_title=Interview Setup Wizard
interview_setup_desc=Setup interviewers and feedback topic for
                                            hire candidate
interview_setup_step1_title=Select interviewers
interview_setup_step1_desc=Select the users or groups of users that
                                  will interview this candidate
interview_setup_step2_title=Specify Setup Options
interview_setup_step2_desc=Specify interview setup options
interview_setup_step3_title=Specify Notification Options
interview_setup_step3_desc=Specify whether or not to notify the
                                        interviewers by email
```

```
interview_setup_finish_instruction=Click finish to set up the
                                                      interview
interviewer={0} has chosen you to interview {1}.
candidate_role=The candidate is interviewing for the position
                                                        of {0}.
resume_link=The candidate''s resume may be downloaded from Alfresco
                                      at the following link: {0}
label_discussion=Create discussion topic:
label_no_discussion=No discussion
label_notify=Send email to interviewers
label_no_notify=Do not send email
default_discussion_topic=Respond with your feedback on
                                                this candidate
```

14. Save the `properties` file.

15. Deploy, restart, and test.

Now when you do the same test you did after stubbing the wizard, you should see the working implementation of each step.

You can launch the wizard through either of the UI actions. That is, through **browse document actions menu**:

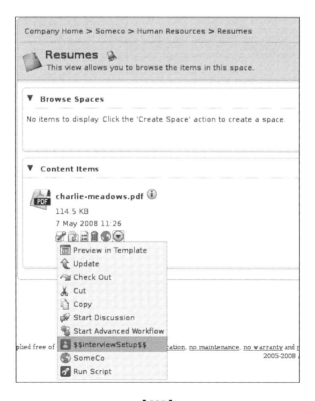

or through properties:

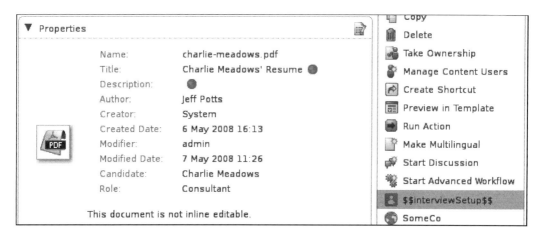

The first dialog allows the user to select the interviewers.

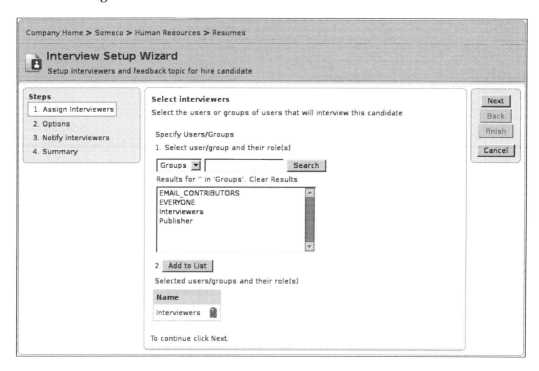

The next step sets the setup options such as whether or not to create a discussion forum and on what topic should it be:

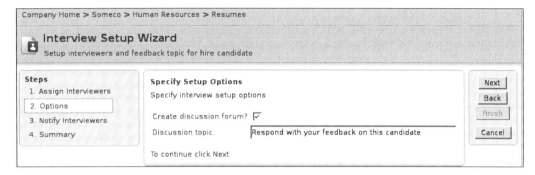

The third step gives the user a chance to send an email to the interviewers:

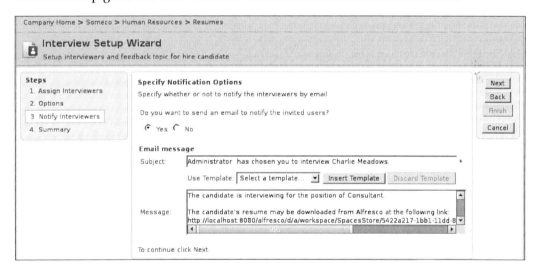

The final step summarizes the choices made in the previous steps:

If you chose to create a discussion topic, you should see the newly added forum:

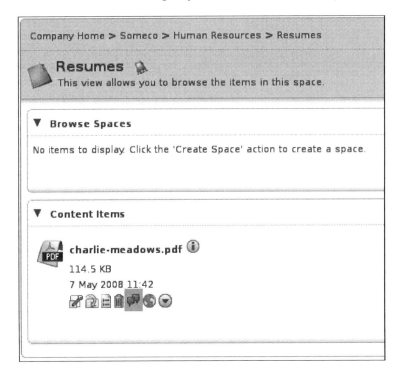

Clicking on the discussion forum link will display the topic the wizard created in the forum:

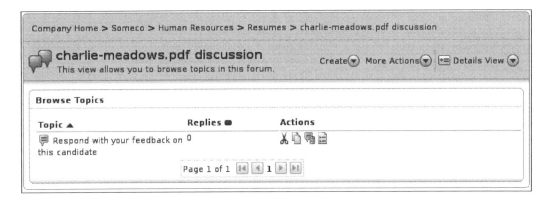

If you chose to send a notification and your test user has an email account on your development machine, there should be an email waiting for the interviewer(s):

From: alfresco@alfresco.org
To: tuser1@localhost
Subject: Administrator has chosen you to interview Charlie Meadows.
Date: Wed, 7 May 2008 11:42:49 -0500 (CDT)

```
Administrator has chosen you to interview Charlie Meadows.

The candidate is interviewing for the position of Consultant.

The candidate's resume may be downloaded from Alfresco at the following link:
http://localhost:8080/alfresco/d/a/workspace/SpacesStore/5422a217-1bb1-11dd-8a25-b78f4690764e/charl
```

 You have two choices to test out the mail notification. You can point Alfresco to an existing SMTP host, or you can install your own SMTP server locally. If you are doing a significant amount of mail-enabled work, I recommend installing an SMTP server on your development machine. Apache JAMES is a Java-based, cross-platform mail server that is easy to install and configure. For more information, see `http://james.apache.org/`. To tell Alfresco to use an existing server, set the following properties in `custom-repository.properties` to match your environment:

```
mail.host
mail.port
mail.username
mail.password
```

Adding Conditions to Wizard Step Pages

There may be times when you want to conditionally choose between two or more pages for a given step. For example, suppose SomeCo wanted to let the recruiter schedule the interviewers in specific time slots. You might want to give them the option of using a free-time lookup to help them with that, or they might want to just put people in slots regardless of what their calendar looks like. You could add a checkbox to the options page that gives them the choice, and configure the `schedule` step to look like this:

```
<step name="schedule" title="Schedule" description="Schedule
  Interviewers">
    <condition if="#{InterviewSetupWizard.useiCal == true}">
        <page path="/jsp/extension/wizards/interview-setup-wizard/
          schedule-ical.jsp"
                    title = "Schedule Interviewers"
```

```
                        description = "Schedule interviewers using
                        free-time lookup"
                        instruction = "Use the dialog below to
                  schedule interviewers based on their availability" />
      </condition>
      <page path="/jsp/extension/wizards/interview-setup-wizard/stub-
            schedule-standalone.jsp"
                  title = "Schedule Interviewers"
                  description = "Schedule interviewers without regard
                                                    to availability"
                  instruction = "Use the dialog below to schedule
            interviewers based on what works best for
            you and the candidate" />
      </step>
```

In this example, if the first condition is met, that page definition will be used. The page definition without a condition is treated as the default if no conditions are met.

Receiving Interview Feedback via Email

As of 2.2 Enterprise and 2.9 Community, Alfresco can be configured to run as an SMTP listener. This means, you can send mail to the repository. A nice enhancement to the example above would be to grab the discussion topic's email ID (which is really just its `node-dbid`) and use it as the reply-to address on the email notification that gets sent to interviewers. Interviewers could then simply reply to the notification with their feedback, which would automatically be stored as part of the feedback discussion thread.

Persisting Interviewer Choices

In this example you did not persist the interviewers anywhere. In a real-world scenario, particularly if you add the ability for recruiters to schedule interviewers, you should consider storing the interviewer selections and maybe other options. The `InterviewSetupWizard` bean can then populate itself with the stored settings so that when the recruiter launches the wizard, the original selections are present.

You could persist the interviewer selection data to the resume object, but a better idea is to create a content-less object (which inherits from `sys:base`) to store the data and then relate it to the resume with an association. That would make it easier to manage cases where there are multiple interviews for the same candidate, and it leaves the resume object only the responsibility of managing resume-related data.

Copying Alfresco's Code into Your Customizations

In this example you used Alfresco's code in several different ways. In one case (summary.jsp) you leveraged a JSP page as is. In another (notify), you copied the page into your source tree and renamed it to work around the location change between Community and Enterprise. For the InterviewSetupWizard bean, you copied methods from the BaseInviteUsersWizard rather than extending the bean.

There are potential copyright and license issues this creates, particularly if you are developing solutions you plan to redistribute, but those won't be discussed here. The more relevant point is that you have to be cognizant of the potential upgrade issues this creates. Of course all customizations, regardless of whether they are from scratch or based on Alfresco's source, need to be tested with each new Alfresco build. When your customizations leverage Alfresco's code, it is wise to add an additional source code compare step to your testing efforts to make sure any changes get incorporated into your source tree.

Customizing Web Client JSP Pages

There may be requirements you can't meet simply by adding new menu items, dialogs, or wizards. Customizing the login page, which you did in Chapter 2, is one example. Regardless of whether you are overriding an existing JSP with your own version or creating a new JSP from scratch, the steps involved are the same:

1. Create (or copy and modify) the JSP using JSF, Alfresco, and custom tag libraries.
2. Write JSF-managed backing beans as necessary to handle logic.
3. Update faces-config.xml with the appropriate navigation rules.
4. Optionally, update web-client-config-custom.xml with navigation rule overrides.
5. Externalize strings to a properties file.

Overriding Navigation Rules with Type-specific Settings

One thing the login page example didn't cover is navigation rule overrides. Let's look at a simple out of the box example to understand how this works.

In Alfresco WCM, web projects are stored in web project folders (`wca:webfolder`). Just like standard folders, you can browse a folder and go to folder details. The out of the box JSF navigation rules related to web folders reside in **WEB-INF|faces-config-navigation.xml**. Look at the navigation case related to the `browse` and `browseWebsite` outcomes:

```
<navigation-rule>
        <from-view-id>/jsp/*</from-view-id>
        <navigation-case>
                <from-outcome>browse</from-outcome>
                <to-view-id>/jsp/browse/browse.jsp</to-view-id>
        </navigation-case>
        ...
</navigation-rule>
...
<navigation-rule>
    <from-view-id>/jsp/*</from-view-id>
    <navigation-case>
        <from-outcome>browseWebsite</from-outcome>
        <to-view-id>/jsp/wcm/browse-website.jsp</to-view-id>
    </navigation-case>
        ...
```

This configuration says that any time the `browse` outcome occurs, JSF should return the `browse.jsp` page and any time the `browseWebsite` outcome occurs, JSF should return the `browse-website.jsp` page.

There are places in the user interface, however, where a component will return the `browse` outcome. But the intent is to browse a website folder, not a regular folder. To handle this situation, Alfresco's web client configuration file allows type-specific navigation overrides to be set. If you look at **WEB-INF|classes|alfresco|web-client-config-navigation.xml**, you'll see the out of the box, type-specific navigation overrides. In this case, the relevant section is:

```
<config evaluator="node-type" condition="wca:webfolder">
        <navigation>
                <override from-view-id="/jsp/browse/browse.jsp"
                                                        to-view-
            id="/jsp/wcm/browse-website.jsp" />
                <override from-outcome="browse" to-view-
            id="/jsp/wcm/browse-website.jsp" />
                <override from-outcome="showSpaceDetails" to-view-
            id="/jsp/wcm/website-details.jsp" />
        </navigation>
</config>
```

This section tells Alfresco that whenever a `browse` outcome occurs in the context of a web folder, instead of showing the `browse.jsp` page, it should show `browse-website.jsp` instead.

Summary

In this chapter, you learned that the Alfresco Web Client is an all-purpose user interface for general document management. It can be easily extended using approaches that range from making XML configuration file changes to writing new JSF-managed beans, JSPs, and navigation rules.

Specifically, you learned how to:

- Add new menu items to the web client
- Show/hide menu items based on things such as permissions or arbitrary logic
- Create custom renderers to change how the web client shows repository data
- Create custom dialogs and wizards to gather information from a user
- Assess whether the solution you are building should be based on a custom version of Alfresco's web client, or would be more appropriate as a custom application

It is important to remember that there are several very basic ways to tweak the user interface that aren't as involved as what has been discussed in this chapter. For example, custom views and Alfresco dashlets can be written in FreeMarker. Web scripts, the topic of the next chapter, can also be used in some cases. Usually, these are faster to develop and easier to maintain than the JSF route. So it pays to spend some time looking for ways to simplify your customizations.

6

Exposing Content through a RESTful API with Web Scripts

There are many ways to interact with the repository programmatically, one of which is via Web Scripts. Then why devote an entire chapter to the Web Script Framework? Web scripts allow you to define a REST API for the content in the Alfresco repository. REST stands for Representational State Transfer. In a nutshell, REST describes an architectural style of interaction based on simple URL-based requests and responses occurring over HTTP. Rolling your own RESTful API offers a huge advantage in terms of flexibility and implementation speed over other forms of web services such as SOAP. Web scripts have quickly become the preferred integration method between the frontend and an Alfresco backend, particularly for portals and dynamic web sites.

Specifically, in this chapter you will learn how to:

- Write web scripts that create, read, and delete data in the backend repository and return responses in HTML, XML, and JSON

- Use both JavaScript and Java to write "controller" logic

- Make asynchronous JavaScript (AJAX) calls to web scripts

- Leverage all three out of the box web script runtimes to execute web scripts in the context of an HTTP request, a JSF tag, and a JSR-168 portlet

- Create a Rating Service that centralizes all logic related to creating Rating nodes and is exposed as a "root object" to the JavaScript API

Introducing the Web Script Framework

Content-centric applications are becoming more and more componentized. This trend is turning traditional content management approaches inside out. Rather than having a single, monolithic system responsible for all aspects of a content-centric web application, loosely coupled subsystems are being integrated to create more agile solutions.

This approach requires that your **Content Management System (CMS)** has a flexible and lightweight interface. You don't want to be locked in to a presentation approach based on the content repository you are working with. In fact, in some cases, you might have very little control over the tools that will be used to talk to your CMS.

Consider the exploding rate of **Next Generation Internet (NGI)** solutions, the growing adoption of wikis and blogs within an Enterprise ("Enterprise 2.0"), and the increasing popularity of mash-ups both inside and outside the Enterprise. These trends are driving implementations where the CMS is seen as a black-box component with the frontend (or perhaps many different frontends) interacting with the CMS and other components via REST. The shorthand way to refer to this is "content-as-a-service".

Among open source CMSs, Alfresco is at the forefront of this trend, and the Web Script Framework is a key enabler of the product in a content-as-a-service world. Historically, there have been two approaches to interacting with Alfresco through services: SOAP-based Web Services and do-it-yourself REST.

Alfresco has had a SOAP-based Web Services API available for quite some time, but SOAP-based Web Services take longer to develop and have heavier client-side requirements than their RESTful cousins. Additionally, some organizations found that Alfresco's out of the box services were too chatty and had too much processing overhead to scale well. So they ended up writing their own services and exposing them through Alfresco's embedded Apache Axis server.

Developers looking for a lighter-weight approach leveraged the fact that objects in the Alfresco repository are URL-addressable. FreeMarker templates and server-side JavaScript can be applied to any node in the repository through a specially formatted URL. So, for example, you can write a FreeMarker template that returns XML or JSON, and then have a frontend application post an XMLHttpRequest to Alfresco that specifies a node reference and a reference to the FreeMarker template. Alfresco will process the FreeMarker template in the context of the node specified and return the results.

This do-it-yourself approach to RESTful interactions works fine, but it feels a little hack-ish. Plus, you wind up with some pretty gnarly-looking URLs.

The Web Script Framework introduced in the 2.1 version essentially improves on the basic idea that started with URL addressability. Think of a web script as a chunk of code that is mapped to a human-readable (and search-engine friendly) URL. So, for example, a URL that returns expense reports that are pending approval might look like:

```
/alfresco/service/expenses/pending
```

While a URL that returns expenses that are pending approval for a specific user might look like:

```
/alfresco/service/expenses/pending/jpotts
```

In this URL, you could read the `jpotts` component of the URL as an implied argument. A more explicit way to provide an argument would be like:

```
/alfresco/service/expenses/pending?user=jpotts
```

You might choose to treat the `pending` component of the URL as an argument as well, which tells the web script what status of expense reports to return. The point is that the Web Script Framework leaves the structure of the URL and how (and if) your URL includes arguments completely up to you.

Step-by-Step: Hello World Web Script

Let's implement the most basic web script possible: a `Hello World` script that echoes back an argument. You'll need one descriptor and one FreeMarker template. Do the following:

1. Log in to Alfresco.

2. Navigate to |**Company Home**|**Data Dictionary**|**Web Scripts Extensions**.

3. Create a file called `helloworld.get.desc.xml` in the `Web Scripts Extensions` folder with the following content:

    ```
    <webscript>
      <shortname>Hello World</shortname>
      <description>Hello world web script</description>
      <url>/helloworld?name={nameArgument}</url>
    </webscript>
    ```

4. Create a file called `helloworld.get.html.ftl` with the following content:

    ```
    <html>
        <body>
            <p>Hello, ${args.name}!</p>
        </body>
    </html>
    ```

5. Go to `http://localhost:8080/alfresco/service/index` and press the **Refresh** button. Click the **List Web Scripts** link—you should be able to find the web script you just defined.

6. Now point your browser to `http://localhost:8080/alfresco/service/helloworld?name=Jeff`. You should see:

   ```
   Hello, Jeff!
   ```

What Just Happened?

You invoked a URL in your web browser (specifically, you made a GET request over HTTP). The Alfresco web application is configured to map all requests matching the pattern `/alfresco/service/*` to the web script request dispatcher servlet. The servlet handed off the request to the Web Script Runtime to process the web script. The Web Script Runtime figured out which web script to execute by matching the remainder of the URL (`"helloworld?name=Jeff"`) to the URL pattern you declared in the web script's descriptor file, `helloworld.get.desc.xml`.

You didn't specify what kind of response you wanted from the web script, and the web script descriptor didn't declare a default, so the framework assumed HTML would be acceptable. It then used file naming convention to find a FreeMarker template to generate an HTML response for this web script. The FreeMarker template formatted a response to send back to the browser that included some HTML and the value of the name argument.

Following the Model-View-Controller Pattern

The Web Script Framework makes it easy to follow the **Model-View-Controller (MVC)** pattern. You don't have to be a hardcore disciple of the Gang of Four to appreciate the value of the MVC pattern. In MVC, all business logic resides in the controller. It is completely separated from the presentation or view. This makes it possible to have as many views as you need without a big maintenance headache because the business logic isn't mugged together with the view. It is centralized in the controller. There is a clear separation of concerns.

In Alfresco's web script framework, the controller is server-side JavaScript, a Java Bean, or both. The controller handles the request, performs any business logic that is needed, populates the model with data, and then forwards the request to the view. The view is one or more FreeMarker templates responsible for constructing a response in the appropriate format. The model is essentially a data structure passed between the controller and the view.

The mapping of URL to controller is done through an XML descriptor that is responsible for declaring the URL pattern, whether the script requires a transaction or not, and the authentication requirements for the script. The descriptor optionally describes arguments that can be passed to the script as well as the response formats that are available.

Adding Controller Logic

The Hello World example consisted of one FreeMarker template and one descriptor XML file. The FreeMarker API is quite extensive, and many out of the box examples rely solely on FreeMarker for light logic processing as well as rendering a response. Ideally, however, FreeMarker templates should be strictly focused on presentation. Logic, such as querying the repository, creating or updating content, executing actions, and so on, should be handled in the JavaScript or Java-based controller.

Try adding a simple controller to the Hello World example:

1. You should still be logged in to the web client.

2. Create a file in **|Company Home|Data Dictionary|Web Scripts Extensions** called `helloworld.get.js` with the following content:

   ```
   model.foo = "bar";
   ```

3. Update your `helloworld.get.html.ftl` file with the following content:

   ```
   <html>
       <body>
           <p>Hello, ${args.name}!</p>
           <p>Foo: ${foo}</p>
       </body>
   </html>
   ```

4. Go to `http://localhost:8080/alfresco/service/index` and press the **Refresh** button. This is required because you added a controller that the web script runtime didn't know about.

5. Now go to your web browser and enter the same URL from the first example, which was `http://localhost:8080/alfresco/service/helloworld?name=Jeff`. You should see:

   ```
   Hello, Jeff!
   Foo: bar
   ```

What's going on here is that the web script framework is executing the controller prior to rendering a response with the FreeMarker template. In the controller you can do anything the Alfresco JavaScript API can do. In this case, you didn't leverage the JavaScript API at all. You just put some data into the "model" object. The "model" variable is a root variable Alfresco makes available to you to enable data sharing between the controller (JavaScript) and the view (FreeMarker).

In subsequent examples the controller will have more work to do and in one case, you'll use Java instead of JavaScript for the controller.

Configuring the Web Script

The three most important settings for any web script are:

1. The HTTP method used to make the request to the web script.

2. The URL and any arguments the web script expects.

3. The response formats the web script supports.

The Web Script Framework defines conventions that make it easy to configure these settings.

Specifying the HTTP Method

In the Hello World example, notice that the file names for the descriptor and the FreeMarker template include `get`. It tells the framework that when someone invokes the web script with a GET, those descriptor and FreeMarker files are applied. By differentiating the HTTP method (such as GET, POST, DELETE, and PUT), you can define multiple web scripts that get invoked depending on the method used to make the request.

Use the following to determine which HTTP method is appropriate for your web script:

- GET: Retrieves the representation of a resource. The URI should return the same resource no matter how many times it is called. Calling this URI should have no effect on the repository. A GET usually doesn't require a transaction.

- POST: Creates a new resource. The server decides on that resource's URI.

- PUT: Creates a new resource. But the client decides on the URI or updates an existing resource. Like a GET, the URI should update the same resource no matter how many times it is called.

- DELETE: Deletes a resource, or stops a resource from being accessible.

Some browsers and some UI toolkits only support GET and POST. In those cases, you may be able to use HTTP method tunneling. Currently only available in Labs, HTTP method tunneling allows you to specify the "real" HTTP method as either an argument in the URL (`alf_method`) or in the request header (`X-HTTP-Method-Override`). For example, a POST could be issued with `alf_method` set to "DELETE". Alfresco would then match the request to the web script configured to handle the DELETE method even though the actual request was a POST.

Specifying Arguments

Arguments are declared as part of the `url` element in the web script's descriptor XML. There are two styles of arguments supported. The Hello World example used explicit arguments—argument names and placeholders appear in the URL as part of the query string:

```
<url>/helloworld?name={nameArgument}</url>
```

The other style is to use implicit arguments in which the arguments are incorporated into components of the path:

```
<url>/helloworld/{nameArgument}</url>
```

The Hello World example only had one argument, but you could add as many as you need. Using the explicit style, each argument is separated with an ampersand. Make sure you escape ampersands in a URL. Web script descriptors must always be valid XML:

```
<url>/helloworld?name={nameArgument}&amp;secondArg={anotherArg}</url>
```

What does Alfresco use to match a URL to a web script? Prior to the release of the 3.0 version, a web script's URL ended as soon as either the first argument or the query string occurred. For example, in the following URL, the web script would be recognized as `helloworld`:
`/helloworld/{nameArgument}`

That meant that prior to release 3.0, you couldn't have a web script URL that included static path elements after an argument. But as of 3.0, the following URL can be used for a web script:
`/helloworld/{nameArgument}/english`

How you choose to structure your URLs is a matter of preference, consistency, and, potentially, search engine friendliness (some search engines may have trouble indexing URLs that include a query string).

Specifying the Response Format

The response formats are mapped to FreeMarker templates through naming convention. In the Hello World example, the FreeMarker template was named `helloworld.get.html.ftl`. So Alfresco interprets that to mean "This is the template to use when someone asks for an HTML response for this web script."

One of the benefits of the MVC pattern is that you can have one set of controller logic with as many different views as you need because the controller logic and view logic are cleanly separated. For example, you could create a second FreeMarker template for the Hello World example named `helloworld.get.xml.ftl` that looked like this:

```
<helloworld>
    <message>Hello, ${args.name}!</message>
    <foo>${foo}</foo>
</helloworld>
```

Response format can be specified via URL either as an extension on the script ID, like this:

```
http://localhost:8080/alfresco/service/someco/helloworld.
xml?name=jeff
```

or with an explicit `format` argument:

```
http://localhost:8080/alfresco/service/someco/helloworld?name=jeff&fo
rmat=xml
```

If a format is not specified, the default format will be returned. The default response format can be specified as part of the descriptor:

```
<format default="xml">any</format>
```

The content of the `format` element specifies the style in which the script expects the format to be provided. In the example, `any` specifies that either one is accepted, but it could be restricted to one or the other, if necessary, using "extension" or "argument".

If no default format is specified in the descriptor, Alfresco assumes a default of HTML.

Deploying Web Scripts

The descriptor, the JavaScript file, and the FreeMarker templates together make up the web script. These files can reside either in the repository or on the file system. If a web script uses a Java Bean, the class must reside somewhere on the classpath.

Regardless of where they are deployed, updates can be picked up without an application server restart. After deploying a new or updated script, go to `http://localhost:8080/alfresco/service/index` and press the **Refresh list of web scripts** button.

Building Solutions with the Web Script Framework

Now that you understand the basics, you may already be thinking of different ways you could leverage web scripts to build your own solutions. For example, you can use web scripts to:

- Enable a frontend web application written in any language that understands HTTP to retrieve repository data in XML, JSON, or any other format
- Populate JSR-168 portlets without coding Java against the portlet API
- Capture and persist user-contributed content/data
- Interact with a business process (for example, a jBPM workflow) through non-web client interfaces such as email
- Create ATOM or RSS feeds for repository content or business process data
- Decompose the existing web client into smaller components that could potentially lend it to being re-born in new and exciting ways!

The last one is exactly what Alfresco decided to do. The Alfresco 3.0 Share client is based entirely on web scripts.

Recall from prior chapters that SomeCo would like to publish Whitepapers on its web site. In addition to making the Whitepapers available on the Web, SomeCo wants to provide a way for web site users to rate the Whitepapers and display the aggregated ratings with each Whitepaper. Earlier, you created a behavior that calculates the ratings summary. Now you are going to make Whitepapers and ratings available via REST.

Planning the SomeCo Whitepapers and Ratings API

Before diving into the examples, let's plan the new API at high level. The following table outlines the URLs, the HTTP methods, and the response formats for each:

URL	Method	Description	Response formats
/someco/ whitepapers	GET	Returns a list of Whitepapers.	HTML, JSON
/someco/ rating?id={id}	GET	Gets the average rating for a given Whitepaper by passing in the Whitepaper's noderef.	HTML, JSON
/someco/rating?id={ id}&rating={rating}& user={user}	POST	Creates a new rating for the specified Whitepaper by passing in a rating value and the user who posted the rating.	HTML, JSON
/someco/ rating?id={id}	DELETE	Deletes all ratings for a specified Whitepaper.	HTML

When this API is in place, frontend developers can incorporate Whitepapers and user-contributed ratings into the SomeCo web site. The following screenshots show pages that use the API you're going to build to query for Whitepaper and ratings data. It looks like the folks at SomeCo have shamelessly ripped off the Optaros news, events, and publications page. At least they changed the logo:

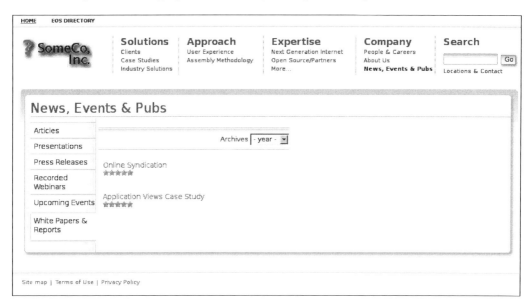

You can't tell from the screenshots, but the ratings widget (the row of five stars beneath each Whitepaper title) is clickable. When a star is clicked, the browser sends an asynchronous post to the /someco/rating URL described in the earlier table. When the Whitepaper title link is clicked, the Whitepaper detail is displayed as follows:

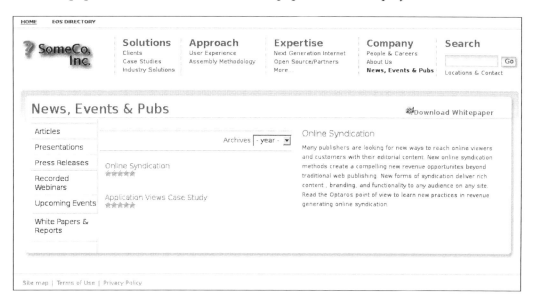

The **Download Whitepaper** link uses the standard "Download URL" to give the user direct access to the content.

By the end of the chapter, you will be able to deploy this web page and have it interact with your web scripts.

Retrieving Data with Web Scripts

The first service that needs to be implemented retrieves the list of Whitepapers enabled for publication. The web script needs to return the list of Whitepapers in two formats: HTML and JSON. HTML will allow you to easily test the service and JSON will make it easy for code on the frontend to process the list. This will require four files: one descriptor, one JavaScript controller, and two FreeMarker templates—one for each format.

New to JSON? It stands for JavaScript Object Notation. It is a way to describe JavaScript objects in plain text. The beauty of it is that it is extremely easy to create and consume, and it isn't as verbose as XML. For more information on JSON, see http://www.json.org.

Step-by-Step: Writing a Web Script to List Whitepapers

To create a web script that retrieves the list of Whitepapers, do the following:

1. First, in your Eclipse project create the descriptor file in **|config|alfresco| extension|templates|com|someco|whitepapers**. Name it `whitepapers. get.desc.xml` and give it the following content:

```
<webscript>
  <shortname>Get all whitepapers</shortname>
  <description>Returns a list of active whitepapers</description>
  <url>/someco/whitepapers</url>
  <url>/someco/whitepapers.json</url>
  <url>/someco/whitepapers.html</url>
  <format default="json">extension</format>
  <authentication>guest</authentication>
  <transaction>none</transaction>
</webscript>
```

2. Next, you need a controller to execute the query to find the Whitepapers. Create a file in the same directory where you created the descriptor called `whitepapers.get.js`. The first thing you're going to do is import the `rating.js` JavaScript file. You're going to add a new function to that file in a moment:

```
<import resource="classpath:alfresco/extension/scripts/rating.js">
```

3. Now add code to execute a search for Whitepapers. You need to use a Lucene search string that grabs every thing in the Whitepapers folder that is a Whitepaper object and has the `isActive` flag set to `true`:

```
var whitepapers = search.luceneSearch("+PATH:\"/app:company_home/
cm:Someco/cm:Marketing/cm:Whitepapers/*\" +TYPE:\"sc:whitepaper\"
+@sc\\:isActive:true");
```

4. If no Whitepapers are found, an error message needs to be returned. Otherwise, build an array of Whitepapers and store that array in the model:

```
if (whitepapers == null || whitepapers.length == 0) {
   logger.log("No whitepapers found");
   status.code = 404;
   status.message = "No whitepapers found";
   status.redirect = true;
} else {
   var whitepaperInfo = new Array();
   for (i = 0; i < whitepapers.length; i++) {
```

```
        var whitepaper = new whitepaperEntry(whitepapers[i],
    getRating(whitepapers[i]));
        whitepaperInfo[i] = whitepaper;
    }
    model.whitepapers = whitepaperInfo;
}
function whitepaperEntry(whitepaper, rating) {
    this.whitepaper = whitepaper;
    this.rating = rating;
}
```

5. Save the JavaScript file.

6. The controller you just wrote imports a script called `rating.js`. Update
    |config|alfresco|extension|scripts|rating.js with a new function called
    `getRating` as shown here. The function is responsible for retrieving the
    rating summary statistics for a given node:

```
function getRating(curNode) {
    var rating = {};
    rating.average = curNode.properties["{http://www.someco.com/
                              model/content/1.0}averageRating"];
    rating.count = curNode.properties["{http://www.someco.com/model/
                                  content/1.0}ratingCount"];
    rating.user = getUserRating(curNode, curUser);
    return rating;
}
```

7. The `getRating` function calls `getUserRating` to see if a specified user
    has already rated this Whitepaper, and if so, retrieves the rating. Add the
    `getUserRating` function to the same JavaScript file as follows:

```
function getUserRating(curNode, curUser) {
    if (curUser == undefined || curUser == "") {
        logger.log("User name was not passed in");
        return 0;
    }
    var results = curNode.childrenByXPath("*//.[@sc:rater='" +
                                          curUser + "']");
    if (results == undefined || results.length == 0) {
        logger.log("No ratings found for this node for user: " +
                                                  curUser);
        return 0;
    } else {
        var rating = results[results.length-1].properties["{http://
                        www.someco.com/model/content/1.0}rating"];
        if (rating == undefined) {
```

```
          return 0;
       } else {
          return rating;
       }
    }
 }
```

8. Save the JavaScript file.

9. As you saw in the Hello World example, one FreeMarker template is needed for each response format. Let's create the HTML response template first. Create a new file in **|config|alfresco|extension|templates|webscripts |com|someco|whitepapers** called `whitepapers.get.html.ftl`. The HTML response is for debugging purposes, so nothing fancy is needed. An HTML table showing the list of Whitepapers will do fine. First, set up a date format variable and then start the table:

```
<#assign datetimeformat="EEE, dd MMM yyyy HH:mm:ss zzz">
<html>
    <body>
        <h3>Whitepapers</h3>
        <table>
```

10. Now iterate over the array of `whitepaperEntry` objects to build the table:

```
<#list whitepapers as child>
    <tr>
        <td><b>Name</b></td><td>${child.whitepaper.
                                 properties.name}</td>
    </tr>
    <tr>
        <td><b>Title</b></td><td>${child.whitepaper.
                                 properties["cm:title"]}</td>
    </tr>
    <tr>
        <td><b>Link</b></td><td><a href="${url.context}${
        child.whitepaper.url}?guest=true">${url.context}${
                                 child.whitepaper.url}</a></td>
    </tr>
    <tr>
        <td><b>Type</b></td><td>${child.whitepaper.
                                     mimetype}</td>
    </tr>
    <tr>
        <td><b>Size</b></td><td>${child.whitepaper.size}
        </td>
    </tr>
```

```
<tr>
   <td><b>Id</b></td><td>${child.whitepaper.id}</td>
</tr>
<tr>
   <td><b>Description</b></td>
     <td><p><#if child.whitepaper.properties["cm:
     description"]?exists && child.whitepaper.
     properties["cm:description"] != "">${child.
     whitepaper.properties["cm:description"]}</#if></p>
     </td>
</tr>
<tr>
   <td><b>Pub Date</b></td><td>${child.whitepaper.
   properties["cm:modified"]?string(datetimeformat)}
   </td>
</tr>
<tr>
   <td><b><a href="${url.serviceContext}/rating.
   html?id=${child.whitepaper.id}&guest=true">Rating
   </a></b></td>
   <td>
   <table>
        <tr>
            <td><b>Average</b></td><td>${child.
            rating.average}</td>
        </tr>
        <tr>
            <td><b>Count</b></td><td>${child.
            rating.count}</td>
        </tr>
      <#if (child.rating.user > 0)><tr><td><b>User
      </b></td><td>${child.rating.user}</td></tr></#if>
   </table>
   </td>
</tr>
<#if !(child.whitepaper == whitepapers?last.
 whitepaper)>
<tr><td colspan="2" bgcolor="999999"> </td></tr>
</#if>
</#list>
</table>
</body>
</html>
```

11. Save the HTML response template.

12. Now create the JSON response template. Create a file called `whitepapers.get.json.ftl` in the directory in which you created the HTML template. The overall logic is exactly the same, but the output format is in JSON instead of HTML:

```
<#assign datetimeformat="EEE, dd MMM yyyy HH:mm:ss zzz">

{"whitepapers" : [
<#list whitepapers as child>
    {
    "name" : "${child.whitepaper.properties.name}",
    "title" : "${child.whitepaper.properties["cm:title"]?j_string}",
    "link" : "${url.context}${child.whitepaper.url}",
    "type" : "${child.whitepaper.mimetype}",
    "size" : "${child.whitepaper.size}",
    "id" : "${child.whitepaper.id}",
    "description" : "<#if child.whitepaper.properties
     ["cm:description"]?exists && child.whitepaper.properties
     ["cm:description"] != "">${child.whitepaper.properties
     ["cm:description"]?j_string}</#if>",
    "pubDate" : "${child.whitepaper.properties["cm:modified"]?string
     (datetimeformat)}",
    "rating" : {
       "average" : "${child.rating.average}",
       "count" : "${child.rating.count}",
       "user" : "${child.rating.user}"
       }
    }
    <#if !(child.whitepaper == whitepapers?last.whitepaper)>,</#if>
</#list>
]
}
```

13. Save the JSON response template.

14. You are going to let Guests run these web scripts. That means they'll need access to the Whitepapers folder. Log in to the web client and add the special Guest user as a Consumer to the Whitepapers folder.

15. Deploy your changes using `ant deploy`.

16. Refresh the list of web scripts by clicking the **Refresh** button at `http://localhost:8080/alfresco/service/index`.

17. Test your changes.

If you haven't already, create one or more SomeCo Whitepaper objects in the
Someco | Marketing | Whitepapers folder in your repository. Execute the
addTestRating.js script a few times to create some test ratings for each test
Whitepaper. (As it stands, the getRating function will bomb if you don't.)

Also, remember to click the **SC Web Enable** UI action link to set the isActive flag
to true.

Because the descriptor specifies that this script requires Guest access or higher, you'll
need to either log in to Alfresco before running the script, authenticate with a valid
user and password when the basic authentication dialog is presented, or append
&guest=true to the URL. For now, use the guest approach, which means the URL
should look like this: http://localhost:8080/alfresco/service/someco/
whitepapers.html?guest=true If you forget the html, you'll get a JSON response
because you set that as the default format in the descriptor.

If all goes well, you should see something similar to the following figure:

	Whitepapers	
Name	application-views.pdf	
Title	Application Views Case Study	
Link	/alfresco/d/d/workspace/SpacesStore/16c15c7f-1de5-11dd-8189-03f52b46d68a/application-views.pdf	
Type	application/pdf	
Size	117,249	
Id	16c15c7f-1de5-11dd-8189-03f52b46d68a	
Description	Executive summary of how brands can use Application Views to engage customers with branded content on the content real estate of chosen partners' sites.	
Pub Date	Sat, 17 May 2008 21:59:07 CDT	
Rating	Average 3 Count 2	
Name	online-syndication.pdf	
Title	Online Syndication	
Link	/alfresco/d/d/workspace/SpacesStore/c1507aa0-2485-11dd-bf67-e5f6287cc1fb/online-syndication.pdf	
Type	application/pdf	
Size	117,249	
Id	c1507aa0-2485-11dd-bf67-e5f6287cc1fb	
Description	Many publishers are looking for new ways to reach online viewers and customers with their editorial content. New online syndication methods create a compelling new revenue opportunites beyond traditional web publishing. New forms of syndication deliver rich content , branding, and functionality to any audience on any site. Read the Optaros point of view to learn new practices in revenue generating online syndication.	
Pub Date	Sat, 17 May 2008 22:01:30 CDT	
Rating	Average 3 Count 3	

Debugging

Did your web script work? If not, it's time to debug. The first thing you will want to do is to go into **WEB-INF|classes|log4j.properties** and set `log4j.logger.org.alfresco.repo.jscript` to DEBUG. This will cause any `logger.log` statements in your controller to write to `catalina.out`.

Another tool you'll want to leverage is the web script list. You can use it to see (1) if Alfresco knows about your script and (2) the version of the scripts the runtime knows about. The starting URL for the web script list is `http://localhost:8080/alfresco/service/`. From there, you can see a list of web scripts by package and by URL. You can also browse the configuration for a specific web script. For example, you can go to `http://localhost:8080/alfresco/service/script/com/someco/whitepapers/whitepapers.get` and Alfresco will dump the descriptor and all of the response templates.

The Node Browser can be helpful to debug problems as well. In this case, for example, you're running a Lucene query in the JavaScript controller to find Whitepapers. If the controller isn't finding any Whitepapers even though you've created test data, try executing the query in the Node Browser. If it doesn't return results, there could be something wrong with either your test data or the query syntax.

Fast Facts

- The descriptor you created has multiple URL elements. There is one URL for each format plus a URL without a format. Because the URLs differ only in format, it isn't strictly required that they be listed in the descriptor. But it is a good practice. A better reason for using multiple URL elements would be if you wanted to use completely different URL formats for the same web script.

- The authentication element declares the lowest level of authentication required for this script. If your script touches the repository, you will want this to be Guest or higher. Other options are **none**, **user**, and **admin**. Authentication will be discussed shortly.

- The transaction element specifies the level of transaction required by the script. Listing Whitepapers doesn't need a transaction so you specified **none**. Other possible values are **required** and **requiresnew**.

- The ability to import a script from another script was added with release 2.1. The import tag also supports including scripts that reside in the repository. Note that the import tag is not native to the Rhino JavaScript implementation. Beware, though. Alfresco compiles all imported JavaScript files into a single file and gives that to Rhino. So when there is an error, the line number Rhino reports is from the compiled set of JavaScript files, which could be hard to map back to the line number in the original JavaScript source.

- The controller builds a new array for the Whitepaper search results. You could have just set `model.whitepapers` equal to the Whitepapers variable that contains the query results but, in this case, you built a new array and set that to the model. You did that because you needed to incorporate a specific user's rating, if one exists, that isn't part of the Whitepaper nodes in the query result set.

- The `getUserRating` function in `rating.js` looks for ratings specific to a particular user by querying the children using an XPath expression (shown as follows). The expression asks for any child of the current node with the `sc:rater` property set to the name of the user passed in to the function:

```
var results = curNode.childrenByXPath("*//.[@sc:rater='" + curUser
                                                         + "']");
```

- The FreeMarker template that renders the JSON response includes output that needs to be escaped. Both the title and the description could potentially contain characters that would make the JSON invalid (such as a quote). To address that, the code uses the FreeMarker built-in `j_string` to escape the string, as follows:

```
"title" : "${child.whitepaper.properties["cm:title"]?j_string}",
```

Organizing Web Scripts

The Web Script Framework allows you to organize script assets into a hierarchical folder or package structure. Just as it is with Java, it is a good idea to do this for all web scripts. That's because the number of web scripts your installation leverages is going to grow over time as you, Alfresco, and third parties add more functionality. Following a reverse domain name pattern is a good convention and is consistent with how Alfresco organizes its scripts.

Alfresco reserves certain package names for its own use. These may change over time, so consult the wiki for the specific list. But if you steer clear of using `org/alfresco`, you'll probably be fine.

Overriding Web Scripts

Alfresco searches for web scripts in the following order:

1. In the repository under **|Company Home|Data Dictionary|Web Scripts Extensions**.
2. In the repository under **|Company Home|Data Dictionary|Web Scripts**.
3. In the classpath under **|alfresco|extension|templates|webscripts**.
4. In the classpath under **|alfresco|templates|webscripts**.

If you want to override an existing web script, just make sure your web script is found first. In addition to overriding an entire web script, you can override components of a web script. For example, suppose a web script in the Web Scripts folder has something in its JavaScript controller you want to override. You can add the controller to the Web Scripts Extensions folder in the same package folder structure to override the lower-level controller.

Choosing a URL

URLs can follow any pattern you want. Because the URL pattern must be unique to a given web application, it makes sense to use the package name partially or completely. For SomeCo, the convention will be to use someco in all URLs, assuming the default Alfresco web application name hasn't been changed. This means that when using HTTP, SomeCo's web script URLs will look like this:

```
/alfresco/service/someco/[web script name].[format]?[arguments]
```

When running web scripts as JSR-168 portlets, the URLs will be:

```
/alfresco/168s/someco/[web script name].[format]?[arguments]
```

When running web scripts as part of the web client UI, the URLs will be:

```
/alfresco/wcs/someco/[web script name].[format]?[arguments]
```

Within a web script, you can use ${url.serviceContext} to refer to the service context component of the URL (/alfresco/, /alfresco/168s, and /alfresco/wcs) to avoid hardcoding within references to other web scripts.

Just like packages, Alfresco already has several URLs mapped to web scripts. Unfortunately, they don't follow a strict pattern. If your URLs don't incorporate a unique string, you may want to do a recursive search through the descriptor XML files in the source or browse the web script directory by URL (http://localhost:8080/alfresco/service/index/uri/) to make sure your URLs are easily distinguishable from Alfresco's.

Choosing between the Repository and the File System

You ran the Hello World web script out of the repository. The Whitepaper listing ran out of the file system. There are trade-offs to consider with each approach.

The advantage of using the file system is that the web scripts that make up your solution can be deployed alongside your other extensions. This can be done using the same deployment tools without requiring the extra step of uploading them to the repository.

The trade-off is that it is a little more work to edit the web scripts when they need to be changed. If they are stored in the repository, they can be easily edited just like any other piece of content. If they are stored in your source code control system and deployed with the rest of your customizations, it's a little more work to make a change. Whether or not you consider this an advantage or a disadvantage depends on the team supporting the solution and the development processes you like to use.

If scripts are defined in the repository as well as the classpath, the files in the repository take precedence over the files on the classpath as mentioned previously in *Overriding Web Scripts*.

Step-by-Step: Retrieving the Rating for a Whitepaper

Getting a specific rating is roughly the same as getting a Whitepaper. A controller searches for ratings and stores them in the model, then two response templates (one for HTML and one for JSON) are used to return the data in the appropriate format.

To create a web script that retrieves a rating for a specific Whitepaper, do the following:

1. Retrieving the rating for a Whitepaper is a bit easier because of the existing `getRating` function in `rating.js`. All the controller has to do is grab the node ID of the Whitepaper in question, locate the node, and then call `getRating` function. Create a new controller in **|config|alfresco|extensio n|templates|webscripts|com|someco|ratings** called `rating.get.js` as shown here:

```
<import resource="classpath:alfresco/extension/scripts/rating.js">
if (args.id == null || args.id.length == 0) {
   logger.log("ID arg not set");
   status.code = 400;
   status.message = "Node ID has not been provided";
   status.redirect = true;
} else {
   var curNode = search.findNode("workspace://SpacesStore/"
                                                 + args.id);

   if (curNode == null) {
      logger.log("Node not found");
      status.code = 404;
      status.message = "No node found for id:" + args.id;
      status.redirect = true;
   } else {
      model.rating = getRating(curNode, args.user);
   }
}
```

2. The descriptor and response templates are very similar to the Whitepaper example. Create a new descriptor called `rating.get.desc.xml` in **|config|alfresco|extension|templates|webscripts|com|someco|ratings** as follows:

```
<webscript>
  <shortname>Get Content Rating</shortname>
  <description>Returns rating data for the specified node</
                                                description>
  <url>/someco/rating?id={id}&amp;user={user?}</url>
  <url>/someco/rating.json?id={id}&amp;user={user?}</url>
  <url>/someco/rating.html?id={id}&amp;user={user?}</url>
  <format default="json">extension</format>
  <authentication>guest</authentication>
  <transaction>none</transaction>
</webscript>
```

3. Create a response template called `rating.get.json.ftl` that retrieves rating data from the model and outputs a JSON `rating` object:

```
{"rating" :
       {
        "average" : "${rating.average}",
        "count" : "${rating.count}",
        "user" : "${rating.user}"
       }
}
```

4. Create a response template called `rating.get.html.ftl`. In a later example you're going to incorporate a graphical ratings widget into this page. You'll use the HTML page this response template creates to test the widget. For now, just output the ratings data and provide a link to get back to the Whitepaper list:

```
<html>
    <head>
    </head>
    <body>
        <script type="text/javascript">
         function deleteRatings(id) {
              alert("Not yet implemented");
         }
        </script>

        <p>
```

```
<a href="${url.serviceContext}/someco/whitepapers.
                                    html?guest=true">
Back to the list</a> of whitepapers</p>
    <p>Node: ${args.id}</p>
    <p>Average: ${rating.average}</p>
    <p># of Ratings: ${rating.count}</p>
    <#if (rating.user > 0)>
       <p>User rating: ${rating.user}</p>
    </#if>
      <p><a href="#" onclick=deleteRatings("${args.id}")>Delete
      ratings</a> for this node</p>
  </body>
</html>
```

5. Deploy, refresh, and test.

Point your browser at the Whitepapers web script. Click the **Rating** link. The **Rating** link invokes the web script you just created. You should see:

> Back to the list of whitepapers
>
> Node: 16c15c7f-1de5-11dd-8189-03f52b46d68a
>
> Average: 3
>
> # of Ratings: 2
>
> Delete ratings for this node

Test out the JSON response by replacing the html string in the URL with json. The rating service should return something similar to:

```
{"rating" :
    {
        "average" : "1.923",
        "count" : "13",
    }
}
```

Specifying Optional Arguments

Did you catch the new twist in the URL declaration for this web script? Here it is again:

```
<url>/someco/rating?id={id}&amp;user={user?}</url>
```

The question mark in the `user` value placeholder declares the argument as optional. Using the optional indicator is, well, optional. Alfresco does not enforce mandatory parameters and it doesn't care if you provide an argument that isn't declared. You may have noticed that the Whitepaper script will show the user's last rating if you pass the `user` argument in even though you may not have included it in the URL declaration.

At some point, Alfresco may start enforcing that web script calls should match the declared URL. Or it might start generating documentation based on the descriptor. So you might as well get in the habit of declaring all of your arguments now. Plus, in the absence of automatically generated documentation, the descriptor is what people will use to figure out how to call your web script (no matter how much time you spend crafting documentation elsewhere).

Handling Errors

In both the Whitepaper examples and the ratings example, you probably noticed some error handling code. For example, in the `rating.get.js` file, if the Whitepaper node cannot be located, the following code is executed:

```
status.code = 404;
status.message = "No node found for id:" + args.id;
status.redirect = true;
```

The response `code` gets set to `404`, which is the standard HTTP response code for **File not found**. An error message is set and the `redirect` property is set to `true`, which tells the web script framework to `redirect` the response to the error handling templates.

For example, if you pass a bad node ID to the `rating.html` web script, you'll get a response that looks like:

 Web Script Status 404 - Not Found

The Web Script /alfresco/service/someco/rating.html has responded with a status of 404 - Not Found.

404 Description: Requested resource is not available.

Message:	No node found for id:16c15c7f-1de5-11dd-8189-03f52b46d68b
Server:	Alfresco Community Network v3.0.0 (dev @build-number@) schema 124
Time:	May 21, 2008 2:43:36 PM
Diagnostics:	Inspect Web Script (com/someco/ratings/rating.get)

Similarly, if you pass a bad node ID to the `rating.json` web script (the same script with a different response format) the JSON that comes back will be:

```
{
    status :
    {
      "code" : 404,
      "name" : "Not Found",
      "description" : "Requested resource is not available."
    },
    "message" : "No node found for id:16c15c7f-1de5-11dd-8189-
03f52b46d68b",
    "exception" : "",
    "callstack" :
    [
    ],
    "server" : "Alfresco Community Network v3.0.0 (dev @build-number@)
schema 124",
    "time" : "May 21, 2008 2:47:25 PM"
}
```

Getting an error back in the request response format is nice. The calling code can handle errors more gracefully when it knows the format that will come back, even when exceptions are thrown.

The examples show the standard response template for error codes. Depending on the solution you are building it might make more sense to customize these, whether simply for look-and-feel or because you want to structure the response differently. You can override the standard error templates with your own by creating FreeMarker files that follow a specific naming convention. When an error occurs, the framework attempts to find a template specific to the HTTP method, response format, and error code. If one does not exist, it looks for a more general fit until it ultimately reaches the default `status.ftl`.

The following table shows the naming convention and location for error templates beginning with the most specific case and ending with the most general:

Naming convention	Location	Example	What it does
`<scriptid>.<method>.<format>.<code>.ftl`	Same as descriptor	`whitepapers.get.html.404.ftl`	Displays when a GET request for an HTML response of the Whitepapers script returns a 404 error.
`<scriptid>.<method>.<format>.status.ftl`	Same as descriptor	`whitepapers.get.html.status.ftl`	Displays when a GET request for an HTML response of the Whitepapers script returns any error.
`<format>.<code>.ftl`	Package hierarchy	`html.404.ftl`	Displays for all HTML responses that return a 404.
`<format>.status.ftl`	Package hierarchy	`html.status.ftl`	Displays for all HTML responses that return any error.
`<code>.ftl`	`WEB-INF/ classes/ alfresco/ webscripts`	`404.ftl`	Default error template for all 404 errors across all packages, scripts, and response formats.
`status.ftl`	`WEB-INF/ classes/ alfresco/ webscripts`	`status.ftl`	Default, out of the box error template for all errors.

Error templates have access to the web script model and the FreeMarker API, like any other response template. Error templates in the package hierarchy have access to the `status` root variable.

Writing Java-Backed Web Scripts

You now have a web script that returns all Whitepapers, and a web script that returns the rating summary for a specific Whitepaper. The next step is to implement a web script that supports the POST method so that people can submit new ratings.

Like all web scripts, the web script that creates ratings will run as the user executing the script. In this case, you are appending **Guest=True** to the URL and so the web script will run as **Guest**. But allowing **Guest** to create data in the repository is not a good idea. That means the web script needs to run as an actual user. One way to handle this would be to set the web script's minimum authentication level to **User**, give named users (or one or more groups) write access to the Whitepapers folder, and make web site users authenticated. But SomeCo doesn't want to set up user accounts for every user who might rate content. Any user ought to be able to rate content whether or not he or she can authenticate with Alfresco as a named user.

The solution is to let **Guest** call the POST URL, but leverage the Alfresco Java API rather than JavaScript as the controller. Why? Because the Java API has the ability to execute code as any named user. In this example, you'll use **admin** as that user. In production, using a user account dedicated to the purpose of creating ratings is a better idea.

> JavaScript or Java controllers? All of the HTTP methods are supported using either API. The JavaScript API is getting more powerful with each release. But in this case, the JavaScript API just doesn't support what's required. Obviously, you can choose what's right for your organization and the task at hand. Some companies choose to standardize on Java controllers across the board. Others prefer the speed of development afforded by JavaScript, using Java only when JavaScript doesn't suffice.

Step-by-Step: Writing a Java-Backed Web Script to Handle Ratings Posts

Let's write a new web script for ratings that handles the POST method to create new rating objects for a specific Whitepaper. Like the web scripts you've seen so far, this is going to involve a FreeMarker template and a descriptor, but instead of using JavaScript for a controller you are going to write a Java class. To let the web script framework know about the Java class, you'll use a new Spring bean configuration file to declare which web script the controller class belongs to.

> Look out for 3.0 package changes. Between 2.2 Enterprise and 3.0 Labs, Alfresco changed some packages and class names in `org.alfresco.web.scripts`. The source code that accompanies the book works with both editions. For Java-based web script controllers, there are two separate Eclipse projects—one for each edition. If you are building as you go and working only with a single edition, there is no need for you to maintain the separation.

Follow these steps:

1. First, create the descriptor. This script handles the POST method, so name the descriptor `rating.post.desc.xml` and populate it as follows:

```
<webscript>
  <shortname>Post Content Rating</shortname>
  <description>Sets rating data for the specified node
  </description>
  <url>/someco/rating</url>
  <url>/someco/rating.json</url>
  <url>/someco/rating.html</url>
  <format default="json">extension</format>
  <authentication>guest</authentication>
  <transaction>requiresnew</transaction>
</webscript>
```

2. The response templates simply echo back the node, rating, and user argument values that were used to create the new rating. First, create the HTML response template called `rating.post.html.ftl`:

```
<html>
    <body>
        <p>Successfully added rating:</p>
        <p>Node:${node}</p>
        <p>Rating:${rating}</p>
        <p>User:${user}</p>
        <p><a href="${url.service}?id=${node}">Show rating</a></p>
    </body>
</html>
```

3. Then, create the JSON response template called `rating.post.json.ftl`:

```
{"rating" :
        {
          "node" : "${node}",
          "rating" : "${rating}",
          "user" : "${user}"
        }
}
```

4. Now write the Java code. First, write the business logic for creating the rating. Just as you did in the JavaScript-based controller when you put the business logic in the `rating.js` file to promote reuse, you're going to use the Rating bean you created in an earlier chapter for the new `create()` method. The class is `com.someco.behavior.Rating`. Begin the new method by accepting the `NodeRef` of the Whitepaper, the rating value, and the user posting the rating as arguments.

5. First, implement the web script's controller logic. All you have to do is write a Java class that grabs the ID, rating, and rater arguments and then creates the new rating node. To do that, create a new class in **src|java** called `com.someco.scripts.PostRating`. The class name isn't significant but following a descriptive naming convention is helpful, particularly if there will be a large number of Java-backed web scripts. The class must extend `org.alfresco.web.scripts.DeclarativeWebScript`:

```
public class PostRating extends org.alfresco.web.scripts.
                                      DeclarativeWebScript {
```

6. The Node Service will be injected as a dependency by Spring:

```
private NodeService nodeService;
```

7. The controller logic goes in the `executeImpl()` method. The first thing you need to do after declaring the method is initialize the `ratingValue` variable and grab the ID, rating, and user arguments:

```
@Override
protected Map<String, Object> executeImpl(WebScriptRequest req,
                                          WebScriptStatus status) {
    int ratingValue = -1;
    String id =      req.getParameter("id");
    String rating = req.getParameter("rating");
    String user = req.getParameter("user");
```

8. Next, attempt to parse the rating value. If an exception is thrown, move forward with the initialized value, which will get caught during the range check:

```
try {
    ratingValue = Integer.parseInt(rating);
} catch (NumberFormatException nfe) {
}
```

9. The parameters are all required. Web scripts do not yet enforce mandatory arguments. So the controller does the checking and sets an error code if there is a problem. If all arguments have been provided and the rating is in the range we are looking for, grab the `NodeRef` based on the ID passed in, check with the `nodeService` to make sure it exists, and then call the `create()` method that you will implement shortly:

```
if (id == null || rating == null || rating.equals("0") ||
                                         user == null) {
    logger.debug("ID, rating, or user not set");
    status.jsSet_code(400);
    status.jsSet_message("Required data has not been provided");
    status.jsSet_redirect(true);
```

```
    } else if ((ratingValue < 1) || (ratingValue > 5)) {
      logger.debug("Rating out of range");
      status.setCode(400);
      status.setMessage("Rating value must be between 1 and 5
                                                  inclusive");
       status.setRedirect(true);
    } else {
      NodeRef curNode = new NodeRef("workspace://SpacesStore/"
                                                  + id);

      if (!nodeService.exists(curNode)) {
         logger.debug("Node not found");
         status.jsSet_code(404);
         status.jsSet_message("No node found for id:" + id);
         status.jsSet_redirect(true);
      } else {
         ratingBean.create(curNode, Integer.parseInt(rating),
                                                  user);

      }

    }
```

10. The rating data that was passed in needs to set on the model so that it can be echoed back by the response templates:

```
   Map<String, Object> model = new HashMap<String, Object>();
   model.put("node", id);
   model.put("rating", rating);
   model.put("user", user);

   return model;
}
```

11. Now implement the `create()` method. This method uses the `runAs` method in `AuthenticationUtil` so that regardless of the permissions of the authenticated user running the web script, the rating node will get created:

```
public void create(final NodeRef nodeRef, final int rating,
                                      final String user) {

         AuthenticationUtil.runAs(new RunAsWork<String>() {
              @SuppressWarnings("synthetic-access")
              public String doWork() throws Exception {
```

12. The method should first ask the `nodeService` if the Whitepaper already has the rateable aspect. If it does, no action is necessary, otherwise, add the aspect:

```
              // add the aspect to this document if it needs it
              if (nodeService.hasAspect(nodeRef, SomeCoModel.ASPECT_
              SC_RATEABLE)) {
```

```
        } else {
            nodeService.addAspect(nodeRef, SomeCoModel.ASPECT_
                                    SC_RATEABLE, null);
        }
```

13. Create a new properties map to store the rating and rater properties:

```
        Map<QName, Serializable> props = new HashMap<QName,
                                            Serializable>();
        props.put(SomeCoModel.PROP_RATING, rating);
        props.put(SomeCoModel.PROP_RATER, user);
```

14. Use the node service to create a new ratings node as a child to the Whitepaper, then close out the method:

```
        nodeService.createNode(
            nodeRef,
            SomeCoModel.ASSN_SC_RATINGS,
            QName.createQName(SomeCoModel.NAMESPACE_
              SOMECO_CONTENT_MODEL, SomeCoModel.PROP_RATING.
                    getLocalName() + new Date().getTime()),
            SomeCoModel.TYPE_SC_RATING,
            props);
        return "";
    }
  },
  "admin");
}
```

15. Complete the class by adding a setter for the `nodeService`:

```
public void setNodeService(NodeService nodeService) {
    this.nodeService = nodeService;
}
}
```

16. Save the class.

17. You need to tweak the Rating behavior class. When a new rating gets added, the properties on the object being rated get set. Just like the create method, the behavior needs to work even for users without the permissions needed to change the object's properties. First update the `addRating()` method:

```
...
total = total + rating;
count = count + 1;
average = total / new Double(count);
setParentProperties(parentRef, average, total, count);
return;
...
```

18. Then, implement the `setParentProperties()` method by wrapping the old property setters with the `AuthenticationUtil.runAs` method:

```
protected void setParentProperties(final NodeRef parentRef, final
            Double average, final int total, final int count) {
    AuthenticationUtil.runAs(new RunAsWork<String>() {
        @SuppressWarnings("synthetic-access")
        public String doWork() throws Exception {
            // store the average on the parent node
            nodeService.setProperty(parentRef, SomeCoModel.
                                    PROP_AVERAGE_RATING, average);
            nodeService.setProperty(parentRef, SomeCoModel.
                                    PROP_TOTAL_RATING, total);
            nodeService.setProperty(parentRef, SomeCoModel.
                                    PROP_RATING_COUNT, count);
            if (logger.isDebugEnabled()) logger.debug("
                                        Property set");
            return "";
        }
    },
    "admin");
}
```

19. Now you need to let the web script framework know that this new class is the controller for the rating web script. Create a new Spring bean configuration file in **|config|alfresco|extension** called `someco-scripts-context.xml` with the following content:

```xml
<?xml version='1.0' encoding='UTF-8'?>
<!DOCTYPE beans PUBLIC '-//SPRING//DTD BEAN//EN' 'http://www.
                    springframework.org/dtd/spring-beans.dtd'>

<beans>
    <bean id="webscript.com.someco.ratings.rating.post" class="com.
                someco.scripts.PostRating" parent="webscript">
        <property name="nodeService">
            <ref bean="NodeService" />
        </property>
    </bean>
</beans>
```

20. Deploy the new web script.

Once you get the UI widget wired in, it will be easier to test. For now, go to the Web Script home page and refresh the list of web scripts. Verify that your new web script shows up. To navigate to the index for the new web script directly, go to this URL:

```
http://localhost:8080/alfresco/service/index/package/com/someco/
ratings
```

You should see:

```
Post Content Rating

POST /alfresco/service/someco/rating

POST /alfresco/service/someco/rating.json

POST /alfresco/service/someco/rating.html

Description:      Sets rating data for the specified node

Authentication:  guest

Transaction:     none

Format Style:    extension

Default Format:  json

Id: com/someco/ratings/rating.post

Description:      classpath:alfresco/extension/templates/webscripts/
com/someco/ratings/rating.post.desc.xml
```

Using the Correct ID for Web Script Beans

The web script framework uses the bean's ID to find Java-based web script controllers. The ID follows a naming convention. The convention is:

```
webscript.package.service-id.method
```

In this example, the package is `com.someco.ratings`, the service ID is `rating`, and the HTTP method is `post`. If you don't follow this convention, the bean won't be registered as a controller for the web script. You won't see an error. The code simply fails to get called.

Another potential gotcha is the "parent" attribute of the "bean" element. The parent bean is the singular "webscript" here versus the plural "webscripts", which is how Data Dictionary web script folders are named. That's an easy one to miss and kind of hard to debug.

Using both Java and JavaScript for Controller Logic

Using a Java-backed web script doesn't exclude the use of JavaScript for a particular web script. If you have both a Java class and a JavaScript file, the Java class gets executed first followed by the JavaScript. The script has access to everything the Java class put in the model, and can update the model before passing it along to the response template.

This is potentially confusing because people who try to support your web script may see the JavaScript controller and initially assume it is solely responsible for the controller logic. Compounding the problem is the fact that Java beans are wired in via Spring, and the context files are not located near the web scripts. To lessen the potential maintenance headaches, put all of your logic for a given web script either in JavaScript or Java, but not both.

Wiring a Web Script to UI Widgets

SomeCo wants to show a graphical ratings widget on its web page. When the user clicks a star, it should post the corresponding rating to Alfresco. In a subsequent example, you'll see how to leverage the widget on SomeCo's web site. For this example, you are going to add the ratings widget to the HTML response for the rating web script. That will let you test both the widget and the rating POST.

The ratings widget is based on code from Laurent Haan's tutorial at `http://www.progressive-coding.com/tutorial.php?id=6`. Most of it is unchanged with the exception of changing the ratings from being 0-indexed to 1-indexed. It's also been modified as per the instructions found at `progressive-coding.com` to leverage the Prototype JavaScript library. Laurent's code is included here with his permission.

Recall that in the earlier rating example, the HTML response simply showed the rating summary data for a given Whitepaper. The goal now is to enhance that response with the rating widget so that the POST can be tested. The following figure shows what the response will look like when you are done. This example Whitepaper node has **2 Ratings** and an average rating of **3**:

Back to the list of whitepapers

Node: 16c15c7f-1de5-11dd-8189-03f52b46d68a

Average: 3

# of Ratings: 2

Rater:

Rating: ☆☆☆☆☆

Delete ratings for this node

The purpose of the rating widget is two-fold. First, it graphically displays the average rating for a Whitepaper. Second, each star in the widget is hot. When you click one of the rating stars, an asynchronous post is made to **|someco|rating**, which causes a new rating object to get created. The value of the rating posted depends on the star clicked. The person submitting the rating would normally be passed in based on some sort of credential, maybe from a portal session or a cookie. In this example, you are going to add a field to the page so that you can specify any value you want for the rater.

Step-by-Step: Using a Widget to Post Ratings

Adding the ratings widget to the rating web script HTML is going to involve creating a new client-side JavaScript file, copying the widget-related icons to the images directory, and modifying the existing FreeMarker template with additional HTML and AJAX calls to make the widget functional.

Here are the steps:

1. First, edit the `rating.get.html.ftl` file to add new HTML related to the rater field and the rating widget. The DIV is where the rating widget will be displayed. Notice how its ID uses the Whitepaper's NodeRef. That makes the ID unique, and allows you to figure out which rating widget got clicked when there is more than one on a page:

    ```
    <p><a href="${url.serviceContext}/whitepapers.
            html?guest=true">Back to the list</a> of whitepapers</p>
    <p>Node: ${args.id}</p>
    <p>Average: ${rating.average}</p>
    <p># of Ratings: ${rating.count}</p>
    <form name="login">
       Rater:<input name="userId"></input>
    </form>
    Rating: <div class="rating" id="rating_${args.id}" style="display:
                                inline">${rating.average}</div>
    ```

2. Now work on the JavaScript. The rating widget has an associated JavaScript file that needs to be referenced in the head element. There is also a dependency on the prototype JavaScript library. Modify the contents as follows:

    ```
    <head>
       <script src="${url.context}/someco/javascript/prototype.js"
                                type="text/javascript"></script>
       <script src="${url.context}/someco/javascript/rating-script.js"
                                type="text/javascript"></script>
    </head>
    ```

3. Now add JavaScript to the "script" section. The `submitRating()` function gets called when a star in the rating widget is clicked. Its job is to figure out the widget that was clicked on (as identified by the node ID), the star that was clicked on, and the user who clicked it:

```
function submitRating(evt) {
var tmp = Event.element(evt).getAttribute('id').substr(5);
var widgetId = tmp.substr(0, tmp.indexOf('_'));
var starNbr = tmp.substr(tmp.indexOf('_')+1);
if (document.login.userId.value != undefined && document.login.
                                        userId.value != "") {
   curUser = document.login.userId.value;
} else {
   curUser = "jpotts";
}
postRating(widgetId, starNbr, curUser);
}
```

Add the `postRating()` function. It is responsible for making the AJAX call to the rating web script. You're already using prototype for the widget. You can leverage prototype's AJAX functions to make the post:

```
function postRating(id, rating, user) {
    var url = "${url.serviceContext}/someco/rating?id=" + id +
              "&rating=" + rating + "&guest=true&user=" + user;
          new Ajax.Request(url, {
             method:"post",
              onSuccess: function(transport) {
               var response = transport.responseText || "no
                                           response text";
               alert("Success: \n\n" + response);
                window.location.reload(true);
              },
              onFailure: function(){ alert('Post not
                                       successful') }
          });
}
```

4. The last bit of JavaScript initializes the rating widget events:

```
function initEvents() {
    init_rating();
    $$('.rating').each(function(n){
          n.immediateDescendants().each(function(c){
          Event.observe(c, 'click', submitRating);
          });
    });
}
Event.observe(window, 'load', initEvents);
```

5. Create a new script in **|src|web|someco|javascript** called `rating-script.js`. This is the rating widget-specific code provided by `progressive-code.com`. The icon references point to the star icons that you are about to copy into the project:

```
var NUMBER_OF_STARS = 5;
function init_rating() {
    var ratings = document.getElementsByTagName('div');
    for (var i = 0; i < ratings.length; i++) {
        if (ratings[i].className != 'rating')
            continue;

        var rating = ratings[i].firstChild.nodeValue;
        ratings[i].removeChild(ratings[i].firstChild);
        if (rating > NUMBER_OF_STARS || rating < 0)
            continue;
        for (var j = 1; j <= NUMBER_OF_STARS; j++) {
            var star = document.createElement('img');
            if (rating >= 1) {
                star.setAttribute('src', '/alfresco/someco/images/
                                        stars/rating_on.gif');
                star.className = 'on';
                rating--;
            } else if(rating > 0 && rating < 1) {
                star.setAttribute('src', '/alfresco/someco/images/
                                        stars/rating_half.gif');
                star.className = 'half';
                rating = 0;
            } else {
                star.setAttribute('src', '/alfresco/someco/images/
                                        stars/rating_off.gif');
                star.className = 'off';
            }
            var widgetId = ratings[i].getAttribute('id').
                                                    substr(7);
            star.setAttribute('id', 'star_'+widgetId+'_'+j);
            star.onmouseover = new Function("evt", "displayHover('
                                    "+widgetId+"', "+j+");");
            star.onmouseout = new Function("evt", "displayNormal('
                                    "+widgetId+"', "+j+");");
            ratings[i].appendChild(star);
        }
    }
}

function displayHover(ratingId, star) {
    for (var i = 1; i <= star; i++) {
```

```
                document.getElementById('star_'+ratingId+'_'+i).
                    setAttribute('src', '/alfresco/someco/images/stars/
                                                rating_over.gif');
        }
    }

    function displayNormal(ratingId, star) {
        for (var i = 1; i <= star; i++) {
            var status = document.getElementById('star_'+ratingId+'_
                                                '+i).className;
            document.getElementById('star_'+ratingId+'_'+i).
                    setAttribute('src', '/alfresco/someco/images/stars/
                                            rating_'+status+'.gif');
        }
    }
```

6. Copy `prototype.js` from the source code that accompanies this chapter into **|src|web|someco|javascript**.

7. Copy the rating widget's star images from the source code that accompanies this chapter into **|src|web|someco|images|stars**.

8. Deploy, restart, and test.

You should now be able to invoke the web script to list the Whitepapers. From there, you can follow the `rating` link to see the rating data for a specific Whitepaper, which includes the rating widget. The ratings widget should be displaying the number of stars based on the current average rating for the Whitepaper. If you click on a star, it should post the appropriate rating to Alfresco.

If you use a specific name in the **Rater** field to post a **Rating**, you can see the value of that user's rating by appending the "user" argument to the URL for either the Whitepaper or rating web scripts:

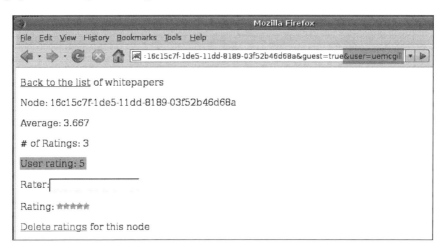

Implementing the Delete Ratings Link

You now know more than enough to implement the **Delete ratings** link on the rating web script HTML response page (`rating.get.html.ftl`) on your own. Here are some hints if you need them:

- In the `rating.get.html.ftl` file, add the AJAX call to the `deleteRatings()` function. The call will be to a new web script you need to write.

- The prototype library handles PUT and DELETE by sending a POST and an argument that specifies the method you really wanted to use. So use a POST instead. The only argument the script needs is the node ID of the Whitepaper that needs to have its ratings cleared.

- Set the required authentication level for the new web script to **admin** to keep guests from deleting ratings. Because you are setting the authentication level to **admin** you won't need to worry about switching the user to **admin** in the controller like you did in the rating post example.

- Decide whether you want to use JavaScript or Java for the controller. If you go the JavaScript route, add a `deleteRatings()` function to the `rating.js` file and call that from your controller. If you go with Java, remember that you'll need to configure the controller as a bean in `someco-scripts-context.xml`.

- If you get stuck, look at the source code that accompanies the chapter.

When you are done, you'll be able to create, read, update, and delete ratings entirely through web scripts.

Adding the Web Script Calls to SomeCo's Whitepaper Web Page

You now have a RESTful API in place for working with Whitepapers and ratings. Now SomeCo's web team can integrate the frontend web site with the Alfresco backend by making calls to the web scripts you created. This book isn't about frontend web development. So rather than having you recreate this code step-by-step, here's a rough outline of the steps the web team went through. At the end of the summary, you can deploy the final product and test it out.

The `|src|web|index.html` page is the only HTML page in SomeCo's web site at the moment. There are three DIVs in the page that need to get updated. If you are following along by looking at the source, search for "GOES HERE" to find the DIVs easily.

Near the top of the page are two references to JavaScript files. The `rating-script-web-site.js` file is a slightly modified version of the `rating-script.js` file used in the earlier `rating.get.html.ftl` example. The `whitepapers.js` file is new. It contains the AJAX and DOM manipulation calls related to retrieving Whitepapers, displaying the Whitepaper detail, and setting the download link:

```
<script type="text/javascript" src="someco/javascript/rating-
script-web-site.js"></script>
<script type="text/javascript" src="someco/javascript/whitepapers.
js"></script>
```

Just below the references to the two JavaScript files is an `init` function. Below that is a **Yahoo User Interface (YUI)** Toolkit event call that calls the `init` function when the DOM has finished loading, which in turn calls `getWhitepapers()`:

```
<script type="text/javascript">
    function init() {
        getWhitepapers("http://localhost:8080/alfresco/service/
        someco/whitepapers?guest=true");
    }
    YAHOO.util.Event.onDOMReady(init);
</script>
```

The `getWhitepapers` function resides in `whitepapers.js`. The function is responsible for using YUI to set up the AJAX call, invoking the call, and setting the callback function. The callback function iterates over the Whitepaper data to build the list of Whitepapers. Once the list is built, it gets set in the DIV on the `index.html` page:

```
function getWhitepapers(url) {
    /*
     * Define the callback object for success and failure
     * handlers as well as object scope.
     */
    var callback =
    {
        success:AjaxObject.handleSuccess,
        failure:AjaxObject.handleFailure,
        scope: AjaxObject
    };

    var AjaxObject = {
        handleSuccess:function(o){
            this.processResult(o);
        },

        handleFailure:function(o){
```

```
                // Failure handler
                alert("Failure");
            },
        processResult:function(o){
            try {
                data = YAHOO.lang.JSON.parse(o.responseText);
                var el = new YAHOO.util.Element("whitepapers-menu");
                el.on('contentReady', function() {
                    for (var i=0; i<data.whitepapers.length; i++) {
                        var whitepaper = data.whitepapers[i];
                        var li = document.createElement('li');
                        var a = document.createElement('a');
                        a.id = "whitepaper-" + i;
                        var div = document.createElement('div');
                          div.id = "rating_" + whitepaper.id;
                        var ratingValue = document.createTextNode
                                            (whitepaper.rating.average);
                        div.appendChild(ratingValue);
                        YAHOO.util.Dom.addClass(div, 'rating');
                        a.href = "javascript:loadWhitepaper(" + i + ");";
                        a.innerHTML = whitepaper.title;
                        a.appendChild(div);
                        li.appendChild(a);
                        YAHOO.util.Dom.addClass(li, 'leaf');
                        el.appendChild(li);
                    }
                    init_rating("http://localhost:8080/alfresco/service/
                                            someco/rating");
                });
            } catch(e) {
                alert("Invalid JSON string");
            }
        },
    startRequest:function(url) {
        YAHOO.util.Connect.asyncRequest('GET', url, callback, null);
        }
    };
    AjaxObject.startRequest(url);
}
```

Each whitepaper title is hot. When it is clicked, the loadWhitepapers function is called. There is no AJAX going on here—the Whitepapers have already been loaded. The loadWhitepapers function simply sets the Whitepaper detail DIV and the download link based on the Whitepaper that was clicked:

```
function loadWhitepaper(index) {
    var whitepaper = data.whitepapers[index];
    var downloadLink = document.getElementById("topFiles");
    var div = document.createElement('div');
    div.id = "csTopDownload";
    var link = document.createElement('a');
    link.href = whitepaper.link;
    var img = document.createElement('img');
    img.src = whitepaper.icon;
    var linkText = document.createTextNode('Download Whitepaper');
    link.appendChild(img);
    link.appendChild(linkText);
    div.appendChild(link);

    if (downloadLink.hasChildNodes()) {
        downloadLink.replaceChild(div, downloadLink.firstChild);
    } else {
        downloadLink.appendChild(div);
    }

    var whitepaperDescription = document.getElementById("newsContent");
    var descriptionDiv = document.createElement('div');
    YAHOO.util.Dom.addClass(descriptionDiv, 'node');
    var descriptionTitle = document.createElement('h2');
    descriptionTitle.innerHTML = whitepaper.title;
    var descriptionText = document.createElement('p');
    descriptionText.innerHTML = whitepaper.description;
    descriptionDiv.appendChild(descriptionTitle);
    descriptionDiv.appendChild(descriptionText);

    if (whitepaperDescription.hasChildNodes()) {
        whitepaperDescription.replaceChild(descriptionDiv,
                                 whitepaperDescription.firstChild);
    } else {
        whitepaperDescription.appendChild(descriptionDiv);
    }
}
```

The code that handles posting the ratings lives in the `rating-script-web-site.js` file. This file is essentially the same as the `rating-script.js` file used in the `rating.get.html.ftl` example earlier, but it has been changed to (1) not require the `prototype.js` toolkit and (2) use YUI for the AJAX call to post the rating:

```
...
 star.setAttribute('onclick', "javascript:postRating('" + widgetId +
"', " + j + ", '" + rater + "', '" + url + "');");
...
function postRating(id, rating, rater, url) {

    var AjaxObject = {

        handleSuccess:function(o){
            alert("Posted rating");
            refresh_ratings("http://localhost:8080/alfresco/service/
            someco/whitepapers?guest=true");
        },

        handleFailure:function(o){
            // Failure handler
            alert("Failed to post rating");
        },

         startRequest:function(url) {
            YAHOO.util.Connect.asyncRequest('POST', url, callback,
                        "id=" + id + "&rating=" + rating + "&user=" +
                                        rater + "&guest=true");
        }
    };

    AjaxObject.startRequest(url);
}
```

The complete source code for this example is included in a separate project called "web-site" in the source code that accompanies this chapter. You can use Ant to deploy it to the root of your Alfresco web application to see it in action.

> This showed you one very basic example of how to make AJAX calls against web scripts. There are a lot of different frontend toolkits available that can be used to do similar things, which is the whole point of creating a REST API. The first example used Prototype, Alfresco 3.0 uses YUI, and Optaros' streamlined web client, DoCASU, uses EXT JS, just to name a few.

Making Other Types of Content "Rateable"

You've just created a RESTful content ratings widget for Alfresco and you used it to let SomeCo web site users rate Whitepaper content. What's cool, though, is that none of the rating logic depends on the specific "Whitepaper" type. Remember that "rateable" was defined as an aspect. It can get added to any object in the repository. And because the rating web scripts deal with Node IDs, the ratings web scripts and widget will work on anything SomeCo decides to make rateable in the future.

Dealing with the Cross-Domain Scripting Limitation

You may have noticed that all the URL examples use localhost. In fact, for development, SomeCo's HTML pages (Whitepaper index and Whitepaper detail) that make AJAX calls are also on localhost. In real life, however, it is highly likely that the code making AJAX calls to your web scripts will reside on a different host than the one where Alfresco lives. This creates a problem called the "cross-domain scripting limitation". The issue is that for security reasons, browsers don't let you open an XMLHttpRequest to a different host than the one serving the page. There are two ways you can handle this depending on your situation:

- Use a proxy servlet. Servers aren't subject to the browser's security constraints. They can make calls to any host they want. You can easily write your own Java servlet that acts as a reverse proxy. AJAX calls go against the proxy servlet hosted on the same domain as the page making the call, and the proxy servlet then invokes the web script on the other domain, and returns the results to the calling client.

- Use a callback mechanism. Alfresco has a callback mechanism built into the web script runtime. Here's how it works. Although the browser prevents XMLHttpRequests from crossing domains, JavaScript source can be loaded from anywhere. Instead of specifying a real JavaScript file, you specify a web script that returns JSON, appended with an argument called `alf_callback` that specifies a function on your page. When the function is called, the JSON your web script returned is passed in. For example, the following could be added to a page on a server in another domain. When the page is loaded in the browser, the rating web script would be called followed by a call to the callback function. It would in turn display an alert with the average rating value:

```
<script>
   function callbackTest(res) {
      alert("Average:" + res.rating.average);
   }
</script>

<script type="text/javascript" src="http://
code.optaros.com/alfresco/service/someco/rating.
json?id=531c4efd-753a-11dd-80a7-45d54d668b8a&guest=true&alf_
callback=callbackTest"></script>
```

In an effort to try to keep things simple, the example corporate web site is deployed to the root of the Alfresco web application. Because everything is on the same server, the cross-domain limitation isn't an issue.

Handling Form Data

The rating example makes an AJAX call using the POST method. What if, instead of using AJAX you were simply posting an HTML form? The web script framework is able to handle form posts, including multi-part forms.

For example, let's re-do the HelloWorld example as a form post instead of passing the name argument in the query string. We can use a static HTML page to render the form, but for the cost of an extra descriptor let's use a web script for both the GET (to render the form) and the POST (to process the form data). To do this, you'll need two descriptors (one for GET and one for POST), two FreeMarker templates, and a JavaScript controller.

Step-by-Step: Implementing a Form-Based Hello World

To convert the Hello World web script to use a form, do the following:

1. Create a descriptor for the GET called `helloworldform.get.desc.xml` in **|config|alfresco|extension|templates|webscripts|com|someco** with the following content:

```
<webscript>
  <shortname>Hello World Form</shortname>
  <description>Hello world form web script</description>
  <url>/someco/helloworldform</url>
</webscript>
```

2. Create a FreeMarker template for the GET called `helloworldform.get.html.ftl` to present a simple form to capture the name. Add the following content:

```
<html>
<body>
    <form action="${url.service}" method="post">
        Name:<input name="name"><br />
        <input type="submit" name="submit" value="Go!">
    </form>
</body>
</html>
```

3. Now write the web script that handles the POST. Create a POST descriptor called `helloworldform.post.desc.xml` by copying the GET descriptor. The two differ only in name and description.

```
<webscript>
  <shortname>Hello World Form Post</shortname>
  <description>Hello world form post web script</description>
  <url>/someco/helloworldform</url>
</webscript>
```

4. Create a JavaScript controller to put the name in the model. This isn't strictly necessary. You could just grab the argument from the FreeMarket template, but you're going to add to this controller in the next example:

```
model.name = args.name;
```

5. Last, add a FreeMarker template for the POST that echoes back the field value:

```
<html>
<body>
        <p>Hello, ${name}!</p>
</body>
</html>
```

6. Deploy, refresh, and test.

When you navigate your browser to `http://localhost:8080/alfresco/service/someco/helloworldform`, you should see the form returned by the GET FreeMarker template:

When you specify a value and click **Go!**, the controller for the POST extracts the field value and adds it to the model, so the FreeMarker template for the POST can display it.

Step-by-Step: Using File Upload in a Multipart Request

Web scripts can handle multipart forms. That means you can add a file upload control to a form and then do something with that file, such as persist it to the repository.

The previous example was not a multipart form—the fields were passed to the controller as part of the `args` array. When using a multipart form, form fields reside in the `formdata` variable. To handle a file upload, all you have to do is know where to get the fields and the file and then do something with it. Let's modify the example you just did to handle a file upload. Do these steps:

1. Edit the `helloworldform.get.html.ftl` file to change the form to a multipart form, and add a file upload control like this:

   ```
   <form action="${url.service}" method="post" enctype="multipart/
                               form-data" accept-charset="utf-8">
       Name:<input name="name"><br />
       File:<input type="file" name="file"><br />
       <input type="submit" name="submit" value="Go!">
       </form>
   ```

2. Change the `helloworldform.post.js` controller. Because this is a multipart form, the fields are in the `formdata` variable. The field object named `file` will have special properties for the filename, mimetype, and the content. First, add the code to extract these values:

   ```
   for each (field in formdata.fields) {
      if (field.name == "name") {
         model.name = field.value;
      }
      if (field.name == "file" && field.isFile) {
         filename = field.filename;
         content = field.content;
         mimetype = field.mimetype;
      }
   }
   ```

3. Then, add code that grabs a folder to save the content to, creates the content, sets some properties, and saves the new node:

```
var results = search.luceneSearch("+PATH:\"app:company_home/*\"
+TYPE:\"cm:folder\" +@cm\\:name:\"Someco\"");
var targetFolder = results[0];
var newDoc = targetFolder.createFile(filename); newDoc.properties.
content.write(content); newDoc.properties.content.mimetype =
mimetype;
newDoc.save();
```

4. The first form example didn't touch the repository, so no authentication or transaction was needed. This one does, though. To avoid making you tweak the permissions in the web client, let's just use admin as the required authentication level. The GET doesn't need a transaction, but the POST does. Modify the `helloworld.get.desc.xml` file as follows:

```
<shortname>Hello World Form</shortname>
<description>Hello world form web script</description>
<url>/someco/helloworldform</url>
<authentication>admin</authentication>
<transaction>none</transaction>
```

5. Modify the `helloworld.post.desc.xml` file as follows:

```
<shortname>Hello World Form Post</shortname>
<description>Hello world form post web script</description>
<url>/someco/helloworldform</url>
<authentication>admin</authentication>
<transaction>required</transaction>
```

6. Deploy, refresh, and test.

Now when you point your browser to `http://localhost:8080/alfresco/service/someco/helloworldform`, you will see the new file upload control:

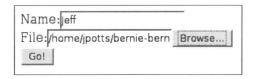

After setting the name, selecting a file, and clicking **Go!**, you'll see the same output as from the previous example. But if you log in to the web client and go to the Someco folder, you should see the newly persisted file.

Customizing the Web Client with Web Scripts

Web scripts are not limited just to being an easy way to interface other applications with the repository. They can be used to customize or extend the existing web client. The web client delivered as part of 3.0 is based entirely on web scripts. The "classic" web client can also leverage web scripts. You could create custom components that make web script calls via AJAX. For example, maybe SomeCo wants Alfresco users to be able to use the ratings widget you created earlier from within the web client.

One hook that can help you leverage web scripts from within the web client is the "webscript" JSP tag. You can use it to call any web script from any JSP running within the Alfresco web application. For example, suppose you wanted to let SomeCo users add the Whitepaper list as a dashlet to the Alfresco dashboard. In the real world, you'd spend some time making it a bit more presentable. For this example, you'll take the HTML response of the Whitepaper list web script and make it display as an Alfresco dashlet.

Step-by-Step: Running a Web Script as a Dashlet

You've already developed the web script. Making it run as a dashlet is a matter of writing a two-line JSP page and configuring the page as a dashlet in `web-client-config-custom.xml`. To do this, follow these steps:

1. Create a new JSP page called `whitepapers.jsp` in **|src|web|jsp|extension |dashlets**. The page uses the `webscript` tag to call the Whitepapers script. The user argument comes from the `NavigationBean's` `currentUser` property:

   ```
   <%@ taglib uri="/WEB-INF/repo.tld" prefix="r" %>
   <r:webScript scriptUrl="/wcs/someco/whitepapers.html?user=#{
                        NavigationBean.currentUser.userName}" />
   ```

2. Configure the JSP as a dashlet in `web-client-config-custom.xml` by adding a new configuration element as follows:

   ```
   <!-- Alfresco dashboard config -->
   <config evaluator="string-compare" condition="Dashboards">
      <dashboards>
         <dashlets>
            <dashlet id="someco-whitepapers-webscript" label="
                                                SomeCo Whitepapers"
                     description="SomeCo Whitepapers WebScript"
   ```

```
                              jsp="/jsp/extension/dashlets/whitepapers.jsp" />
                </dashlets>
              </dashboards>
            </config>
```

3. Deploy, restart, and test.

To test the new dashlet, log in to the web client and click the **Configure** button on the Alfresco dashboard. After selecting the desired layout, you should see the new dashlet in the list. After you add it and return to the dashboard, you'll see the web script results:

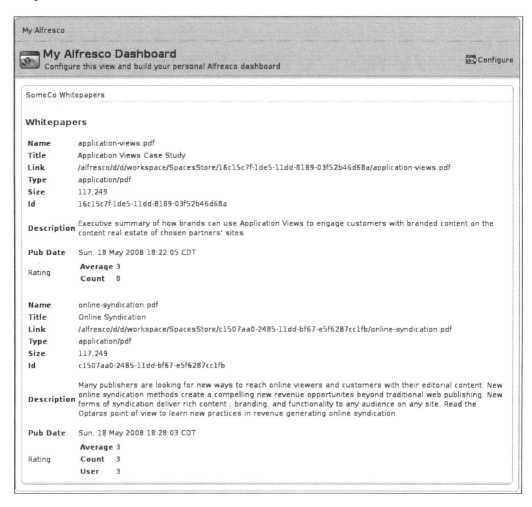

This was a simple example, but it should have your wheels turning. Remember the custom component renderer you created in an earlier chapter in which you told Alfresco to use a graphical traffic light to display the project status instead of the boring text output? Now that you know how to write web scripts, you could follow the same recipe to create a custom component renderer for the average rating property on any object with the rateable aspect. The component could use the "webscript" tag to call a web script. The web script would return all the HTML and JavaScript needed to produce a clickable ratings widget in the property sheet. Similarly, you can create custom dialogs that are populated by web scripts.

Understanding Web Script Runtimes

Web Scripts are executed in a "Web Script Runtime". There are three runtimes available that are out of the box:

1. The servlet runtime executes all web scripts requested via HTTP.
2. The JSF runtime allows JSF components to execute scripts. The dashlet example you just saw leverages the JSF runtime.
3. The JSR-168 runtime allows web scripts to run as portlets.

You can write your own runtime if these don't meet your needs. Alfresco may add more in the future.

Advanced Web Scripts

Now that you have the basics under your belt, let's look at a few advanced web scripts topics.

Running Web Scripts as JSR-168 Portlets

All web scripts are automatically available as JSR-168 portlets. What does this mean? Most portals available today have support for JSR-168, otherwise known as the Portlet 1.0 API (The JSR-286 specification is essentially the next version of the standard or Portlet 2.0.) Theoretically, any portlet developed purely to the portlet API can be run in any portal that is compliant to the specification. The web script framework wraps the web script output in a JSR-168 portlet.

For example, out of the box, Alfresco comes with a **My Spaces** dashlet. The dashlet is implemented as a couple of web scripts (one calls the other via AJAX). If you point your browser to the following URL:

```
http://localhost:8080/alfresco/service/ui/myspaces?p=/Company%20Home/
Someco
```

You can see the web script just as you would if you had added the dashlet to your Alfresco Dashboard:

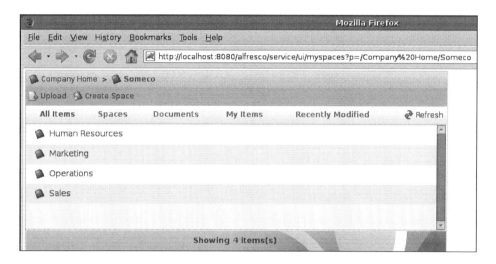

Now suppose you would like to implement an open source portal such as JBoss Portal or Liferay. (Yes, this should work on closed-source portals too, but why would you want to use one of those?) You can run the **My Spaces** web script as a portlet without touching the web script code. Setting up a portal is beyond the scope of this book. The Appendix includes high-level instructions for deploying Alfresco and Liferay to the same application server instance, which is the easiest way to get web script-based portlets running. Here is a screenshot showing Liferay with the out of the box **My Spaces** web script:

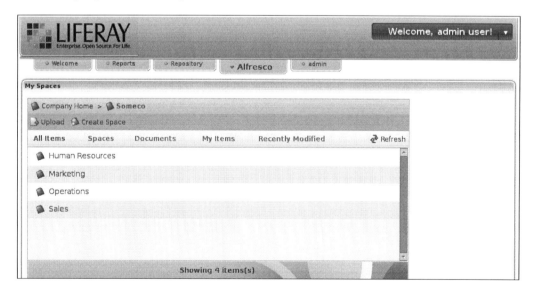

Of course, this works with custom web scripts as well. Here is an example showing a custom **Report Search** portlet. It is backed by two custom web scripts. One web script renders the search form. When the **Search** button is clicked, the query is posted via AJAX to the other web script. It runs the query and returns the **Results**:

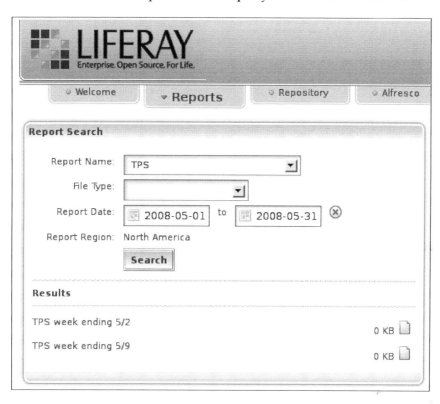

In both examples, what's happening behind the scenes is that the portal is running an instance of a JSR-168 portlet that knows how to execute web scripts. Take a look at a snippet from the `portlet.xml` file used in the **My Spaces** example:

```
<portlet>
    <description>My Spaces</description>
    <portlet-name>AlfrescoMySpaces</portlet-name>
    <portlet-class>org.alfresco.web.scripts.portlet.WebScriptPortlet
    </portlet-class>
        <init-param>
            <name>authenticator</name>
            <value>webscripts.authenticator.jsr168.webclient</value>
        </init-param>
```

```
<init-param>
    <name>scriptUrl</name>
    <value>/alfresco/168s/ui/myspaces</value>
</init-param>
<supports>
    <mime-type>text/html</mime-type>
    <portlet-mode>VIEW</portlet-mode>
</supports>
<portlet-info>
    <title>My Spaces</title>
    <short-title>My Spaces</short-title>
</portlet-info>
    </portlet>
```

The `portlet.xml` file tells vital information about the portlets it has available to the portal container. Look at the portlet-class. The `org.alfresco.web.scripts.portlet.WebScriptPortlet` class comes out of the box with Alfresco. Every web script you run as a portlet will use this class.

One of the parameters the `WebScriptPortlet` expects is `scriptUrl`. As you might expect, this parameter points to the URL of the web script the portlet should invoke. Notice that because you are running the web script as a portlet, you need to use the JSR-168 service context, which is `/alfresco/168s`. So, if you were to run the Whitepaper list web script as a portlet, the URL specified in `portlet.xml` would be `/alfresco/168s/someco/whitepapers.html`.

If you need to provide a query string that includes spaces or other characters, don't escape the URL in `portlet.xml`. For example, if SomeCo wanted to run the **My Spaces** web script as a portlet with a hardcoded path pointing to the Human Resources folder, the URL would be:

```
/alfresco/168s/ui/myspaces?p=/Company Home/Someco/Human Resources
```

The obvious exception is any character that prevents the portlet XML from being well-formed such as an ampersand ("&").

Using web scripts to implement portlets can be very efficient from a development perspective. And a portal can often provide a richer, more flexible end user experience than what is currently available with Alfresco alone.

For more information on installing and configuring Liferay, including integrating Liferay with Alfresco and a Single Sign-On (SSO) solution, see *Liferay Portal Enterprise Intranets*, Jonas X. Yuan, Packt Publishing, April 2008.

Dealing with Web Script Authentication

How web scripts authenticate depends on the runtime you are using. HTTP-based web scripts, such as the ones you built to work with Whitepapers and ratings, are configured out of the box to use basic authentication. If you invoke a web script that requires a higher level of authentication than what's already taken place, the browser will present a basic authentication login dialog.

Web scripts executing in the context of the JSF runtime run within the web client. They simply leverage the web client's session.

Web scripts running in the context of the JSR-168 runtime will use the web client session if it is there. If it isn't, they will try to use the JSR-168 authenticator that uses the portal credentials. These portal credentials in turn try to establish a session with Alfresco. If that doesn't work, a Basic Authentication dialog will be displayed.

If you have Alfresco configured to leverage an SSO provider such as CAS, web scripts will leverage the session created when the user logs in to the centralized login page. Although a specific web script example isn't provided, the Appendix contains high-level instructions for installing CAS and integrating it with Alfresco.

If you are writing your own web pages that need to invoke authenticated web scripts, one approach is to use a web service call to get a ticket. The ticket is then added to the request header. Here is snippet from com.someco.examples. SomeCoWebScriptInvoker (included with your source) that shows how to use this approach:

```
AuthenticationUtils.startSession(getUser(), getPassword());
setTicket(AuthenticationUtils.getTicket());
URL scriptUrl = (new URI(getScriptUrl())).toURL();

System.out.println("Invoking: " + scriptUrl);

conn = (HttpURLConnection)scriptUrl.openConnection();

conn.setRequestMethod(getMethod());

conn.setRequestProperty("Authorization", "Basic " + Base64.
                encodeBytes((getTicket()).getBytes()));
conn.connect();
```

In this case, `SomeCoWebScriptInvoker` is a runnable class that uses the Alfresco Web Services API to get the ticket, and then invokes the web script via HTTP. A web page could work similarly. The web site would have a login page. The code handling the login post would make the web service call to get the ticket, and the ticket would be added to the header of subsequent web script requests.

If you don't want to go the Web Services API route, there is a web script that can give you a ticket based on username and password:

```
http://localhost:8080/alfresco/service/api/login?u=admin&pw=admin
```

This method isn't preferred, though, because the username and password are included in the query string.

Controlling Web Script Cache

The web script descriptor includes a `cache` element that can be used to attempt to influence how the web script response is cached. The following snippet shows how the cache is configured by default:

```
<webscript>
...
  <cache>
    <never>true</never>
    <public>false</public>
    <mustrevalidate>true</mustrevalidate>
  </cache>
</webscript>
```

The cache settings are used as follows:

- Setting the `never` element to `true` says that the response should never be cached.
- Specifying `false` for the `public` element means that the response should not be stored in a public cache.
- Setting the `mustrevalidate` element to `true` indicates that the response contains dynamic content, and that the cache should always check to ensure it has the most up-to-date response.

As you can see, by default, web scripts are not configured to be cache-friendly. It is important to remember, however, that the web script runtime may or may not support the cache settings, and that caching the response is not the responsibility of the web script run time. It is handled by the proxy sitting in front of the web script and the client making the request.

In the case of HTTP web scripts, the default settings create the following cache-related HTTP response headers:

```
Cache-Control: no-cache

Pragma: no-cache
```

The most cache-friendly configuration for a web script would look like this:

```
<cache>
  <never>false</never>
  <public>true</public>
  <mustrevalidate>false</mustrevalidate>
</cache>
```

With this configuration in place, the cache-related response headers no longer contain the `pragma` setting, and `Cache-Control` is set to `public`.

Cache settings made in the descriptor can be overridden at runtime by manipulating the `cache` root object from within the controller. See the Appendix for a complete listing of JavaScript root objects, including the cache variable.

Executing Remote Web Scripts

Up to this point, all of the web scripts you've executed have run in the same process as the Alfresco repository. You can run web applications on other servers that talk to those web scripts. But the actual execution of the web scripts takes place within the web script runtime executing inside the Alfresco process. But what if you wanted to execute web scripts in a separate process or even on a different physical machine?

Beginning in the 2.9 Labs release, the web script framework can be run separately from the core Alfresco web application. Building the "webscript framework" project produces not only the `alfresco-webscript-framework.jar`, which contains the classes needed to compile and execute web scripts, but also the `alfwsf.war`. The WAR can be deployed to a servlet container (and embedded in your own custom web applications) to provide a standalone web script execution environment.

In 3.0 Labs, the concept of de-coupling the web script framework from the Alfresco repository process has evolved into a full-fledged web application framework called **Surf**. Surf gives you all the power of the web script framework without being tied to the Alfresco repository. You can deploy Surf web applications anywhere and still make remote calls to web scripts running on the Alfresco server. Because Surf is based on web scripts, you build Surf apps with the tools you are already familiar with: FreeMarker and Java or JavaScript. The Appendix has further details on the new framework.

Refactoring the Rating Service

The examples in this chapter centered on enabling user-generated ratings for content in the repository. Ratings can be added by JavaScript or Java code simply by creating Rating nodes and letting the behavior kick in to calculate the actual rating statistics.

Everything works, but the logic used to create ratings nodes is a bit scattered. In some cases, logic is duplicated across JavaScript libraries and Java classes. Partly that was done on purpose to show both Java and JavaScript examples, but that kind of sprawl could easily happen on a real-world project. Wouldn't it be better if there was a true service for handling ratings? Alfresco does this all the time. The Node Service, Search Service, and Person Service are just a few examples. (There's a list in the Appendix.)

There are several reasons why creating a Rating Service makes sense:

- It centralizes all business logic
- It is consistent with Alfresco's pattern
- We can easily add method security, transaction requirements, and auditing annotations
- It can be easily wrapped to expose the service as a root object accessible by server-side JavaScript

Those are convincing points, but what's involved? Rather than provide a step-by-step guide, here is a summary that outlines how to establish the service and then modify the examples in this chapter to take advantage of it. Look at the source code that accompanies this chapter to see the code in full.

Start by defining an interface. The `com.someco.service.RatingService` interface should not have any implementation-specific methods. In other words, if someone else wanted to implement a Rating Service that used database tables instead of Alfresco to persist ratings, the interface should still be valid.

Next, write a JUnit test for the interface. You can execute JUnit tests from within Eclipse. If you want to use the same repository as your MySQL-backed development instance, you can. Just make sure the JUnit test can find your configuration. The `setUp()` and `tearDown()` methods might look something like this:

```
public void setUp() throws Exception {
        nodeService = (NodeService) ctx.getBean("NodeService");
        ratingService = (RatingService) ctx.getBean("
                                        RatingService");
        authenticationComponent = (AuthenticationComponent) ctx.
        getBean("authenticationComponent");

        this.authenticationComponent.setSystemUserAsCurrentUser();
```

```
    }
    @Override
    protected void tearDown() throws Exception {
        authenticationComponent.clearCurrentSecurityContext();
        super.tearDown();
    }
```

With a repeatable way to test the service, the next step is to implement the interface. The `com.someco.service.RatingServiceImpl` class should contain only the logic to get and create rating nodes and properties. Let the behavior continue to hold the calculation logic. In fact, the `create()` method you added to the PostRating rating controller can be moved over pretty much as is.

Once the implementation class is done, it is time for the Spring setup. Follow the same pattern that Alfresco does. Define a `RatingService` bean as the `public` bean—it will be a proxy to your implementation bean. This is where things such as security, transaction, and audit interceptors can be added if needed. Here is the definition for the `RatingService`:

```
<bean id="RatingService" class="org.springframework.aop.framework.
ProxyFactoryBean">
        <property name="proxyInterfaces">
            <list>
                <value>com.someco.service.RatingService</value>
            </list>
        </property>
        <property name="target">
            <ref bean="ratingServiceImpl"/>
        </property>
        <property name="interceptorNames">
            <list>
                <idref local="RatingService_transaction" />
                <idref local="RatingService_security" />
            </list>
        </property>
    </bean>
```

The `RatingService_transaction` bean defines the transaction modes needed for each of the methods in the service:

```
<bean id="RatingService_transaction" class="org.springframework.
transaction.interceptor.TransactionInterceptor">
        <property name="transactionManager">
            <ref bean="transactionManager"/>
        </property>
```

```
                <property name="transactionAttributes">
                    <props>
                        <prop key="delete*">${server.transaction.mode.
                                                    default}</prop>
                        <prop key="get*">${server.transaction.mode.readOnly}
                        </prop>
                        <prop key="has*">${server.transaction.mode.readOnly}
                        </prop>
                        <prop key="rate*">${server.transaction.mode.default}
                        </prop>
                        <prop key="*">${server.transaction.mode.default}
                        </prop>
                    </props>
                </property>
            </bean>
```

The `RatingService_security` bean declares the permissions needed to execute the service's methods. Here is a snippet:

```
...
<property name="objectDefinitionSource">
    <value>
    com.someco.service.RatingService.hasRatings=ACL_ALLOW
    com.someco.service.RatingService.rate=ROLE_AUTHENTICATED
    com.someco.service.RatingService.deleteRatings=ACL_METHOD.ROLE_
                                                        ADMINISTRATOR
com.someco.service.RatingService.getRatingData=ROLE_AUTHENTICATED
com.someco.service.RatingService.getUserRating=ROLE_AUTHENTICATED
            </value>
</property>
...
```

The bean for the implementation class rounds out the Spring configuration needed for the new service:

```
<bean id="ratingServiceImpl" class="com.someco.service.
RatingServiceImpl" >
    <property name="nodeService">
        <ref bean="NodeService" />
    </property>
    <property name="searchService">
        <ref bean="SearchService" />
    </property>
</bean>
```

At this point, the `RatingService` can be used from anywhere in the Java Foundation API. But what about JavaScript? If the service was a root object available to the JavaScript API, then your new service could be used regardless of the language chosen for the web script controller, and basically anywhere in Alfresco. Doing this involves writing a new class that extends `BaseProcessorExtension` and then configuring it with Spring. Here is a snippet of `com.someco.jscript` to give you a taste:

```
public class Ratings extends BaseProcessorExtension {

    private RatingService ratingService;

    private final ValueConverter valueConverter = new ValueConverter();

    public void rate(ScriptNode scriptNode, int rating, String user) {
        ratingService.rate((NodeRef)valueConverter.convertValueForRepo(s
criptNode), rating, user);
    }

    public void deleteRatings(ScriptNode scriptNode) {
        ratingService.deleteRatings((NodeRef)valueConverter.convertValu
eForRepo(scriptNode));
    }
...
```

The Spring bean for the new class declares the `RatingService` dependency and specifies the name of the root object:

```
<bean id="ratingScript" parent="baseJavaScriptExtension" class="com.
someco.jscript.Ratings">
    <property name="extensionName">
        <value>ratings</value>
    </property>
    <property name="ratingService">
        <ref bean="RatingService" />
    </property>
</bean>
```

Using the service from JavaScript would look like this:

```
ratings.rate(document, 2, person.properties.userName);
logger.log("User rating:" + ratings.getUserRating(document, person.
properties.userName));

var ratingData = ratings.getRatingData(document);

logger.log("Average:" + ratingData.getRating());
logger.log("Count:" + ratingData.getCount());
logger.log("Total:" + ratingData.getTotal());
```

With the `RatingService` in place, the rating-related JavaScript files and Java controllers can be re-factored. Suggestions include:

- Editing `rating.js` to remove anything not used by the JavaScript behavior, which is everything but the `computeAverage` function

- Editing `whitepapers.get.js`, `rating.get.js`, and `addTestRating.js` to use the `ratings` root object to create and retrieve rating data

- Editing `ratingDelete.post.js` to use the `ratings` root object to delete ratings

- Editing `PostRating.java` to make a call to `RatingService` instead of using its own `create()` method to create new rating nodes

The source code that accompanies this chapter includes the Rating Service and the recommended changes mentioned. The original code you wrote during the exercises has been commented out for comparison.

Summary

This chapter gave you an introduction to the Alfresco Web Script Framework. You began with a very simple Hello World script and then gradually moved to more complex examples culminating in a REST API for retrieving Whitepapers, getting the average rating for a specific Whitepaper, posting new ratings for a given Whitepaper, and deleting all ratings for a specific Whitepaper.

The SomeCo web site was able to leverage the web scripts to add a Whitepaper listing along with a graphical ratings widget. The widget, the web scripts, and the backend model are generic enough to be used for other types of content as well.

Other takeaways from this chapter include:

- Web scripts are composed of an XML descriptor, one or more FreeMarker templates (one for each response format), and, optionally, a controller.

- Controllers can be implemented as JavaScript or Java, and have full access to the Alfresco API. Controllers share data with the view via the model, which is essentially a HashMap.

- The URL structure and the arguments a web script accepts are completely up to you.

- Web Scripts execute in a runtime. Alfresco ships with a servlet runtime for HTTP requests, a JSF runtime used by the `r:webScript` tag, and a JSR-168 runtime used to run web scripts as JSR-168 portlets.

- The level of authentication (**none**, **guest**, **user**, **admin**) required for a web script is defined in the descriptor. How a web script authenticates depends on the runtime.

- Web scripts can be deployed to either the file system or the repository. Regardless of where they are deployed, the web script directory can be used to browse and refresh the available web scripts.

- The 3.0 Surf web application framework is based on web scripts. Unlike 2.x web scripts, Surf components do not have to run on the same server as the Alfresco repository process.

- Centralizing business logic into a service is a good practice. In this chapter, you created a Rating Service that centralized all logic related to creating Rating nodes. It then exposed the service as a root object to the JavaScript API to make it available to both Java and JavaScript code.

Alfresco's Web Script Framework provides an easy way to integrate with the Alfresco repository. It is especially attractive when you are writing frontend code that leverages JavaScript toolkits, because those toolkits heavily utilize REST and AJAX. The framework will become even more important as Alfresco rolls out its new web script-based clients, and, hopefully, as you and others develop interesting and useful web script-based modules for the community.

7
Advanced Workflow

Every organization has business processes that lend themselves to automation. Often, these business processes are content-centric. In Chapter 1, you learned that Alfresco has two separate approaches to handling content-centric business processes: simple or basic workflows and advanced workflows. In this chapter, you'll explore Alfresco's advanced workflow capability provided by the embedded JBoss jBPM workflow engine.

Specifically, in this chapter you will learn:

- What workflow is and why you need a workflow engine
- How to create business process definitions using both a text editor and the JBoss Graphical Process Designer
- The steps required to expose a custom business process to the Alfresco web client user interface
- How to add logic to workflows using Beanshell expressions, JavaScript, and Java
- How to create an asynchronous process involving the Workflow Service, Alfresco Web Scripts, and actions
- How to debug workflows using Alfresco's workflow console
- How to compare Alfresco's two options for workflow (advanced workflows and basic workflows)

What is a Workflow?

When Alfresco released version 1.4, it made a huge leap forward in enterprise readiness. That was the release when Alfresco embedded the JBoss jBPM engine into the product, which meant that enterprises could route Alfresco repository content through complex business processes. Most content has some sort of process around it. That's why content repositories almost always have a mechanism to streamline, facilitate, and report against the business processes that produce, consume, or transform the content within them.

[The terms "workflow" and "business process" will be used interchangeably throughout this book.]

But before geeking out on the wonders of graph-based execution languages, let's agree on what the term **workflow** means. Generically, workflow is *a reliably repeatable pattern of activity enabled by a systematic organization of resources...that can be documented and learned* (http://en.wikipedia.org/wiki/Workflow). The term has been around since people started studying the nature of work in the early 20th century in an effort to streamline manufacturing processes.

In fact, in the world of ECM, it is sometimes helpful to think of an assembly line or manufacturing process when thinking about how content flows through an organization. Content is born of raw material (data), shaped and molded by one or more people (collaboration) or machines (systems), reviewed for quality, and delivered to consumers. Content may go through a single process or many subprocesses. Content may take different routes through a process based on certain aspects of that content. The output of an organization or department of knowledge is essentially the content that comes rolling off the assembly line (the collection of workflows that define that organization's business processes).

Although not always formalized or automated, almost everyone in modern society has been involved in a workflow in some way:

- When you submit an insurance claim, you are initiating a workflow.
- If you witness drunk and disorderly conduct on an airline flight and are asked to provide a statement to the airline, you are participating in a workflow. (Seriously, it happens more often than you'd think.)
- When you check on the status of your loan application, you are asking for metadata about a running workflow.

- When someone brings you a capital request that requires your approval because it is over a certain dollar amount, a characteristic of that request (the dollar amount) has triggered a decision within the workflow that routes the capital request to you.

- When you give the final approval for a piece of web content to be published, it is likely that you are completing a workflow.

As varied as these examples are, all of them have a couple of things in common that make them relevant to ECM: (1) they are examples of human-to-human and, in some cases, human-to-machine interaction and (2) they are content- or document-centric.

These are two very important characteristics that help clarify the kind of workflow most relevant to the ECM space. There are standalone workflow engines (jBPM is one of them) that can be used to model and execute all sorts of "repeatable patterns of activity" with or without content. But in the world of ECM, patterns involving humans working with content are the focus. Of course, document-centric workflows may include fully automated steps and machine-to-machine interactions. The point is that document-centric workflows in which humans review, approve, or collaborate in some way are in the scope of the discussion, while processes that run lights-out system-to-system orchestration or integration are not.

Workflow Options

Some of you are saying, "You're right. Workflows are everywhere. I could really streamline my organization by moving processes currently implemented with email, phone calls, and cubical drive-bys into a more formalized workflow. What are my options?" Let's talk about three: roll your own, standalone workflow engines, and embedded workflow engines.

Roll your own. People are often tempted to meet their workflow requirements with custom code. Very basic systems might be able to get by with a single flag on a record or an object that declares the status of the content such as "Draft", or "In Review", or "Approved". But flags only capture the "state" of a piece of content. If you want to automate how content moves from state to state, the coding and maintenance becomes more complex. Sure, you can write code as part of your application that knows that once Draft documents are submitted for review, they need to go to Purchasing first, and then to Finance, if and only if the requested cash outlay is more than $10m. But do you really want to write it?

People intent on rolling their own workflow often realize the maintenance problem this creates. So they create an abstraction used to describe the flow from state to state that keeps them from embedding that logic in compiled code. Once they've done that, they've essentially created their own proprietary workflow engine that no one else in the world knows how to run or maintain. And with all of the open source workflow engines available, this seems like a particularly flagrant waste of resources.

For these reasons, the "roll your own" option is really not recommended for any but the most basic workflow requirements.

Standalone engines. There are a number of standalone workflow engines, both open source and proprietary. They are sometimes more broadly referred to as **BPM** (**Business Process Management**) systems. These are often extremely robust and scalable solutions that can be used to model, simulate, and execute any process you can think of, from high-volume loan processing to call center queue management. Often, these workflow engines are implemented in conjunction with a rules engine that lets business users have control over complicated if-then-else decision trees.

Standalone engines are most appropriate for extremely high volume or exceedingly complex solutions involving multiple systems. Another good use for standalone engines is when you are developing a custom application that has workflow requirements. Standalone engines can usually talk to any database or content management repository you might have implemented. But they won't be as tightly integrated into the content management system's user interface as the workflow engine built into a CMS. For this reason, for content-centric solutions that operate mostly within the scope of a CMS, it is usually less complicated (and less expensive) to use the workflow engine embedded within the CMS, provided it has enough functionality to meet the workflow requirements of the business.

Embedded workflow engines. Almost every CMS available today, whether open source or proprietary, has a workflow engine of some sort embedded within it. However, the capability of each of these varies widely.

The major benefit of leveraging an embedded workflow engine is the tight level of integration for users as well as developers. Users can initiate and interact with workflows without leaving the CMS client. Typically, developers customizing or extending the CMS can work with workflows using the core CMS API.

Alfresco is an "embedded workflow engine" example. It embeds JBoss jBPM, which is an example of a standalone engine.

Creating Process Definitions

JBoss jBPM is an open source, standalone workflow engine. OK, it is more than just a standalone workflow engine. JBoss rightly calls jBPM a "platform for graph-based execution languages". Workflow is one of several different domains that can be addressed with a graph-based execution language, but it is the only one this book concerns itself with.

The jBPM engine is responsible for managing deployed processes, instantiating and executing processes, persisting process state and metadata to a relational database (via Hibernate), and tracking task assignment and task lists.

jBPM is built on the idea that any process can be described as a graph or a set of connected nodes. Workflows are described with "process definitions" using an XML-based language called **Java Process Definition Language (jPDL)**. jPDL is one example of a graph-based execution language. Others include BPEL for service orchestration and SEAM pageflow.

In jPDL, each node represents a step in a workflow. Connections between nodes signify the transition from one step to another. Creating a process definition is a matter of creating nodes to represent steps in the process and connecting them with transitions.

Step-by-Step: Creating a Hello World Process Definition

Let's get your feet wet by writing a simple process. Conceptually, the process looks like this:

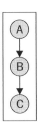

The process has three nodes. Node A and Node C are the Start and Stop nodes. Node B will write a message to the log. For now, you'll implement this process using raw XML and deploy and run it using Alfresco's workflow console. In later examples, you'll use the jBPM Graphical Process Designer to design and deploy the process, and Alfresco's web client to instantiate and run the workflow.

To create a simple Hello World process, follow these steps:

1. In your Eclipse project, create a new folder structure called **|config|alfresco |extension|workflows|HelloWorld**.

2. Within the new `HelloWorld` folder, create a new XML file called `processdefinition.xml` with the following content:

```
<?xml version="1.0" encoding="UTF-8"?>
<process-definition xmlns="urn:jbpm.org:jpdl-3.1"
name="helloWorld">
    <start-state name="start">
        <transition name="" to="hello"></transition>
    </start-state>
    <node name="hello">
        <transition name="" to="end1">
            <action class="org.alfresco.repo.workflow.jbpm.
              AlfrescoJavaScript">
                <script>
                    logger.log("Hello World!");
                </script>
            </action>
        </transition>
    </node>
    <end-state name="end1"></end-state>
</process-definition>
```

3. Save the file.

4. Double-check that in **WEB-INF|classes|log4j.properties** you've got `log4j.logger.org.alfresco.repo.jscript` set to debug.

5. Deploy the customizations using **ant deploy**, and then restart Tomcat.

6. Log in to the web client as admin.

7. Go to the workflow console. The workflow console isn't yet linked in to the UI. You must go directly to the console via `http://localhost:8080/alfresco/faces/jsp/admin/workflow-console.jsp`.

8.   Use the console to deploy the workflow. Type **deploy alfresco | extension | workflows | Hello-world | processdefinition.xml**, and click **Submit**. The console should respond with something similar to:

```
Last command: deploy alfresco/extension/workflows/hello-world/
processdefinition.xml
Duration: 68ms
-----
deployed definition id: jbpm$31 , name: jbpm$helloWorld , title:
helloWorld , version: 8
definition: jbpm$31 , name: helloWorld , version: 8
workflow: None
path: None
```

9.   Now start a workflow using this process definition. The console already has the newly deployed workflow in context, so type **start** and click **Submit**. The console should respond with something similar to:

```
Last command: start
Duration: 84ms
-----
started workflow id: jbpm$8 , def: helloWorld
path: jbpm$8-@ , node: start , active: true
 transition id: [default] , title: Task Done
```

10. As you can see by the console output, the workflow (technically, the workflow's token) is currently sitting on the `start` node. You need to tell it to move to the next node. The path ID in the example above is `jbpm$8-@`, so the command to signal the token is `signal jbpm$8-@`. Type the command appropriate to your path ID and click **Submit**.

11. Check the Alfresco log. The `Hello World!` message should have been printed in the log.

This was almost the simplest process you could possibly define, but you learned that:

*   Processes can be defined with plain XML.

*   Processes can reside in the Alfresco classpath. In this case, you used the extension directory.

*   Processes can be deployed and started using the Alfresco workflow console.

If you were to make changes to the process definition and deploy them, you would need to restart Alfresco. That's because the classloader already has the original definition loaded in memory.

Organizing Processes

If you look at the out of the box process definitions stored in **WEB-INF | classes | alfresco | workflow**, you'll notice that Alfresco chose to put all process definitions in the same directory. I recommend that you do not follow this example because it breaks the deployment tool in the jBPM **Graphical Process Designer** (GPD). Instead, when organizing your own workflows, follow the example in this chapter. Put each process definition in its own directory and name the jPDL file `processdefinition.xml`.

Using the jBPM Graphical Process Designer

One of the nice things about jBPM is that a graphical tool is available as an Eclipse plug-in for creating and deploying process definitions, called the jBPM **Graphical Process Designer** (GPD). The GPD is sometimes called the jBPM jPDL Designer, but that's a relatively recent change. So you'll still see GPD on the JBoss site and that's what this book will use.

There are people in the business of marketing workflow tools who love to say things such as "Using the graphical process designer, business analysts can create advanced workflows without writing any code!" Graphical process designers are definitely useful, but be realistic. Code has to be written. The GPD is most useful for quickly designing the process, setting node properties, and connecting nodes. Once that's done, you will switch over to the XML to finish out the definition.

The GPD also includes the ability to deploy a process directly to the jBPM engine running within Alfresco without leaving Eclipse. That can be a real timesaver, especially when you are still developing the process.

The jBoss GPD is freely available from `http://www.jboss.org/jbossjbpm/ gpd_downloads/`. It installs as an Eclipse plug-in. There are a few different ways to install an Eclipse plug-in. The GPD archive contains a `features` folder and a `plugins` folder. To install the plug-in, expand those folders right over the top of the corresponding folders in your Eclipse home directory and then restart Eclipse. If you do **File | New | Other** and see JBoss jBPM Process Definition as shown below, you've successfully installed the plug-in. If not, try restarting using **eclipse-clean**. If that still doesn't work, double-check that you expanded the GPD archive into the correct location:

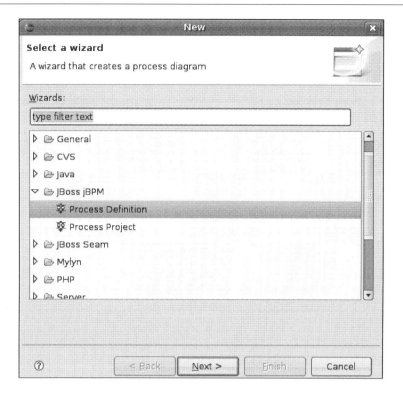

Step-by-Step: Using jBPM Process Designer to Create and Deploy Processes

Let's jazz up the process a bit and this time, instead of raw XML, let's use the GPD to create and deploy the process definition file.

The HelloWorld process definition had a single path. Execution progressed from node A to node B to node C. In practice, however, most workflows have multiple execution paths. Consider the following figure:

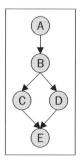

By looking at the transitions, you can see that the path of execution will always be from node A to node B. Node B has two outgoing paths. One path is to node C and the other to node D. The paths converge on node E. Note that from the diagram it is impossible to tell which path will be taken. It's also possible that both could be followed simultaneously.

Let's implement the process described by the diagram using the GPD. The result of that will be a `processdefinition.xml` file just like before. But the GPD will enable you to create it more quickly than you would be able to by writing the XML from scratch. To do this, follow these steps:

1. In the client-extensions Eclipse project, navigate to the `Workflows` directory you created for the Hello World example.

2. Select **File | New | Other | JBoss jBPM Process Definition**. Specify `helloWorldFork` as the process name and click **Finish**.

3   The **Diagram** tab of the GPD should be displayed. The **Diagram** tab is used to lay out the process by selecting node types from the palette (such as **Start**, **End**, **Fork**, **Join**, and **Node**) and clicking on the canvas. Add a **Start**, an **End**, a **Fork**, a **Join**, and two **Nodes** to the canvas.

4. Organize the nodes to appear roughly as they do in the node diagram shown earlier in this section.

5. Node properties can be edited in the tree view of the process or nodes can be double-clicked to open a properties editor. Set the names of the two nodes to **Node C** and **Node D** respectively.

6. The **Transition** tool is used to connect the nodes. Connect the nodes to match the node diagram. When you are done, the process should look like this:

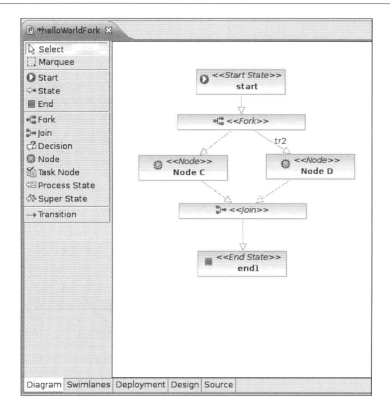

7. Switch to the **Source** tab to see the underlying XML. The XML namespace attribute (xmlns) does not get filled in by the GPD. Specify it now:

```xml
<?xml version="1.0" encoding="UTF-8"?>
<process-definition xmlns="urn:jbpm.org:jpdl-3.1"
                    name="helloWorldFork">
   <start-state name="start">
...
```

8. Add two Hello World messages to this process, one for each transition from nodes **C** and **D**:

```xml
<node name="Node C">
   <transition name="" to="join1">
      <action class=
      "org.alfresco.repo.workflow.jbpm.AlfrescoJavaScript">
         <script>
            logger.log("Hello World! From Node C!");
         </script>
      </action>
   </transition>
```

```
            </node>
            <node name="Node D">
                <transition name="" to="join1">
                    <action class=
                    "org.alfresco.repo.workflow.jbpm.AlfrescoJavaScript">
                        <script>
                            logger.log("Hello World! From Node D!");
                        </script>
                    </action>
                </transition>
            </node>
```

9. Save the file.

10. You could take the process and deploy it right now by running the **ant deploy** task and then deploying from the classpath using the workflow console as you did in the HelloWorld example. But the GPD has a **Deployment** tab that makes deployment a bit easier and has the advantage of allowing repeated deployments without a restart, unlike the classpath method. Switch to the **Deployment** tab. Specify **|alfresco|jbpm|deployprocess** in the **Server Deployer** field and click **Test Connection**. If the server is running, you should see a success message:

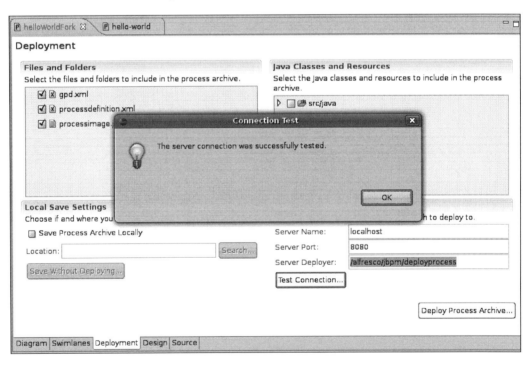

11. Click **Deploy Process Archive** to deploy the process to Alfresco.

 If either the **Test Connection** button or the **Deploy Process Archive** button results in an error, check the application server log for clues.

12. Now test out the new process with the workflow console. Log in to the web client as admin, and go to the workflow console URL (`http://localhost:8080/alfresco/faces/jsp/admin/workflow-console.jsp`).

13. Type **show definitions all** and click **Submit**. You should see an entry for **jbpm$helloWorldFork**. Make a note of its ID, which will look something like **jbpm$32**.

14. Tell the console you want to work in the context of the **helloWorldFork** definition. Type **use definition jbpm$32**, replacing **jbpm$32** with your specific ID, and then click **Submit**.

15. Start a new workflow. Type **start** and click **Submit**. The console should respond with something similar to:

```
started workflow id: jbpm$10 , def: helloWorldFork
path: jbpm$10-@ , node: start , active: true
 transition id: [default] , title: Task Done
```

16. Type **show paths** and click **Submit**. The console should respond with:

```
path id: jbpm$10-@ , node: start
```

17. Signal the path ID. Type **signal jbpm$10-@** and click **Submit**. Check the Alfresco console. You should see that the Hello World string printed for both node transitions.

Tokens

A token is like the "You Are Here" flag for a process—it points to the execution state. The token moves from node-to-node as the process is executed. But it doesn't move on its own. Tokens only move when they are signaled. Let's look at an example. In the figure, when you initially execute the process, the token is at node **A**. Remember in the example that the next step after starting the workflow is to run the **Signal** command. When you signal the token, it will take the only path available to it, which is to move to node **B** where it will wait for a signal. From node **B** there are multiple paths available. If you signal the token without specifying which path to take, it will take a default path. Or, you can tell it which path to take when you send it the signal.

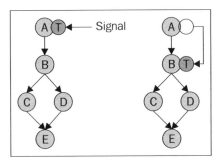

In the HelloWorldFork example, both paths were executed. In the example, the token spawned two child tokens, one for the path from node **B** (the fork) to node **C**, and one from node **B** to node **D**. When the paths converge, the child tokens go away and the parent token resumes.

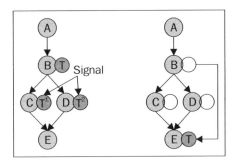

Most of the time, you won't have to concern yourself with token-level detail. There are a few times you might want to know about them:

1. When you write your own node types you are responsible for how tokens are signaled.

2. Process variables (more on those shortly) are scoped to a token.

3. If a process ever gets stuck, you may need to signal the token manually.

Node Types

Nodes are typed (in a Java sense, not in a content sense). A node's type determines how it behaves. You saw in the previous example that both branches in the execution path were executed because both hello world messages showed up in the log. Why didn't the execution proceed down only in a single path? It was because you used a fork, which is a special type of node that spawns concurrent paths of execution. The following table summarizes the node types available in jBPM out of the box:

Node Type	Description
Start State	Only one allowed per process definition. Only outgoing transitions are allowed.
Fork	Spawns multiple concurrent paths of execution.
Join	Joins multiple paths into a single path. A Join acts like a wait state (see below) until all tokens have reached the Join.
Decision	Choice between multiple paths of execution. You'll see examples of how to implement the logic for a decision later in the chapter.
Node	Plain old node. Good for containing an action that might execute business logic.
State	A wait state. Execution does not proceed until the node is explicitly signaled.
Process State	Executes a subprocess. Behaves as a wait state while the subprocess executes.
Task Node	A node that contains one or more tasks assigned to humans.
End State	Only one allowed per process definition. Only incoming transitions are allowed.

It is important to note that if your application has a requirement that isn't addressed by one of the out of the box node types, you can add your own by writing Java code. And, if the behavior of a node type isn't exactly what you need, you can extend it just like you can any Java class.

Versioning Process Definitions

When you check in an updated process definition to the jBPM runtime, jBPM automatically versions the process. On the workflow console, when you run `show definitions all`, the response includes every version of every process definition currently deployed.

You may be wondering what happens to running workflow instances when a new version of the process definition is checked in. The answer is that jBPM handles that gracefully. It makes sure that running workflows continue to run with their original process definition. All new workflows will use the most current process definition.

Deploying Dependencies

If you are writing complex processes that depend on resources beyond just the definition, you can optionally package those dependencies along with your process definition into a **Process Archive (PAR)** file (like a JAR file, a PAR file is just a ZIP). The **Java Classes and Resources** section of the **Deployment** tab is used to associate dependencies with the process, so the GPD knows to include them with the PAR. If you choose not to create a PAR, dependent classes can reside anywhere on the Alfresco classpath, preferably right alongside your other classes in the extension directory.

Using Alternative Deployment Methods

So far you've seen how to deploy process definitions to Alfresco through the workflow console and the GPD. Processes can also be deployed through Spring, via Ant (jBPM ships with an Ant task called deploypar), and through the jBPM API.

Of these, the most common in the Alfresco world is through Spring. The snippet below shows how to point to a single process definition. If you have multiple workflows to deploy using this approach, use multiple props elements:

```
<bean id="extension.workflows.workflowBootstrap" parent="workflowDepl
oyer">
    <property name="workflowDefinitions">
        <list>
            <props>
                <prop key="engineId">jbpm</prop>
                <prop key="location">alfresco/extension/workflows/simple-
                    process/processdefinition.xml</prop>
                <prop key="mimetype">text/xml</prop>
                <prop key="redeploy">true</prop>
            </props>
        </list>
    </property>
</bean>
```

The engineId must be set to jbpm. Maybe at some point other engines will be supported. But for now, jBPM is the only choice.

The `location` is any location on the classpath. But to be consistent with how customizations are deployed, I recommend standardizing on the Alfresco extension directory or more specifically in a directory called `workflows` within `alfresco/extension`.

The `mimetype` setting is **text|xml** when deploying the `processdefinition.xml` file. If you choose to deploy the process as a PAR, set the location to the path of the PAR file and set the `mimetype` to `application/zip`.

The `redeploy` flag tells Alfresco whether or not it should automatically redeploy the process on startup. During development if you are deploying your processes via Spring, you probably want this to be set to `true`. Once you get to production, set it to `false` to avoid needlessly creating new versions of the process definition every time the server is restarted.

Wiring a Process to the Alfresco UI

So far you've learned the definition of workflow, specifics around the jBPM engine, and how to deploy processes. But the discussion up to this point hasn't been specific to Alfresco. In Alfresco, web client users need to:

- Start workflows
- Add one or more pieces of content to a workflow ("Approve this piece of web content", for example)
- Assign tasks to users and/or groups, and work with the tasks assigned to them
- Provide process-specific metadata for a specific workflow such as due dates, priority, special processing instructions, or any other custom metadata you can think of

JBoss jBPM is just an engine—it is up to the application embedding the engine to expose the capabilities of the engine to the user interface. Alfresco's already done that work for you. Figuring out how to wire your custom workflows into the Alfresco web client UI is just a matter of following Alfresco's framework.

Alfresco uses the same mechanism to model workflow process data and the corresponding web client user interface as it does to define custom content models. You learned how to extend Alfresco's content model in Chapter 3. The steps for integrating a custom workflow with the Alfresco web client UI are identical. At a high level it involves:

- Defining a content model for your workflow in which workflow tasks map to content types (Alfresco-provided types, custom types, or both)

- Updating `web-client-config-custom.xml` to tell Alfresco how to expose the process metadata to the web client user interface

- Externalizing the strings

Let's see how this works by wiring the Hello World process you created earlier to the Alfresco UI. After that, you'll work through a more complex example for SomeCo.

Step-by-Step: Grabbing the Hello World Argument from the User

The Hello World process you created at the start of the chapter didn't require any user involvement other than signaling the start node. Once you did that, it ran to completion. Certainly, you'll have workflows like this. Workflows can be useful for chaining together several automated operations that don't need human involvement. In this example, though, you need to learn how to integrate a custom workflow with the Alfresco web client user interface. So let's modify the Hello World example to say hello to a name specified when the workflow is launched. This will involve creating a custom workflow content model, configuring the web client user interface, and modifying the process definition to retrieve the string from the model.

Let's get started. Follow these steps:

1. First, in the workflows folder in your Eclipse project make a copy of the `helloWorld` folder and its contents. Call the new folder `helloWorldUI`.

2. Now edit the `processdefinition.xml` file. There are three areas that need to be addressed. First, the process name needs to change. Process names need to follow Alfresco's content type naming convention. Change the name to `scwf:helloWorldUI`. The `scwf` string is the namespace of a new custom content model you are going create shortly:

```
<?xml version="1.0" encoding="UTF-8"?>
<process-definition xmlns="urn:jbpm.org:jpdl-3.1" name="scwf:
                                                    helloWorldUI">
```

3. Next, the goal is to have the person starting the workflow specify a string when the workflow is launched. To do this, add a task to the start node and name it `scwf:submitHelloWorldTask`. The start-state element should look like this after you've made the modification:

```
<start-state name="start">
   <task name="scwf:submitHelloWorldTask" />
   <transition name="" to="hello"></transition>
</start-state>
```

4. The final change to the process is to read the string that was set by the workflow initiator. The string will be stored in a property as defined in the yet-to-be-created custom workflow content model. All you have to do is declare a variable that matches the property name, and then reference it in the log statement. Note the use of an underscore ("_") instead of a colon (":") to separate the namespace from the property name. Modify the `hello` node as follows:

```
<node name="hello">
    <transition name="" to="end1">
        <action class=
        "org.alfresco.repo.workflow.jbpm.AlfrescoJavaScript">
            <script>
                <variable name="scwf_helloName" access="read"/>
                <expression>
                    logger.log("Hello, " + scwf_helloName + "!");
                </expression>
            </script>
        </action>
    </transition>
</node>
```

5. Save the `processdefinition.xml` file.

6. When the workflow is launched, the initiator specifies a name string. Alfresco has to know how to handle that data. Alfresco uses a content model to do that. Create a new content model XML file in **config | alfresco | extension | model** called `scWorkflowModel.xml` with the following content:

```
<?xml version="1.0" encoding="UTF-8"?>
<!-- Definition of new Model -->
<model name="scwf:workflowmodel"
    xmlns="http://www.alfresco.org/model/dictionary/1.0">

    <!-- Optional meta-data about the model -->
    <description>Someco Workflow Model</description>
    <author>Optaros</author>
    <version>1.0</version>

    <!-- Imports are required to allow references to
      definitions in other models -->
    <imports>
        <import uri=
        "http://www.alfresco.org/model/dictionary/1.0"
          prefix="dz" />
        <import uri="http://www.alfresco.org/model/bpm/1.0"
            prefix="bpm" />
```

```
    </imports>
    <!-- Introduction of new namespaces defined by this model -->
    <namespaces>
        <namespace uri="
         http://www.someco.com/model/workflow/1.0"
            prefix="scwf" />
    </namespaces>
```

7. Add to it a type that corresponds to the task you created in the start-element, which was called `scwf:submitHelloWorldTask`. The type only needs one property, which is the name string:

```
    <types>
        <type name="scwf:submitHelloWorldTask">
            <parent>bpm:startTask</parent>
            <properties>
                <property name="scwf:helloName">
                    <type>d:text</type>
                    <mandatory>true</mandatory>
                    <multiple>false</multiple>
                </property>
            </properties>
        </type>
    </types>
</model>
```

8. Save the model XML file.

9. Create a new properties file in **config | alfresco | extension** called `scWorkflow.properties`. The properties file for workflows follows a specific syntax. First, add properties related to the custom workflow model. These properties describe the type and the property you added to the model:

```
#
# Hello World UI Workflow
#

# scWorkflowModel related strings
scwf_workflowmodel.type.scwf_submitHelloWorldTask.title=Start
Hello World UI Workflow
scwf_workflowmodel.type.scwf_submitHelloWorldTask.
description=Submit a workflow that says hello in the log
scwf_workflowmodel.property.scwf_helloName.title=Name
scwf_workflowmodel.property.scwf_helloName.description=Say hello
to this person
```

10. Then, add properties that relate to the process. In this example, the only process-related properties are used to give the workflow a title and a description. Alfresco will display the title and description in the Start Advanced Workflow wizard:

```
# processdefinition related strings
scwf_helloWorldUI.workflow.title=Hello World UI
scwf_helloWorldUI.workflow.description=A simple hello
world process
```

11. Save the properties file.

12. You have to tell Alfresco about the new model. Recall that models are configured in a Spring context bean. You created a context file specifically for models in an earlier chapter called `someco-model-context.xml`. Edit the context file to add a reference to the new model XML you just created:

```
<bean id="extension.dictionaryBootstrap" parent="
dictionaryModelBootstrap" depends-on="dictionaryBootstrap">
    <property name="models">
        <list>
        <value>alfresco/extension/model/scModel.xml</value>
        <value>alfresco/extension/model/scWorkflowModel.xml</value>
        </value>
        </list>
    </property>
</bean>
```

13. Alfresco also needs to know about the `scWorkflow.properties` file. It makes sense to add it to the model context. Add the following bean to the context file:

```
<bean id="extension.workflowBootstrap"
          parent="workflowDeployer">
    <property name="labels">
        <list>
            <value>alfresco.extension.scWorkflow</value>
        </list>
    </property>
</bean>
```

14. Save the context file.

15. Deploy your changes using Ant and restart Tomcat to pick up the new model and UI configuration.

16. Use the GPD **Deployment** tab to deploy the new process.

17. Test the process by starting an advanced workflow on any piece of content.

Here's a tip. Every time you open the GPD **Deployment** tab, the **Server Deployer** field gets reset to the default. You can fix that by setting the **Server Deployer** value as a preference. Go to **Window | Preferences | JBoss jBPM | Server Deployment** and set the **Server Deployer** field to **| alfresco | jbpm | deployprocess**.

To start an advanced workflow in the UI, navigate to any piece of content. Then select its actions menu, either from the browse list or from the details page, and click **Start Advanced Workflow**:

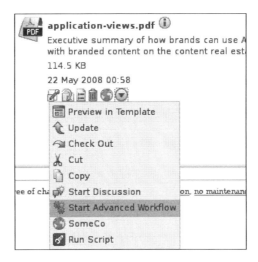

You should see your workflow listed as well as the other Hello World workflow examples and the out of the box workflows:

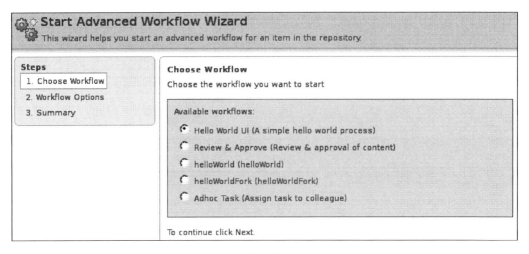

On the **Workflow Options** page, you should see the text field you defined, as well as the externalized string for the label:

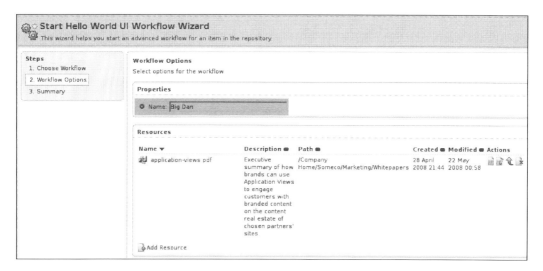

When the workflow runs, the log should show the personalized Hello World message:

```
10:48:28,161 User:admin DEBUG [repo.jscript.ScriptLogger] Hello,
Big Dan!
```

Understanding Workflow-Specific Content Models

The workflow-specific content model defines the data structure for the process. Workflow models use the same fundamental building blocks—types, properties, aspects, and associations—as "normal" Alfresco content model definitions. In fact, if you already have a custom model, you can define your workflow-specific model in the same content model XML file. But to reduce confusion, I recommend you do what you did here and keep your content types separate from your workflow types using at least two different model files.

What is the purpose of the workflow-specific model? Think of it like any other content model. Custom content models are used to define the metadata you want to capture about a piece of content. The metadata (properties) is grouped into types and aspects. By virtue of defining these properties as part of the content model, Alfresco takes care of persisting the data to the underlying database.

Workflow models function in the same way. Suppose you have a process in which three different departments are involved in an approval process. Maybe you'd like the workflow initiator to be able to define which of those departments are required approvers and which are optional or "FYI" reviewers. The workflow model defines how that information is going to be stored.

As in other content models, you don't have to start from scratch. Alfresco ships out of the box with some workflow-specific types already defined. There are two model definition files related to this. One is called `bpmModel.xml`. It resides in the Alfresco web application root under **WEB-INF | classes | alfresco | model**. The other is called `workflowModel.xml` and it resides under **WEB-INF | classes | alfresco | workflow**.

The bpmModel file contains the lowest-level workflow classes such as the base definition for all tasks and the default start task. It also contains important aspects such as a set of "assignee" aspects that define associations between tasks and users or groups.

The workflowModel file contains the content model for the out of the box process definitions. This model file offers a lot of potential for reuse in your custom processes. For example, if your process starts by allowing the submitter to specify a list of several people to receive a task, you could use the `submitParallelReviewTask`. If you want to base an approval on the percentage of individuals who approve a task, you can use the `submitConcurrentReviewTask`. Of course, just like any model, you are free to use these as is, extend them, or not use them at all.

When users interact with the workflow via the web client, Alfresco will use the workflow content model and the `web-client-config-custom.xml` file to figure out what metadata to expose to the UI, and how to present it just as it does when viewing content properties. Alfresco uses the name of the workflow task to figure out the appropriate workflow content type. So, all tasks in which there are Alfresco web client user interactions must be given a name that corresponds to the name of a workflow content type.

You may have noticed that the custom type you created (`scwf:startHelloWorldTask`) was a subtype of `bpm:workflowTask`. Doing that added key properties and aspects to your workflow, including the ability to associate content with the workflow. If you look at the `bpmModel.xml` file, you'll see that the `bpm:workflowTask` includes an association called `bpm:package`. That's what is used to relate workflow instances with the content being routed by the workflow.

Assigning Tasks to Users and Groups

A task is a step in a workflow that requires human interaction. jBPM maintains a list of tasks assigned to each participant. How users interact with the task list is up to the application embedding the jBPM engine. In Alfresco, a dashlet displays a to-do list for the currently logged in user. As users complete their tasks, the tasks are removed from the to-do list. An empty to do list is shown here:

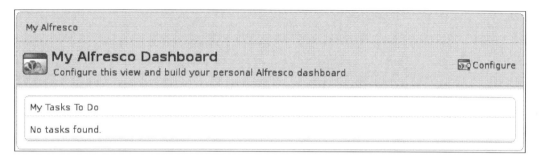

If tasks are steps a human performs, how do tasks get associated with the people who need to perform them (actors)? One of the child elements of the "task" element is "assignment". The assignment element points to a Java class that is an instance of `AssignmentHandler`. The Java class uses the jBPM API to handle assigning the task to an actor. Alfresco saves us some work here. It provides an `AssignmentHandler` out of the box. You'll see an example of how it can be used soon.

Often, a process has the notion of a role in which multiple tasks during the process get assigned to the same actor playing that role. For example, suppose you are defining a process that contains multiple tasks performed by "marketing". Rather than assign the marketing group or individual repeatedly to each task, it would be nice if you could make the assignment once, and then tell the other tasks to use the same assignment. In jBPM this is implemented through swimlanes. An actor can be assigned to a swimlane, and then all tasks that need to be performed by the same actor refer to the swimlane.

Alfresco creates one swimlane for you automatically called "initiator". The initiator swimlane is a convenient way to assign tasks to whoever started the workflow.

When defining a business process, it is important to understand how the participants in the process will do the work. One specific area that needs to be considered is whether to use pooled actors for a given task. Suppose you assigned a task to a group of ten people. You could iterate through the group and assign a task to each and every member of the group, and then not consider the task complete until all actors have taken action. An alternative is to use pooled actors. Using a pool, all members of a group are notified of the task. But as soon as one actor takes "ownership" of the task, it is removed from everyone else's to-do list. The owner can then either complete the task or return it to the pool. If it is returned to the pool, all members of the group see the task in their to-do list until another person takes ownership or completes the task. To use pooled actors, use the `pooledactors` child element of the `assignment` element instead of the `actor` element. The SomeCo Whitepaper Submission workflow you are about to build uses pooled actors.

The decision to use pooled actors depends entirely on the business process. There is no preferred approach.

Step-by-Step: Creating the Initial Whitepaper Submission Workflow

In earlier chapters, you created a UI action linked to a rule action that enables and disables Whitepapers for publication to the Web. You used an evaluator to show or hide the UI action link based on whether or not the user was a member of the `Publisher` group. That approach works fine in cases where the action doesn't require review or approval. But SomeCo wants anyone in the company to be able to submit a Whitepaper for publication to the web site, as long as the right people review the document before it is published. This process is well-suited to an advanced workflow.

The Whitepaper needs to be reviewed by the Operations team as well as the Marketing team. It doesn't matter who on the team does the review. SomeCo wants to notify each team and then let one representative from each team "own" the review task. This means the process needs to use pooled actors for the review tasks.

Either team can reject the Whitepaper. If it is rejected, the person who submitted the Whitepaper can make revisions and re-submit. If both teams approve, the Whitepaper moves on to the next step.

Here are the high-level steps involved in implementing this process:

1. Lay out the process using the JBoss jBPM Graphical Process Designer.
2. Configure swimlanes and add tasks to task nodes with appropriate assignments.
3. Wire the process to the Alfresco web client UI by updating the SomeCo Workflow Content Model and modifying the web client configuration.

To get this done, follow these steps:

1. Create a new process in **alfresco | extension | workflows** called `publishWhitepaper`.

2. Using the GPD **Diagram** tab and the description of the business process, lay out the process as shown in the diagram that follows. Note that the reason the transition labels between the **Operations Review** and **Marketing Review** task nodes and the **Join** are hard to read is because there are two transitions for each and the GPD overlays them. So each **Review** task node has two leaving transitions—one for **approve** and one for **reject**:

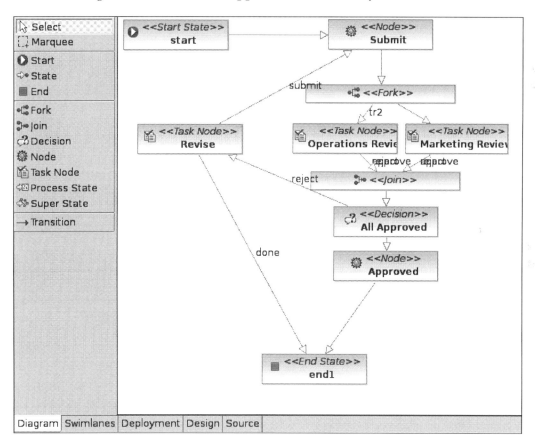

3. If you haven't already done so, name the transitions as shown in the diagram. Any transition leaving a task node should be labeled because a human is going to see that (or its externalized equivalent) in the UI. Everywhere else it is convenient if the transitions have names, but it isn't required.

4. Now edit the source of `processdefinition.xml`. First, fix the process definition element by setting the `xmlns` and `name` attributes:

```
<process-definition xmlns="urn:jbpm.org:jpdl-3.1" name="scwf:
publishWhitepaper">
```

5. Now drop in the swimlanes. You need the built-in `initiator swimlane` discussed earlier, plus one for `Marketing` and one for `Operations`. The out of the box processes show you how to use a picker to let the initiator specify a user or a group. In this example, you're going to hardcode the Alfresco group assignment in the swimlanes because you know which groups need to be assigned. There's no reason to make the initiator pick in this case. Also, you're going to use the `pooledactors` element because the entire team needs to get a task with one person taking ownership of and completing that task. The swimlanes use the `AlfrescoAssignment` class to assign the actor. In this case, you're using an expression that leverages the Alfresco `people` object because you need the actor to be a reference to the group object, not just a string containing the group name. Add the swimlanes to the start of the process definition:

```
<swimlane name="initiator" />

<swimlane name="marketing">
   <assignment class=
    "org.alfresco.repo.workflow.jbpm.AlfrescoAssignment">
       <pooledactors>#{people.getGroup('GROUP_marketing')}
       </pooledactors>
   </assignment>
</swimlane>

<swimlane name="operations">
   <assignment class=
    "org.alfresco.repo.workflow.jbpm.AlfrescoAssignment">
<pooledactors>#{people.getGroup('GROUP_operations')}
</pooledactors>
   </assignment>
</swimlane>
```

6. The process has three task nodes and a start-state node. Each of these needs a task. The task gets assigned to a `swimlane`. Update the `processdefinition.xml` file as follows (only the nodes needing tasks are shown):

```
<start-state name="start">
   <task name="scwf:submitReviewTask" swimlane="initiator" />
   <transition name="" to="Submit"></transition>
</start-state>

<task-node name="Marketing Review">
```

```
<task name="scwf:marketingReview" swimlane="marketing" />
<transition name="approve" to="join1"></transition>
<transition name="reject" to="join1"></transition>
</task-node>

<task-node name="Operations Review">
<task name="scwf:operationsReview" swimlane="operations" />
<transition name="approve" to="join1"></transition>
<transition name="reject" to="join1"></transition>
</task-node>

<task-node name="Revise">
<task name="scwf:revise" swimlane="initiator"></task>
<transition name="submit" to="Submit"></transition>
<transition name="done" to="end1"></transition>
</task-node>
```

7. The shell of the process is now complete. It doesn't do anything special yet, but once you wire in the UI, you'll be able to test that the assignment works as you expect. Now let's integrate the process with Alfresco by defining the content model and updating the client configuration. Update **config | alfresco | extension | model | scWorkflowModel.xml** by adding the following types:

```
<type name="scwf:submitReviewTask">
    <parent>bpm:startTask</parent>
    <mandatory-aspects>
       <aspect>scwf:thirdPartyReviewable</aspect>
    </mandatory-aspects>
</type>

<type name="scwf:marketingReview">
    <parent>bpm:workflowTask</parent>
    <overrides>
       <property name="bpm:packageItemActionGroup">
          <default>read_package_item_actions</default>
       </property>
    </overrides>
</type>

<type name="scwf:operationsReview">
    <parent>bpm:workflowTask</parent>
    <overrides>
       <property name="bpm:packageItemActionGroup">
          <default>read_package_item_actions</default>
       </property>
     </overrides>
</type>
```

```
    <type name="scwf:revise">
      <parent>bpm:workflowTask</parent>
      <overrides>
         <property name="bpm:packageItemActionGroup">
            <default>edit_package_item_actions</default>
         </property>
      </overrides>
   </type>
</types>
```

8. Now the `web-client-config-custom.xml` file. Add the web client configuration for the new workflow types and properties. You can see that although the BPM model defines several properties, you're only exposing the workflow description and comment properties for this particular process. The description is editable only when submitting the workflow or doing a revision, and is read-only everywhere else:

```
<!-- workflow property sheets -->
<config evaluator="node-type" condition="scwf:submitReviewTask"
 replace="true">
   <property-sheet>
      <separator name="sep1" display-label-id="general"
       component-generator="HeaderSeparatorGenerator" />
      <show-property name="bpm:workflowDescription" component-
         generator="TextAreaGenerator" />
   </property-sheet>
</config>

<config evaluator="node-type" condition="scwf:marketingReview"
   replace="true">
   <property-sheet>
      <separator name="sep1" display-label-id="general"
         component-generator="HeaderSeparatorGenerator" />
      <show-property name="bpm:description" component-
         generator="TextAreaGenerator" read-only="true"/>
      <show-property name="bpm:comment" component-
         generator="TextAreaGenerator" />
   </property-sheet>
</config>

<config evaluator="node-type" condition="scwf:operationsReview"
replace="true">
   <property-sheet>
      <separator name="sep1" display-label-id="general"
      component-generator="HeaderSeparatorGenerator" />

      <show-property name="bpm:description" component-
```

```
                generator="TextAreaGenerator" read-only="true"/>
            <show-property name="bpm:comment" component
            generator="TextAreaGenerator" />
        </property-sheet>
    </config>

    <config evaluator="node-type" condition="scwf:revise"
    replace="true">
        <property-sheet>
            <separator name="sep1" display-label-id="general"
              component-generator="HeaderSeparatorGenerator" />
            <show-property name="bpm:description" component-
              generator="TextAreaGenerator" read-only="false"/>
            <show-property name="bpm:comment" component-
              generator="TextAreaGenerator" />
        </property-sheet>
    </config>
```

9. The last step is to externalize the strings. Update **config | alfresco | extension | scWorkflow.properties** with the model-related strings:

```
# scWorkflowModel related strings
scwf_workflowmodel.type.scwf_submitReviewTask.title=Start SC Web
Review
scwf_workflowmodel.type.scwf_submitReviewTask.description=Submit
SC Web documents for review & approval to a group of people
scwf_workflowmodel.type.scwf_marketingReview.title=Marketing
Review
scwf_workflowmodel.type.scwf_marketingReview.description=Review
documents for impact on SomeCo marketing message
scwf_workflowmodel.type.scwf_operationsReview.title=Operations
Review
scwf_workflowmodel.type.scwf_operationsReview.description=Review
documents for technical accuracy and best practices
scwf_workflowmodel.type.scwf_revise.title=Revise
scwf_workflowmodel.type.scwf_revise.description=Make changes then
resubmit or abort
```

10. Next, add the process-related strings:

```
# processdefinition related strings
scwf_publishWhitepaper.workflow.title=Publish Whitepaper to SC Web
scwf_publishWhitepaper.workflow.description=Review and approve SC
Whitepaper content

scwf_publishWhitepaper.node.Marketing\ Review.transition.approve.
title=Approve
scwf_publishWhitepaper.node.Marketing\ Review.transition.approve.
description=Approve this change
```

```
scwf_publishWhitepaper.node.Marketing\ Review.transition.reject.
title=Reject
scwf_publishWhitepaper.node.Marketing\ Review.transition.reject.
description=Reject this change
scwf_publishWhitepaper.node.Operations\ Review.transition.approve.
title=Approve
scwf_publishWhitepaper.node.Operations\ Review.transition.approve.
description=Approve this change
scwf_publishWhitepaper.node.Operations\ Review.transition.reject.
title=Reject
scwf_publishWhitepaper.node.Operations\ Review.transition.reject.
description=Reject this change
scwf_publishWhitepaper.node.Revise.transition.submit.
title=Resubmit
scwf_publishWhitepaper.node.Revise.transition.submit.
description=Resubmit after revision
scwf_publishWhitepaper.node.Revise.transition.done.title=Abort
scwf_publishWhitepaper.node.Revise.transition.done.
description=Stop the review process for this content
```

11. Save the properties file.

12. Deploy the changes by running Ant and then restart Tomcat.

13. Deploy the process using the **Deployment** tab in the GPD.

14. Test the process.

To test the process, do the following:

1. If you haven't done so already, create a group called `operations` and one called `marketing`. Create a couple of test users for each group.

2. In the repository, create a test Whitepaper in **Someco | Marketing | Whitepapers**, if you don't have any already.

3. Configure the permissions on the Whitepapers folder such that the marketing and engineering groups have Editor access or higher.

4. Start an Advanced Workflow on your test Whitepaper.

5. You should see the newly-deployed workflow in the list of available workflows:

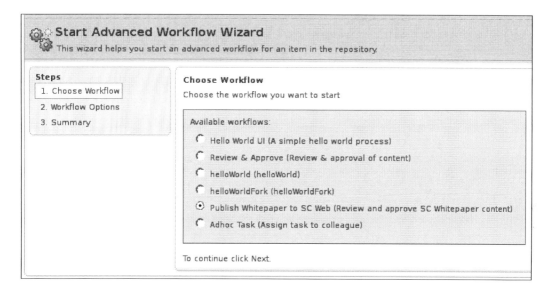

6. Log in as one of your test users. Because the process uses pooled tasks, you'll need to add the **My Pooled Tasks** dashlet to your **My Alfresco Dashboard**. Don't remove the **My Tasks To Do** dashlet:

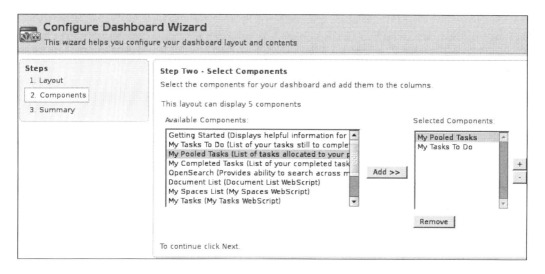

7. After configuring the dashboard to include the **My Pooled Tasks** dashlet, you should see the task:

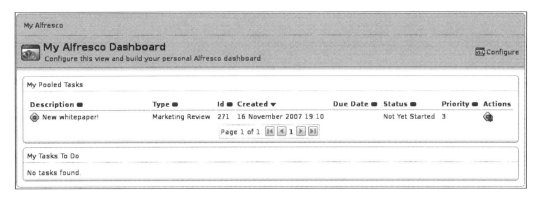

8. Either take ownership of the task so that you can see how the task moves to your **My Tasks To Do** list and gets removed from the other users' inboxes (if the users are members of the same group) or simply Approve the task.

9. Use the workflow console to verify that the process completed. If you submit **show workflows all** on the workflow console, you should see no running workflows after both Marketing and Operations have approved the Whitepaper.

In the real world, you'd run several tests as you have to make sure you test every possible path through the workflow. This can be tedious. So if you are doing several complex workflows as part of your project, make sure you allocate enough time to test them adequately. Bumpy workflows are a surefire way to erode user adoption.

Controlling What Actions Can Be Taken from the Task Management Dialog

The `bpm:packageItemActionGroup` defines what actions are available for working with the content in the workflow at that particular step in the process. In this example, the initiator needs to be able to change the contents of the workflow when the workflow is started and when making revisions. So for the `scwf:revise` type in the `scWorkflowModel.xml` file, the `packageItemActionGroup` property is overridden with `edit_package_item_actions`:

```
<overrides>
   <property name="bpm:packageItemActionGroup">
      <default>edit_package_item_actions</default>
   </property>
</overrides>
```

Resources

Name ▼	Description ●	Path ●	Created ●	Modified ●	Actions
📄 application-views.pdf	Executive summary of how brands can use Application Views to engage customers with branded content on the content real estate of chosen partners' sites.	/Company Home/Someco/Marketing/Whitepapers	28 April 2008 21:44	1 June 2008 21:33	

📄 Add Resource

The reviewers should not be able to add or remove anything to or from the workflow. So for the rest of the types, the property is set to have `read_package_item_actions` as the default:

```
<overrides>
    <property name="bpm:packageItemActionGroup">
        <default>read_package_item_actions</default>
    </property>
</overrides>
```

Resources

Name ▼	Description ●	Path ●	Created ●	Modified ●	Actions
📄 application-views.pdf	Executive summary of how brands can use Application Views to engage customers with branded content on the content real estate of chosen partners' sites.	/Company Home/Someco/Marketing/Whitepapers	28 April 2008 21:44	1 June 2008 21:33	

Page 1 of 1 |◄ ◄ **1** ► ►|

Other out of the box package item action groups include: `edit_and_remove_package_item_actions`, `remove_package_item_actions`, and `add_package_item_actions`. These are just UI action groups (see Chapter 5), so if one of the out of the box groups doesn't meet your needs, you can create your own.

Enabling the Workflow Initiator to Select Users and Groups

If you have run any of the out of the box advanced workflows, you've seen that it is possible to let the workflow initiator select users and/or groups, which are then used to assign tasks. In SomeCo's example, you hardcoded the groups in the swimlane assignment, but doing something user-configurable is easy.

Alfresco's out of the box process definitions reside in **WEB-INF | classes | alfresco | workflow**. You'll notice there are a number of processes that don't get deployed out of the box although they are defined and ready to use. Deploying, running, and dissecting these are helpful self-study exercises. Let's look at `adhoc_processdefinition.xml` to see an example of how initiator-specified user and group assignment works.

There are two things of interest in this file related to how the task assignment works. First, note that the start task is called `wf:submitAdhocTask`:

```
<start-state name="start">
   <task name="wf:submitAdhocTask" swimlane="initiator"/>
   <transition name="" to="adhoc"/>
</start-state>
```

You know from the previous examples that there must be a corresponding type in Alfresco's model of the same name. You'll see that soon.

Next, notice that the swimlane uses an actor (rather than a pooled actor as in the SomeCo example) and that it uses a Beanshell expression for the actor value. The expression will resolve to an association called `assignee` in the `bpm` namespace that points to the "person" object being assigned to the swimlane:

```
<swimlane name="assignee">
   <assignment class=
    "org.alfresco.repo.workflow.jbpm.AlfrescoAssignment">
      <actor>#{bpm_assignee}</actor>
   </assignment>
</swimlane>
```

Alfresco's workflow model, which resides in **WEB-INF | classes | alfresco | workflow | workflowModel.xml**, includes the `wf:submitAdhocTask` type and the `bpm:assignee` association as expected. (The association defined as part of a mandatory aspect, also called `bpm:assignee`, lives in the BPM model.)

```
<type name="wf:submitAdhocTask">
   <parent>bpm:startTask</parent>
   ...
   <mandatory-aspects>
      <aspect>bpm:assignee</aspect>
   </mandatory-aspects>
</type>
```

The user picker component appears in the start workflow dialog because the web client configuration has a `show-association` element for the property sheet of `wf:submitAdhocTask`. Associations to "person" objects automatically render with the user picker component:

```
<config evaluator="node-type" condition="wf:submitAdhocTask"
  replace="true">
    <property-sheet>
        <show-association name="bpm:assignee" display-label-
        id="wf_adhoc_assign_to" />
    </property-sheet>
</config>
```

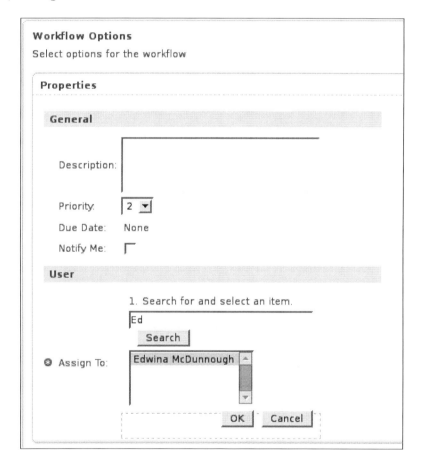

You can set up user and group selection in your own process definitions by following the same pattern.

Adding Logic to Workflows with Actions and Process Variables

So far you've seen that a process can be modeled as a collection of nodes connected via paths or transitions. A common requirement is to be able to execute some code or business logic at certain points within the process. For example, maybe you want to send an email or want to increment a counter that keeps track of how many times a node has been executed. Actions are the hooks that make this happen. (Yes, this is yet another use for the word "action" within Alfresco. But, to be fair, this one occurs within the context of jBPM.)

What triggers an action? As a token propagates through the workflow, it fires events. Examples include things such as entering a node, leaving a node, or following a transition.

Actions can be a Beanshell expression or a Java class. In the context of Alfresco, actions can also be written using JavaScript, which can make use of the Alfresco JavaScript API.

Storing Data in Process Variables

Often, there is metadata about a process that needs to be tracked. A due date or a priority flag are two examples. A due date isn't really a property of the content being routed through the workflow—it's a property of the process. jBPM gives us the ability to store this kind of data as part of the running process through process variables.

Process variables are name-value pairs that get persisted with the rest of the process state. Variables can be scoped to a specific token. By default, they are scoped to the root token so that they are effectively global.

In the following example, the `script` element sets a variable called `scwf_tempCnt` equal to `0` when the token enters the node:

```
<event type="node-enter">
   <script>
      <variable name="scwf_tempCnt" access="write"/>
      <expression>
         scwf_tempCnt = 0;
      </expression>
   </script>
</event>
```

Elsewhere in the process, you can read the value of the variable with an expression like:

```
#{scwf_tempCnt}
```

In this example, a Beanshell expression is being used for the logic. But actions can also be implemented in Java. In Alfresco's case, Alfresco has written a jBPM action in Java that allows you to execute Alfresco server-side JavaScript from within a process. You'll see both jBPM expressions and Alfresco JavaScript in the coming example.

All process variables are available to Beanshell, JavaScript, and Java.

Step-by-Step: Adding Logic to the Whitepaper Submission Workflow

The process you've built so far assigns tasks to the appropriate groups. But you should have noticed during your test that whether the marketing or operations users approved or rejected the content, the workflow always routed to the `Revise` node. That's because you have yet to add any logic to the process definition. The workflow was simply taking the default transitions.

The `All Approved` decision node has to figure out if all required approvals have been obtained. If they have, the process continues. If not, the initiator should get a chance to either make revisions or abort the workflow. The logic that makes that decision will depend on a process variable. When someone approves the Whitepaper, a counter will get incremented. The decision will check the value. If the counter is equal to 2, both approvals have been received and the workflow can continue down the "happy path". Otherwise, a revision is necessary and so the content should be routed back to the initiator.

The other thing that still needs to be resolved is that once an approval is given, the document needs to be enabled for the Web. In an earlier chapter you wrote an action that sets the web flag and publication date. Now you can benefit from encapsulating that operation into an action by reusing it here. The approved node will use the Alfresco JavaScript API to execute the action.

Implementing this logic involves adding expressions and Alfresco JavaScript to the appropriate events and transitions in the process, and then re-deploying the process definition for testing. To do this, follow these steps:

1. Edit the `processdefinition.xml` file for the `publishWhitepaper` process. You're going to use a counter to keep track of the number of approvals received. You need to be careful to initialize the counter to `0` because it's possible that a Whitepaper may go through several review cycles. The `Submit` node is a convenient place to do the initialization. Add a `node-enter` event to the `Submit` node with a declaration for the variable and logic to initialize it to `0`:

```
<node name="Submit">
        <event type="node-enter">
```

```
      script>
         <variable name="approveCount" access="read,write"/>
         <expression>
            approveCount = 0;
         </expression>
      </script>
   </event>
   <transition name="" to="fork1"></transition>
</node>
```

2. Now you need to increment the counter when the approve transition is taken out of the `Operations Review` node. Add a script to the `approve` transition to increment the counter:

```
<task-node name="Operations Review">
   <task name="scwf:operationsReview" swimlane="operations" />
   <transition name="approve" to="join1">
      <script>
         <variable name="approveCount" access="read,write"/>
         <expression>
            approveCount = approveCount + 1;
         </expression>
      </script>
   </transition>
   <transition name="reject" to="join1"></transition>
</task-node>
```

3. Do the same for the `Marketing Review` node.

4. With the counter logic in place, the `All Approved` decision node can conditionally transition based on the counter. The transition to the `Revise` node doesn't need a condition. It will be used as the default:

```
<decision name="All Approved">
   <transition name="reject" to="Revise"></transition>
   <transition name="" to="Approved">
      <condition>#{approveCount == 2}</condition>
   </transition>
</decision>
```

5. When a Whitepaper is approved, it should have the `sc:webable` aspect added to it and the `isActive` and `published` properties set. The `set-web-flag` action you wrote in an earlier chapter does just that. So all you have to do is tell the process to execute it for each piece of content in the workflow package using Alfresco JavaScript. Update the `Approved` node as follows:

```
<node name="Approved">
   <transition name="" to="end1">
      <action class=
```

```
    "org.alfresco.repo.workflow.jbpm.AlfrescoJavaScript">
     <script>
        <variable name="bpm_package" access="read" />
        <expression>
           var setWebFlagAction = actions.create("set-
             web-flag");

          setWebFlagAction.parameters["active"] = true;
             for (var i = 0; i &lt; bpm_package.children.
             length; i++)
          {

             setWebFlagAction.execute(bpm_package.
             children[i]);
          }
        </expression>
     </script>
  </action>
 </transition>
 </node>
```

6. Save the `processdefinition.xml` file. Use the **Deployment** tab in Eclipse to deploy the updated process, and then test it out.

To test out the updated process, run an advanced workflow on a Whitepaper that does not have its `isActive` flag set to `true`. In your test, if both approvers approve the content, the workflow should complete successfully and the flag should be set to `true`. Otherwise, the initiator will get a chance to make revisions or abort the workflow.

 Watch out for inline comments. The JavaScript expressions in process definitions get rolled up into a single file. So inline comments starting with double slash ("//") will effectively disable all code following the comment, even if it appears to you to be on a different line.

Using Java Classes for Decisions

You didn't need it in this example, but if the decision was more complex than could easily be handled with an expression or JavaScript, you could have used a Java class to implement the decision logic. To do that, you would have used a `handler` tag to point to a Java class that implements the `DecisionHandler` interface:

```
<decision name="CapEx Decision">
    <handler class="com.someco.bpm.CapExDecisionHandler" />
    <transition name="transBoard" to="Board Review"></transition>
    <transition name="transMgt" to="Management Review"></transition>
</decision>
```

The `decide()` method of the handler class performs the logic it needs to and then returns the name of the transition to take.

Getting Access to the Content in the Workflow

Recall from this chapter that the `scwf:submitReviewTask` type has an ancestor type that adds an association called `bpm:package`. That's what allows the JavaScript in the `Approved` node to iterate over the content that is being routed through the workflow. Always remember that unless you've done something to prevent it, the workflow initiator can add multiple files to a workflow.

Selecting the Right Event for Your Logic

Notice that in one case, you've placed code in the "node-enter" event while in other cases, you've used the node's transition. The difference is a matter of when the code is executed and whether or not the node is automatically signaled. For example, in the `Approved` node, if you were to move the JavaScript to an action outside of the transition (it then behaves like a node-enter event), you may find that the action will get executed, but won't automatically signal the node when it is complete. With the action on the transition, the node immediately takes the default transition and performs the action as part of that step.

Using ForEachFork

In the SomeCo example, you created two explicit review task nodes in your process: The `Marketing Review` node's task was assigned to the `marketing` swimlane and the `Operations Review` node's task was assigned to the `operations` swimlane.

But what if, instead, the workflow initiator was able to pick as many actors as thought necessary? There are two out of the box processes that show an example of this: `parallelreview_group_processdefinition` and `parallelreview_processdefinition` (the former is for groups, while the latter is for individual users).

These processes use an Alfresco jBPM action called `ForEachFork` to dynamically create and assign one task for every user in the list. A counter is then used to track how many approvals are obtained, similar to the counter used in the SomeCo example.

Looking at `parallelreview_group_processdefinition.xml`, you can see that the `for each` is iterating over each person in the selected group. The person will be in a process variable called `reviewer`:

```
<node name="startreview">
   <action class="org.alfresco.repo.workflow.jbpm.ForEachFork">
      <foreach>#{people.getMembers(bpm_groupAssignee)}</foreach>
      <var>reviewer</var>
   </action>
   <event type="node-enter">
      <script>
         <variable name="wf_approveCount" access="write" />
         <expression>
            wf_approveCount = 0;
         </expression>
      </script>
   </event>
   <transition name="review" to="review" />
</node>
```

The `review task-node` then makes an assignment using the value of the reviewer process variable. When this process is actually running, there will be one task node for each person in the group. If the approve transition is taken, the counter will be incremented:

```
<task-node name="review">
   <task name="wf:reviewTask">
      <assignment class=
       "org.alfresco.repo.workflow.jbpm.AlfrescoAssignment">
         <actor>#{reviewer}</actor>
      </assignment>
   </task>
   <transition name="reject" to="endreview" />
   <transition name="approve" to="endreview">
      <script>
         <variable name="wf_approveCount" access="read,write" />
            <expression>
               wf_approveCount = wf_approveCount +1;
            </expression>
      </script>
   </transition>
</task-node>
```

The `isapproved` decision then calculates the number of actual approvals received, and compares that to the total number of reviewers to come up with a percentage. If the percentage meets a threshold, the process continues along the `approved` transition, otherwise it is rejected:

```
<decision name="isapproved">
    <event type="node-enter">
        <action class=
        "org.alfresco.repo.workflow.jbpm.AlfrescoJavaScript">
            <script>
                <variable name="wf_reviewerCount" access="write"/>
            <expression>people.getMembers(bpm_groupAssignee).length;
            </expression>
            </script>
        </action>
        <action class=
         "org.alfresco.repo.workflow.jbpm.AlfrescoJavaScript">
            <script>
                <variable name="wf_requiredPercent" access="write"/>
                <expression>wf_requiredPercent =
                wf_requiredApprovePercent;</expression>

            </script>
        </action>
        <action class=
         "org.alfresco.repo.workflow.jbpm.AlfrescoJavaScript">
            <script>
                <variable name="wf_actualPercent" access="write"/>
                    <expression>wf_actualPercent = ((wf_approveCount *
                    100) / people.getMembers(bpm_groupAssignee).length);
                    </expression>
            </script>
        </action>
    </event>
    <transition name="reject" to="rejected" />
    <transition name="approve" to="approved">
        <condition>#{wf_actualPercent >=
        wf_requiredApprovePercent}</condition>
    </transition>
</decision>
```

The use of `ForEachFork` action is not limited to dealing with assignment. It is a generic construct that could be used any time you need to spawn parallel flows based on a list.

Using the Workflow API

In the previous example, the logic was easily handled by either expressions or JavaScript within the business process. However, there may be cases when jBPM actions are better implemented in Java. For example, there might be an API readily available in Java that isn't available in JavaScript. Or suppose you want to manipulate workflows from outside a business process. May be you want to complete tasks, add items to a workflow, or start a workflow from an action, a web script, or a custom dialog. You could use the jBPM API directly to do these things, but a better approach is to go through Alfresco's Workflow Service. That way, you are insulated from any changes to the jBPM engine and, at least theoretically, from more drastic changes such as if Alfresco ever decides to swap out the workflow engine entirely.

The next example gives you a chance to try out both of these scenarios. In one, you're going to write a custom jBPM action. In the other, you are going to use the Workflow Service to signal a node.

SomeCo would like to update the Whitepaper submission workflow to optionally include review by an external third party. The third party might be a SomeCo partner, for example, that does not have login credentials for Alfresco, but still needs to be able to approve or reject content. You will give external third parties the ability to approve or reject a task via URL by writing a web script that uses Alfresco's Workflow Service to signal the node to take the appropriate approve or reject transition.

The third party needs to know they need to review content. Alfresco has a mail action available out of the box that could be called from JavaScript. But Java is better suited for grabbing everything needed for the body of the email. So you'll write a custom jBPM action class, and then invoke the out of the box mail action from there.

Step-by-Step: Implementing Third-Party Review

Someday there will be an out of the box mechanism for exposing business processes to external parties. Until then, you can roll your own using the out of the box mail action and web scripts. There are two pieces required to make this work. First, you need a web script that signals the node to take either the approve or reject transition. Second, when the token arrives in the **Third Party Review** node, an email should go to the third party with **approve** and **reject** links. The recipient will open the email and click on either the **approve** link or the **reject** link. Both links are calls to the same web script—the path that needs to be taken is passed as an argument to the web script.

Implementing this is going to involve:

1. Updating the process definition to include a new decision that figures out whether or not to do a third-party review, a third-party review node (a state), and the associated transitions.

2. Updating the workflow model to include a new aspect representing "third-party reviewable" metadata. This also requires corresponding updates to the `web-client-config-custom.xml` file and the `scWorkflow.properties` file.

3. Writing a web script that figures out the appropriate workflow, node, and transition, and then uses the Workflow Service from a Java-based controller to take the appropriate transition. This includes configuring the controller as a Spring bean.

4. Writing a jBPM action class to compose the email body, and then send it to the third-party recipient using the out of the box email action via Alfresco's Action Service.

At the end of this example, SomeCo will be able to involve third parties who know nothing about Alfresco in an Alfresco-managed business process using everyone's favorite Knowledge Management and collaboration application: email.

To put this in place, follow these steps:

1. First, update the `publishWhitepaper` process definition to include a new decision and a new task node. The third-party review is optional. Therefore, you need to add a new decision node between **All Approved** and **Approved**. The reason it goes after the **All Approved** decision is that you don't want to bother the third party with a review task if the internal reviewers aren't going to approve the content. Add the decision node and name it **Third Party**. Don't delete the existing transition from **All Approved** to **Approved**. There is code on that transition that will be lost if you do. You'll reset the transitions using the source tab soon:

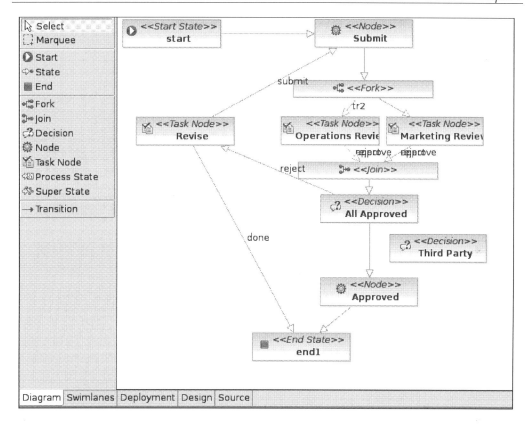

2. Next, add the **Third Party Review** node as a state. It is a state because it is going to sit and wait for the web script to signal it.

3. Add transitions connecting **Third Party** to **Third Party Review**, **Third Party** to **Approved**, **Third Party Review** to **Revise** named **reject**, and **Third Party Review** to **Approved** named **approve**.

4. Now, switch over to the source tab. Change the transition in **All Approved** from **Approved** to **Third Party**.

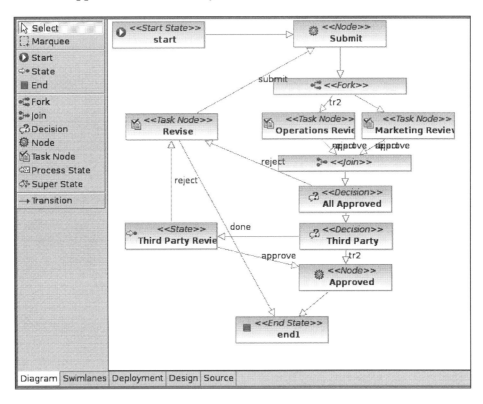

5. Save the process definition for now. You'll return to add logic to the new node in a minute.

6. Edit the **config | alfresco | extension | model | scWorkflowModel.xml** file. Add the following aspect to track the email address of the third party:

```
<aspects>
    <aspect name="scwf:thirdPartyReviewable">
        <title>Someco Third Party Reviewable</title>
        <properties>
            <property name="scwf:reviewerEmail">
                <type>d:text</type>
                <mandatory>false</mandatory>
                <multiple>false</multiple>
            </property>
        </properties>
    </aspect>
</aspects>
```

7. Update the `scwf:submitReviewTask` to include the new `thirdPartyReviewable` aspect as mandatory so that any time anyone launches this workflow, they have the opportunity to specify a third-party email address if they'd like:

```
<type name="scwf:submitReviewTask">
    <parent>bpm:startTask</parent>
    <mandatory-aspects>
        <aspect>scwf:thirdPartyReviewable</aspect>
    </mandatory-aspects>
</type>
```

8. Save the `scWorkflowModel.xml` file.

9. Edit the **config | alfresco | extension | scWorkflow.properties** file. Add the following model-related strings:

```
scwf_workflowmodel.property.scwf_reviewerEmail.title=Reviewer
email
scwf_workflowmodel.property.scwf_reviewerEmail.description=Third-
party reviewer email address
```

10. Add the following process-related strings:

```
scwf_publishWhitepaper.node.Third\ Party\ Review.transition.
approve.title=Approve
scwf_publishWhitepaper.node.Third\ Party\ Review.transition.
approve.description=Approve this change

scwf_publishWhitepaper.node.Third\ Party\ Review.transition.
reject.title=Reject
scwf_publishWhitepaper.node.Third\ Party\ Review.transition.
reject.description=Reject this change
```

11. Save the `scWorkflow.properties` file.

12. Edit **config | alfresco | extension | web-client-config-custom.xml** to add the client configuration related to the email address:

```
<!-- add third-party reviewable related aspect properties to
property sheet -->
<config evaluator="aspect-name" condition="scwf:
thirdPartyReviewable">
    <property-sheet>
        <show-property name="scwf:reviewerEmail" display-label
        id="email" />
    </property-sheet>
</config>
```

13. Save the `web-client-config-custom.xml` file.

14. Now implement the web script. Create a descriptor in **config | alfresco | extension | templates | webscripts | com | someco | bpm** called `review.get.desc.xml` with the following content:

```
<webscript>
  <shortname>BPM Review</shortname>
  <description>Review and approve a BPM task</description>
  <url>/someco/bpm/review?id={idArgument}&amp;action=
  {transArgument}</url>
  <format default="html">extension</format>
  <authentication>guest</authentication>
  <transaction>none</transaction>
</webscript>
```

15. Create a FreeMarker template in the same directory named `review.get.html.ftl` with HTML that simply echoes back the arguments that were passed in (obviously, SomeCo is going to want to make this a bit friendlier at some point):

```
<html>
<body>
<p>Signaled ${args.id} for transition ${args.action}</p>
</body>
</html>
```

16. Now write the Java controller. Create a new class called `com.someco.scripts.GetReview`. The class extends `DeclarativeWebScript` and has a dependency that will be passed in via Spring, which is the `WorkflowService` bean:

```
public class GetReview extends org.alfresco.web.scripts.
DeclarativeWebScript {
        private WorkflowService workflowService;
```

17. The `executeImpl()` method reads the arguments, then uses the Workflow Service to signal the workflow. So, for example, if someone were to invoke `http://localhost:8080/alfresco/service/someco/bpm/review?id=jbpm$89-@&action=approve&guest=true`, the controller would signal the node identified by `jbpm$89-@` with the `approve` transition. All the controller needs to do in its `executeImpl` method is to call the signal method on the `workflowService`. You'll notice that the `AuthenticationUtil.runAs` method is being used to allow guests to successfully execute the action:

```
    protected Map<String, Object> executeImpl(WebScriptRequest req,
WebScriptStatus status) {

        String id = req.getParameter("id");
        String action = req.getParameter("action");
```

```
        if (id == null || action == null) {
            status.jsSet_code(400);
            status.jsSet_message("Required data has not been
                             provided");
                  status.setRedirect(true);
        }
        Map<String, Object> model = new HashMap<String, Object>();

        model.put("response", AuthenticationUtil.runAs(new
        RunAsWork<String>() {
        @SuppressWarnings("synthetic-access")
            public String doWork() throws Exception {

                logger.debug("About to signal id:" + id + " with
                 transition:" + action);

                workflowService.signal(id, action);
                logger.debug("Signal sent.");

                return "Success";
            }
        },
        "admin"));

        return model;
    }
```

18. Save the controller.

19. Java controllers need to be configured as Spring beans. Use the existing **config | alfresco | extension | someco-scripts-context.xml** file to add the bean:

```
<bean id="webscript.com.someco.bpm.review.get" class="com.someco.
scripts.GetReview" parent="webscript">
    <property name="workflowService">
        <ref bean="WorkflowService" />
    </property>
</bean>
```

20. Create a new class called `com.someco.bpm.ExternalReviewNotification` that extends `JBPMSpringActionHandler`. Begin the class as:

```
public class ExternalReviewNotification extends
JBPMSpringActionHandler {
    private static final String FROM_ADDRESS =
    "alfresco@localhost";
    private static final String SUBJECT = "Workflow task
    requires action";
```

```
private static final String RECIP_PROCESS_VARIABLE =
"notificationRecipient";
private ActionService actionService;
protected void initialiseHandler(BeanFactory factory) {
   actionService = (ActionService)factory.getBean
                     ("actionService");
}
```

21. The URL for the BPM web script you just implemented contains the path ID that needs to get signaled. The path ID is an Alfresco concept that can be equated to jBPM's `token`. It is a string created by concatenating the workflow engine identifier (`jbpm`) with the jBPM process instance ID, which you can get from the jBPM API. Begin the `execute()` method as follows:

```
public void execute(ExecutionContext executionContext)
throws Exception {
```

22. The first thing the method does is grab the recipient from a process variable. The process variable is different than the one in the `scwf` namespace to avoid coupling this action class with a specific workflow model:

```
String recipient = (String) executionContext.getVariable(
                     ExternalReviewNotification.RECIP_
                     PROCESS_VARIABLE);
```

23. Next, start building the message body with a string buffer:

```
StringBuffer sb = new StringBuffer();
sb.append("You have been assigned to a task named ");
```

24. Get the token and then the current node from the `executionContext` to include the task name (**Third Party Review**) in the email:

```
sb.append(executionContext.getToken().getNode().getName());
sb.append(". Take the appropriate action by clicking one of
             the links below:\r\n\r\n");
```

25. Rather than hardcode "approve" and "reject", iterate over the leaving transitions to spit out their names followed by the appropriate web script URL. That way, if the process ever changes, there's a chance the action class won't need to be touched. In a production environment, you'd obviously need to either hardcode the appropriate host name to be used as part of the URL or place it in a configuration file:

```
List transitionList = executionContext.getNode().
                     getLeavingTransitions();

for (Iterator it = transitionList.iterator(); it.hasNext(); ) {
   Transition transition = (Transition)it.next();
   sb.append(transition.getName());
   sb.append("\r\n");
```

```
sb.append("http://localhost:8080/alfresco/service/someco/bpm/
review?id=jbpm$");
sb.append(executionContext.getProcessInstance().getId());
sb.append("-@");
sb.append("&action=");
sb.append(transition.getName());
sb.append("&guest=true");
sb.append("\r\n\r\n");
}
```

26. Now that the message body is built, use the Alfresco mail action to send it. You could leverage the Java mail API to do it yourself, but leveraging the mail action means you can leverage the same SMTP configuration settings Alfresco already uses:

```
Action mailAction = this.actionService.createAction
(MailActionExecuter.NAME);
mailAction.setParameterValue(
        MailActionExecuter.PARAM_SUBJECT,
        ExternalReviewNotification.SUBJECT);
mailAction.setParameterValue(MailActionExecuter.
PARAM_TO,  recipient);
mailAction.setParameterValue(
        .PARAM_FROM,
        ExternalReviewNotification.FROM_ADDRESS);
mailAction.setParameterValue(MailActionExecuter.PARAM_TEXT,
sb.toString());

this.actionService.executeAction(mailAction, null);

return;
}
```

27. Save the class.

28. The last step is to make two final updates to the process definition. The `Third Party` decision and the `Third Party Review` nodes need logic. The `Third Party` decision needs to know how to figure out whether or not the third-party review should take place. Add the following expression that checks to see if the third-party reviewer email address is set:

```
<decision name="Third Party">
    <transition name="tr2" to="Approved"></transition>
    <transition name="" to="Third Party Review">
        <condition>#{scwf_reviewerEmail!=""}</condition>
    </transition>
</decision>
```

29. The `Third Party Review` state node needs an action that sends the email notification:

```
<state name="Third Party Review">
    <event type="node-enter">
        <script>
            <variable name="notificationRecipient"
             access="read,write" />
            <variable name="scwf_reviewerEmail" access="read" />
            <expression>
                notificationRecipient = scwf_reviewerEmail;
            </expression>
        </script>
        <action class=
        "com.someco.bpm.ExternalReviewNotification"/>
    </event>
    <transition name="reject" to="Revise"></transition>
    <transition name="approve" to="Approved"></transition>
</state>
```

30. Save the process definition.

31. Deploy your changes using **ant deploy**, deploy the updated process using the GPD, and then test.

 When testing the notification piece, you'll need access to an SMTP server. For developing and testing locally, Apache James works great. If the SMTP server you use is running somewhere other than localhost, you'll have to tell Alfresco about it via the `mail.host` setting in `custom-repository.properties`.

To test this out, launch the workflow for a piece of test content. Remember to specify an email address for the third-party reviewer that corresponds to a valid account on your email server. Log in as your test Marketing and Operations users to approve the content. If all goes well, you should get an email that looks like this:

Subject:	**Workflow task requires action**
From:	alfresco@localhost
Date:	02:57 PM
To:	tuser1@localhost

You have been assigned to a task named Third Party Review. Take the appropriate action by clicking one of the links below:

reject
http://localhost:8080/alfresco/service/someco/bpm/review?id=jbpm$23-@&action=reject&guest=true

approve
http://localhost:8080/alfresco/service/someco/bpm/review?id=jbpm$23-@&action=approve&guest=true

If you click on a link, it should signal the task-node and the workflow should continue on the appropriate path.

Using a Task-Node Instead of a State

The **Third Party Review** node in this case was implemented as a state instead of a task node. But you might want it to be a task node to make it easier for someone internal to SomeCo to approve the review on behalf of the third party. To do that, you would need to:

1. Change the node from **state** to **task-node**.

2. Add a task with the appropriate swimlane assignment (initiator, for example).

3. Create the corresponding workflow model changes (new type, web client configuration, properties).

4. Update the web script to complete the task rather than simply signaling the **task-node**. If you don't, the transition will be followed, but the task will hang around.

Making the Third-Party Review More Robust

The third-party review is a good example of wait-state/asynchronous behavior in a process, and shows how web scripts can interact with workflows via the Alfresco Workflow Service. But there are a few open items that would need to be addressed before you use it in production. Some of these issues include:

- The email recipient doesn't get a copy of the documents being reviewed. One way to address this would be to have the notification action create a ZIP of the documents in the workflow package and then attach that ZIP to the email that gets sent. Another option would be to write additional web scripts to implement a mini-workflow task management user interface that third-party recipients could use to review content and assigned tasks. But then you've moved beyond the simple email interaction into custom client land.

- It'd be really easy for an unauthorized person to signal any node in the system because the controller class doesn't do any validation whatsoever and the path IDs are sequential. In production, you'd want to check that:

  ◦ The person making the request is the person assigned to the task

  ◦ That the task is still active

  ◦ A shared secret of some kind was generated, stored as process metadata, and passed back in as an argument in the URL for validation

- The email body should probably come from a FreeMarker template. That way you could reuse the notification class in any number of processes. Plus, it simplifies email body maintenance.

- The web script response should be a lot friendlier.

Most of these shortcomings have very little to do with advanced workflows specifically, so they are left up to you to address on your own.

Using Timers

Timers are a common requirement for business processes. The most common functionality is around doing something if someone doesn't respond to a task fast enough. That something might be reassigning the task or sending a nasty email to the assignee's boss. Another use might be to purposefully postpone all or part of a process until a specific day and time occurs.

Timers have been a part of jBPM for quite some time, but weren't enabled in Alfresco until release 2.1. In 2.1, timers had to be on task nodes. The ability for a timer to be added to other node types was added in 2.2 Enterprise.

Timers get set on a node either using the **create-timer** tag or via the **timer** tag. When a timer expires, the process can take a transition, execute a script, or call an action.

Step-by-Step: Adding a Timer to the Third-Party Review

In the previous example, you added the ability for the web site submission workflow to incorporate an external third party in the process. SomeCo is glad that its partners will be involved in the process, but it doesn't want them to become an unnecessary bottleneck. To address this, you are going to add a timer to the **Third Party Review** node so that if there is no response after a certain period of time has elapsed, an assumed approval will take place.

Adding a timer is really simple. It involves updating the process definition with the timer tag and redeploying the process. Follow these steps:

1. Edit the `processdefinition.xml` file for the publish-whitepaper process. After 10 minutes (Man, SomeCo has its partners on a short leash!), the `approve` transition should be signaled and a message written to the log. To make that happen, update the `Third Party Review` node as follows:

```
<state name="Third Party Review">
<event type="node-enter">
    <script>
```

```
            <variable name="notificationRecipient" access=
             "read,write" />
            <variable name="scwf_reviewerEmail" access="read" />
            <expression>
               notificationRecipient = scwf_reviewerEmail;
            </expression>
          </script>
          <action class=
          "com.someco.bpm.ExternalReviewNotification"/>
       </event>
       <timer name="thirdPartyTimer" duedate="10 minutes"
         transition="approve">
           <action class=
           "org.alfresco.repo.workflow.jbpm.AlfrescoJavaScript">
              <script>
                 logger.log("Third-party timer expired
              ...approving");
              </script>
           </action>
       </timer>
       <transition name="reject" to="Revise"></transition>
       <transition name="approve" to="Approved"></transition>
    </state>
```

2. If the timer trips, the action in the Approved node will be running without a user context, and the change to the isActive flag will fail with an AuthenticationException. Whether this is a bug or a feature, as of 2.2 Enterprise and 2.9 Community there is a workaround, which is to add the runas element as a child of the action to specify that the action should run as admin. Modify the Approved node as follows:

```
<node name="Approved">
     <transition name="" to="end1">
         <action class=
         "org.alfresco.repo.workflow.jbpm.AlfrescoJavaScript">
            <runas>admin</runas>
            <script>
              <variable name="bpm_package" access="read" />
              <expression>
                 var setWebFlagAction = actions.create("set-web-
                 flag");
                 setWebFlagAction.parameters["active"] = true;
                  for (var i = 0; i &lt;
                  bpm_package.children.length; i++) {
              setWebFlagAction.execute(bpm_package.children[i]);
```

```
                }
            </expression>
        </script>
    </action>
  </transition>
</node>
```

3. Save the process, redeploy it using the GPD, and then test.

To test the updated process, start an advanced workflow making sure to specify the third-party reviewer email address to trigger the third-party review. After 10 minutes, the approve transition should be taken automatically.

If you prefer not to wait for the countdown to verify that your timer was set correctly, log in to the web client, go to the workflow console, then type **show timers all** and click **Submit**. You should see a response like:

```
id: jbpm$1 , name: thirdPartyTimer , due date: 2008-06-02 17:49:42.0 ,
path: jbpm$25-@ , node: Third Party Review , process: jbpm$25
```

Understanding Timer Syntax

Using the `timer` tag is a shortcut. The long way to do it is to use a `create-timer` element on a `node-enter` event, as well as a `cancel-timer` on the `node-leave` event. If you need to create and cancel timers this granularly, consult the jBPM documentation for details.

The due date on a timer can be an absolute date or it can be relative, like the one you used in the `Third Party Review` example. You can also add a `business` modifier if you want to use business units instead of calendar units, as shown here:

```
<timer name='reminder'
    duedate='8 business hours'
    repeat='30 business minutes'
    transition='transToSetup' >
<action class='com.someco.bpm.TimerExpirationHandler' />
</timer>
```

Just like any other attribute value in your process definition, the due date could be the result of an expression. For example, the out of the box workflow used by Alfresco Web Content Management (WCM) allows the workflow initiator to select a launch date for web content, which is then set as the due date on a timer using a Beanshell expression:

```
<timer duedate="#{wcmwf_launchDate}" transition="launch" >
```

Timers can execute Alfresco JavaScript using the `AlfrescoJavaScript` action class, which you've seen in multiple examples. If the Alfresco JavaScript API doesn't have what you need, you can use Java to write your own custom jBPM action handler that will get executed when the timer expires.

Debugging Workflows

If something goes wrong or you just want to get up close and personal with the execution of a process, you can use the workflow console. Unfortunately, there's not a link in the UI for it just yet. The URL is `http://localhost:8080/alfresco/faces/jsp/admin/workflow-console.jsp`. The following table shows some common commands and what they do:

Command	What it does
`show workflows all`	Shows all running workflows.
`use workflow <workflow id>` where <workflow id> is something like jbpm$71	Makes all subsequent commands happen in the context of the specified workflow.
`show transitions`	Shows all leaving transitions for the current workflow.
`signal <path id> <transition>` where <path id> is something like jbpm$71-@ and <transition> is the name of the leaving transition you want to take. Leave off the transition to take the default.	Signals the token. Good when your workflow is stuck on a node or when you want to take a transition without going through the task management UI.
`desc path <path id>` where <path id> is something like jbpm$71-@	Dumps the current context. Great for debugging process variables.
`end workflow <workflow id>`	Cancels the specified workflow.
`show definitions all`	Shows the current deployed workflow definitions.
`undeploy definition <workflow id>` or `undeploy definition name <workflow name>`	Undeploys the specified workflow and stops any workflows running with that definition. The <workflow id> variant undeploys a specific version of a workflow.

These are a subset of the commands available. Type **help** and click **Submit** to see the full list of commands.

Other debug aids include using `logger.log` statements in Alfresco JavaScript actions (with `log4j.logger.org.alfresco.repo.jscript` set to DEBUG) and using `System.out` statements in Beanshell expressions.

As mentioned in Chapter 2, the Eclipse remote debugger is very helpful when trying to troubleshoot Java-based nodes, decisions, and action handlers.

Comparing Alfresco Workflow Options

You have now seen how Alfresco leverages the embedded JBoss jBPM engine to provide advanced workflow capability. Let's take a look at how advanced workflows compare to basic workflows, so you can make good decisions about which one is more appropriate in a given situation.

Basic workflows are nice end-user tools. Basic workflows use folders and a "forward step/backward step" model to implement serial processes. When a piece of content is dropped in a folder, a rule is triggered that associates a **forward step** and a **backward step** (one or the other or both) with the content. These steps are tied to Alfresco actions such as **Set a property** or **Move the content to a specified folder**. End users can then click on the appropriate step for a given piece of content.

For example, suppose there are requirements for a simple submit-review-approve process in which content is submitted, then reviewed, and then approved or rejected. One way to implement this with basic workflows is to use three folders. Let's say they are called **Draft**, **In Review**, and **Approved**, each of which has a rule set that applies a basic workflow. The workflow for content in the **Draft** folder would have a single forward step labeled **Submit**, and its action would move content to the **In Review** folder and send an email to the approver group. The **In Review** folder would have a workflow in which the forward step would be labeled **Approve**, and it would copy the content to an **Approved** folder. The backward step would be labeled **Reject**, and its action would move the content back to the **Drafts** folder.

You can see that basic workflows are useful, but limited with regard to the complexity of the business processes they can handle. A summary of the differences between basic workflows and advanced workflows appears in the following table:

Alfresco basic workflows	Alfresco advanced workflows
• Are configurable by non-technical end users via the Alfresco web client	• Are defined by business analysts and developers via a graphical Eclipse plug-in or by writing XML
• Leverage rules, folders, and actions	• Leverage the power of the embedded JBoss jBPM workflow engine
• Can only handle processes with single-step forward and/or backward, or serial flows	• Can model any business process including decisions, splits, joins, parallel flows, subprocesses, wait states, and timers
• Do not support decisions, splits, joins, or parallel flows	• Can include business logic written either in JavaScript or Java, either of which can access the Alfresco API
• Do not maintain state or metadata about the process	• Maintain state and process variables (metadata) about the process

Summary

In this chapter, you learned:

- A workflow is a business process and Alfresco embeds the JBoss jBPM workflow engine to execute advanced workflows.

- Business process definitions can be created using a text editor or the JBoss Graphical Process Designer (GPD).

- Logic can be added to workflows using Beanshell expressions, JavaScript, and Java.

- Workflows are well suited to long-running processes and can include asynchronous steps triggered by external programs. In the example, you used the Workflow Service, Alfresco web scripts, and actions to implement a process involving non-Alfresco users via email.

- Timers can be added to a process using relative or absolute dates. Alfresco's workflow console is a handy debugging tool.

- Alfresco's basic workflows are configurable by end users but aren't as powerful or flexible as advanced workflows.

When setting up an advanced workflow for the first time, there are a lot of steps involved because you have to do all the work from mapping the process to custom workflow types. Once the model and web client configuration are in place, additional development iterations on the process tend to move quickly.

The following summarizes the advanced workflow implementation steps:

1. Model the process using the jBPM Process Designer. Just get the process right — don't worry about node names, events, or actions just yet.

2. Add tasks, swimlanes, and any other necessary assignment logic.

3. Define a workflow content model. If you use a new content model file, remember to update the custom `model-context.xml` file to point to the new content model definition XML file.

4. Update `web-client-config-custom.xml` to expose workflow tasks to the Alfresco web client.

5. Create or update a workflow-specific properties file to externalize the strings in both the workflow model and the process definition.

6. Add logic to decisions, events, and transitions using Beanshell expressions, Alfresco JavaScript, or Java classes.

7. Deploy the process definition using either the **Deployment** tab in the GPD, or by copying the process definition to your extension directory and deploying with a Spring bean configuration file.

Web Content Management
8

People have been using Alfresco to manage web content since the early days of the product. When using that approach, however, content authoring and deployment are completely customized. In 2007, Alfresco released its formal web content management functionality that added features most people expect when they think of a **Web Content Management (WCM)** offering, including templating, site preview, snapshots, virtualization, and deployment.

Although Alfresco's WCM offering is built on top of Alfresco's core repository, there are differences in the underlying stores and the underlying Alfresco features that are (and aren't) exposed to Alfresco WCM. This chapter is about those differences and also the specific customization points within WCM, but is not an exhaustive how-to on all capabilities of Alfresco's WCM offering. Specifically, in this chapter you'll learn how to:

- Define web forms using XML Schema to allow non-technical users to create content
- Write presentation templates using XSLT and FreeMarker to enable the transformation of web form data into multiple rendition formats
- Use Alfresco's WCM API from JavaScript and Java to query the repository from a frontend web site
- Implement content deployment to publish content from the repository to a file system or another Alfresco instance
- Leverage advanced workflows to route web content for review and approval
- Use the API to work with WCM assets from JavaScript and Java

Understanding the Difference between Alfresco DM and Alfresco WCM

In previous chapters, you've been dealing strictly with documents and have been using Alfresco's web-based client to manage those files. Some of the files have been made available on SomeCo's web site, but the solution thus far has been about **Document Management (DM)**, not Web Content Management (WCM).

WCM is a specialized subset of the larger **Enterprise Content Management (ECM)** umbrella that is focused specifically on authoring, managing, and publishing files used to produce a web site.

Alfresco's WCM solution is built on top of the core product. It adds the following functionality:

- **Web forms**. Web forms (sometimes called "templating" in other WCM solutions) are used to enable content contribution from non-technical content authors. Rather than using specialized content authoring tools, content authors can log in to the Alfresco web client, and create and save content using a web form. The resulting data is stored as XML. The XML can optionally be transformed into one or more publication formats such as XML, HTML, PDF, JSP, RSS, or any other format that's needed, and then published to the live web site.

- **Sandboxes**. Every user responsible for maintaining a web site gets his/her own virtual copy of the entire web site. This virtual area or "sandbox" includes everything that's currently on the live site, plus any changes made within the sandbox.

- **Preview**. Preview functionality allows the authors contributing content, and the reviewers reviewing and approving content to see changes in the context of the live site before they are published. Any asset, including the entire site, can be previewed to see what it will look like when the changes go live.

- **Virtualization**. Virtualization is what helps make preview and sandboxing possible. Virtualization allows content authors and reviewers to work within the context of the entire site without physically duplicating site assets. The Alfresco Virtualization Server runs a virtual copy of the web site as a web application. This means if you preview a Java-based web application, you'll see not only the site content and graphic assets, but also running Java code.

- **Workflow**. Alfresco WCM uses the same jBPM engine that Alfresco DM uses, and so the chapter on advanced workflows applies here. In addition to a simple business process used to submit web content, Alfresco WCM adds additional WCM process functionality such as link checking, publication dates, and expiration dates.

- **Deployment**. There are several options for content deployment. In addition to doing it yourself (copying content out of the repository via CIFS, for example), Alfresco WCM adds a file system deployment tool and an Alfresco deployment tool. The file system deployment tool can copy content to any file system that is running an Alfresco **File System Receiver** (**FSR**). The Alfresco deployment tool is used to deploy content between Alfresco repositories.

- **Snapshots and Rollback**. Every change is captured in a "snapshot" before it goes live. Snapshots are what they sound like—a snapshot of the web site as it existed at a moment in time. Rollback is used to back out of changes. Using rollback, you can revert your site to any previous snapshot.

When the Alfresco engineers began working on this WCM-specific functionality, they decided that the "Spaces Store" implementation wouldn't be adequate. So they created a new store implementation called the **Advanced Versioning Manager** (**AVM**). While this did give the WCM product the functionality it needed, it had the unpleasant side effect of creating a separation between DM and WCM from an API perspective. For example, a piece of content is not simply a Node system-wide. It is only a node on the DM side of Alfresco. In WCM, it is an "AVMNode". Rather than working with the NodeService, you have to use the AVMNodeService (or its equivalent in the JavaScript API) to work with WCM content programmatically.

There are differences beyond the API. For example:

- Rule actions aren't supported in WCM.
- Auditing is not fully supported in WCM.
- File-level permissions are not supported in the WCM user interface.
- Full-text indexing of web project folders only includes the Staging sandbox and does not include individual user sandboxes. What's more, you cannot execute a search from the UI that crosses multiple web projects.
- WebDAV is unsupported for WCM stores.
- In DM, all content lives in a single store called the SpacesStore. In WCM, each web project, each sandbox within a web project, and each workflow running with web project content resides in a separate store.

WCM isn't always a subset of the DM functionality. Some features, such as the deployment tools and web forms, are only available in WCM (but web forms have been added to Alfresco Labs as "ECM Forms" to enable structured authoring outside of a web project).

The lack of fidelity between DM and WCM isn't always a problem, but it is an issue you should be aware of when you are planning your solution. Don't assume that a feature that works on the DM side will automatically work on the WCM side. And some features (such as object-level permissions) may be supported by the underlying WCM store, but don't have a corresponding user interface. Hopefully, over time, the discrepancies between the two sides will diminish. Content managers (and implementation teams) shouldn't care which store the content is in—logically, there should just be "Alfresco". Until the gaps are bridged, it may take some creativity to work around some of these issues.

Obtaining Alfresco WCM

You must obtain and install an additional download to enable Alfresco WCM functionality. The download includes a new Spring bean configuration file, a standalone Tomcat instance pre-configured with JARs, and server settings that allow a separate Tomcat instance (which is called "the virtualization server") to run web applications stored in Alfresco WCM web folders. This capability is used when content managers "preview" an asset or a web site.

Just as in the core Alfresco server, you can either build the WCM distribution from source or obtain a binary distribution.

Step-by-Step: Installing Alfresco WCM

If you are building from source, the source code for Alfresco WCM is included with the source code for the rest of the product. If you don't know where to get the source code, see Chapter 2. Once the source code is checked out, all you have to do is run the "distribute" Ant task as follows:

```
ant -f continuous.xml distribute
```

After several minutes, the WCM distribution will be placed in the **build|dist** directory of your source code's root directory.

Alternatively, if you are using binaries, download the binary distribution of the Alfresco WCM extension. Where you get it depends on whether you are running Labs or Enterprise. The Labs version is available for download from http://www.alfresco.com. The Enterprise version can be downloaded from the customer or partner site using the credentials provided by your Alfresco representative.

Regardless of whether you chose source or binary, you should now have an Alfresco WCM archive. For example, the Labs edition for Linux is named alfresco-labs-wcm-3b.tar.gz.

To complete the installation, follow these steps:

1. Expand the archive into any directory that makes sense to you. For example, on my machine I use **|usr|local|bin|alfresco-labs-3.0-wcm**.

2. Copy the `wcm-bootstrap-context.xml` file to the Alfresco server's extension directory **($TOMCAT_HOME|shared|classes|alfresco|extension)**.

3. Edit the startup script (`virtual_alf.sh`) to ensure that the APPSERVER variable is pointing to the virtual-tomcat directory in the location to which you expanded the archive. Using the example from the previous step, the APPSERVER variable would be:

   ```
   APPSERVER=|usr|local|bin|alfresco-labs-3.0-wcm|virtual-tomcat
   ```

4. Start the virtual server by running:

   ```
   .|virtual_alf.sh start
   ```

5. Start the Alfresco server (or restart it if it was already running).

You now have Alfresco with Alfresco WCM up and running. You'll test it out in the next section, but you can do a "smoke test" by logging in to the web client and confirming that you see the `Web Projects` folder under `Company Home`.

Creating Web Projects

A web project is a collection of assets, settings, and deployment targets that make up a web site or a part of a web site. Web projects are stored in web project folders, which are regular folders with a bunch of web project metadata.

The number of web project folders you use to represent a site, or whether multiple sites are contained within a single web project folder is completely up to you. There is no "right way" that works for everybody. Permissions are one factor. The ability to set permissions stops at the web site. Therefore, if you have multiple groups that maintain a site that are concerned with the ability of one to change the other's files, your only remedy is to split the site across web project folders.

Web form and workflow sharing is another thing to think about. As you'll soon learn, workflows and web forms are defined globally, and then selectively chosen and configured by each site. Once made available to a web project, they are available to the entire web project. For example, you can't restrict the use of a web form to only a subset of the users of a particular site.

SomeCo has chosen the approach of using one web project folder to manage the entire `SomeCo.com` web site.

Step-by-Step: Creating the SomeCo Web Project

The first thing you need to do is create a new web project folder for the SomeCo web site. Initially, you don't need to worry about web forms, deployment targets, or workflows. The goal is simply to create the web project and import the contents of the web site.

To create the initial SomeCo web project, follow these steps:

1. Log in as admin. Go to **Web Projects** under **Company Home**.

2. Click **Create**, and then **Create Web Project**.

3. Specify the name of the web project as **SomeCo Corporate Site**.

4. Specify the DNS name as **someco-site**.

5. Click **Next** for the remaining steps, taking all defaults. You'll come back later and configure some of these settings.

6. On the summary page, click **Finish**.

7. You now have a web project folder for the SomeCo corporate site. Click **SomeCo Corporate Site**. You should see one **Staging Sandbox** and one **User Sandbox**. Click the **Browse Website** button for the **User Sandbox**.

8. Now you can import SomeCo's existing web site into the web project folder. Click **Create**, and then **Bulk Import**. Navigate to the "web-site" project in your Eclipse workspace. Assuming you've already run Ant for this project, there should be a ZIP file in the build folder called **someco-web-site.zip**. Select the file. Alfresco will import the ZIP into your **User Sandbox**.

What Just Happened

You just created a new web project folder for SomeCo's corporate web site. But upon creation of a web project folder, there is no web site to manage. This is a big disappointment for some people. The most crestfallen are those who didn't realize that Alfresco is a "decoupled" content management system—it has no frontend framework and no "default" web site like "coupled" content management systems such as Drupal. This will change in the 3.0 releases as Alfresco introduces its new set of clients. But for now, it's up to you to give Alfresco a web site to manage.

You just happened to have a start on the SomeCo web site sitting in your Eclipse workspace. Alfresco knows how to import WAR and ZIP files, which is a convenient way to migrate the web site into Alfresco for the first time. Because web project sandboxes are mountable via CIFS, simply copying the web site into the sandbox via CIFS is another way to go. The difference between the two approaches is that the WAR/ZIP import can only happen once. The import action complains if an archive contains nodes that already exist in the repository.

If you haven't already done so, take a look at the contents of your sandbox. You should see index.html in the root of your **User Sandbox** and a someco folder that contains additional folders for CSS, images, JavaScript, and so on. The HTML file in the root is the same index.html file you deployed to the Alfresco web application (in an earlier chapter) in order to implement the AJAX ratings widget. Click the preview icon. (Am I the only one who thinks it looks eerily similar to the Turkish nazar talisman used to ward off the "evil eye"?) You should see the index page in a new tab or window. The list of Whitepapers won't be displayed. That's because the page is running in the context of the virtualization server, which is a different domain than your Alfresco server. Therefore, it is subject to the cross-domain restriction, which will be addressed later.

Playing Nicely in the Sandbox

Go back to the root of your web project folder. The link in the breadcrumb trail is likely to be the fastest way to navigate back. Click the **Browse Website** link in the **Staging Sandbox**. It's empty. If you were to invite another user to this web site, his/her sandbox would be empty as well. Sandboxes are used to isolate changes each content owner makes, while still providing him/her the full context of the web site. The **Staging Sandbox** represents your live web site. Or in source code control terms, it is the HEAD of your site. It is assumed that whatever is in the **Staging Sandbox** can be safely deployed to the live web site at any time. It is currently empty because you have not yet submitted any content to staging.

Let's go ahead and do that now. If you click the **Modified Items** link in the User Sandbox, you'll see the index.html file and the **someco** folder. You could submit these individually. But you want everything to go to staging, so click **Submit All**:

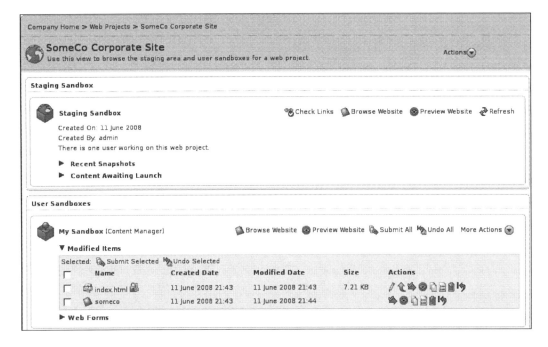

Provide a label and a description such as **initial population** and click **OK**. It is safe to ignore the warning that a suitable workflow was not found. That's expected because you haven't configured a workflow for this web project yet.

Now the files have been submitted to staging. Here are some things to notice:

- If you click the **Preview Website** link in the **Staging Sandbox**, you'll see the web site just as you did in the User Sandbox earlier.

- If you browse the web site in the **Staging Sandbox**, you'll see the same files currently shown when you browse the web site in your User Sandbox.

- A snapshot of the site was automatically taken when the files were committed and is listed under **Recent Snapshots**:

Inviting Users

To get a feel for how sandboxes work, invite one or more users to the web project (**Actions, Invite Web Project Users**). The following table describes the out of the box web project roles:

WCM User Role	Can do these things
Content Contributor	Create and submit new content; but cannot edit or delete existing content
Content Reviewer	Create, edit, and submit new content; but cannot delete existing content
Content Collaborator	See all sandboxes, but only have full control over their own
	Create, edit, and submit new content; but cannot delete existing content
	Edit web project settings
Content Manager	See and modify content in all sandboxes; exert full control over all content
	See and deploy snapshots and manage deployment reports
	Edit web project settings
	Invite new users to the web project
	Delete the web project and individual sandboxes

You'll notice that each new user gets his/her own sandbox, and that the sandbox automatically contains everything that is currently in staging. If a user makes a change to his/her sandbox, it is only visible within their sandbox until they commit the change to staging. If this is done, everyone else sees the change immediately. Unlike some content management and source code control systems, there is no need for other users to do an "update" or a "get latest" to copy the latest changes from staging into their sandbox.

 It is important to note that Alfresco will not merge conflicts. When a user makes a change to a file in his/her sandbox, it will be locked in all other sandboxes to prevent conflicts. If you were to customize Alfresco to disable locking, the last change would win. Alfresco would not warn you of the conflict.

The Alfresco admin user and any user with Content Manager Access can see (and work within) all User Sandboxes. Everyone else sees only their own sandboxes.

Mounting Sandboxes via CIFS

All sandboxes are individually mountable via CIFS. In fact, in staging, each snapshot is individually mountable. This gives content owners the flexibility to continue managing content in their sandbox using the tools they are familiar with.

The procedure for mounting a sandbox is identical to that of mounting the regular repository via CIFS, except that you use "AVM" as the mount point instead of "Alfresco".

One difference between mounting the AVM repository through CIFS and mounting the DM repository is that the AVM repository directory structure is more complicated. For example, the path to the root of admin's sandbox in the SomeCo site is:

```
|someco-site--admin|HEAD|DATA|www|avm_webapps|ROOT
```

The first part of the path, `someco-site`, is the DNS name you assigned when you set up the web project. The `admin` string indicates which User Sandbox we are looking at. If you wanted to mount to the **Staging Sandbox**, the first part of the path would be `someco-site` without `--admin`. The next part of the path, `HEAD`, specifies the latest-and-greatest version of the web site. Alternatively, you could mount a specific snapshot like this:

```
|someco-site--admin|VERSION|v2|DATA|www|avm_webapps|ROOT
```

As you might expect, the normal permissions apply. Users who aren't able to see another user's sandbox in the web client won't be able to do so through CIFS.

Virtualization and Layering

The AVM store makes use of "layered directories" to make virtualized copies of underlying directories available while isolating changes to individual layers. A user sandbox, for example, is simply a layer on top of the Staging directory. Let's look at a simple example.

Suppose we have a layer with a folder and a piece of content. This base layer could be the Staging Sandbox or just as easily be any other AVM store in the repository:

A **Transparent Layer** on top of the **Base Layer** can see the objects beneath it:

When new objects are added to the lower layer, they are immediately visible in the top layer:

Objects can be added to the top layer without affecting objects in lower layers:

If a background object is edited, a copy is placed in the upper layer:

When modified items are submitted to staging, an AVM merge is performed that merges the **Transparent Layer** with the **Base Layer**. This explains why all changes committed to Staging are automatically visible to all other User Sandboxes immediately with no further synchronization required:

Note that using the AVM API, you can arbitrarily create as many layers as you want.

Creating Web Forms

In the previous example you created a web project folder and imported the SomeCo web site. For some sites, that may be enough. In a bare bones implementation, once the site is migrated to the repository, life continues pretty much as normal. Content providers use authoring tools to save content via CIFS or edit content directly in the web client, and the system handles review and approval, snapshots, and deployment.

The next step for many people, however, is to identify subsections of the site that lend themselves to being managed through web forms. Web forms allow non-technical content owners to manage, approve, and deploy their own web content. Good candidates for web forms include content that:

- Is managed by non-technical content owners. Technical people such as designers, developers, and technical writers are not the target audience for web forms.

- Changes fairly often. You don't want to go to the trouble of creating templates if the content is created once and never changed again.

- Is more than one or two pages. Similar to the previous point, you may not want to invest time in creating and maintaining a web form if there are only a handful of pages that will ever be created using that web form.

- Has multiple output formats. One of the beauties of a web form is that its data is stored as XML, and then optionally transformed into one or more output formats. Content that needs to be available as HTML, RSS, and mobile-friendly HTML, for example, might be good to manage with web forms because it can be entered once and rendered in each desired format.

- Has a structure that might be generic enough to be reused in multiple places within a site or across multiple sites. Examples include content types such as "alert", "news item", "contact information", or "information request form".

- Has a relatively fixed and simple structure. If you think of the spectrum of structured content from SGML-like structured authoring tools on one end to very unstructured tools such as word processors, page layout tools, or graphics tools on the other, web forms are somewhere to the left of center. A web form is structured—it has a fixed number of fields that are ordered a certain way. But a web form would never be used as a replacement for editing highly complex XML documents such as flight maintenance manuals.

These are not hard-and-fast rules. There are those that will move 100% of their site into web forms. As long as the ultimate value of WCM is achieved, making it easier to manage your web site, by all means go for it!

Step-by-Step: Creating a SomeCo Press Release Web Form

SomeCo has decided to use web forms to manage press releases because the corporate communications team is looking to remove the web team bottleneck. The web team is happy because it is looking forward to getting away from mundane "please convert this from Microsoft Word to HTML and post it" tasks and moving toward more value-added tasks such as information architecture and user interface design.

The press release is simple. It includes a title, subtitle, location, date, body, contact information, and footer. The index or list of press releases will be addressed in another example.

Creating the press release web form involves creating an XML Schema (XSD) document to define the data structure and a presentation rendering file (you'll use FreeMarker in this example), configuring the web form in the data dictionary, and finally, adding the web form to the SomeCo web site.

Web forms may seem similar to content types, and they are. But don't be confused. A web form XSD defines the structure of an XML document. The data saved by the web form will be XML conforming to the XSD. A customized content model, on the other hand, defines metadata on the object. Web form data lives in a file. Object metadata lives in the relational database. If you need to extract selected elements from the web form XML and store them in properties on the object, you can see Metadata Extractors in Chapter 4.

To implement a simple press release form, follow these steps:

1. Create a new XML Schema file in Eclipse in the **| src | forms** folder. This book won't cover XSD in any depth. I recommend you to pick up a book on XML Schema, use XSD creation tools to save some time, or refer to other XSDs in the source code as examples, or all three. For SomeCo's press release, the XSD begins by defining the XML Schema, Alfresco, and SomeCo Press Release namespaces:

```
<?xml version="1.0"?>
<xs:schema xmlns:xs="http://www.w3.org/2001/XMLSchema"
      xmlns:pr="http://www.someco.com/corp/pr"
      xmlns:alf="http://www.alfresco.org"
      targetNamespace="http://www.someco.com/corp/pr"
      elementFormDefault="qualified">
```

2. Next, add the root element for `press_release`. In schema terms, the `press_release` element is a complex type made up of a sequence that includes the fields you need to capture in order to produce a press release. Add the schema definition XML to define the fields (`title`, `sub_title`, `location`, `date`, `body`, `company_footer`, and `company_info`) and close out the `xs:schema` tag:

```
<!-- defines the form for creating a press release -->
<xs:element name="press_release">
   <xs:complexType>
      <xs:sequence>
         <xs:element name="title" type="xs:normalizedString"/>
         <xs:element name="sub_title" type=
           "xs:normalizedString"/>
         <xs:element name="location" type=
           "xs:normalizedString" default="Austin, TX"/>
         <xs:element name="date" type="xs:date"/>
         <xs:element name="body" type="xs:string" minOccurs=
           "1" maxOccurs="1">
            <xs:annotation>
```

```
                  <xs:appinfo>
                     <alf:appearance>custom</alf:appearance>
                  </xs:appinfo>
               </xs:annotation>
             </xs:element>
           <xs:element name="company_footer" type="xs:string"
             minOccurs="0" maxOccurs="unbounded"/>
           <xs:element name="contact_info" type="xs:string"
             minOccurs="0" maxOccurs="unbounded"/>
         </xs:sequence>
       </xs:complexType>
     </xs:element>
   </xs:schema>
```

3. Save the XSD file.

4. Create a new FreeMarker file in **| src | forms** called `press-release.ftl` to use as the rendering engine presentation file. The FreeMarker needs to convert the XML saved by the web form into an HTML version of the press release. You'll see an XSLT example shortly. Begin the FTL by declaring the press release prefix and assigning the root `press_release` element to a variable:

```
<#ftl ns_prefixes={"pr":"http://www.someco.com/corp/pr"}>
<#assign press_release = .vars["pr:press_release"]>
```

5. Then, add the markup for the press release, inserting FreeMarker calls to extract data from the XML where necessary:

```
<div class="node">
  <h2>${press_release["pr:sub_title"]}</h2>
  <p><p>${press_release["pr:location"]} - ${press_release
       ["pr:date"]} - ${press_release["pr:body"]}
            <#list press_release["pr:company_footer"] as cf>
            <p>${cf}</p>
         </#list>
            <#list press_release["pr:contact_info"] as ci>
            <p>${ci}</p>
         </#list>
  </p></p>
  <div class="clearfix"></div>
</div>
<div class="clearfix"></div>
```

6. Save the FTL file.

7. Log in as admin.

8. Go to **Data Dictionary**, and then **Web Forms**.

9. Click **Create**, and then **Create Web Form**.

10. Browse for the schema.

11. Alfresco needs to know where to store the web form XML. In this example, you'll store it in **|news|press-releases|data**. So specify the output path pattern:

    ```
    /${webapp}/news/press-releases/data/${name}.xml
    ```

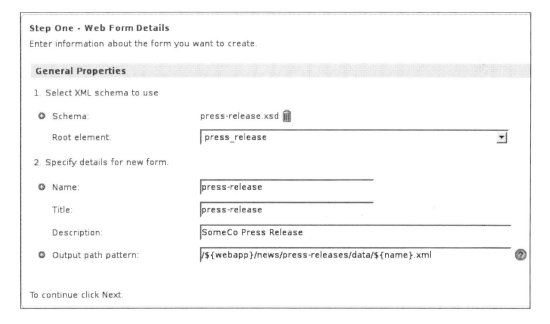

12. Click **Next**.

13. Select the Rendering Engine template file you created earlier. It should be in **src|web|forms|press-release.ftl**.

14. Alfresco needs to know where to store the rendition. This markup is going to eventually be read by an AJAX call from the press release list page. The call expects the press release to reside in **|ajaxnews|news|press-releases,** so specify the following output path pattern:

```
/${webapp}/ajaxnews/news/press-releases/${name}.${extension}
```

Step Two - Configure Templates

Enter information about the rendering engine templates you want to use for form press-release.

1. Select the rendering engine template to use

   Rendering Engine Template File: press-release.ftl 🗑

2. Specify details for the new rendering engine template

   ⊙ Rendering Engine: ⊙ FreeMarker ⊙ XSLT ⊙ XSL-FO

   ⊙ Name: | press-release.ftl |

      Title: | press-release |

      Description: | Transforms press release XML into HTML |

   ⊙ Rendition mimetype: | HTML   ▾ |

   ⊙ Output path pattern: | /${webapp}/ajaxnews/news/press-releases/${name}.${extension} | ⊙

3. [Add to List]

   Selected Rendering Engines
   No selected items.

To continue click Next.

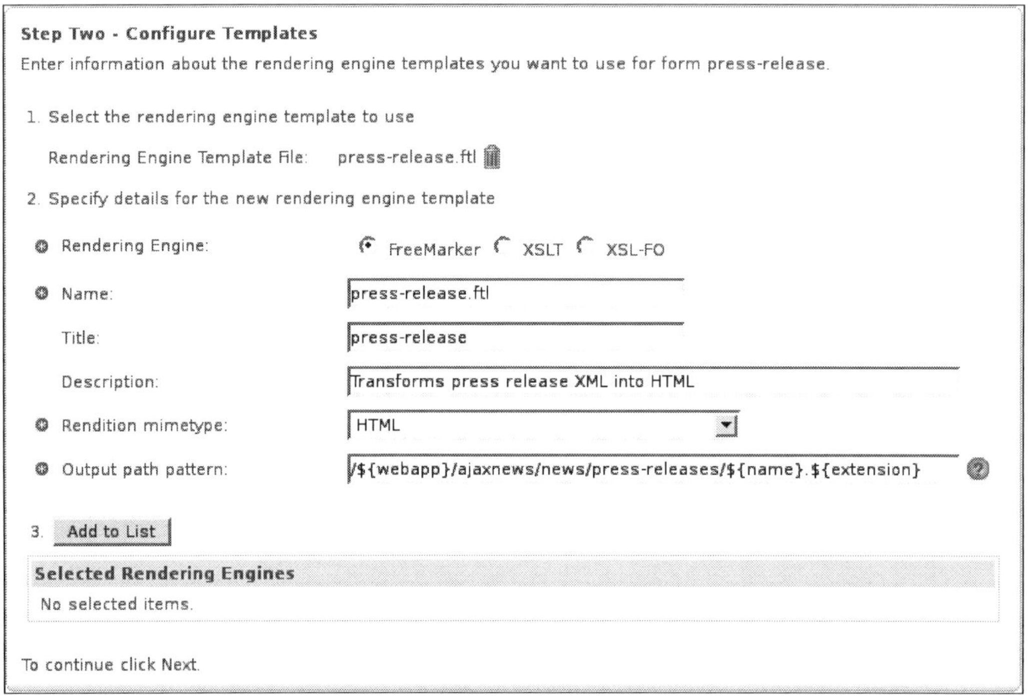

15. Click **Add to List**.

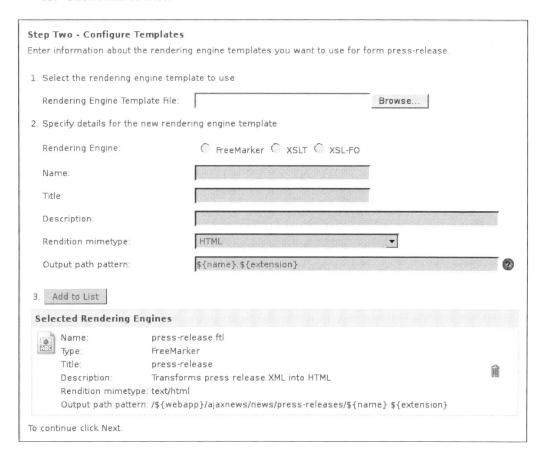

16. Click **Next**. Specify **No, not now** to defer associating a workflow with this web form.

17. Click **Next**, then **Finish**.

18. The web form has been defined in the data dictionary. Now, any web project can choose to use it. You need to make sure the SomeCo web project is configured to use the form. Go to the web project then click **Actions**, and then **Edit Web Project Settings**.

19. Click **Next** until you get to the web form step. Click **Add to list**.

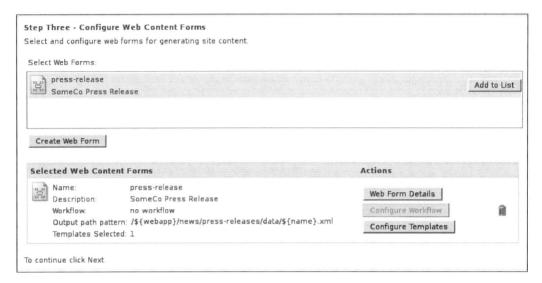

20. Click **Finish**.

Test the web form. You can either create content using the web form by using the **Create Content** link from the list of web forms in the sandbox as shown here, or you can browse the web site and click **Create**, and then **Create Web Content**:

Either way, you will launch the create web content wizard. In the first step, specify a name for the content. The next step launches the web form:

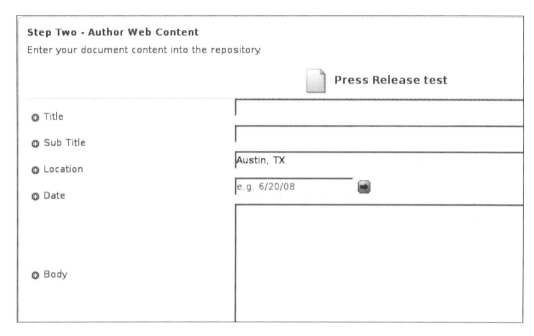

Click the **preview** icon (the little eyeball) to preview the generated press release HTML:

When you are happy with the content, click **Finish** to save the content to the repository.

 Did preview work? If not, the first thing to check is whether your virtualization server is running. Preview depends on it. Next, are you connected to the Internet? Unless you've changed the `alfresco-virtserver.properties` file in the virtualization server's **virtual-tomcat|conf** directory, Alfresco expects connectivity to the `alfrescodemo.net` domain.

Mapping XML Schema Types to Web Form Controls

The type of control that appears in the web form depends on the XML Schema data type. In the press release example, you saw that the XSD type `xs:normalizedString` maps to a text input field, the `xs:date` type maps to a date picker, and an `xs:string` maps to a rich text editor.

In addition to types, XSD supports annotations. In the context of XForms and Alfresco, annotations allow you to fine-tune the appearance of web form controls. For example, in the press-release XSD, you used an annotation to set the appearance attribute of the `body` element to `custom`. If you take a look at `web-client-config-wcm.xml`, you'll see where this is configured:

```
<widget xforms-type="xf:textarea"
        appearance="custom"
        javascript-class-name="alfresco.xforms.RichTextEditor">
    <param name=
     "theme_advanced_buttons1">bold,italic,underline,strikethrough,
       separator,fontselect,fontsizeselect</param>
    <param name=
     "theme_advanced_buttons2">link,unlink,image,separator,justifyleft,
      justifycenter,justifyright,justifyfull,separator,bullist,numlist,
      separator,undo,redo,separator,forecolor,backcolor</param>
    <param name="height">600</param>
    <param name="mode">exact</param>
    <param name="force_p_newlines">true</param>
    <param name="apply_source_formatting">true</param>
    <param name="plugins">table</param>
    <param name="theme_advanced_buttons3">tablecontrols</param>
</widget>
```

Here's how to make sense of what's happening:

1. You declared `body` to be an `xs:string`.

2. Alfresco's embedded XForms implementation, Chiba, maps `xs:string` to `xf:textarea`.

3. You annotated `body` to have an appearance of `custom`.

4. In `web-client-config-wcm.xml`, the `xf:textarea` widget is defined for the `custom` appearance as being implemented with the TinyMCE Rich Text Editor, with a specific set of buttons, the table plug-in, and so on. When the form is rendered, the widget uses the parameters from `web-client-config-wcm.xml` to render itself. The parameters include things such as the editor component to use, the specific set of buttons to display, and so on.

The following table, a subset of what's on the Alfresco wiki, shows some of the more common XSD datatypes supported by Alfresco, the appearance annotations they support, and how they map to Alfresco web form controls:

XML Schema Datatype	"alf:appearance" Annotations Supported	XForms Control	Alfresco Web Form UI Control
`xs:string`	Full	`xf:textarea`	Rich text editor
	Default	`xf:textarea`	Rich text editor, min.
	Minimal	`xf:textarea`	Text area
`xs:normalizedString`	None	`xf:input`	Text field
`xs:boolean`	None	`xf:input`	Checkbox
`xs:double`	None	`xf:input`	Text field
`xs:decimal`	None	`xf:input`	Text field
`xs:float`	None	`xf:input`	Text field
`xs:integer, xs:double, xs:decimal, xs:float` with inclusive bounds	None	`xf:range`	Slider
`xs:anyType`	None	`xf:textarea`	Rich text editor
`xs:anyURI`	Full	`xf:upload`	File picker
	Minimal	`xf:upload`	Text field
	Configurable	`xf:upload`	File picker with filters
`xs:anyType`	None	`xf:textarea`	Rich text editor

Localizing Web Forms with Labels and Alerts

In addition to using annotations to customize the appearance of a control, you can also use annotations to override the default label and field validation alert message. The override can be static text or a localized string.

In the press release example, you created an element called sub_title. By default, this results in a label called Sub Title and the alert message: "Please provide a valid value for Sub Title. Sub Title is a required NormalizedString value". What if, instead of Sub Title, you wanted to keep the sub_title element in the XML, but have the web form show Lead-in and maybe give a friendlier alert message? Annotations let you do that. In this case, the sub_title element would be updated as follows:

```
<xs:element name="sub_title" type="xs:normalizedString">
   <xs:annotation>
      <xs:appinfo>
         <alf:label>${leadIn}</alf:label>
         <alf:alert>${leadInAlert}</alf:alert>
      </xs:appinfo>
   </xs:annotation>
</xs:element>
```

The corresponding key and value for the label and alert would then be added to one of three places:

- A strings.properties file in the web form's folder (**Data Dictionary | Web Forms | press-release**, in this example)
- A strings.properties file in the Web Forms folder, which would be used globally across all web forms
- Within the custom webclient.properties file, which would be packaged and deployed with your other extensions

Externalizing labels and alerts to properties files isn't required. You could have put the values directly in the annotations as string literals, but externalizing the strings is better because the web form labels and alerts can then be localized.

If you were to compose a web form with these changes in place, the label and alert message would show the annotated values as shown here:

Step Two - Author Web Content

Enter your document content into the repository.

Please provide values for all required fields

- Please provide a valid value for 'Title'. 'Title' is a required 'NormalizedString' value.
- Please provide a lead-in
- Please provide a valid value for 'Date'. 'Date' is a required 'Date' value.
- Please provide a valid value for 'Body'. 'Body' is a required 'String' value.

Press Release test-local

- Title
- Lead-in
- Location   Austin, TX
- Date   e.g. 7/2/08

Generating XSD Dynamically

You didn't have a reason to do this for SomeCo, but there might be times when the XSD cannot be fully expressed at design time. For example, suppose you wanted to populate a drop-down list on a web form with the results of an SQL query to some external database. Alfresco's sample web site that ships with Alfresco WCM has an example of this. In this case, it uses a query against the web project rather than a database, but the same technique applies. In its press release XSD (every WCM vendor on Earth uses "press release" as an example), it uses an xs:include tag that points to a JSP, which defines part of its schema:

```
<xs:include schemaLocation="/media/releases/get_company_footer_
choices_simple_type.jsp"/>
```

Later in the XSD, it adds an element that refers to a type defined by the dynamic schema:

```
...
    <xs:element name="include_company_footer" type=
    "pr:company_footer_choices" minOccurs="1" maxOccurs="unbounded"/>
...
```

Where does that `pr:company_footer_choices` XSD type get defined? When the `include` is processed and the JSP is invoked, the result is the XML Schema that defines the type and includes the query results. Here is the relevant chunk of the JSP referred to by the `xs:include`:

```
<jsp:root>
   ...
    <xs:schema xmlns:xs="http://www.w3.org/2001/XMLSchema"
             xmlns:alf="http://www.alfresco.org"
             elementFormDefault="qualified">
    <xs:simpleType name="company_footer_choices">
      <xs:restriction base="xs:normalizedString">
        <!-- call into CompanyFooterBean to retrieve all company
footers -->
        <c:forEach items="${pr:getCompanyFooterChoices(pageContext)}"
         var="companyFooter">
          <jsp:element name="xs:enumeration">
           <!-- this is the file name of the company footer -->
           <jsp:attribute name="value"><c:out value=
           "${companyFooter.fileName}"/></jsp:attribute>
           <jsp:body>
             <xs:annotation>
               <xs:appinfo>
                 <!-- this produces the label displayed in the
combobox within the press release form -->
                 <alf:label><c:out value=
                 "${companyFooter.name}"/></alf:label>
               </xs:appinfo>
             </xs:annotation>
           </jsp:body>
          </jsp:element>
        </c:forEach>
      </xs:restriction>
    </xs:simpleType>
  </xs:schema>
```

You can use this same pattern in your projects to dynamically generate XSD. But remember that the JSP is invoked in the context of the web project. That means the virtualization server has to be running and the web project has to have everything it needs to render the JSP. In Alfresco's press release example, that includes the JSP, a tag library, a bean, and dependent JARs.

Step-by-Step: Creating a Press Release Index Page

You now have a press release web form that has one presentation rendition. But SomeCo's web site needs to show a list of press releases. The user experience team wants to create a press release index page that shows a list of press release titles alongside the body of the first press release in the list. Clicking another press release title should load the body of the press release without requiring an entire page refresh.

The trick here is deciding how to grab the list of press releases and when to generate the press release index page. There are a few options:

- Build a static version of the press release index page. Use XSLT or FreeMarker to build the list of press release titles. Either add the index page generation as an additional rendition to the press release web form or create a separate web form just for the press release index.

- Use JSP to dynamically render the press release index page. The JSP can build the list of press release titles and links by querying the repository with the AVMRemote API.

- Use JSP as in the previous option, but use a call to a web script to build the list of press release titles instead of the AVMRemote API. Web scripts are preferred over the AVM Remote API.

The best choice depends entirely on how you've chosen to set up your site and deploy content. In a completely static site, your only choice will be to render the press release list prior to deployment. You'll have to decide whether you want to generate the list every time a web form is saved, in which case you could add the press release list as an additional rendition to the existing press release web form, or you can create a separate web form for the list.

If you've decided to include dynamic calls to Alfresco as a part of your site's architecture, you may decide that generating the press release list dynamically (either through the AVMRemote API or a web script) makes the most sense. The nice thing about this approach is that you don't have to worry about when to generate the list, but you do have to pay attention to potential timing issues. If your pages depend on any content that is statically deployed (maybe a video that accompanies the press release, for example), the query on the index page might pick up a press release title by querying staging. However, the static assets have yet to be deployed to the frontend.

Let's run through the "static index page, list generated at press release author time" example. The previous example used FreeMarker. Let's use XSLT this time, though FreeMarker would have worked just as well. By the end of this example, you'll have a new XSLT presentation file to add as an additional rendition to the existing press release web form. Every time a press release gets saved, the index page will be regenerated.

To implement the press release list page, follow these steps:

1. Create a new XSL file in the client-extensions Eclipse project under **src | forms** called `press-release-index.xsl` by copying the `press-release-index.xsl.sample` file from the source code that accompanied this chapter.

2. The HTML for the press release index page is a bit involved. It has been copied into the `press-release-index.xsl.sample` file for you with the sections relevant to this example flagged with "TODO" comments. Search for the first "TODO". Add an XSL variable that makes a call to the `AVMRemote` function, `parseXMLDocuments`, to retrieve a list of press release XML:

```
<xsl:variable name="pressReleaseList" select="alf:
parseXMLDocuments('press-release', '/news/press-releases/data')"
/>
```

3. Now search for the next "TODO". This is where the list of press release titles should go. Use an `xsl:for-each` to iterate over the list, and output the press release title and a link to the press release HTML. This snippet includes a call to an XSL function you are about to add, which is used to change the suffix of the target press release file from `xml` to `html`:

```
<xsl:for-each select="$pressReleaseList">
  <xsl:variable name="selectedVar">
    <xsl:choose>
      <xsl:when test="position() = 1">selected</xsl:when>
          <xsl:otherwise>leaf</xsl:otherwise>
    </xsl:choose>
  </xsl:variable>

  <li class="{$selectedVar}">
    <xsl:variable name="fileNameFixed"><xsl:call-template name=
     "fixFileName"><xsl:with-param name="fileName"><xsl:value-of
      select="@alf:file_name" /></xsl:with-param>
        </xsl:call-template></xsl:variable>
    <a href="{$fileNameFixed}"><xsl:value-of select="pr:title" />
    <span class="bioListTitle"></span>
            </a>
  </li>
</xsl:for-each>
```

4. The next "TODO" is to use a couple of `xsl:value-of` statements to output the title and body of the first press release in the list:

```
<h2>
  <xsl:value-of select="$pressReleaseList[1]/pr:title" />
</h2>
<p></p><p></p>
<xsl:value-of select="$pressReleaseList[1]/pr:body" />
<div class="clearfix"></div>
```

5. The final "TODO" is to add the `fixFileName` function referred to in the press release iterator. The function simply does a substring replacement on the `xml` suffix:

```
<xsl:template name="fixFileName">
  <xsl:param name="fileName" />
  <xsl:value-of select="concat(substring-before($fileName, '.xml')
    , '.html')" />
</xsl:template>
```

6. Save the file.

7. Now you need to add the new press release index presentation as an additional rendering engine template to the press release web form. This will cause the index page to be regenerated every time a new press release is created. Go to **Data Dictionary | Web Forms** and click the **Edit Web Form** icon.

8. Click **Next** to display the **Configure Templates** dialog.

9. Browse for the newly created **press-release-index.xsl** file.

10. Set the output path to:

```
${webapp}/news/press-releases/index.${extension}
```

11. Click **Add to List**.

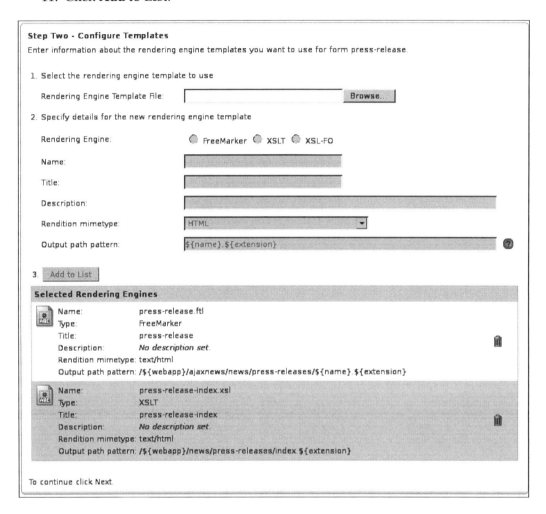

12. Click **Next** until the **Finish** button is enabled, and then click **Finish**.

13. You may find that the existing web project needs to have the web form dropped and re-added for the new change to take effect smoothly. Go to the web project, click **Actions** and then **Edit Web Project Settings**, and then click **Next** until you get to the **Configure Web Forms** step in the wizard. Click the trash can icon to remove it from the list, and then click **Add to List**, and then **Finish**.

Now test your change. You should be able to edit the existing web content or create a new press release, and see that both the press release and the press release list get generated. Preview the index page to validate that the AJAX call works appropriately.

Making Changes to an Existing Web Form

As you saw in the previous example, certain changes made to the web form definition in the data dictionary may require touching the web form configuration in the individual web project. If these are repeatable in your environment, they should probably be logged as bugs in Jira. If you do see quirky behavior after making a web form change, it can usually be addressed by removing and re-adding the web form to the web project. Of course, if you have many web projects this could get tedious quickly.

Changes to an XSD when web form data has already been created can be tricky. If you are just doing something simple such as adding annotations, you can make the change and update the XSD using the **Update** action on the XSD object in the web form folder. But if you are changing the data structure, you should first test that change on a development Alfresco instance to see how existing web form XML content will behave after the change. Depending on how that goes, you may have to use a script to update the existing XML to be compatible with the new XSD.

Using Web Forms Outside the WCM User Interface

In the Labs edition, Alfresco has added forms capability to the web client without requiring a web project. This is handy when you need non-technical users to author XML, which you then subsequently process with rules, actions, web scripts, or some other mechanism.

All of the discussion in this chapter on web forms applies to non-WCM forms, or simply, "Forms". The differences between WCM forms and non-WCM forms are:

- Non-WCM forms do not have associated presentation rendition files. Forms simply save as XML. If you need to transform the XML into one or more renditions, you can use rule actions to fire when the XML gets created.

- Correspondingly, because there is no transformation, there is no need for a **Preview** to see how the renditions transformed the XML.

- Forms do not have an output path. XML data is saved where the user is sitting in the folder structure when he/she clicks **Create Content**.

The ability to do simple XML authoring in the web client outside a web site's context is often requested as a feature. So, hopefully, it will "graduate" from the Labs edition to the Enterprise edition soon.

Deploying Content

Once content is committed to staging, it is ready to be delivered to the live web site. What's the best way to get content out of Alfresco and onto the frontend application or web servers? There are several options to consider:

- **CIFS**. One option is to serve the content directly out of the **Staging Sandbox**. The web server or application server points its document root to the **Staging Sandbox** via CIFS. Although people have done this in the past, it is no longer recommended.

- **File-level copy**. Another CIFS-based approach is to copy the content from a CIFS-mounted sandbox to the web server's file system. This copy could be scheduled by a cron job or initiated manually. Alfresco's file system deployment functionality really makes this option obsolete. It addresses the many drawbacks to this approach, which include lack of transactional deployment and no integration with the web client user interface.

- **File System Receiver (FSR)**. The FSR is used for Alfresco-to-file system content deployments. An Alfresco FSR is a small Spring application that runs on each file system you want to deploy to. The Alfresco WCM web client communicates with it over RMI. Further details on the FSR will be provided shortly.

- **Alfresco Server Receiver (ASR)**. The ASR is used for Alfresco-to-Alfresco deployments. The ASR is built into the Alfresco server and, like the FSR, communicates via RMI. The ASR copies objects between web projects, which means that, unlike FSR, metadata is preserved.

FSR and ASR deployments are the recommended approach and will suffice in most cases. If, for some reason, none of these options addresses your specific needs, you can always develop your own deployment mechanism. For example, one Optaros client wanted to convert JSP pages to rendered HTML prior to deployment. If one of the methods mentioned were used to deploy the page, the JSP would be copied to the target file system. Instead, we wrote a process that invoked the JSP and deployed the resulting HTML page so that the deployment target contained only static HTML.

Step-by-Step: Deploying Content Using the File System Receiver (FSR)

Let's work through an example to deploy the SomeCo web site to a directory on your file system. This will involve obtaining, installing, and configuring the FSR on your local machine, creating the target directory, and adding an FSR host to the SomeCo web project.

To test out FSR locally, follow these steps:

1. The FSR is distributed as a separate download. For example, if you are running Labs, you need the `alfresco-labs-deployment.zip` file. Enterprise users running binaries will download `alfresco-enterprise-deployment.zip`. If you are building from source, the deployment code is included with the rest of the source code in the "deployment" project.

2. Regardless of the distribution you are using, unzip the archive to a place that makes sense to you on the file system. On my machine, that's **|usr|local|bin|alfresco-enterprise-2.2-wcm|deploy**.

3. Edit the startup script appropriate to your operating system. Depending on your setup, you may have to modify the classpath in the startup script. For example, on my system, I modified the startup script to look like this:

```
#!/bin/sh
DEPLOY_HOME=/usr/local/bin/alfresco-enterprise-2.2-wcm/deploy

nohup java -server -cp $DEPLOY_HOME/alfresco-deployment.
jar:$DEPLOY_HOME/spring-2.0.2.jar:$DEPLOY_HOME/commons-logging-
1.0.4.jar:$DEPLOY_HOME/alfresco-core.jar:$DEPLOY_HOME/jug.
jar:$DEPLOY_HOME org.alfresco.deployment.Main application-context.
xml >>$DEPLOY_HOME/deployment.log 2>&1 &
```

4. If any of the JARs referenced in the startup script are missing, either adjust the path in the startup script to point to the valid location for those JARs or copy the JARs from the Alfresco SDK dependency library (**$SDK_HOME|lib|server and $SDK_HOME|lib|server|dependencies**) to the deployment program directory.

5. Edit the `application-context.xml` file in the deployment program directory. Create an FSR target as an entry in the `targetData` property map. The FSR target maps an FSR target name (the `key` attribute) to a directory on the file system (the value of the `entry` element with the `key` attribute set to `root`):

```
<!-- Target Configuration. Modify for your site. -->
<property name="targetData">
    <map>
        <entry key="someco-live">
            <map>
                <entry key="root"><value>/var/www/someco-live
                </value></entry>
                <entry key="user"><value>admin</value></entry>
                <entry key="password"><value>admin</value></entry>
            </map>
        </entry>
        . . .
```

6. Save the `application-context.xml` file.

7. If it does not exist already, create the target deployment directory on the file system. The directory can be anywhere, but in this example, the directory is **|var|www|someco-live**.

8. Start the FSR deployment listener process by executing the startup script. If you used the startup script provided here, you can monitor the `deployment.log` file to watch for errors.

9. Log in to the web client as admin (project coordinators can do this too).

10. Edit the web project settings for the SomeCo web site. Click **Next** until the **Configure Deployment Servers** page is displayed. Click **Add File System Receiver**.

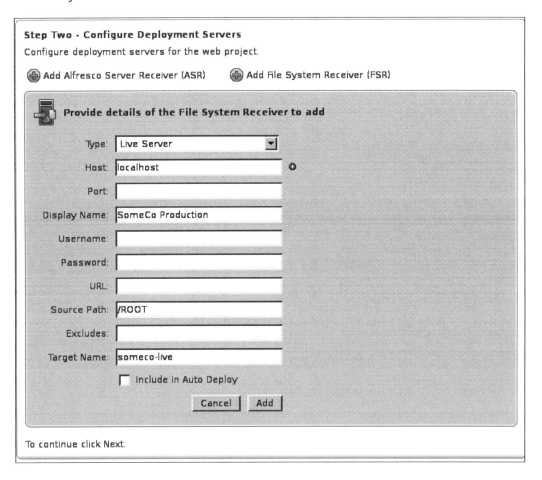

11. Complete the form as follows:

    ° Specify **localhost** for the **Host** field.

    ° Provide a user-friendly **Display Name** such as **SomeCo Production**.

    ° You want all web project content to be deployed, so specify **/ROOT** as the **Source Path**.

    ° The **Target Name** needs to match the FSR target you configured in `application-config.xml`, so specify **someco-live**.

12. Click **Add** (or, depending on the release, it may be **Save**).

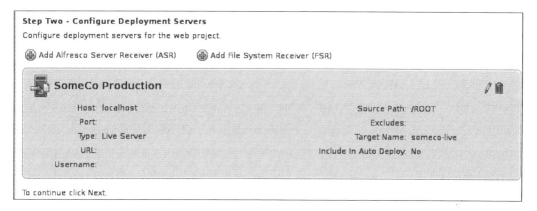

13. Click **Finish** to exit out of the web project wizard.

14. You now have a configured FSR target and you are ready to test it out. You should have at least one snapshot in your **Staging Sandbox**. Snapshots are automatically created when content is submitted to staging. When you click the twisty to view **Recent Snapshots**, you will notice that now that the web project has at least one deployment target, a **Deploy** action icon is shown.

15. To initiate a deployment, click the icon, make sure the deployment target is selected, and then click **OK**. The deployment target will update with the status of the deployment.

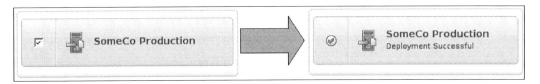

16. Close out of the deployment status page and notice a new link in the **Staging Sandbox** called **View Deployments**. Click the link to see the detailed list of the files that were deployed.

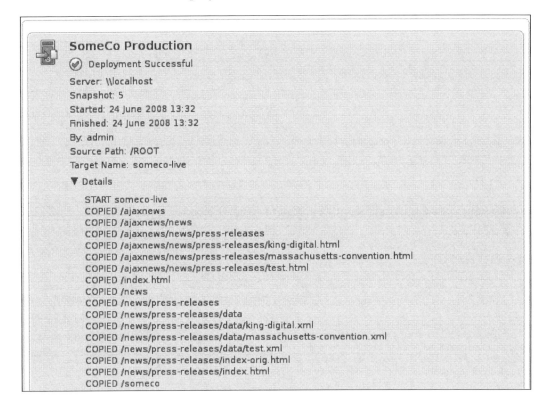

17. You should also check the target directory (| **var** | **www** | **someco-live** in this example) to validate that the content was copied from Alfresco to the file system. Finally, note that the **Status** column in the list of snapshots now includes **LIVE** next to the successfully deployed snapshot.

If the snapshot does not deploy successfully, check the deployment log and the Alfresco server log. If you are running on Linux, make sure that the user running the deployment process has write access to the target directory.

FSR deployments are transactional only within a given FSR target. In other words, if something goes wrong with the deployment to a specific target, the deployment will be rolled back automatically for that target only. If you are deploying to multiple targets and one fails and the others succeed, the successful deployments will not be rolled back.

To manually roll back a deployment, you simply deploy the previous snapshot to that deployment target.

Running Multiple FSR Hosts and Multiple FSR Targets

A given physical host can run multiple File System Receivers. Each FSR must run on its own port. The RMI port is specified in the `deployment.properties` file in the deployment program directory.

Each FSR can contain multiple FSR target directories. For example, each web project in your organization might deploy to a different directory on the target file system. In fact, different web projects should never deploy to exactly the same FSR target. That's because the web projects will try to make the target directory look like their own **Staging Sandbox**—each deployment will wipe the other web project's deployment out.

Setting the FSR Target User and Password

You probably noticed the username and password entries in the deployment program's `application-context.xml` file. If these are set to anything other than `admin` and `admin` respectively, the web project's FSR configuration has to specify a matching username and password or the deployment will fail. The ports the FSR uses are well known. So it is a good idea to set the username and password to keep someone from intentionally or unintentionally deploying content to your FSR.

Viewing Deployment Reports

Alfresco keeps track of what gets deployed. These are persisted to the spaces store as `{http://www.alfresco.org/model/wcmappmodel/1.0}deploymentreport` objects, which are the children of `{http://www.alfresco.org/model/wcmappmodel/1.0}deploymentattempt` objects stored in the web folder. These are accessible through the WCM user interface by clicking on **View Deployment Reports** in the **Staging Sandbox** and, like any other node in the repository, via the API.

Deploying to Test Servers

In the example, you took the defaults when you configured the FSR host in the web project settings. The server type defaults to "Live Server". The other choice in that drop-down is "Test Server". So what's a test server? Suppose you are managing a .NET-based web site. (I know it is painful—don't worry, this is just a thought exercise). When you click **Preview**, the virtualization server will have no way to render the .NET pages because the virtualization server is a Tomcat application server. In this case, you need a deployment target running Windows Server and the .NET Framework so that you can deploy and test the site.

The solution is to install the FSR on a set of Windows Servers. Then, in the web project settings, each of the FSR targets that point to the Windows Servers can be flagged as a "Test Server". This group of test servers effectively establishes a pool of servers that sandbox users and content reviewers can deploy to. When someone deploys to a test server, the test server is allocated to that individual for that web project so that no one else can deploy to it until it is released back to the pool.

Note that the test servers don't have to be separate physical servers. An FSR can contain many targets. And, you could run multiple FSRs on a given box if needed.

If the web project contains at least one test server, individuals can deploy from their sandbox using **More Actions**, and then **Deploy** from the sandbox page:

When the user is done testing their changes, he/she can use **More Actions**, and then **Release Server** to return the server to the pool:

Reviewers can also deploy to test servers. The deploy button for reviewers is located on the task management page for the workflow that gets initiated when content is submitted:

Test servers allocated to workflow reviewers are returned to the pool when the review task is completed.

Enabling Deployment Targets for Auto Deploy

Remember that once content is committed to staging, it has to be deployed somewhere. Even if content is routed through a workflow and approved, it still sits in staging and waits to be deployed.

For some people, this makes sense. They like to be able to control exactly when content moves to the live servers by manually triggering the deployment using the **Deploy** link for a particular snapshot as you've already seen. For others, once content is approved it should be deployed immediately without human intervention. That's a job for "auto deploy".

There are two steps to enabling auto deploy. First, at least one deployment target (either ASR or FSR) has to be flagged for auto deploy. There is a checkbox on the deployment server configuration page in web project settings that you can check to indicate that the target is eligible for auto deploy.

Second, when content is submitted via workflow, the submitter has to check the **Auto Deploy** checkbox.

When these two conditions are met, a workflow task in the default **submit to web** workflow will kick off a deployment to all deployment targets that have the auto deploy flag set to true.

In order to bulletproof this a bit, if you are looking to leverage auto deploy, it would be a good idea to customize the default workflow (or make the change in your custom workflows) to make the auto deploy flag read-only, or, better yet, just set it to true behind the scenes and hide it from the user entirely.

Step-by-Step: Deploying to an Alfresco System Receiver (ASR)

You've worked through an Alfresco-to-File System deployment using FSR. But what if your web site is going to be dynamically querying the Alfresco repository? In those cases, you'll probably want to deploy the content from a web project on your authoring server to one (or more, preferably) "rendering" server. A rendering server is just another Alfresco server that is used to expose the web content as a service by responding to queries from the frontend.

The only requirement on the target is that Alfresco must be up and running. In fact, for testing and development purposes, Alfresco can even deploy to itself. That's what we're going to do in this example. Setting this up involves creating a new web project to expose the deployed content, editing the web project settings with the new ASR target, and then running the deployment.

To try this out, follow these steps:

1. Create a new web project. The name isn't important, but the DNS name is. When Alfresco deploys the project it will take the source project's DNS name and append "live" to the end. So if the DNS name for the SomeCo Corporate Site is **corporate-site** the target store (and therefore the DNS name of the new web project) will be **corporate-sitelive**.

2. Edit the web project settings for the SomeCo Corporate Site. Add a new ASR target. Take the defaults, but provide a host name of **localhost**.

3. Initiate a deployment for a snapshot. Select the newly created deployment target.

Upon successful deployment, you should be able to browse the target web project's **Staging Sandbox** and see the same content you have in your source web project's **Staging Sandbox**.

Note that the earlier discussion regarding auto deploy and live versus test servers applies to ASRs as well. But unfortunately, treating localhost as a test server does not seem to work.

Performing Post-Deployment Processing

There may be cases when you need to perform some tasks on the local deployment target after the files have been delivered. A good example of this might be loading metadata into an external relational database. Another example might be requesting indexing by an external search engine. In both examples, you need to be able to call a program after the deployment runs.

Step-by-Step: Running Post-Deployment Code in an FSR Deployment

In this case of an FSR deployment, the logic you want to execute after a deployment resides in a Java class that implements the `org.alfresco.deployment.FSDeploymentRunnable` interface. There are two examples that ship out of the box with Alfresco. One is called `org.alfresco.deployment.SampleRunnable` and the other is called `org.alfresco.deployment.ProgramRunnable`. The `SampleRunnable` class writes a deployment log file starting with `dep-log` to the deployment program's root directory. The `ProgramRunnable` class shows one way to run executables external to Java. It writes a temporary file containing a list of the deployed assets, and then calls `cp` to copy the file to a directory specified as an argument in the bean configuration.

As long as you implement the interface, you are free to do anything Java can do as part of your post-deployment processing. Just remember that the class is running in the context of the deployment target. If you need to connect back to Alfresco for some reason, you'll need to do so via the Web Services API or by invoking a web script. It also means the code that is being executed will need to be on the deployment target's classpath.

Let's walk through an example using the two samples provided out of the box. To do that, follow these steps:

1. Look at the source for the two sample `FSDeploymentRunnable` classes. From within Eclipse, if you don't already have the full source code imported, you can look at the classes by borrowing the `alfresco-deployment.jar` in the SDK Alfresco Embedded project. The classes are in the `org.alfresco.deployment` package.

2. Edit the `application-context.xml` file in the root of your deployment program directory. You'll notice the two sample beans, `sampleRunnable` and `sampleProgramRunnable`, are already defined. The `sampleRunnable` has no properties to define. The `sampleProgramRunnable` bean needs to know the program to run. As the first argument, the class will provide the full path to the temporary file containing the deployed assets. It is up to you to provide further arguments. The bean is configured to do a copy out of the box. Change the target filepath to something that makes sense to your environment. For example, on my machine I'm using:

```
<property name="arguments">
    <list>
            <value>/home/jpotts/dump.txt</value>
        </list>
</property>
```

3. Add bean references for both beans to the list of "runnables" in the deployment target configuration for "someco-live":

```
<entry key="runnables">
    <list>
        <ref bean="sampleRunnable" />
        <ref bean="sampleProgramRunnable" />
    </list>
</entry>
```

4. Save `application-context.xml`.

5. Restart the deployment process.

Now test out your "SomeCo Production" FSR deployment by deploying (or redeploying) a recent snapshot. You should see a deployment log file in the root of your deployment program directory that starts with `dep-log`. You should also see a log file matching the filepath you provided as an argument to the `sampleProgramRunnable` bean.

Handling Deletes

Did your change set include deleted assets as well as new or modified assets? Make sure that when you implement your post-processing logic, you've accounted for the fact that deleted files are included in the list of deployed files. You can use the `getType()` method of `DeployedFile` to figure out if a file is actually a delete (`FileType.DELETED`).

Step-by-Step: Implementing ASR Deployment Callbacks

Unfortunately, ASR deployments don't have a similar mechanism for running post deployment processing on the target host. You could incorporate post-deployment processing into a workflow step. Another alternative is to use a deployment callback. A `DeploymentCallback` is a class that implements the `org.alfresco.service.cmr.avm.deploy.DeploymentCallback` interface. When an ASR deployment runs, it fires events. Classes that implement `DeploymentCallback` can listen for those events and decide whether or not to take action.

You have to be careful how much logic you put into your callback. Long-running code could seriously affect the performance of your deployments.

Let's look at a simple example that writes a log4j log message when a deployment completes. This involves writing a new Java class and creating a new Spring configuration file to declare the new bean and to override the out of the box `avm-deploy-website` bean.

Follow these steps:

1. Write a new Java class called `com.someco.avm.DeploymentLogger` that implements `org.alfresco.service.cmr.avm.deploy.DeploymentCallback`. The class just needs to call `logger.debug` when the deployment fires an event of `Type.END`. Implement the class as follows:

```
public class DeploymentLogger implements DeploymentCallback {
    private Logger logger = Logger.getLogger
    (DeploymentLogger.class);
    public void eventOccurred(DeploymentEvent event) {
        if (event.getType() == DeploymentEvent.Type.END) {
            if (logger.isDebugEnabled()) logger.debug("The deployment
            to " + event.getDestination() + " has ended.");
        }
    }
}
```

2. Create a new Spring configuration file called `someco-avm-context.xml`. You are going to override the `avm-deploy-website` bean to add your new callback class to the list of callbacks. Start the file as follows:

```
<?xml version='1.0' encoding='UTF-8'?>
<!DOCTYPE beans PUBLIC '-//SPRING//DTD BEAN//EN' 'http://www.
springframework.org/dtd/spring-beans.dtd'>
<beans>
        <bean id="someco-deployment-logger" class=
    "com.someco.avm.DeploymentLogger" />
```

3. Now override the out of the box `avm-deploy-website` bean to include your new bean in the list of callbacks:

```
<bean id="avm-deploy-website" class=
"org.alfresco.repo.avm.actions.AVMDeployWebsiteAction" parent=
"action-executer">
   <property name="deploymentService">
         <ref bean="DeploymentService"/>
     </property>
   <property name="contentService">
       <ref bean="ContentService"/>
   </property>
   <property name="nodeService">
        <ref bean="NodeService"/>
   </property>
   <property name="publicAction">
       <value>false</value>
   </property>
   <property name="defaultRemoteUsername">
        <value>admin</value>
   </property>
   <property name="defaultRemotePassword">
        <value>admin</value>
   </property>
   <property name="defaultAlfrescoRmiPort">
        <value>${alfresco.rmi.services.port}</value>
   </property>
   <property name="defaultReceiverRmiPort">
       value>44100</value>
   </property>
   <property name="defaultTargetName">
        <value>default</value>
   </property>
   <property name="delay">
        <value>30</value>
   </property>
   <property name="callbacks">
        <list>
            <ref bean="someco-deployment-logger" />
        </list>
   </property>
</bean>
</beans>
```

4. Save the `someco-avm-context.xml` file.

5. Run **ant deploy** to compile and deploy the callback class and the Spring configuration file, and then restart Alfresco.

To test the change, fire off an ASR deployment. Assuming you've set `com.someco` equal to "debug" in `log4j.properties`, you should see the log message show up on the console.

Modifying and Creating WCM Workflows

Alfresco uses the same JBoss jBPM engine for WCM workflows as it does for the advanced workflow functionality you learned about in Chapter 7. Alfresco ships with one WCM-specific workflow. It is called "Web Site Submission", and its process definition file is **WEB-INF|classes|alfresco|workflow|submit_processdefinition.xml**.

If you open the out of the box process definition in the jBPM GPD, you'll see a diagram that looks like this:

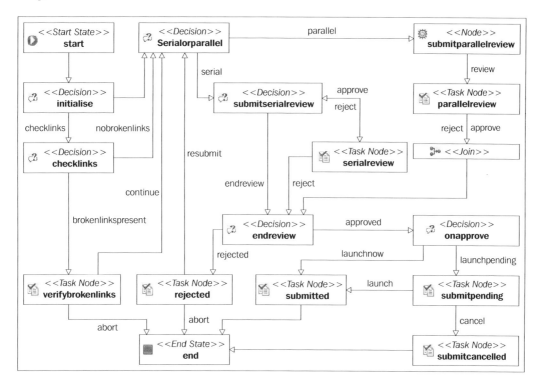

Well, it doesn't really look like that initially. You've got to use a little elbow grease to pretty up the diagram because Alfresco doesn't ship the diagram JPG files that GPD saves. Regardless, by perusing either the diagram or the underlying process definition XML source, you will learn that:

- The workflow uses non-pooled tasks (see Chapter 7). If the workflow is assigned to a group, every member of the group will have to take action. The person configuring the workflow specifies whether each member of the group should be notified in turn (**serial**) or all at once (**parallel**).

- Link checking is an optional step. If broken links are found, a task is queued to the initiator so that it can either resolve (or ignore) the issues or **abort** the workflow.

- Once content is approved, if a launch date has been set, the **submitpending** node sets a timer and waits for the publish date and time to occur. Otherwise, it immediately performs a submit.

- The submitted node has two actions. One action is used to merge the modified items into the **Staging Sandbox**. The other action is only used if the initiator chose the **deploy automatically** checkbox. If that checkbox was enabled, the action deploys the new snapshot to all deployment targets with **Auto Deploy** enabled.

There is nothing particularly special about WCM workflows. It's the same underlying engine you've already learned about. For example, there is a WCM-specific workflow model that defines metadata specific to WCM. You are free to customize the out of the box WCM workflow as needed, or create entirely new workflows using the same techniques discussed in Chapter 7.

Deploying WCM workflows works a bit differently, however. Unlike advanced workflows on the DM side of the house, WCM workflows aren't available to the user interface as soon as they are deployed. They must be added to the list of available WCM workflows by editing the WCM web client configuration. You'll see how to do that in the next example.

Using Launch Dates, Expiration Dates, and Link Checking

You won't be doing any exercises specifically around launch dates, expiration dates, or link checking, but you might be curious how these are implemented in case you want to leverage or change the out of the box behavior.

Launch Dates

When a launch date is set, Alfresco will not immediately merge the content in the workflow with the Staging store. Instead, a timer starts and the content sits in the workflow-specific store. When the timer expires, the submit happens, and the content is merged with Staging.

Content that is pending a launch date is visible from the **Staging Sandbox** in the list of **Content Awaiting Launch**:

It is important to remember that each workflow store is layered on top of Staging. There is no out of the box ability to preview a "roll-up" of all pending changes between now and some future date. For example, suppose you have submitted one asset to go live on July 1 called `foo.html` and another asset called `bar.html` to go live on July 4. Assuming today's date is in June, when you preview the content waiting for launch on July 4, you'll see the change in the context of the current live web site, not as the site will actually look on July 4. This means you will only see `bar.html`, not `foo.html`. That's because the July 4 preview is the set of July 4 changes (`bar.html`) plus what is currently in staging. It does not include `foo.html` because that change doesn't go live until July 1. If today's date was July 4, the site would contain both `foo.html` and `bar.html`.

Similarly, when you preview content submitted with a launch date set to the same day and the exact same time as another piece of content, you will only see the changes submitted as part of the same workflow. You will not see other changes pending for the same launch date/time.

Expiration Dates

A more accurate name for the expiration date field on the submit dialog page is "Reminder date". In Alfresco, content expires in the same way as milk does—after a certain date it may start to stink up the place, but it isn't going to remove itself from the refrigerator. The odor is your reminder to do something about the situation. If you set an expiration date for a piece of content, Alfresco will remind you about it when the date passes by creating a workflow with the expired content, But it is up to you to do something about it. The only action Alfresco will take against the expired content is starting the workflow.

The expiration isn't handled through a workflow timer. Instead, a scheduled bean runs every night to find expired content. When content is submitted with an expiration date, Alfresco adds the `wca:expires` aspect to it, which includes a property called `wca:expirationDate`. Expired content is content with a `wca:expirationDate` value equal to today or any earlier date.

Alfresco keeps track of the expired content keyed by the last user who modified the content. Once it has processed the list of expired content, it starts a "change request" workflow for each user in the map with all of that user's content. It's then up to the user to do something about the expired content.

The schedule for the job that checks expired content as well as the class that does the checking can be modified by overriding the `avmExpiredContentTrigger` bean in the `scheduled-jobs-context.xml` file:

```xml
<!-- Job to scan for expired content in website staging areas -->
<bean id="avmExpiredContentTrigger" class=
"org.alfresco.util.CronTriggerBean">
    <property name="jobDetail">
        <bean id="avmExpiredContentJobDetail" class=
        "org.springframework.scheduling.quartz.JobDetailBean">
            <property name="jobClass">
                <value>org.alfresco.repo.avm.AVMExpiredContentJob
                </value>
            </property>
            <property name="jobDataAsMap">
                <map>
                    <entry key="expiredContentProcessor">
                        <ref bean="avmExpiredContentProcessor" />
                    </entry>
                </map>
            </property>
        </bean>
    </property>
```

```
        <property name="scheduler">
            <ref bean="schedulerFactory" />
        </property>
        <!-- trigger at 3:30am each day -->
        <property name="cronExpression">
            <value>0 30 3 * * ?</value>
        </property>
    </bean>
```

Out of the box, the workflow to which the job starts to route expired content is specified in a bean named `avmExpiredContentProcessor` that is found in `avm-services-context.xml`:

```
    <!-- Bean used to process content that has expired in AVM staging
areas -->
    <bean id="avmExpiredContentProcessor" class=
     "org.alfresco.repo.avm.AVMExpiredContentProcessor">
      <property name="adminUserName">
        <value>admin</value>
      </property>
      <property name="workflowName">
        <value>jbpm$wcmwf:changerequest</value>
      </property>
      ...
    </bean>
```

Link Checking

The intent of the link checking mechanism is to proactively warn content contributors if the content they are submitting contains broken links. This is implemented with a step in the out of the box "Web Site Submission" workflow that runs an action if the workflow initiator checked the **validate links** checkbox when the content was submitted.

The action class is `org.alfresco.repo.avm.wf.AVMSubmitLinkChecker`. This class invokes an action called `avm-link-validation` that is implemented by the `org.alfresco.linkvalidation.LinkValidationAction` action executer class. That class produces a link validation report. The `AVMSubmitLinkChecker` inspects the report and sets the jBPM process variable called `wcmwf:broken_links` to the number of broken links. If the number is greater than 0, the workflow queues a `wcmwf:verifyBrokenLinksTask` to the initiator so that they can resolve (or ignore) the issues.

The details around exactly how the link validation engine works are beyond the scope of this book. The source code is not included with the SDK. If you want to walk through it, start with the `org.alfresco.linkvalidation.LinkValidationServiceImpl` class in the `link-validation` project in the source tree.

If you want to disable the link validation service entirely, override the `linkValidationService` bean in `linkvalidation-service-context.xml` to change the polling interval to `0`:

```
<bean id="linkValidationService"
      class="org.alfresco.linkvalidation.LinkValidationServiceImpl"
      lazy-init="true"
      init-method="register">

  <!-- Poll interval to check getLatestSnapshotID (in milliseconds).
-->
  <!-- Note:  If pollInterval is 0, link validation is disabled.
-->
  <property name="pollInterval" value="0"/>
  ...
```

Step-by-Step: Creating a No-Approval Workflow for Job Postings

SomeCo wants to tweak the out of the box WCM workflow. Here is a list of the changes it would like to see:

- SomeCo wants a workflow that does not require an approval step. It has a small, very flat team. It may add an approval step at some point. But for now, when someone submits content, they want it to be automatically approved. This means that when someone configures the workflow, they should not see the "serial or parallel" dropdown or the user/group selection component.

- SomeCo does not want to perform link checking. It has a third-party tool that performs continuous link checking, and so it would like to disable Alfresco's link checking feature. This means no one should see (or have to de-select) the **validate links** checkbox.

- SomeCo always wants content to be deployed to auto deploy targets if any targets are configured for auto deploy. It does not want the submitter to have to check the **deploy automatically** box.

Implementing these changes will require creating and deploying a new WCM workflow, updating the custom workflow model and the associated properties file, modifying `web-client-config-custom.xml`, and touching a new configuration file called `web-client-config-wcm.xml`.

At the end of the example, you'll be able to submit content that is immediately deployed to all auto deploy targets without requiring intermediate approval or deployment steps.

You're going to implement this in two chunks. First, you are going to implement the "no approval" workflow, then clean up the workflow configuration dialog, hide the unnecessary checkboxes, and clean up the process definition.

Follow these steps:

1. Create a new folder in your Eclipse project called `no-approval-submit` under **config | alfresco | extension | workflows**.

2. Import the out of the box submit-to-web process definition from **WEB-INF | classes | alfresco | workflow | submit_processdefinition.xml** into your Eclipse project's **config | alfresco | extension | workflows | no-approval-submit folder**.

3. Remove the unnecessary nodes related to link checking, review, and approval. Remove the following nodes:
    - checklinks
    - verifybrokenlinks
    - serialorparallel
    - submitserialreview
    - serialreview
    - submitparallelreview
    - parallelreview
    - joinparallelreview
    - endreview
    - rejected

4. Now clean up the `initialise` node. Change the node type from `decision` to `node`, remove the event, and use a single transition to `onapprove`. It looks like a pointless node, but you are going to come back later and add a new event to it:

```
<node name="initialise">
    <transition name="" to="onapprove" />
</node>
```

5. Rename the process to `scwf:noApprovalSubmit`:

```
<process-definition xmlns="urn:jbpm.org:jpdl-3.1" name="scwf:
noApprovalSubmit">
```

6. Look at the diagram for your workflow. Rearrange the nodes until they are somewhat presentable, and then compare it to the following diagram. Your nodes and transitions should match:

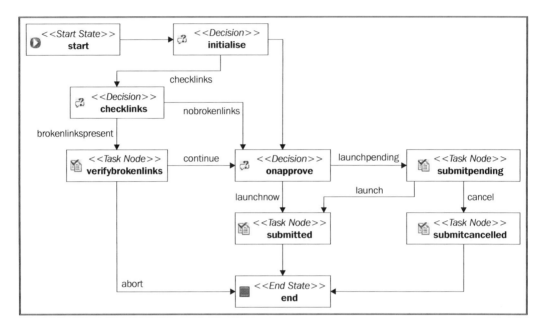

7. At the time of this writing, there is a bug related to overriding the list of WCM workflows (Jira #ETWOTWO-119). The list can't be customized without changing a core Alfresco configuration file. Until the bug is fixed, you're going to purposefully break the "don't touch the source" rule. Copy `web-client-config-wcm.xml` from **WEB-INF | alfresco | classes** into your Eclipse project under **config | alfresco**. (Note: Don't just copy the one from the source code that accompanied this chapter. If you are running Labs, that file may have changed).

8. Edit `web-client-config-wcm.xml` to add `scwf:noApprovalSubmit` to the list of workflows:

```
<workflows>
wcmwf:submit,scwf:noApprovalSubmit
</workflows>
```

9. Modify your Eclipse project's `build.xml` to package `web-client-config-wcm.xml` appropriately:

```
<target name="package-extension" depends="setup, package-jar"
 description="Creates a zip called ${package.file.zip} which can be
 unzipped on top of an exploded Alfresco web app">
    <delete file="${package.file.zip}" />
    <zip destfile="${package.file.zip}" update="true">
        <zipfileset dir="${config.dir}${extension.dir}" prefix=
          "WEB-INF/classes${extension.dir}" />
        <zipfileset file="${config.dir}/alfresco/web-client-
          config-wcm.xml" prefix="WEB-INF/classes/alfresco"/>
        <zipfileset file="${package.file.jar}" prefix="WEB- INF
          /lib" />
        <zipfileset dir="${lib.dir}" prefix="WEB-INF/lib" />
        <zipfileset dir="${web.dir}" excludes="META-INF/**" />
    </zip>
</target>
```

10. Run **ant deploy** then restart Tomcat.

11. After Alfresco comes back up, deploy the new process using the **Deployment** tab on the jBPM Graphical Process Designer, as described in Chapter 7.

At this point you should be able to configure your web form and non-web form content to use the new workflow. And, you can submit content into the workflow. But you'll notice we haven't fully met the requirements yet. The **Configure Workflow** button launches a dialog that still has the review type and user/group assignment, shows the **validate links** and **auto deploy** checkboxes, and the auto deploy isn't automatically taking place. Continue on to address these issues.

1. To get rid of the link check and auto deploy checkboxes, we need to override the JSP used by the submit dialog. A quick search of **WEB-INF|classes |alfresco|web-client-config-dialogs.xml** shows that the JSP that handles the submit dialog is called **jsp|wcm|submit-dialog.jsp**. Import it into your Eclipse project under **src|web|jsp|extension|dialogs|submit-dialog.jsp**.

2. Edit the `submit-dialog.jsp` file you just imported. Remove the following code to get rid of the two checkboxes:

```
<h:panelGrid columns="2" cellspacing="0" cellpadding="2"
style="margin-left: 20px; margin-top: 6px;" rendered="#{DialogMana
ger.bean.workflowListSize != 0}">
<h:selectBooleanCheckbox id="links-chkbox" value="#{DialogManager.
bean.validateLinks}" />
<h:outputText value="#{msg.check_links} (#{msg.check_links_
info})" escape="false" />
```

```
    </h:panelGrid>

    <h:panelGrid columns="2" cellspacing="0" cellpadding="2"
    style="margin-left: 20px; margin-top: 6px;" rendered="#{DialogMana
    ger.bean.workflowListSize != 0}">
    <h:selectBooleanCheckbox id="deploy-chkbox"
    value="#{DialogManager.bean.autoDeploy}" />
    <h:outputText value="#{msg.deploy_automatically} (#{msg.
    deploy_automatically_info})" escape="false" />
    </h:panelGrid>
```

3. Now edit `web-client-config-custom.xml` to override the submit dialog's JSP with a pointer to the new JSP:

```
<!-- Dialogs -->
   <config>
      <dialogs>
         dialog name="executeScript"    page=
         "/jsp/extension/dialogs/execute-script.jsp" managed-bean=
         "ExecuteScriptDialog"
          icon="/someco/images/icons/execute_script_large.gif"
          title="Execute Script"
          description="Executes a script against the selected
          node" />
          <dialog name="submitSandboxItems" page=
          "/jsp/extension/dialogs/submit-dialog.jsp" managed-bean=
          "SubmitDialog" icon="/images/icons/submit_large.gif"
           title-id="submit_items_title"
           description-id="submit_items_desc" />
      </dialogs>
   </config>
```

4. Without a checkbox that the user can set, you need a way to tell the workflow to always perform the auto deploy step. You could modify the action that executes the auto deploy. But a less invasive approach is to use an expression to set the value of the `wcmwf:autoDeploy` property to true. Use the `initialise` node in `processdefinition.xml` to do this:

```
<node name="initialise">

   <event type="node-enter">
      <script>
         <variable name="wcmwf_autoDeploy" access="read,write" />
            <expression>
              wcmwf_autoDeploy = true;
            </expression>
```

```
        </script>
      </event>

    <transition name="" to="onapprove" />
</node>
```

5. The process definition can reuse some of the existing workflow types, but others have mandatory aspects that include properties you no longer want to set such as bpm:assignee and wcmwf:reviewType. In the processdefinition.xml file for the no-approval-submit workflow, change the type names as follows:

   ○ Rename wcmwf:submitReviewTask to scwf: submitNoApprovalTask

   ○ Rename wcmwf:submitcancelledTask to scwf: submitCancelledNoApprovalTask (note capitalization change)

   ○ Rename wcmwf:submittedTask to scwf: submittedNoApprovalTask

6. Now add the corresponding type definitions to SomeCo's workflow model. In your Eclipse project, edit **config | alfresco | extension | model | scWorkflow Model.xml**. Add the following new types:

```
<type name="scwf:submitNoApprovalTask">
    <parent>wcmwf:startTask</parent>
    <associations>
       <association name="wcmwf:webproject">
          <source>
             <mandatory>false</mandatory>
                <many>false</many>
          </source>
          <target>
             <class>wca:webfolder</class>
             <mandatory>true</mandatory>
             <many>false</many>
          </target>
       </association>
    </associations>
    <mandatory-aspects>
        <aspect>wcmwf:submission</aspect>
    </mandatory-aspects>
</type>

<type name="scwf:submitCancelledNoApprovalTask">
    <parent>wcmwf:workflowTask</parent>
```

```
        <mandatory-aspects>
            <aspect>wcmwf:submission</aspect>
        </mandatory-aspects>
    </type>
    <type name="scwf:submittedNoApprovalTask">
        <parent>wcmwf:workflowTask</parent>
        <mandatory-aspects>
            <aspect>wcmwf:submission</aspect>
        </mandatory-aspects>
    </type>
```

7. The new types import namespaces that weren't declared previously. Add new namespace declarations to the model file as follows:

```
<imports>
    <import uri="http://www.alfresco.org/model/dictionary/1.0"
     prefix="d" />
    <import uri="http://www.alfresco.org/model/bpm/1.0"
    prefix="bpm" />
        <import uri="http://www.alfresco.org/model/wcmmodel/1.0"
        prefix="wcm" />
        <import uri="http://www.alfresco.org/model/wcmworkflow/1.0"
        prefix="wcmwf" />
        <import uri="http://www.alfresco.org/model/wcmappmodel/1.0"
        prefix="wca"/>
</imports>
```

8. Save the model file.

9. You'll recall that content models are declared in a model context file. Workflow content models can be declared using the Dictionary Bootstrap, but using that approach, the wcmwf model can't be extended (Jira #ETWOTWO-385). So let's adjust how the custom workflow model is declared to use the Workflow Bootstrap instead. Modify **config|alfresco |extension|someco-model-context.xml** as follows:

```
<bean id="extension.dictionaryBootstrap" parent="dictionaryModelBo
otstrap" depends-on="dictionaryBootstrap">
        <property name="models">
            <list>
                <value>alfresco/extension/model/scModel.xml</value>
            </list>
        </property>
    </bean>

    <bean id="extension.workflowBootstrap"
          parent="workflowBootstrap">
```

```
        <property name="models">
            <list>
             <value>alfresco/extension/model/scWorkflowModel.xml
             </value>
            </list>
        </property>
    </bean>

    <!-- Registration of resource bundles -->
    <bean id="parallel.workflowBootstrap"
          parent="workflowDeployer">
        <property name="labels">
            <list>
                <value>alfresco.extension.scWorkflow</value>
            </list>
        </property>
    </bean>
```

10. Update `web-client-config-custom.xml` with property sheet configurations for the new types. Add the following to the bottom of the file before the closing `alfresco-config` tag:

```
<!-- WCM settings -->
<config evaluator="node-type" condition=
 "scwf:submitNoApprovalTask" replace="true">
    <property-sheet>
        <separator name="sep1" display-label-id=
        "nothing_to_configure" component-generator=
        "HeaderSeparatorGenerator" />
    </property-sheet>
</config>

<config evaluator="node-type" condition=
"scwf:submitCancelledNoApprovalTask" replace="true">
    <property-sheet>
        <separator name="sep1" display-label-id="general"
        component-generator="HeaderSeparatorGenerator" />
        <show-property name="bpm:taskId" />
        <show-property name="bpm:description" component-
        generator="TextAreaGenerator" read-only="true"/>
        <show-property name="wcmwf:label" read-only="true" />
        <show-property name="wcmwf:launchDate" read-only="true"/>
        <show-property name="wcmwf:autoDeploy" read-only="true"/>
        <show-property name="bpm:comment" component-generator=
          "TextAreaGenerator" />
    </property-sheet>
```

```
    </config>
    <config evaluator="node-type" condition=
    "scwf:submittedNoApprovalTask" replace="true">
        <property-sheet>
            <separator name="sep1" display-label-id="general"
            component-generator="HeaderSeparatorGenerator" />
            <show-property name="bpm:taskId" />
            <show-property name="bpm:description" component-
            generator="TextAreaGenerator" read-only="true"/>
            <show-property name="wcmwf:label" read-only="true" />
            <show-property name="wcmwf:launchDate" read-only="true"
            />
            <show-property name="wcmwf:autoDeploy" read-only="true"
            />
          <show-property name="bpm:comment" component-generator=
          "TextAreaGenerator" />
        </property-sheet>
    </config>
```

11. Update `scWorkflow.properties` **with externalized strings for the UI:**

```
#
# Submit no-approval workflow
#

# scWorkflowModel related strings
scwf_workflowmodel.type.scwf_submitNoApprovalTask.title=Submit
scwf_workflowmodel.type.scwf_submitNoApprovalTask.
description=Submit content

scwf_workflowmodel.type.scwf_submitCancelledNoApprovalTask.
title=Submit cancelled
scwf_workflowmodel.type.scwf_submitCancelledNoApprovalTask.
description=Submission of content cancelled

scwf_workflowmodel.type.scwf_submittedNoApprovalTask.
title=Submitted
scwf_workflowmodel.type.scwf_submittedNoApprovalTask.
description=Submitted content

# processdefinition related strings
scwf_noApprovalSubmit.workflow.title=Submit Content Directly
to Web
scwf_noApprovalSubmit.workflow.description=Submit content that
does not require approval
```

12. When users click **Configure Workflow** for this workflow, they will see a blank page because we don't have any configurable properties. For this exercise, you used a separator that points to a **nothing_to_configure** label. Add the text for the label to `webclient.properties`:

```
# Custom WCM workflow
nothing_to_configure=Nothing to configure
```

13. Deploy your changes using **ant deploy**, then restart Tomcat.

14. Once Alfresco has restarted successfully, deploy the process definition using the **Deployment** tab in the GPD.

15. Test your changes.

To test out the custom workflow and the associated web client configuration changes, first edit the **press-release** web form in the data dictionary. You should now see **Submit Content Directly to Web** as a selectable default workflow:

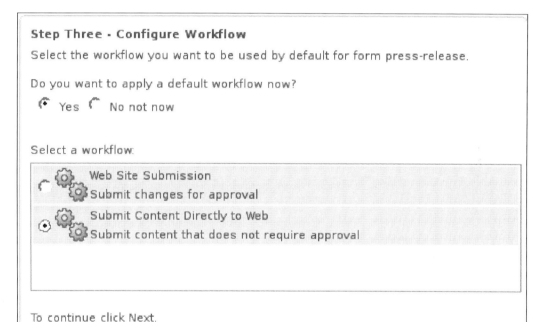

Next, edit the web project settings for SomeCo's Corporate Site. When you open the **web form details**, the new workflow should be in the list:

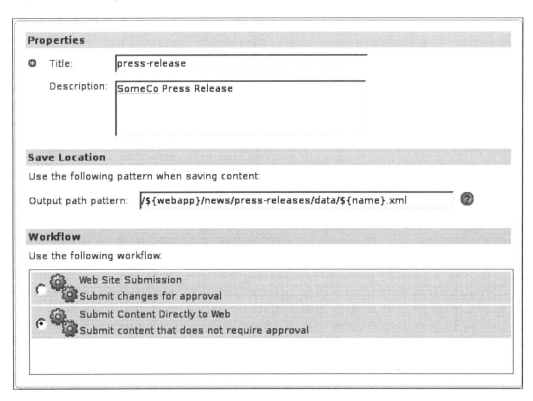

Any time you click **Configure Workflow**, the **Nothing to configure** message should display. With a bit more work you might be able to disable the **Configure Workflow** button using client-side logic when the approval-less workflow is selected:

Similarly, the workflow configuration for non-web form assets should also show your custom workflow:

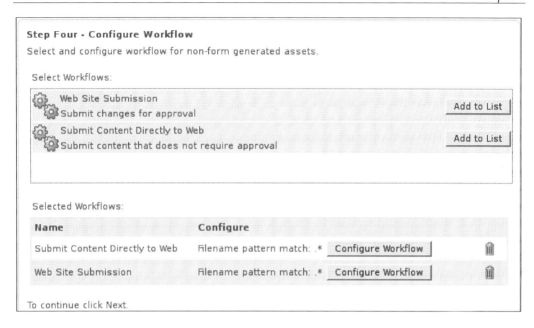

When you submit items, you should no longer see the **link checking** and **auto deploy** checkboxes:

Items submitted into the workflow without a publish date should immediately be committed to staging, a snapshot should be taken, and that snapshot should get deployed to all deployment targets that have the **auto deploy** flag set to true:

Working with the AVM API

You've already seen one aspect of working with the AVM API. You used the `parseXMLDocuments()` call from an XSLT stylesheet to grab the press release XML nodes out of the repository in order to build the press release list. But the AVM API goes much deeper. Using the AVM API you can do things such as:

- Creating new stores, layered directories, and branches using the AVMService
- Comparing and merging two stores using the AVMSyncService
- Initiating deployments using the DeploymentService

Just as in the Foundation API, many of these objects and methods are available from server-side JavaScript.

Step-by-Step: Writing a Web Script to Query AVMNodes

Let's start with a simple example using JavaScript. You've already seen how to create a static list of press releases using an XSLT transformation that is triggered when a press release is saved. What if, instead, you wanted to dynamically return a list of press releases? One way to do this would be to create a web script that gathers up the press release nodes and hands them to a FreeMarker template to render a response. This is similar to the Whitepapers web script you created in Chapter 6, but instead of working with "regular" nodes, you'll be using the AVM API to find AVM nodes.

You are already familiar with the ingredients for this recipe. By now you should be an old hand at web scripts. The difference is in the controller code. To implement the web script, follow these steps:

1. Create a web script descriptor called `pressreleases.get.desc.xml` in your Eclipse project under **|config|alfresco|extension|templates|webscripts| com|someco|avm**. The descriptor is simple. We just need the AVM store and the folder path to have `Press Releases` as arguments:

```
<webscript>
   <shortname>Press Releases</shortname>
   <description>Retrieves press release web form data</description>
   <url>/someco/pressreleases?s={store}&amp;p={path}</url>
   <authentication>user</authentication>
   <transaction>none</transaction>
</webscript>
```

2. Now write the JavaScript controller. Create `pressreleases.get.js` in the same folder as the descriptor. In this example, rather than using an if-then-else for the argument check and subsequent code execution, use the "enclosing code block" approach. It makes it easier to break out of the script if an argument is missing or invalid. Start the script with some checks for the two arguments:

```
script : {
   // store and path provided as args
   if (args.s == null || args.s.length == 0) {
      status.code = 400;
      status.message = "Store is a required argument.";
      status.redirect = true;
      break script;
   }
   if (args.p == null || args.p.length == 0) {
      status.code = 400;
      status.message = "Path is a required argument.";
      status.redirect = true;
      break script;
   }
```

3. Now use the `avm` object to find the store:

```
// get avm node
var store = avm.lookupStore(args.s);
if (store == null || store == undefined) {
   status.code = 404;
   status.message = "Store " + args.s + " not found.";
   status.redirect = true;
   break script;
}
```

4. If the store is OK, you should be able to find the folder node that contains the press release XML:

```
// get press release data folder
var pressReleaseNode = avm.lookupNode(args.s + ":" + args.p);
if (pressReleaseNode == undefined) {
    status.code = 404;
    status.message = "Could not find press release folder.
    Path:" + args.p + " Store:" + args.s;
    status.redirect = true;
    break script;
}
```

5. Finally, add the store and the folder node to the model:

```
// set store and folder in the model
    model.store = store;
    model.folder = pressReleaseNode;
}
```

6. Save the controller.

7. Create two FreeMarker templates, one for HTML and one for RSS. Create a FreeMarker file called `pressreleases.get.html.ftl`. The code simply iterates over the children in the folder and outputs some metadata about the nodes:

```
<html>
    <head>
        <title>Press releases in folder: ${folder.displayPath}/
        ${folder.name}</title>
    </head>
    <body>
        <p><a href="${url.serviceContext}/sample/avm/stores">AVM
        Store</a>: ${store.id}</p>
        <p>AVM Folder: ${folder.displayPath}/${folder.name}</p>
        <table>
            <#list folder.children as child>
                <tr>
                    <td>${child.properties.creator}</td>
                    <td>${child.size}</td>
                    <td>${child.properties.modified?datetime}</td>
                    <td><a href="${url.serviceContext}
                    /api/node/content/${child.nodeRef.storeRef.protocol}
                    /${child.nodeRef.storeRef.identifier}/
                    ${child.nodeRef.id}/${child.name?url}">${child.name}
                    </a>
```

```
        </tr>
      </#list>
    </table>
  </body>
</html>
```

8. Now create the RSS version called `pressreleases.get.rss.ftl`. It too iterates over the children, but this one actually parses the press release XML to include in the RSS markup. The first line tells FreeMarker to use our press release namespace as the default namespace:

```
<#ftl ns_prefixes={"D", "http://www.someco.com/corp/pr"}>
```

9. Then comes the general information about the RSS feed:

```
<?xml version='1.0' encoding='UTF-8'?>
<rss version="2.0"
   xmlns:content="http://purl.org/rss/1.0/modules/content/"
   xmlns:dc="http://purl.org/dc/elements/1.1/">
   <channel>
      <title>someco.com</title>
      <link>http://localhost</link>
      <description>SomeCo Corporate Press Releases</description>
      <pubDate>${folder.parent.properties.modified?datetime}
      </pubDate>
   <generator>http://www.alfresco.com</generator>
      <language>en</language>
```

10. Next, iterate over the child objects. The assign statement (highlighted) is using `xmlNodeModel` to parse the press release XML content:

```
<#list folder.children as child>
  <#assign pr_doc=child.xmlNodeModel>
  <item>
    <title>${pr_doc.press_release.title}</title>
    <link>http://localhost:8080${url.serviceContext}/api/
    node/content/${child.nodeRef.storeRef.protocol}/
    ${child.nodeRef.storeRef.identifier}/${child.nodeRef.
    id}/${child.name?url}</link>
      <pubDate>${child.properties.modified?datetime}
      </pubDate>
      <dc:creator>${child.properties.creator}
      </dc:creator>
      <guid isPermaLink="false">${child.properties
      ["sys:node-dbid"]?c}</guid>
        <description><![CDATA[${pr_doc.press_release.
        sub_title}]]>
        </description>
```

```
                            <content:encoded><![CDATA[${pr_doc.
press_release.body}]]>
    </content:encoded>
        </item>
      </#list>
    </channel>
</rss>
```

11. Save all files, run **ant deploy**, and check the web script console (`http://localhost:8080/alfresco/service/`) to make sure your script loaded OK.

12. Test your changes.

To test the script, invoke the web script in your web browser. For example, for the SomeCo Corporate Site, you would use `someco-site` as the `store` argument (because that's the DNS name you assigned when you created the web project) and `/www/avm_webapps/ROOT/news/pressreleases/data/` as the "path" argument as follows:

```
http://localhost:8080/alfresco/service/someco/pressreleases.
rss?s=someco-site&p=/www/avm_webapps/ROOT/news/press-releases/data/
```

Using that URL, the web script will run against the press release XML stored in the **Staging Sandbox**. When shown in Firefox, the RSS appears as follows:

someco.com

SomeCo Corporate Press Releases

Optaros Assembles Syndication Application Widget to Increase Revenues for King Digital

Solution assembled from open source

Massachusetts Convention Center Authority (MCCA) Selects Optaros for Event Management EMS System

Optaros' open source assembly methodology shines

Optaros Assembles New Online Shopping Concept for Wonderbox

Private boutique shopping concept implemented with open source

If, instead, you wanted to run the web script against a User Sandbox (or any other sandbox for that matter), you simply need to change the store ID that gets passed to the web script. For example, admin's User Sandbox would be **someco-site--admin** (note that there are two dashes separating the site DNS and the username).

Step-by-Step: Writing a Web Script to Trigger Deployments

Some of the SomeCo web developers want to write all of their code with Emacs. They plan to use CIFS to save changes directly to their sandboxes. But they'd like a way to invoke User Sandbox deployments to FSR test servers. That way, they can develop, deploy, and test without ever leaving the comfort of their favorite text editor.

To meet this requirement, you're going to develop two web scripts. One web script deploys the User Sandbox to test the server selected from the pool. The other releases the test server back into the pool. The controller code here is a little involved, so you'll use Java instead of JavaScript for this example.

The web script descriptor and the FreeMarker template are all standard fare. The Java-based controller is going to have to:

1. Determine if a test server has already been allocated to the user's sandbox.

2. If not, try to allocate a test server if one is available.

3. Prepare a `deployment attempt` object.

4. Use the action service to invoke a deployment.

When it is done, any time someone wants to do a deployment, they'll be able to do so by invoking the web script from the command line or from within a tool that can be extended to issue HTTP GETs. The test server can then be used to validate changes. When testing is over, the server can be returned to the pool by invoking the "release" web script.

If all goes well, you could take this a step further by creating a "submit" web script that would commit the modified items in the user's sandbox to Staging so that the developers would never have to log in to the web client. But let's not get ahead of ourselves.

Do this:

1. In your Eclipse project's **config | alfresco | extension | templates | webscripts | com | someco | avm** folder, create the web script descriptors for both the `deploy` and `release` web scripts. These are both simple URLs that only require one argument: the store to be deployed. The `deploy.get.desc.xml` file should look like this:

    ```
    <webscript>
        <shortname>Deploy</shortname>
        <description>Deploys the user's sandbox to a test server.</
    description>
        <url>/someco/deploy?s={store}</url>
    ```

```
<format default="xml">extension</format>
<authentication>user</authentication>
<transaction>none</transaction>
</webscript>
```

2. And the `release.get.desc.xml` file should look like this:

```
<webscript>
   <shortname>Release</shortname>
   <description>Releases a test server, if allocated, back to the
    pool</description>
   <url>/someco/release?s={store}</url>
   <format default="xml">extension</format>
   <authentication>user</authentication>
   <transaction>none</transaction>
</webscript>
```

3. Go ahead and do the response templates. XML seems like a good choice because it is easy to read if someone's using a command-line tool such as curl and easy to parse if someone's adding an Emacs extension to invoke the script. The response doesn't need much. The critical information is the server name, so the developer knows which test server from the pool they grabbed. Create a `deploy.get.xml.ftl` file with:

```
<?xml version='1.0' encoding='UTF-8'?>
<deploy>
   <store>${store}</store>
   <server>${serverName}</server>
   <status>${status}</status>
   <url><#if serverUrl?exists>${serverUrl}</#if></url>
</deploy>
```

4. For the release script, the server name won't be returned if there was nothing to release. So the FTL needs to handle a missing value. Create the `release.get.xml.ftl` file with:

```
<?xml version='1.0' encoding='UTF-8'?>
<release>
   <store>${store}</store>
   <server><#if serverName?exists>${serverName}</#if></server>
   <status>${status}</status>
</release>
```

5. The response templates are out of the way. Now comes the fun part: writing the controller. After that you'll wire it up with a Spring bean configuration and you'll be ready to test. Create a new Java class in **src | java** called `com.someco.scripts.GetDeploy.java`. There is a decent amount of code here. So let's take it in chunks. First of all, it is a plain old web script and so it extends from `DeclarativeWebScript` and has several dependencies:

```
public class GetDeploy extends DeclarativeWebScript {

    // Dependencies
    private AVMService avmService;
    private ActionService actionService;
    private NodeService nodeService;
    private PermissionService permissionService;
    private ImporterBootstrap importerBootstrap;
    private SearchService searchService;

    private static final String PROP_ROOT_FOLDER = "spaces.company_home.childname";
    private static final String PROP_WCM_FOLDER = "spaces.wcm.childname";
```

6. Like all web scripts, most of the work is in the `executeImpl` method. Start it by doing standard checks for the required `store` parameter:

```
@Override
    protected Map<String, Object> executeImpl(WebScriptRequest req,
            Status status, Cache cache) {
        // declare the model object we're going to return
        Map<String, Object> model = new HashMap<String, Object>();

        String store = req.getParameter("s");

        // echo back the store that was passed in
        model.put("store", store);

        if (store == null || store.length() == 0) {
            status.setCode(400);
            status.setMessage("Store is a required parameter.");
            status.setRedirect(true);
            return model;
        }
```

7. The store that gets passed in has to exist. A fast way to figure that out is to call `AVMUtil`'s `lookupStoreDNS` method. It'll throw an exception and stop the script if the store is bogus:

```
// check to see if store exists
        // if it does not, an exception will get thrown
        AVMUtil.lookupStoreDNS(store);
```

8. A couple of your calls will rely on a `NodeRef`, which points to the web project folder. You can get to that from a store by first getting the Staging store, then getting a property off that:

```
String stagingStore = AVMUtil.buildStagingStoreName(
AVMUtil.getStoreId(store));
NodeRef webProjectNodeRef = (NodeRef) avmService.getStorePro
perty(stagingStore,SandboxConstants.PROP_WEB_PROJECT_NODE_
REF).getValue(DataTypeDefinition.NODE_REF);

if (webProjectNodeRef == null || !nodeService.exists
(webProjectNodeRef)) {
        status.setCode(500);
        status.setMessage("Web project does not exist.");
        status.setRedirect(true);
        return model;
}
```

9. Next, you need to figure out whether or not the store is already allocated to a test server in the pool. If it is, great. If it isn't, you have to see if one is available and allocate it. You'll implement the `findDeployToServers` shortly. If there aren't any more test servers in the pool, return an error message:

```
// if this store is already allocated, use that, otherwise
        // try to find a new server available in the pool
        NodeRef serverRef = null;
        List<NodeRef> allocServerList = findDeployToServers
    (webProjectNodeRef, store);
        if (allocServerList.isEmpty()) {
                List<NodeRef> serverList = findDeployToServers
        (webProjectNodeRef, null);
                if (serverList.isEmpty()) {
                        status.setCode(500);
                        status.setMessage("No test servers are
                        available.");
                        status.setRedirect(true);
                        return model;
        }
                serverRef = serverList.get(0);
        } else {
                serverRef = allocServerList.get(0);
        }
```

10. Next, after checking to make sure the test server's node ref actually exists, grab some properties from it. Then use the regular node service to update the property on the server node that keeps track of who's using the test server:

```
// if the node exists, we're good
    if (nodeService.exists(serverRef)) {
      // get all properties of the target server
      Map<QName, Serializable> serverProps = nodeService.
      getProperties(serverRef);

      String url = (String)serverProps.get
      (WCMAppModel.PROP_DEPLOYSERVERURL);
      String serverUri = AVMDeployWebsiteAction
      .calculateServerUri(serverProps);
      String serverName = (String)serverProps
      .get(WCMAppModel.PROP_DEPLOYSERVERNAME);
      if (serverName == null || serverName.length() == 0) {
            serverName = serverUri;
      }

      // Allocate the test server to the current sandbox
      String allocatedTo = (String)serverProps.get(WCMAppModel.
      PROP_DEPLOYSERVERALLOCATEDTO);
      if ((allocatedTo != null) && !(allocatedTo.equals(store))) {
            throw new AlfrescoRuntimeException("testserver.
            taken", new Object[] {serverName});
      } else {
            nodeService.setProperty(serverRef, WCMAppModel.
            PROP_DEPLOYSERVERALLOCATEDTO, store);
      }
```

11. This next part is a bit of a nuisance. It seems like the work of creating a deployment attempt ought to be incorporated into the deployment action or some higher-level service. But it isn't, so it is up to you:

```
// create a deploymentattempt node to represent this deployment
        String attemptId = GUID.generate();
        Map<QName, Serializable> props = new HashMap<QName,
        Serializable>(8, 1.0f);
        props.put(WCMAppModel.PROP_DEPLOYATTEMPTID,
        attemptId);
        props.put(WCMAppModel.PROP_DEPLOYATTEMPTTYPE,
        WCMAppModel.CONSTRAINT_TESTSERVER);
        props.put(WCMAppModel.PROP_DEPLOYATTEMPTSTORE, store);
        props.put(WCMAppModel.PROP_DEPLOYATTEMPTVERSION, "1");

        props.put(WCMAppModel.PROP_DEPLOYATTEMPTTIME, new
        Date());
```

```
props.put(WCMAppModel.PROP_DEPLOYATTEMPTSERVERS,
serverName);
NodeRef attempt = nodeService.
createNode(webProjectNodeRef,
WCMAppModel.ASSOC_DEPLOYMENTATTEMPT, WCMAppModel
.ASSOC_DEPLOYMENTATTEMPT,
        WCMAppModel.TYPE_DEPLOYMENTATTEMPT, props)
        .getChildRef();

// allow anyone to add child nodes to the
deploymentattempt node
permissionService.setPermission(attempt,
 PermissionService.ALL_AUTHORITIES,
            PermissionService.ADD_CHILDREN, true);
```

12. Now that the deployment attempt object is created, you can set up and invoke the deployment action:

```
// store the server deployed to in the model
model.put("serverName", serverName);
if (url != null) {
    model.put("serverUrl", url);
}

String storeRoot = AVMUtil.
buildSandboxRootPath(store);
NodeRef websiteRef = AVMNodeConverter.ToNodeRef(-1,
storeRoot);

// create and execute the action asynchronously
Map<String, Serializable> args = new HashMap<String,
Serializable>(1, 1.0f);
args.put(AVMDeployWebsiteAction.PARAM_WEBPROJECT,
webProjectNodeRef);
args.put(AVMDeployWebsiteAction.PARAM_SERVER,
serverRef);
args.put(AVMDeployWebsiteAction.PARAM_ATTEMPT,
attempt);
Action action = actionService.createAction
(AVMDeployWebsiteAction.NAME, args);
actionService.executeAction(action, websiteRef, false,
true);
```

13. Before closing out the method, you have to update a property on the sandbox that keeps track of the most recent deployment attempt:

```
            // set the deploymentattempid property on the store
            this deployment was for
        avmService.deleteStoreProperty(store, SandboxConstants.
        PROP_LAST_DEPLOYMENT_ID);
        avmService.setStoreProperty(store, SandboxConstants.PROP_
        LAST_DEPLOYMENT_ID,
            new PropertyValue(DataTypeDefinition.TEXT, attemptId));

        }

    return model;
    }
```

14. The controller is done except for this last bit of logic. Alfresco's `DeploymentUtil` class has methods for returning available deployment targets. But it doesn't discriminate between FSR and ASR targets. So you're going to implement your own version, borrowing heavily from Alfresco's existing logic:

```
private List<NodeRef> findDeployToServers(NodeRef webProjectRef,
String store) {
        // get folder names
        Properties configuration = this.importerBootstrap.
        getConfiguration();
        String rootFolder = configuration.getProperty(PROP_ROOT_
        FOLDER);
        String wcmFolder = configuration.getProperty(PROP_WCM_
        FOLDER);

        // get web project name
        String webProjectName = (String)
        this.nodeService.getProperty(
                webProjectRef, ContentModel.PROP_NAME);
        String safeProjectName = ISO9075.encode(webProjectName);

        // build the query
        StringBuilder query = new StringBuilder("PATH:\"/");
        query.append(rootFolder);
        query.append("/");
        query.append(wcmFolder);
        query.append("/cm:");
        query.append(safeProjectName);
        query.append("/*\" AND @");
        query.append(NamespaceService.WCMAPP_MODEL_PREFIX);
        query.append("\\:");
```

```
        query.append(WCMAppModel.PROP_DEPLOYSERVERTYPE.
getLocalName());
        query.append(":\"");
        query.append(WCMAppModel.CONSTRAINT_TESTSERVER);
        query.append("\" AND @");
        query.append(NamespaceService.WCMAPP_MODEL_PREFIX);
        query.append("\\:");
        query.append(WCMAppModel.PROP_DEPLOYTYPE.getLocalName());
        query.append(":\"");
        query.append(WCMAppModel.CONSTRAINT_FILEDEPLOY);
        query.append("\"");

        // if we got a store, include it
        if (store != null && !store.equals("")) {
            query.append(" AND @");
            query.append(NamespaceService.WCMAPP_MODEL_PREFIX);
            query.append("\\:");
            query.append(WCMAppModel.PROP_DEPLOYSERVERALLOCATEDTO.
getLocalName());
            query.append(":\"");
            query.append(store);
            query.append("\"");
        } else {
            // otherwise, explicitly search for objects where the
attr is NULL
            query.append(" AND ISNULL:\"");
            query.append(WCMAppModel.PROP_DEPLOYSERVERALLOCATEDTO.
toString());
            query.append("\"");
        }

        // execute the query
        ResultSet results = null;
        List<NodeRef> servers = new ArrayList<NodeRef>();
        try {
            results = searchService.query(webProjectRef.
getStoreRef(),
                    SearchService.LANGUAGE_LUCENE, query.
toString());
            for (NodeRef server : results.getNodeRefs()) {
                servers.add(server);
            }
        } finally {
            if (results != null) {
                results.close();
```

```
            }
        }
        return servers;
    }
```

15. Now finish off the class by adding the necessary imports and setters for the dependencies, and then save the class.

16. The last thing you have to do is configure a Spring bean for the controller. Edit the existing `someco-scripts-context.xml` file to add the new beans. Don't worry about the "release" bean for now. You will be doing that one on your own in a bit:

```xml
<bean id="webscript.com.someco.avm.deploy.get" class="com.someco.
scripts.GetDeploy" parent="webscript">
        <property name="avmService">
                <ref bean="AVMService" />
        </property>
        <property name="actionService">
                <ref bean="ActionService" />
        </property>
        <property name="nodeService">
                <ref bean="NodeService" />
        </property>
        <property name="permissionService">
                <ref bean="PermissionService" />
        </property>
        <property name="importerBootstrap">
                <ref bean="spacesBootstrap" />
        </property>
        <property name="searchService">
                <ref bean="SearchService" />
        </property>

</bean>
```

17. You are ready to run **ant deploy**, restart, and test.

When testing, you'll probably want to have two browser tabs open. One is for your web client. The other is for the web script invocation. Log in and go to the SomeCo Corporate Site web project folder. If you don't have a test server, add one. If you do have a test server, check to see if any of the test servers are allocated so that you know what to expect when you run the deploy script.

For a more realistic test, you might also want to add one or more additional users to the web project if you currently are using only admin.

To perform a simple test, follow these steps:

1. Add a new piece of content in your User Sandbox. It doesn't matter what kind or where.

2. Point your browser to the deploy web script:

```
http://localhost:8080/alfresco/service/someco/release?s=someco-
site--admin
```

3. You should get the following XML back:

```
<?xml version='1.0' encoding='UTF-8'?>
<deploy>
        <store>someco-site--admin</store>
        <server>SomeCo Test Server</server>
        <status>200</status>
        <url>http://localhost:8081</url>
</deploy>
```

4. You should also be able to browse the directory your FSR is pointing to and see that the content was successfully deployed.

5. Now point your browser to the same web script, but change the store to `someco-site--tuser2` (or whatever the second user you added is named). Assuming you've only configured one test server, there are no more test servers available. So you should see the following XML:

```
<?xml version="1.0" encoding="UTF-8"?>
<response>
  <status>
    <code>500</code>
    <name>Internal Error</name>
    <description>An error inside the HTTP server which prevented
it from fulfilling the request.</description>
  </status>
  <message>No test servers are available.</message>
  <exception></exception>
  <callstack>
  </callstack>
  <server>Alfresco Community Network v3.0.0 (dev @build-number@)
schema 124</server>
  <time>Jul 3, 2008 12:46:16 AM</time>
</response>
```

6. Now release the server by going into the first user's sandbox and clicking **More Actions**, and then **Release Server**. (If you do not see **Release Server**, try **More Actions**, and then **Refresh**. If you still don't see it, something's gone horribly wrong and it is time to hit the node browser.)

7. Now try the deploy for the second user again. It should succeed this time.

```
<?xml version='1.0' encoding='UTF-8'?>
<release>
        <store>someco-site--tuser2</store>
        <server>SomeCo Test Server</server>
        <status>200</status>
</release>
```

That worked well. But you don't want the developers to have to log in to the web client to release the test server back to the pool when they are done with it. You need to implement the controller for the release script. Rather than walking you through the steps to do that, try it on your own. The steps are generally the same. But this time, when you find the server that has already been allocated to the store, unallocate it by setting the `WCMAppModel.PROP_DEPLOYSERVERALLOCATEDTO` property to null. And obviously, you won't be triggering any deployments in this controller.

If you need a web scripts refresher, pay a visit to Chapter 6. If you're still stuck, look at the `com.someco.scripts.GetRelease` Java class that is in the source code that accompanies the chapter.

Implementing a Web Script for Submit

The majority of the code for the deploy web script example came from the Alfresco source. If you are looking for extra credit, try implementing a `submit` web script on your own. You should be able to get most of what you need from Alfresco's `org.alfresco.repo.avm.wf.AVMSubmitHandler`. It uses the `AVMSyncService` to find and then merge the diffs. Using that approach will put the content right in to Staging, completely bypassing the workflow (and link checking, auto-deploy, launch dates, expiration dates, and so on).

An alternative to doing a direct submit would be to do the same thing that a `Submit All` or `Submit Selected` does in the web client—start a workflow with the modified items as part of the change set. Your web script can take arguments for things such as the "label" and "description", and then start the default workflow with the appropriate settings.

Using the AVM Console

Although it is not currently linked from the Administrator Console, the web client contains an "AVM Console" at `http://localhost:8080/alfresco/faces/jsp/admin/avm-console.jsp`. Similar to the workflow console, the AVM Console can be used almost as a command-line interface to the AVM repository. One of the most useful commands is `rmrep`, which is the only non-API way to make sure a repository goes away.

The **Help** link provides the full list of available commands and their syntaxes. A subset of the list of commands includes:

- `lsrep`: Lists all of the AVM store
- `mkbr`: Creates a branch
- `mkldir`: Creates a layered directory on top of a target directory
- `snap`: Takes a snapshot of a store
- `compare`: Compares two trees
- `flatten`: Flattens a layer onto a target tree

Summary

In this chapter you learned about the differences between Alfresco's DM store and the AVM store. The intent was not to provide an end-user how-to for Alfresco's WCM functionality, but rather to show the customization and extension points you'll see during a typical implementation.

Specifically, in this chapter you learned how to:

- Define web forms using XML Schema to allow non-technical users to create content
- Write presentation templates using XSLT and FreeMarker to enable the transformation of web form data into multiple rendition formats
- Use Alfresco's WCM API from JavaScript and Java to query the repository from a frontend web site
- Implement content deployment for both Alfresco-to-file system (FSR) and Alfresco-to-Alfresco (ASR) deployments
- Leverage advanced workflows to route web content including creating your own custom WCM workflow
- Use the AVM API to work with WCM assets from JavaScript and Java, which included finding and parsing web form XML data as well as invoking test server deployments from a web script

9
Security

This chapter is all about security from both an authentication and an authorization perspective. By the end of this chapter, you'll know how to configure Alfresco to authenticate against LDAP, how to set up Single Sign-On (SSO), and how to work with Alfresco's security services. Specifically, you are going to learn how to:

- Install a basic OpenLDAP implementation
- Configure Alfresco to authenticate against LDAP, including "chaining" LDAP with Alfresco authentication
- Configure LDAP synchronization
- Install and configure a popular open source SSO solution from JA-SIG called CAS
- Establish SSO between Alfresco and two of Tomcat's sample servlets
- Create users and groups with the Alfresco API
- Understand the out of the box permissions
- Define a custom permission group or role, which you will then leverage to refactor how the SomeCo Web Enable/Disable links work

Authenticating and Synchronizing with LDAP

Most production Alfresco implementations use something other than Alfresco to authenticate. That's because many enterprises already have a central user directory, and it makes a lot of sense to have Alfresco take advantage of that. There are almost as many different approaches to authentication as there are applications. Microsoft shops will often run NTLM or Kerberos authentication, both of which are supported by Alfresco. Most of the time, though, companies store users in one or more LDAP directories and then configure applications to authenticate against those directories.

In this chapter, the directions refer to OpenLDAP. There are other open source LDAP servers available such as Fedora Directory Server and Apache Directory. Proprietary directory servers also work with Alfresco. The most common one is Microsoft Active Directory, but others such as Sun ONE Directory Server and Novell eDirectory are known to work with Alfresco as well.

Step-by-Step: Setting Up a Local OpenLDAP Server

When testing out authentication against LDAP, you will want a local LDAP directory so that you can have full knowledge and control of the schema and other settings. If you are lucky enough to be running Ubuntu or some other Debian distribution of Linux, installing OpenLDAP is as easy as running `sudo apt-get install slapd` on the command line. Windows users will either have to compile the source (available at `http://www.openldap.org`) or download a pre-compiled binary from one of the many sources available on the Internet.

> Windows users may find it easier to use Apache Directory Server because Windows binaries are readily available. Apache Directory is available for download at `http://directory.apache.org/`. For the examples in this chapter to work, you'll still want to use the same LDAP schema structure as outlined here, but the specific setup instructions will be different. Instead of using the command-line tools for searching and importing LDAP, you can use Apache Directory Studio, which is an Eclipse plug-in available from the Apache Directory web site

Now let's do some basic OpenLDAP configuration, and then set up a simple directory for SomeCo. If you are going to use an existing LDAP or Active Directory server rather than run your own locally, skip to the next Step-by-Step: *Configuring Alfresco to Authenticate against LDAP*. Otherwise, follow these steps:

1. Regardless of the operating system, after installing OpenLDAP you should have a `slapd.conf` file. On Linux, the file is usually in **|etc|ldap**. Edit the file. First, add the directory suffix:

   ```
   suffix          "dc=someco,dc=com"
   ```

2. Next, create the root DN for the directory. This is essentially the admin or superuser account. In production, you'll want to encrypt the password. In the following code it is shown in plain text:

   ```
   rootdn          "cn=Manager,dc=someco,dc=com"
   rootpw          somepassword
   ```

3. Next, specify how the user passwords are encrypted. For development, it is easier to use clear text as opposed to MD4, MD5, or SHA:

```
password-hash    {CLEARTEXT}
```

4. Save the `slapd.conf` file and restart OpenLDAP.

The directory is now configured, but it needs some data before it can be used. It needs:

- A root entry under which all other entries will be stored. The root entry will be called `dc=someco,dc=com`.

- A place to store SomeCo employees. It is common to call this `people`, so the entry will be named `ou=people,dc=someco,dc=com`.

- A place to store groups. Keeping it simple, the groups will live under an entry named `ou=groups,dc=someco,dc=com`.

This structure isn't required for the directory to work with Alfresco—your production directory is probably very different. In fact, trying to wrangle a directory that has grown in fits and starts over time like an unkempt hedgerow is where you'll spend most of your time getting Alfresco to work against your real-life LDAP directory.

> LDAP and CIFS: If you configure Alfresco to authenticate against LDAP and have a requirement to use CIFS, realize that the passwords in your LDAP directory must be either clear text or MD4, otherwise, CIFS won't work. See the Alfresco wiki and Jira for more details.

The easiest way to get things into and out of LDAP is by using LDIF files. An LDIF file is a plain-text file that follows a specific format. Once you create an LDIF file you can import it from the command line using `ldapadd`.

Populate the root directory entry, the people and group entries, and some test users by following these steps:

1. Create an LDIF file called `root.ldif` with the following content:

```
dn: dc=someco,dc=com
dc: someco
description: Root LDAP entry for someco.com
objectClass: dcObject
objectClass: organizationalUnit
ou: rootobject

dn: ou=people,dc=someco,dc=com
ou: people
description: All people in organization
```

```
objectClass: organizationalUnit

dn: ou=groups,dc=someco,dc=com
ou: groups
description: All groups in organization
objectClass: organizationalUnit
```

2. Import it into the LDAP directory using ldapadd as follows:

```
ldapadd -x -f root.ldif -Dcn=Manager,dc=someco,dc=com -
wsomepassword
```

3. Now create a new LDIF file called test-users.ldif with the following content, repeating (and modifying) the block to create as many test users as you want:

```
dn: uid=tuser7,ou=people,dc=someco,dc=com
cn: tuser7
sn: User7
givenName: Test
objectclass: top
objectclass: person
objectclass: organizationalPerson
objectclass: inetOrgPerson
ou: People
l: Dallas
uid: tuser7
mail: tuser7@localhost
telephonenumber: +1 972 555 1212
facsimiletelephonenumber: +1 972 555 1313
roomnumber: 111
userpassword: password
```

4. Again, use ldapadd to import the test-users.ldif file into the directory:

```
ldapadd -x -f test-users.ldif -Dcn=Manager,dc=someco,dc=com -
wsomepassword
```

5. Now query the directory using ldapsearch to verify that you can find one of your test users. For example, the command to search for tuser7 is shown below. The -LLL flag specifies that the results should be returned in LDIF format, which gives you a nice way to export data from the directory in a format that can be easily shared:

```
ldapsearch -x -LLL -Dcn=Manager,dc=someco,dc=com -wsomepassword -b
"ou=people,dc=someco,dc=com" "uid=tuser7"
```

The command-line tools `ldapadd`, `ldapdelete`, `ldapsearch`, and `ldapmodify` are common, easy-to-use tools for doing things such as validating an LDAP query, inspecting an attribute, or exporting directory data. If you don't have these, or you'd just rather use a GUI, there are several open source, graphical LDAP clients available. One of them is Apache Directory Studio, which can optionally run as an Eclipse plug-in and can talk to other LDAP-compliant directories. It isn't restricted to Apache Directory Server.

6. Finally, import a test group. Create a new LDIF file called `test-groups.ldif`. Use the following example to create as many test groups as you'd like. Then import the LDIF file using `ldapadd` just like you've done in the previous steps:

```
dn: cn=Test Group 1,ou=groups,dc=someco,dc=com
objectClass: top
objectClass: groupOfUniqueNames
cn: Test Group 1
uniqueMember: uid=tuser1,ou=people,dc=someco,dc=com
uniqueMember: uid=tuser2,ou=people,dc=someco,dc=com
```

Assuming your data was loaded OK, you've now got a working directory server with a set of test users and a test group. Using an LDAP server in development can be helpful. For example, if you need a large number of test users, it is a lot easier to generate an LDIF file using a Perl script or something similar and then import that into LDAP, rather than either manually creating the users or using the Alfresco API to do it.

For more information on working with OpenLDAP, take a look at *Mastering OpenLDAP: Configuring, Securing and Integrating Directory Services*, by Matt Butcher, Packt Publishing.

Step-by-Step: Configuring Alfresco to Authenticate against LDAP

Pointing Alfresco at LDAP is pretty easy. It involves copying over the sample `ldap-authentication-context.xml` and properties file, modifying the properties file to fit your environment, and restarting Alfresco. At that point, Alfresco will use LDAP to authenticate. You may want to use a mix of Alfresco and LDAP, which is called "chaining". It's covered in the next exercise. It's a good idea, though, to get non-chained LDAP working first, and then modify the configuration to set up chaining. That way, if it doesn't go as planned, you can tell whether it is your LDAP server settings or the chaining configuration that's the culprit.

For this chapter, I chose to create a new Eclipse project called "server-extensions". There are differences in the configuration files between Community and Enterprise, but they reside in the same Eclipse project that accompanies this chapter. There is an Ant property in `build.properties` that distinguishes between the two so that Ant knows which set of files to deploy. If you are only running one distribution, you don't have to distinguish between the two flavors of Alfresco in your Eclipse project if you don't want to. However, you'll have to adjust the `build.xml` file accordingly.

Lastly, notice that the deployment produces two different ZIPs that are deployed to two different locations. The `someco-server-alfresco.zip` file is deployed to the Alfresco web application root (specified by the Ant property `alfresco.web.dir`) and the `someco-server-alfresco-shared.zip` contains the "server-extensions", which in Tomcat get deployed to Tomcat's **shared | classes** directory (specified by the Ant property `alfresco.shared.dir`).

To configure Alfresco to authenticate against LDAP, do this:

1. Create a new Eclipse project called "server-extensions". You're going to use this for your LDAP configuration and the chaining and SSO configuration later in the chapter.

2. Copy the `ldap-authentication-context.xml.sample` file from your distribution into the **config | [community or enterprise] | alfresco | extension** directory in the server-extensions project. Rename the file to remove `.sample` from the end. In the WAR-only distribution, you can find the file in the **extensions | extension** directory. This file points to a properties file so that you don't have to edit the XML.

3. Copy the `ldap-authentication.properties` file from the same directory where you found the sample context file into your Eclipse project under **config | alfresco | extension** (this file is common between Community and Enterprise). The properties file tells Alfresco how to connect to your LDAP directory.

4. Edit `ldap-authentication.properties`. Specify the format of the usernames in the directory:

   ```
   ldap.authentication.userNameFormat=uid=%s,ou=people,dc=someco,
   dc=com
   ```

5. Specify the host name and port of the LDAP directory:

   ```
   # The URL to connect to the LDAP server
   ldap.authentication.java.naming.provider.url=ldap://localhost:389
   ```

6. Change the authentication mechanism from DIGEST-MD5 to simple:

```
# The authentication mechanism to use
ldap.authentication.java.naming.security.authentication=simple
```

7. Specify the Domain Name (DN) of a user entry that can read people and groups. This will be used later when you configure synchronization. It isn't used for authentication. Alfresco binds as the authenticating user when attempting to authenticate:

```
# The default principal to use (only used for LDAP sync)
ldap.authentication.java.naming.security.principal=cn=Manager,
dc=someco,dc=com
```

8. Specify the password of the user provided in the previous step:

```
# The password for the default principal (only used for LDAP sync)
ldap.authentication.java.naming.security.credentials=somepassword
```

9. Save the properties file.

10. To deploy the changes, run `ant deploy-shared`, and then restart Alfresco.

To test the setup, attempt to log in. Unless you set up an **admin** entry in your LDAP directory, you won't be able to log in as **admin**. You'll fix that shortly. Instead, try one of the test users you imported in the LDIF file.

You probably noticed that when you logged in with an LDAP user that had never logged in to Alfresco, Alfresco created the user object at the time of login. The username was set as the user's first name and none of the other user metadata was pulled over. The user metadata will get cleaned up when the LDAP synchronization job runs.

Step-by-Step: Configuring Chaining

With LDAP authentication turned on, you are no longer able to log in as **admin**. That's because you essentially swapped out Alfresco's out of the box authentication component for an LDAP authentication component, and **admin** doesn't exist in LDAP.

Sometimes, there is a requirement to configure Alfresco to try one authentication source and, if it fails, try another. Suppose, for example, that SomeCo's operational staff has a tight grip on the LDAP directory. The Alfresco team might need to troubleshoot a problem and would like to use test IDs, but the turnaround time on getting new entries added to LDAP is too lengthy. Plus, the directory team would rather not pollute the production server with a bunch of fake users named after characters from your favorite movies. One solution is to chain LDAP authentication to Alfresco's authentication so that if a user isn't found in LDAP, Alfresco will attempt to find a matching entry in its own repository.

Of course, there are other reasons to use chaining. Maybe in your organization, users aren't all centrally managed—some might be in LDAP, while others are in some other proprietary store.

Let's set up SomeCo to chain LDAP to Alfresco. This will involve copying and modifying the out of the box chaining context sample file, and tweaking the existing LDAP authentication context file.

Here are the steps:

1. Copy the `chaining-context.xml.sample` file from your Alfresco distribution into the **config | [community or enterprise] | alfresco | extension** directory in the server-extensions project. Rename the file to remove `.sample` from the end. You can find the file in the same place you found `ldap-authentication-context.xml.sample`.

2. The sample chaining file chains JAAS to Alfresco. But SomeCo wants to chain LDAP to Alfresco. The easiest way to get LDAP chaining set up without getting your beans mixed up is to walk through the chaining context file and change bean IDs containing "JAAS" to bean IDs containing "LDAP". The first change is to the `authenticationService` bean. Change `authenticationServiceImplJAAS` to `authenticationServiceImplLDAP`:

    ```
    <bean id="authenticationService" class="org.alfresco.repo.
    security.authentication.ChainingAuthenticationServiceImpl">
        <property name="authenticationServices">
            <list>
                <ref bean="authenticationServiceImplLDAP"/>
            </list>
        </property>
        <property name="mutableAuthenticationService">
            <ref bean="authenticationServiceImplAlfresco"/>
        </property>
        <property name="sysAdminCache">
            <ref bean="sysAdminCache"/>
        </property>
    </bean>
    ```

3. Next, change the `authenticationComponent` bean. This is the bean that lists the authentication sources in the chain. In this example, you need two sources: LDAP and Alfresco. Again, the only difference between what you need and the sample is the reference to `authenticationComponentImplLDAP`:

    ```
    <bean id="authenticationComponent" class="org.alfresco.repo.
    security.authentication.ChainingAuthenticationComponentImpl">
    ```

```
<property name="authenticationComponents">
   <list>
      <ref bean="authenticationComponentImplLDAP"/>
   </list>
</property>
<property name="mutableAuthenticationComponent">
   <ref bean="authenticationComponentImplAlfresco"/>
</property>
</bean>
```

4. Leave the Alfresco-related beans alone. Nothing needs to change there.

5. Delete the `authenticationDaoJAAS` bean. The LDAP equivalent will live in the `ldap-authentication-context.xml` file.

6. Now edit `ldap-authentication-context.xml`. In the earlier example, when you configured Alfresco to use LDAP instead of Alfresco's authentication, you used the same bean IDs because you were replacing the Alfresco authentication implementation components. Now that you will be running both, you have to make sure the LDAP beans have unique IDs. The new IDs should match the bean references set up in the chaining context file. First, change the `authenticationDao` bean ID:

```
<bean name="authenticationDaoLDAP" class="org.alfresco.repo.
security.authentication.DefaultMutableAuthenticationDao" >
   <property name="allowDeleteUser">
      <value>true</value>
   </property>
</bean>
```

7. Next, change the bean ID of the `authenticationComponent`:

```
<bean id="authenticationComponentImplLDAP"
 class="org.alfresco.repo.security.authentication.ldap.
LDAPAuthenticationComponentImpl">
   <property name="allowGuestLogin">
      <value>true</value>
   </property>
   <property name="LDAPInitialDirContextFactory">
      <ref bean="ldapInitialDirContextFactory"/>
   </property>
   <property name="userNameFormat">
      <value>${ldap.authentication.userNameFormat}</value>
   </property>
   <property name="nodeService">
      <ref bean="nodeService" />
```

```
            </property>
            <property name="personService">
                <ref bean="personService" />
            </property>
            <property name="transactionService">
                <ref bean="transactionService" />
            </property>
        </bean>
```

8. Save the file.

9. Deploy the changes by running **ant deploy-shared**, and then restart Alfresco.

You should now be able to log in using **admin**, one of the test users you created in a previous chapter, or one of the test users in LDAP.

> At the time of this writing, the Community version of Alfresco was throwing a NullPointerException on startup when using chaining. The solution is to add a parent attribute set to authenticationComponentBase to the authenticationComponentImplAlfresco and authenticationDaoAlfresco beans in the chaining context file. This issue has been filed in Jira (ALFCOM-1824) and may be resolved by the time you read this.

Step-by-Step: Synchronizing LDAP with Alfresco

Alfresco stores all its users in the repository, even when using an external authentication mechanism. This makes sense because when inviting users to a web project or setting permissions on an object, you don't necessarily want to make a trip to the authentication source every time to build the list of possible users. Plus, you might not want everyone in the corporate directory to be stored in or have access to the Alfresco repository.

This implies that a synchronization of some kind takes place between Alfresco and the authentication source. Alfresco's out of the box LDAP authentication component knows how to synchronize users and groups from LDAP.

Let's set up synchronization for SomeCo so that the users and groups in the LDAP directory will be imported into Alfresco. This involves copying the sample synchronization context file and modifying the sample synchronization properties file to match the directory setup.

Follow these steps:

1. The synchronization context file is the same for both Community and Enterprise editions. So, copy the `ldap-synchronisation-context.xml` (there's that endearing UK spelling again!) file into the server-extensions project under **config | alfresco | extension**. The file is already configured to pull all of its settings from a properties file, so no changes are needed.

2. Now copy the `ldap-synchronisation.properties` file from the same source directory into the **config | alfresco | extension** directory within your Eclipse project. Edit this file.

3. Modify the set of properties that tell Alfresco how to query for users and groups to match how you've set up your LDAP directory:

```
# The query to find the people to import
ldap.synchronisation.personQuery=(&(objectclass=inetOrgPerson)(uid
=*)(givenName=*)(sn=*)(mail=*))

# The search base of the query to find people to import
ldap.synchronisation.personSearchBase=ou=people,dc=someco,dc=com

# The query to find group objects
ldap.synchronisation.groupQuery=(objectclass=groupOfUniqueNames)

# The search base to use to find group objects
ldap.synchronisation.groupSearchBase=ou=groups,dc=someco,dc=com
Next, edit the set of properties that tell Alfresco about the LDAP
schema:
# The attribute name on people objects found in LDAP to use as the
uid in Alfresco
ldap.synchronisation.userIdAttributeName=uid

# The attribute on person objects in LDAP to map to the first name
property in Alfresco
ldap.synchronisation.userFirstNameAttributeName=givenName

# The attribute on person objects in LDAP to map to the last name
property in Alfresco
ldap.synchronisation.userLastNameAttributeName=sn

# The attribute on person objects in LDAP to map to the email
property in Alfresco
ldap.synchronisation.userEmailAttributeName=mail

# The attribute on person objects in LDAP to map to the
organizational id  property in Alfresco
ldap.synchronisation.userOrganizationalIdAttributeName=SomeCo

# The attribute on LDAP group objects to map to the gid property
in Alfrecso
ldap.synchronisation.groupIdAttributeName=cn
```

```
# The group type in LDAP
ldap.synchronisation.groupType=groupOfUniqueNames
```

```
# The person type in LDAP
ldap.synchronisation.personType=inetOrgPerson
```

```
# The attribute in LDAP on group objects that defines the DN for
its members
ldap.synchronisation.groupMemberAttributeName=uniqueMember
```

4. The `defaultHomeFolderProvider` property is used to specify how to create home folders for new users. The value of the property is a bean reference. In this case, replace what's provided in the sample, `personalHomeFolderProvider`, with `userHomesHomeFolderProvider`. The former creates a home folder in Company Home, while the latter creates a home folder under the `User Homes` folder, which is the default behavior for Alfresco authentication. (If you are curious, these beans are defined in `authentication-services-context.xml` and point to the same class, `org.alfresco.repo.security.person.UIDBaseHomeFolderProvider`. The difference is in the properties passed to the bean class.)

```
# The default home folder provider to use for people created via
LDAP import
ldap.synchronisation.defaultHomeFolderProvider=userHomesHomeFolder
Provider
```

5. If LDAP is the sole source for groups, setting this property to true is a good way to keep the groups in Alfresco clean because all groups will be removed every time a group synchronization runs. In SomeCo's case, you don't want to lose the `Publisher` group you created earlier in the book. So set this to false:

```
# Should all groups be cleared out at import time?
ldap.synchronisation.import.group.clearAllChildren=false
```

6. Last, provide cron expressions that tell Alfresco when to initiate the user and group synchronization jobs. The sample properties file includes property values that will run the person sync every hour on the hour and the group sync every hour on the half hour. In other words, if you use the sample properties file, the "person sync"—the process that synchronizes users between LDAP and Alfresco—will run every hour, on the hour, for example. 7:00, 8:00, 9:00, and so on. The process that synchronizes groups will run every hour on the half hour, for example. 7:30, 8:30, 9:30, and so on.

```
# The cron expression defining when people imports should take
place
ldap.synchronisation.import.person.cron=0 0 * * * ?
```

```
# The cron expression defining when group imports should take
place
ldap.synchronisation.import.group.cron=0 30 * * * ?
```

7. Save the properties file.

8. To deploy your changes, run **ant deploy-shared**, and then restart Alfresco.

The sync jobs will now run according to the schedule you set. If you want to see exactly what each job is doing, add the following to `log4j.properties`:

```
log4j.logger.org.alfresco.repo.security.authentication.ldap=debug
```

Handling Large Directories

If your directory is in the tens or hundreds of thousands of entries, you need to give serious thought to how synchronization is going to work or whether you will use it at all. You can split the sync up into multiple jobs, each handling different parts of the directory tree if needed, and that may help.

In the past, I've seen clients with large directories handling user and group synchronization in real time via a message queue—when changes are made in the identity management system, a message is queued with the nature of the change. A process on the server subscribes to the queue and handles messages appropriately by adding users, removing users, or updating group membership. This is obviously a highly scalable solution, but is not provided out of the box.

Setting Up Single Sign-On (SSO)

If multiple applications in the enterprise use the same LDAP server to authenticate, why force your users to re-enter the same username and password just because they are moving from one application to another? The answer, as usual, is time and money. However, implementing a Single Sign-On (SSO) solution and configuring Alfresco to leverage it may be easier than you think.

There are many SSO providers available and specific implementations can vary dramatically from company to company. In the next exercise, you'll install an open source SSO server called CAS from JA-SIG, and then configure Alfresco to use it. This should give you just enough of a taste of SSO to determine if it makes sense in your organization and what might be involved for a full production rollout, whether using CAS or some other SSO package.

Step-by-Step: Implementing SSO

This exercise involves downloading, installing, and configuring a base install of CAS, and then updating the out of the box `web.xml` file to configure the authentication filter. Finally, you will add an LDAP authentication adapter to CAS to use the same LDAP directory for its authentication that you used by configuring Alfresco in an earlier exercise. When that's done, you'll be able to visit Alfresco and other CAS-protected web applications (we'll use two of the sample Tomcat servlets) without requiring more than one login.

To install CAS and configure Alfresco for SSO, follow these steps:

1. You're going to install CAS in a separate application server from Alfresco. Set up another Tomcat instance on your machine. You'll need to change its HTTP, SSL, and shutdown ports. For example, I used 8081, 8444, and 8006 respectively. If you are running a separate web server, you'll need to modify the AJP connector port as well. These ports are all specified in Tomcat's `conf/server.xml` file:

```
...
<Server port="8006" shutdown="SHUTDOWN">
...
<Connector port="8081" maxHttpHeaderSize="8192"
               maxThreads="150" minSpareThreads="25"
maxSpareThreads="75"
               enableLookups="false" redirectPort="8444"
acceptCount="100"
               connectionTimeout="20000" disableUploadTimeout="tru
e" />
...
<!-- Define a SSL HTTP/1.1 Connector on port 8443 -->
<Connector port="8444" maxHttpHeaderSize="8192"
               maxThreads="150" minSpareThreads="25"
maxSpareThreads="75"
               enableLookups="false" disableUploadTimeout="true"
               acceptCount="100" scheme="https" secure="true"
               clientAuth="false" sslProtocol="TLS"
...
<!-- Define an AJP 1.3 Connector on port 8010 -->
<Connector port="8010"
               enableLookups="false" redirectPort="8444"
protocol="AJP/1.3" />
...
```

2. Start up the new Tomcat instance. You shouldn't have any trouble starting and stopping Tomcat, or running any of the example servlets even with Alfresco's Tomcat running simultaneously.

3. Download the CAS server from JA-SIG at `http://www.ja-sig.org/products/cas/` and extract the archive.

4. When you invoke a CAS-protected URL, the browser will be redirected to the CAS authentication page. For security reasons, the CAS URLs are protected with SSL. It is easier to generate a self-signed certificate and add it to your JRE's keystore than re-configuring CAS not to use SSL. Creating the certificate and adding it to the JRE's keystore is a multi-step process. First, navigate to **$JAVA_HOME|bin** from the command line.

5. Create the SSL key for your machine using Java's `keytool` program. When asked to specify your first and last name, use the name of the machine running the CAS Tomcat server. For example, on my machine, I used `jpotts.optaros-laptop.com`:

```
keytool -genkey -alias tomcat -keypass changeit -keyalg RSA
```

6. You now have a keystore in the current user's home directory. Now you need to add the certificate to your JRE's `cacerts` file. Export the certificate you just generated:

```
keytool -export -alias tomcat -keypass changeit -file server.crt
```

7. Now, add the exported certificate (`server.crt`) to your JRE's `cacerts` file again using Java's `keytool` program, as follows:

```
keytool -import -file server.crt -keypass changeit -keystore ..\
jre\lib\security\cacerts
```

8. The last step in setting up SSL is to tell Tomcat about the `keystore`. Edit the `server.xml` file again. Modify the SSL connector definition with the lines highlighted below. Note that the `keystoreFile` is the full path to the current user's home directory where the keystore resides:

```
<Connector port="8444" maxHttpHeaderSize="8192"
           maxThreads="150" minSpareThreads="25"
           maxSpareThreads="75"
           enableLookups="false" disableUploadTimeout="true"
           acceptCount="100" scheme="https" secure="true"
           clientAuth="false" sslProtocol="TLS"
           keystoreFile="/root/.keystore"
           keystorePass="changeit"
           truststoreFile="/usr/lib/jvm/java-1.5.0-sun/jre/lib/
security/cacerts" />
```

9. Copy the CAS webapp WAR to the webapps directory in the new Tomcat instance you just installed, which will be referred to as "CAS Tomcat" from now. The CAS webapp WAR is in the directory where you expanded CAS under "modules". The file is called `cas-server-webapp-3.2.1.war`.

10. Start CAS Tomcat. You should be able to see the login screen by pointing your browser at `https://[machine name]:8444/cas-server-webapp-3.2.1`.

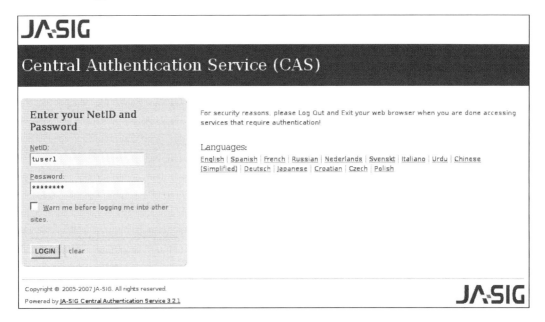

11. Now it is time to test your base CAS installation. Shut down the Alfresco Tomcat instance if it is running. Edit **$TOMCAT_HOME|webapps|servlets-examples|WEB-IN|web.xml**. Add a filter definition for the Yale CAS Client after the webapp description:

```
<!-- cas client filter -->
<filter>
   <filter-name>CAS Filter</filter-name>
   <filter-class>
    edu.yale.its.tp.cas.client.filter.CASFilter</filter-class>
   <init-param>
       <param-name>
       edu.yale.its.tp.cas.client.filter.loginUrl</param-name>
       <param-value>https://jpotts.optaros-laptop.com:8444/cas-
         server-webapp-3.2.1/login</param-value>
   </init-param>
   <init-param>
   <param-name>
```

```
      edu.yale.its.tp.cas.client.filter.validateUrl</param-name>
      <param-value>https://jpotts.optaros-laptop.com:8444/cas-
        server-webapp-3.2.1/serviceValidate</param-value>
    </init-param>
    <init-param>
    <param-name>
      edu.yale.its.tp.cas.client.filter.serverName</param-name>
        <param-value>jpotts.optaros-laptop.com:8080</param-value>
    </init-param>
  </filter>
```

12. Now that the filter is defined, you can add filter mappings for two of the sample servlets. This will cause Tomcat to redirect the browser to the CAS login if anyone without a valid ticket attempts to run one of the servlets:

```
<filter-mapping>
    <filter-name>CAS Filter</filter-name>
    <url-pattern>/servlet/HelloWorldExample</url-pattern>
</filter-mapping>
<filter-mapping>
    <filter-name>CAS Filter</filter-name>
    <url-pattern>/servlet/RequestInfoExample</url-pattern>
</filter-mapping>
```

13. Copy the `casclient-2.1.1.jar` file from the CAS server webapp's **WEB-INF|lib** into Alfresco Tomcat's **common|lib** folder. The JAR contains the CASFilter filter class you specified when you defined the filter in `web.xml`.

14. Now start Alfresco's Tomcat and point your browser to `http://localhost:8080/servlets-examples/servlet/HelloWorldExample`. You should see the CAS login screen, but don't log in.

15. Point your browser to `http://localhost:8080/servlets-examples/servlet/HelloWorldExample`. Again, you should see the CAS login screen, but don't log in.

16. If you go to any other example servlet (or Alfresco, for that matter), you will not see the CAS login screen because you have only enabled the CAS Filter for those two servlets.

17. Go back to the `HelloWorldExample`, and this time log in. Out of the box, CAS runs with an authentication adapter that just checks to see if the username and password are identical. So log in as **admin** with a password of **admin**. You should see the Hello World Servlet. This time, when you go to the `RequestInfoExample` servlet, you will not be challenged for a login. If this works, it means CAS is working and you've got Single Sign-On established between two servlets. Adding a third application (Alfresco) to the setup should be easy at this point, shouldn't it?

18. Stop Alfresco's Tomcat.

19. Import Alfresco's **WEB-INF | web.xml** file into your server-extensions Eclipse project under **src | web | [enterprise or community] | WEB-INF**.

20. Edit the `web.xml` file. Add the same filter definition to Alfresco's `web.xml` that you did for the servlets-example web application. As a reminder, it starts out like this:

```
<filter>
    <filter-name>CAS Filter</filter-name>
    <filter-class>edu.yale.its.tp.cas.client.filter.CASFilter</
filter-class>
...
```

21. Next, add the filter mapping. The syntax is the same that you used for the two sample servlets, but the `url-pattern` is different. For Alfresco, the URL pattern should be:

```
<filter-mapping>
    <filter-name>CAS Filter</filter-name>
    <url-pattern>/faces/*</url-pattern>
</filter-mapping>
```

22. Save the `web.xml` file. At this point, you could restart Alfresco Tomcat and open the web client and you'd be redirected to the CAS login page. But Alfresco doesn't yet know how to extract the credentials from CAS to use to start an Alfresco session. To do that, you have to write an `AuthenticationFilter`. Luckily, someone's already done that for you and posted it on the Alfresco Wiki at `http://wiki.alfresco.com/wiki/Central_Authentication_Service_Configuration`. The class is also included in the source code that accompanies this chapter in the server-extensions project. It is called `com.someco.servlets.AuthenticationFilter`. Copy the `AuthenticationFilter` class provided with the chapter source code into your version of the server-extensions Eclipse project.

23. You have to tell Alfresco to use the new `Authentication Filter` in place of the out of the box `Authentication Filter`. Do that by editing `web.xml` and modifying the `Authentication Filter` filter as follows:

```
<filter>
    <filter-name>Authentication Filter</filter-name>
    <!--
    <filter-class>
     org.alfresco.web.app.servlet.AuthenticationFilter
    </filter-class>
    -->
```

```
<filter-class>
com.someco.servlets.AuthenticationFilter</filter-class>
<init-param>
    <param-name>cas.user.label</param-name>
    <param-value>
    edu.yale.its.tp.cas.client.filter.user</param-value>
</init-param>
</filter>
```

24. To deploy the `AuthenticationFilter` class and the updated `web.xml`, run **ant deploy-web**.

25. Start Alfresco. You should now be able to log in to any of the three web applications (the two test servlets or Alfresco) and not have to log in again when visiting one of the others. Remember that at this point, CAS is still using its default adapter, which grants successful logins when the username and password match.

Logging Out

You'll notice that when you click Alfresco's logout link, you are taken to a "logout" JSP:

If you click the login link at that point (not shown in the screenshot), you'll go right in to Alfresco because CAS still knows about your session. If you want to log out permanently, you can either close your browser window or go to `https://[your machine name]:8444/cas-server-webapp-3.2.1/logout`. Make special note of the `https` protocol and port for the logout. If you use the non-SSL version, you won't be logged out.

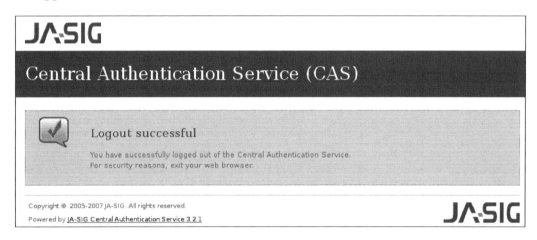

Most people will want the logout link in Alfresco to completely log the user out. So in production, you'll either change the logout link to point to the CAS logout URL, or you'll add a redirect to the logout JSP that redirects to the CAS logout URL.

Step-by-Step: Configuring CAS to Use LDAP for Authentication

This really has nothing to do with Alfresco, but it completes the picture. At this point, CAS is letting in anyone who specifies a username that matches their password. What it needs to do is use the same `OpenLDAP` directory for authentication we pointed Alfresco to earlier. This involves copying a JAR into your CAS webapp's **WEB-INF | lib** directory and updating a couple of configuration files.

To get CAS working with LDAP, do this:

1. Edit the **WEB-INF | deployerConfigContext.xml** in the CAS webapp's **WEB-INF | lib**. Add the following bean:

```
<bean id="contextSource"
     class="org.jasig.cas.adaptors.ldap.util.
AuthenticatedLdapContextSource">
  <property name="pooled" value="true"/>
  <property name="urls">
```

```
        <list>
            <value>ldap://localhost:389</value>
        </list>
    </property>
    <property name="userName" value="cn=Manager,dc=someco,dc=com"/>
    <property name="password" value="somepassword"/>
    <property name="baseEnvironmentProperties">
        <map>
            <entry>
                <key>
                  <value>java.naming.security.authentication</value>
                </key>
                <value>simple</value>
            </entry>
        </map>
    </property>
</bean>
```

2. Elsewhere in this same file, there is a list of authentication handlers. Do a search for `authentcationHandlers` to find it. Comment out the test authentication handler to turn off the `username matches password` behavior:

```
<!--
<bean
class="org.jasig.cas.authentication.handler.support.
SimpleTestUsernamePasswordAuthenticationHandler" />

-->
```

3. Then, add the `Fast Bind` LDAP authentication handler bean to the list. This authentication handler is equivalent to Alfresco's `simple` bind. CAS will try to bind to the directory as the user, and return a successful login if that succeeds:

```
<bean class=
"org.jasig.cas.adaptors.ldap.FastBindLdapAuthenticationHandler" >
    <property name="filter"          value=
        "uid=%u,ou=people,dc=someco,dc=com" />
    <property name="contextSource" ref="contextSource" />
</bean>
```

4. The last step is to copy `cas-server-support-ldap-3.2.1.jar` from the modules directory of your CAS distribution to the CAS webapp's **WEB-INF|lib** directory.

5. Now restart your CAS Tomcat server and attempt to log in. You should be able to log in using any of the test users you loaded into LDAP.

You now have SSO working between Alfresco and two other webapps, and CAS is using your OpenLDAP directory for authentication.

In development mode, you may get tired of having to run your CAS server every time you want to start up Alfresco. If you want to "undo" SSO, all you have to do is revert Alfresco's `web.xml` file back to the original out of the box version. Alternatively, you can simply comment out the filter and filter-mapping you added earlier, and switch the Authentication Filter's filter class back to Alfresco's OOTB filter class.

Working with Security Services

The first part of this chapter was about authentication, or knowing who the user is. This section is about authorization, which is about specifying what the user can do once he/she is authenticated. First, you'll see how to secure the admin user and give additional users admin rights. Then you'll learn how to use Alfresco's security services classes to create users and groups with the API. And finally, you'll see how to declare your own custom permission groups when the out of the box permission groups don't meet your needs.

Securing the Admin User

As you and everyone else in the world knows, the default password for Alfresco's admin account is **admin**. If you are using Alfresco for authentication (and even if you aren't), you should change the password for the admin user after you set up your Alfresco instance. If you use LDAP or some other source for authentication and create an entry in the directory for **admin**, change the password for the admin user in that system. The admin is the all-powerful super user, and so securing the admin account is an important step.

Granting Additional Users Admin Rights

Most organizations have more than one person helping support the Alfresco infrastructure. You could share the admin password with whoever needs it, but a better practice is to assign admin rights to specific users.

Unfortunately, in the current release, this must be done through XML. There is no way to go in through the web client and simply tag a user as having administrative privileges. It is an easy change to make, but it does require a restart.

Step-by-Step: Making tpublisher1 an Admin

Suppose SomeCo wants to grant `tpublisher1` admin privileges. You should have that user from earlier exercises. If not, use any of the test users you've created (Alfresco or LDAP—it doesn't matter). Follow these steps to grant admin rights:

1. Create a new file called `someco-authority-context.xml` in **config|alfresco |extension** in your Eclipse server-extensions project.

2. Add a single bean called `authorityService` to replace the out of the box bean of the same ID. The `adminUsers` property lists the Alfresco usernames that should be given administrative privileges. In this case, the admin ID has been removed from the list making `tpublisher1` the sole administrative account:

```xml
<?xml version='1.0' encoding='UTF-8'?>
<!DOCTYPE beans PUBLIC '-//SPRING//DTD BEAN//EN' 'http://www.
springframework.org/dtd/spring-beans.dtd'>

<beans>
    <bean id="authorityService" class=
    "org.alfresco.repo.security.authority.AuthorityServiceImpl">
        <property name="authenticationComponent">
            <ref bean="authenticationComponent" />
        </property>
        <property name="personService">
            <ref bean="personService" />
        </property>
        <property name="nodeService">
          <ref bean="nodeService" />
        </property>
        <property name="authorityDAO">
            <ref bean="authorityDAO" />
        </property>
        <property name="permissionServiceSPI">
            <ref bean="permissionServiceImpl" />
        </property>
        <property name="adminUsers">
            <set>
            <!--
            <value>admin</value>
            <value>administrator</value>
            -->
                <value>tpublisher1</value>
        </set>
        </property>
    </bean>
</beans>
```

3. Save the context file.

4. Run **ant deploy-shared** to deploy the new context file, and then restart Alfresco.

You should now be able to log in as `tpublisher1` and see the link to the admin console. You can also do things such as invoking a web script that requires admin rights.

Creating Users and Groups Programmatically

As mentioned earlier, the easiest way to load users into Alfresco is to configure Alfresco to use LDAP, and then use an LDIF import. But there may be times when you need to create users or groups with the API. For example, you might be writing a custom client that enables user or group management.

First, you should understand how users are stored. Every Alfresco user, whether or not Alfresco is handling authentication, is stored in the `SpacesStore` as a `cm:person` object. You can see these objects by using the node browser to navigate to System/People:

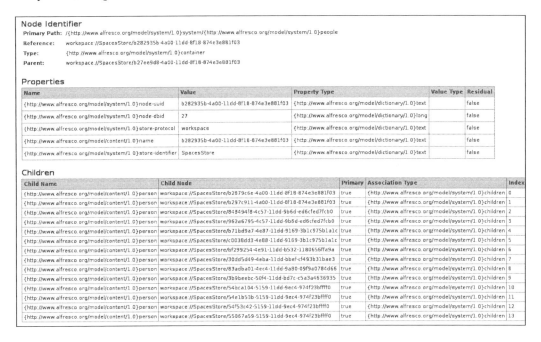

Users managed by Alfresco (where Alfresco is the authentication source) are stored in the `alfrescoUserStore` as `usr:user` objects under System/People. Again, using the node browser you can see these objects:

Node Identifier

Primary Path: /{http://www.alfresco.org/model/system/1.0}system/{http://www.alfresco.org/model/system/1.0}people

Reference: user://alfrescoUserStore/b09bf8c6-4a00-11dd-8f18-874e3e881f03

Type: {http://www.alfresco.org/model/system/1.0}container

Parent: user://alfrescoUserStore/b0919883-4a00-11dd-8f18-874e3e881f03

Properties

Name	Value	Property Type	Value Type	Residual
{http://www.alfresco.org/model/system/1.0}node-uuid	b09bf8c6-4a00-11dd-8f18-874e3e881f03	{http://www.alfresco.org/model/dictionary/1.0}text		false
{http://www.alfresco.org/model/system/1.0}node-dbid	5	{http://www.alfresco.org/model/dictionary/1.0}long		false
{http://www.alfresco.org/model/system/1.0}store-protocol	user	{http://www.alfresco.org/model/dictionary/1.0}text		false
{http://www.alfresco.org/model/content/1.0}name	b09bf8c6-4a00-11dd-8f18-874e3e881f03	{http://www.alfresco.org/model/dictionary/1.0}text		false
{http://www.alfresco.org/model/system/1.0}store-identifier	alfrescoUserStore	{http://www.alfresco.org/model/dictionary/1.0}text		false

Children

Child Name	Child Node	Primary	Association Type	Index
{http://www.alfresco.org/model/user/1.0}user	user://alfrescoUserStore/b0a0b3b9-4a00-11dd-8f18-874e3e881f03	true	{http://www.alfresco.org/model/system/1.0}children	0
{http://www.alfresco.org/model/user/1.0}user	user://alfrescoUserStore/8491663c-4c57-11dd-9b6d-ed6cfed7fcb0	true	{http://www.alfresco.org/model/system/1.0}children	1
{http://www.alfresco.org/model/user/1.0}user	user://alfrescoUserStore/9632a4f9-4c57-11dd-9b6d-ed6cfed7fcb0	true	{http://www.alfresco.org/model/system/1.0}children	2

Groups are stored in `alfrescoUserStore` as well under System/Authorities as `usr:authorityContainers`. The node browser for groups looks like this:

Node Identifier

Primary Path: /{http://www.alfresco.org/model/system/1.0}system/{http://www.alfresco.org/model/system/1.0}authorities

Reference: user://alfrescoUserStore/b10ff04c-4a00-11dd-8f18-874e3e881f03

Type: {http://www.alfresco.org/model/system/1.0}container

Parent: user://alfrescoUserStore/b0919883-4a00-11dd-8f18-874e3e881f03

Properties

Name	Value	Property Type	Value Type	Residual
{http://www.alfresco.org/model/system/1.0}node-uuid	b10ff04c-4a00-11dd-8f18-874e3e881f03	{http://www.alfresco.org/model/dictionary/1.0}text		false
{http://www.alfresco.org/model/system/1.0}node-dbid	7	{http://www.alfresco.org/model/dictionary/1.0}long		false
{http://www.alfresco.org/model/system/1.0}store-protocol	user	{http://www.alfresco.org/model/dictionary/1.0}text		false
{http://www.alfresco.org/model/content/1.0}name	b10ff04c-4a00-11dd-8f18-874e3e881f03	{http://www.alfresco.org/model/dictionary/1.0}text		false
{http://www.alfresco.org/model/system/1.0}store-identifier	alfrescoUserStore	{http://www.alfresco.org/model/dictionary/1.0}text		false

Children

Child Name	Child Node	Primary	Association Type	Index
{http://www.alfresco.org/model/user/1.0}GROUP_Test Group 1	user://alfrescoUserStore/4e0d3e49-521e-11dd-b480-03dcf7deb0fd	true	{http://www.alfresco.org/model/system/1.0}children	0
{http://www.alfresco.org/model/user/1.0}GROUP_Publisher	user://alfrescoUserStore/d932a2f0-52ad-11dd-be6b-e1b39046d0f7	true	{http://www.alfresco.org/model/system/1.0}children	1

You may have taken a look at the **WEB-INF|classes|alfresco|model** folder to see what the `usr` model looks like. It shows you've been paying attention—you learned way back in Chapter 3 that that's where most of the Alfresco models reside. Alfresco got the best of you this time, though. The user model is not with the rest of the models. It is stored in the `alfresco-repository.jar` under **org|alfresco|repo| security|authentication**.

As you can tell by inspecting the model file, the `usr:user` type inherits from `usr:authority`. And groups aren't called groups at all. They are `usr: authorityContainers`, which also inherit from `usr:authority` and have an association to other authority objects (groups can contain both users and other groups).

Knowing where and how users and groups are stored is important for troubleshooting and administrative tasks. It also explains why, when you create users through the API and if you are creating an Alfresco user (that is, Alfresco manages the user instead of LDAP), you have to create both the usr:user object and the cm:person object. As you'll see in the next exercise, the AuthenticationService manages usr:user objects while the PersonService is in charge of cm:person objects.

Step-by-Step: Creating Users and Groups through the API

In the Appendix you'll find a section on building Alfresco Module Package (AMP) files. One of the cool things you can do with an AMP is run bootstrap code. The Appendix example takes advantage of this to execute a bean that creates a couple test users and groups. Let's looks at the code to get an idea of how you might use the AuthenticationService, PersonService, and AuthorityService to create users and groups.

If you want to follow along, the code is in **com | someco | module | BootstrapAuthorit yCreator** in the client-extensions Eclipse project that accompanies this chapter.

The goal of the class is to create four test users (tuser1 through tuser4) and two test groups (sales and marketing).

These test users are Alfresco—not LDAP—users. So the first thing that happens is that the code checks to see if an authentication (a usr:user object) exists, and if it doesn't, it creates one by calling the AuthenticationService:

```
if(!authenticationService.authenticationExists("tuser1")) {
   authenticationService.createAuthentication("tuser1", "password".
toCharArray());
}
```

Next, the PersonService is used to check to see if a cm:person object exists, and if not, it creates one:

```
if (!personService.personExists("tuser1")) {
   personService.createPerson(createDefaultProperties("tuser1",
"Test", "User1", "tuser1@localhost", "password"));
}
```

The createDefaultProperties method is a little helper method that returns a map of property QNames and property values, which is what the createPerson method is expecting:

```
private Map<QName, Serializable> createDefaultProperties(String
userName, String firstName, String lastName, String email, String
password) {
```

```
    HashMap<QName, Serializable> properties = new HashMap<QName,
Serializable>();
    properties.put(ContentModel.PROP_USERNAME, userName);
    properties.put(ContentModel.PROP_FIRSTNAME, firstName);
    properties.put(ContentModel.PROP_LASTNAME, lastName);
    properties.put(ContentModel.PROP_EMAIL, email);
    properties.put(ContentModel.PROP_PASSWORD, password);
    return properties;
}
```

Because you are using Alfresco's services classes, you don't have to worry about the details around creating the user home folder or where the objects actually reside in the underlying store.

As mentioned, Alfresco groups are instances of the `usr:authorityContainer` type with a `usr:authorityName` value that starts with `GROUP_`. So to create a group, use the `authorityService` to create a new authority, making sure to specify that the authority type is `AuthorityType.GROUP`. In this case, if the group already exists, the code gets a handle to it; otherwise it creates a new one:

```
if (authorityService.authorityExists(authorityService.
getName(AuthorityType.GROUP, "sales"))) {
    salesGroup = authorityService.getName(AuthorityType.GROUP,
"sales");
} else {
    // create the sales group
    salesGroup = authorityService.createAuthority(AuthorityType.GROUP,
null, "sales");
}
```

The last step is to add new authorities (users or groups) to the authority container (the group). In this example, `tuser1` and `tuser2` are being added to the `salesGroup`:

```
        authorityService.addAuthority(salesGroup, "tuser1");
        authorityService.addAuthority(salesGroup, "tuser2");
```

You should now have a basic idea about how to work with the three main security services: `AuthenticationService`, `AuthorityService`, and `PersonService`. Take a look at the source and/or the Javadoc for additional details on each of these interfaces. All of them are in the `org.alfresco.service.cmr.security` package.

Understanding Permission Definitions

Alfresco's out of the box permission definitions are stored in **WEB-INF | alfresco | cla sses | alfresco | mode | permissionDefinitions.xml**. If you've ever wondered what the difference is between a Contributor and Editor, this is the file that holds the answer.

Like just about everything else in Alfresco, the permission definitions can be extended. This can be really helpful when the out of the box permissions don't give you exactly what you need. You'll work through such an example in a bit. But first, let's take a peek at how the five permission groups or "roles" you see in the web client are defined. Note that this discussion also holds true for the four WCM roles available in a web project.

Permission Groups

Permission Groups roll up other **Permission Group**(s) and **Permission**(s) into higher-level concepts that make sense to people who have to deal with permissions. In the web client, these are labeled as "roles", although technically they are permission groups.

In Alfresco, users are assigned to groups. Groups are assigned to roles for specific folders and objects. Individual users can also be assigned roles, but using groups is a much better practice. When an individual changes job roles, it is much easier to simply change his/her group membership than updating every object where he/she has been given individual access.

Suppose Caroline is in a group called "HR Administrators", which is given the role of **Contributor** on the "resume" folder. Using the following diagram, let's figure out what Caroline can do.

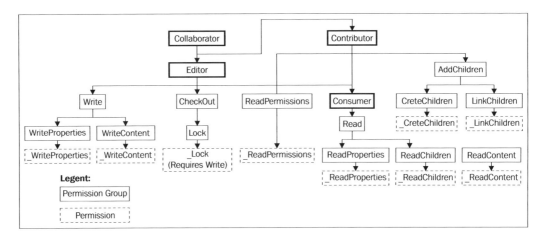

The diagram shows that **Contributor** is a permission group that includes the **Consumer**, **AddChildren**, and **ReadPermissions** permission groups. Each of these permission groups includes others, eventually leading to the following list of low-level permissions for a **Contributor**:

- _ReadProperties
- _ReadChildren
- _ReadContent
- _CreateChildren
- _LinkChildren
- _ReadPermissions

So Caroline can read the resume folder's properties, can see the children listed in the folder, and can even read the content of the folder object. She can add new files to the folder and can read the permissions of the folder. But Caroline can't change anything she doesn't own because she lacks **_WriteProperties** and **_WriteContent** permissions.

The "can't change anything she doesn't own" caveat is important to understand. Owners have full control over their content. An owner can be explicitly set or can be implicitly based on the creator of the content. So in this case, even though Caroline is just a **Contributor**, she'd still be able to change anything she created unless the ownership of those objects is changed.

Because Caroline is in a group, if she were to move to a different department and be back-filled by another person—Justin, for example—it would be easy to simply remove Caroline from the group and add Justin. Now Caroline would no longer be able to add content to the folder, but Justin would. Unless the ownership is changed, though, she will continue to be able to make changes to any content she owns unless a script is run to change the ownership to Justin or someone else.

Permissions

As shown in the table, at some point, permission groups stop including additional permission groups. In other words, you get to the lowest level in the tree. How, then, do permission groups get tied to actual, low-level permissions? Each permission is granted to a permission group, sometimes conditionally. In the table, you may have noticed that the **_Lock** permission is only granted to the **Lock** permission group when the user also has **Write** permission on that node.

Permission Sets

Permission sets are collections of permission groups specific to an Alfresco type. For example, the permission groups applicable to a `cm:folder` object are:

- Coordinator
- Collaborator
- Contributor
- Editor
- Consumer
- RecordsAdministrator (not exposed to the UI out of the box)

On the other hand, the permission groups relevant to an `avm:folder` (a folder in a web project) are:

- ContentManager
- ContentPublisher
- ContentContributor
- ContentReviewer

Permission sets can also be tied to aspects. For example, when an object has the `cm:ownable` aspect applied, one of the things you can do is take ownership of that object (that is, set the "owner" attribute). But you have to have a specific permission level to do that. So, there is a permission set tied to the `cm:ownable` aspect called `TakeOwnership` that includes the permission group `SetOwner`":

```
<permissionSet type="cm:ownable" expose="selected">

    <!-- Permission control to allow ownership of the node to be
    taken from others -->
    <permissionGroup name="TakeOwnership" requiresType="false"
    expose="false">
        <includePermissionGroup permissionGroup="SetOwner"
        type="cm:ownable" />
    </permissionGroup>

    <permissionGroup name="SetOwner" requiresType="false"
    expose="false"/>

    <!-- The low level permission to control setting the owner of a
    node -->
    <permission name="_SetOwner" expose="false"
    requiresType="false">
      <grantedToGroup permissionGroup="SetOwner" />
```

```
        <requiredPermission on="node" type="sys:base" name="_
        WriteProperties" />
    </permission>
</permissionSet>
```

 Node-level permissions are as granular as Alfresco gets. If you want security down to an individual property level, you can make properties read-only through the UI configuration. But this doesn't stop someone with write access on the node from changing the property through the UI.

Step-by-Step: Setting Up A Portal Publisher Custom Role

In Chapter 5, you implemented action evaluator classes that made sure only members of the Publisher group would see the UI action links related to setting the flag that determines if a piece of content should show up on the portal or not. Further, the UI action links were defined in `web-client-config-custom.xml` to only appear if the current user had Write permission or higher. It worked fine at the time, but now that you know about customizing the out of the box permissions, you can do better. First, here are some of the issues with the original approach:

- The group name was hardcoded as a constant in the Java code. You could have fixed this by pulling the group out into a configuration file, but it still would have required a developer to make changes if the group name changed.

- It assumed that the list of people who were allowed to use the action links was the same across the entire organization. If, for example, Sales wanted to use the action to publish something on the portal as well as Marketing, individuals from both teams would have to be added to the Publisher group (or groups within that group) meaning they could publish or un-publish each other's content.

- It assumed that if you had Write permissions on the node, you should see the link. The evaluator then performed the group check. So users still had to belong to the Publisher group, even if they had Write permission. But because not everyone who has Write is in the Publisher group, it is a bit inefficient.

- People who can publish content to the portal can also change the content. Let's suppose that SomeCo wants more fine-grained control. Thus, people who are only supposed to enable or disable the web flag should not be able to actually change any content.

You can address these issues by implementing a custom role. Let's call it PortalPublisher. Instead of having an evaluator check for membership in a particular group, groups can be assigned to the PortalPublisher role. The UI action can then check to see if the current user has that role, and hide the link if he/she doesn't.

This also has the advantage of being able to split up responsibilities more granularly. In one folder, the Sales group could be assigned to PortalPublisher, while in another folder the Marketing group could have that role.

Because it is a custom role, you have more control over what people with that permission can do. In this case, a PortalPublisher should be able to read everything but edit only the properties. (They have to be able to edit the properties because the sc:isActive flag is a property on the object.)

Finally, this gives your administrator accounts access to the UI actions. In the old approach, you had to remember to add **admin** to the Publisher group. Because administrators get all permissions, when the UI action checks to see if the administrator has PortalPublisher permissions, it will return true and the link will be displayed (subject to the logic in the evaluator classes).

Now that you're convinced this is a great idea, go do it. This is going to involve defining a new permission group (PortalPublisher) in the permission definitions file, externalizing the role name, changing the permission required to see the UI action, and refactoring the evaluator classes to skip the group membership check.

Here are the steps:

1. Copy the out of the box permissionDefinitions file into your client-extensions Eclipse project under **config | alfresco | extension | model**.

2. Rename the file to scPermissionDefinitions.xml.

3. Modify the scPermissionDefinitions.xml to include your custom permission group. The first thing to do is add a new permission group to cm:cmobject. Add the following below the ContentReviewer permission group:

```
    <!-- A PortalPublisher is someone who can read everything
and write properties -->
    <permissionGroup name="PortalPublisher" allowFullControl=
    "false" expose="false" >
      <includePermissionGroup type="cm:cmobject" permissionGroup
       ="Consumer"/>
      <includePermissionGroup type="sys:base" permissionGroup=
       "WriteProperties"/>
    </permissionGroup>
```

4. You want web client users to be able to grant people the `PortalPublisher` permission on individual objects as well as on folders, so it can then be inherited to multiple objects. Add the `permissionGroup` to the list of `cm:content`-specific roles:

```
<permissionSet type="cm:content" expose="selected">
   <!-- Content specific roles.
                     -->
   <permissionGroup name="Coordinator" extends="true" expose=
    "true"/>
   <permissionGroup name="Collaborator" extends="true" expose=
    "true"/>
   <permissionGroup name="Contributor" extends="true" expose=
    "true"/>
   <permissionGroup name="Editor" extends="true" expose="true"/>
   <permissionGroup name="Consumer" extends="true" expose="true"/>
   <permissionGroup name="PortalPublisher" extends="true" expose=
    "true"/>
   <permissionGroup name="RecordAdministrator" extends="true"
    expose="false"/>
</permissionSet>
```

5. Also add the `permissionGroup` to the list of `cm:folder`-specific roles:

```
<permissionSet type="cm:folder" expose="selected">
   <!-- Content folder specific roles.
                       -->
   <permissionGroup name="Coordinator" extends="true" expose=
   "true"/>
   <permissionGroup name="Collaborator" extends="true" expose=
   "true"/>
   <permissionGroup name="Contributor" extends="true" expose=
    "true"/>
   <permissionGroup name="Editor" extends="true" expose="true"/>
   <permissionGroup name="Consumer" extends="true" expose="true"/>
   <permissionGroup name="PortalPublisher" extends="true" expose=
   "true"/>
   <permissionGroup name="RecordAdministrator" extends="true"
   expose="false"/>
</permissionSet>
```

6. Save the `scPermissionDefinitions.xml` file.

7. Edit **config | alfresco | extension | someco-model-context.xml**. Override the out of the box `permissionsModelDAO` bean with your own to point to the custom permissions definition file you were just modifying:

```
<bean id='permissionsModelDAO' class="org.alfresco.repo.security.
permissions.impl.model.PermissionModel">
    <property name="model">
        <value>alfresco/extension/model/scPermissionDefinitions.xml
         </value>
    </property>
    <property name="nodeService">
        <ref bean="nodeService" />
    </property>
    <property name="dictionaryService">
        <ref bean="dictionaryService" />
    </property>
</bean>
```

8. The custom role will be shown in the web client, so it needs to be externalized. Edit **config | alfresco | extension | webclient.properties** to add the externalized string for the role name:

```
# Custom PortalPublisher role
PortalPublisher=Portal Publisher
```

9. With the `PortalPublisher` role in place, there is no longer any need to specifically check group membership to determine whether or not to show the **SC Web Enable** and **SC Web Disable** UI action links. Instead, you can configure the UI action link to only show for users with the `PortalPublisher` permission. Edit **config | alfresco | extension | web-client-config-custom.xml** and change the permission required for the two UI action links from `Write` to `PortalPublisher`:

```
<!-- set sc:isActive to true -->
<action id="web_enable">
    <permissions>
        <!-- each permission can be an Allow or Deny check -->
        <permission allow="true">PortalPublisher</permission>
    </permissions>
    <evaluator>com.someco.action.evaluator.WebEnableEvaluator
    </evaluator>
    <label-id>enableWeb</label-id>
    ...
</action>
<!-- set sc:isActive to false -->
<action id="web_disable">
    <permissions>
        <!-- each permission can be an Allow or Deny check -->
        <permission allow="true">PortalPublisher</permission>
    </permissions>
```

```
    <evaluator>com.someco.action.evaluator.WebDisableEvaluator
    </evaluator>
    <label-id>disableWeb</label-id>
    ...
</action>
```

10. Save the `web-client-config-custom.xml` file.

11. The evaluator classes are still needed — they just don't need to perform the group membership check anymore. Edit the `WebEnableEvaluator` and `WebDisableEvaluator` classes to remove the group membership check. Only a subset of the `WebEnableEvaluator` is shown here:

```
// check the group
// DISABLING in favor of custom PortalPublisher permission
/*
if (!GroupMembershipCheck.isCurrentUserInGroup(context, Constants.
GROUP_WEB_PUBLISHER)) {
        return false;
}
*/
```

12. Save the changes you made to the two classes.

13. Deploy your changes using **ant deploy**, and then restart Alfresco.

To test out your changes, log in to the web client as an administrator. (Hopefully, after the earlier exercises you can recall exactly who is now an admin!) Go to the Whitepapers folder and edit the permissions. Assign the **Publisher** group to the **Portal Publisher** role:

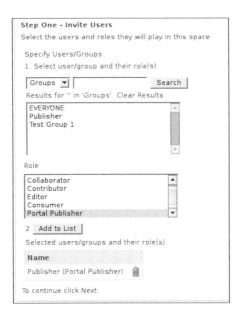

When you log out and log in again as someone who is a member of the Publisher group, you should see and be able to successfully execute the enable and disable actions. (Don't use an administrator because you want to test that your fine-grained, custom permission works on a non-admin account).

Global Permissions

The last section in the `permissionDefinitions.xml` file is a set of global permissions. Global permissions, as the name implies, apply to everything and supersede any other permissions that might be set on the object. The list of global permissions is short:

- Those belonging to the Administrator role always have full control
- Content owners (people belonging to the Owner role for a particular piece of content) always have full control
- Lock owners (people belonging to the Lock Owner role for a particular piece of content) always have Unlock, CheckIn, and Cancel Checkout permissions

Mapping Permissions to Methods

The names of the low-level permissions are pretty descriptive, but you might be wondering how these permissions are hooked in to the Alfresco API. As mentioned earlier in the chapter, Alfresco uses Spring Security. Spring Security bean configurations map methods in Alfresco's service classes to permissions. You can see the mapping in **WEB-INF | classes | alfresco | model | public-services-security-context.xml**. Following is a portion of the mapping for the NodeService with methods requiring the `ReadProperties` permission highlighted, as an example:

```
<bean id="NodeService_security" class="net.sf.acegisecurity.intercept.
method.aopalliance.MethodSecurityInterceptor">
        <property name="authenticationManager"><ref bean=
        "authenticationManager"/></property>
        <property name="accessDecisionManager"><ref local=
        "accessDecisionManager"/></property>
        <property name="afterInvocationManager"><ref local=
        "afterInvocationManager"/></property>
        <property name="objectDefinitionSource">
            <value>
                org.alfresco.service.cmr.repository.NodeService.
    getStores=AFTER_ACL_NODE.sys:base.ReadProperties
                org.alfresco.service.cmr.repository.NodeService.
    createStore=ACL_METHOD.ROLE_ADMINISTRATOR
                org.alfresco.service.cmr.repository.NodeService.
    exists=ACL_ALLOW
```

```
                org.alfresco.service.cmr.repository.NodeService.
        getNodeStatus=ACL_NODE.0.sys:base.ReadProperties
                org.alfresco.service.cmr.repository.NodeService.
        getRootNode=ACL_NODE.0.sys:base.ReadProperties
                org.alfresco.service.cmr.repository.NodeService.
        createNode=ACL_NODE.0.sys:base.CreateChildren
                org.alfresco.service.cmr.repository.NodeService.
        moveNode=ACL_NODE.0.sys:base.DeleteNode,ACL_NODE.1.sys:base.
        CreateChildren
                org.alfresco.service.cmr.repository.NodeService.setChil
        dAssociationIndex=ACL_PARENT.0.sys:base.WriteProperties
                org.alfresco.service.cmr.repository.NodeService.
        getType=ACL_ALLOW
                . . .
```

If you develop your own services, you can follow the same pattern to secure your methods using the same set of permission definitions.

Summary

When you started out the chapter, you had an Alfresco server that only knew about the users stored in its repository. By now, your server is not only authenticating against an external LDAP directory, but also sharing a session with other web applications through the magic of Single Sign-On (SSO).

You saw some sample code for working with three of Alfresco's security services classes (`AuthenticationService`, `AuthorityService`, and `PersonService`) and also learned where Alfresco keeps its permission definitions (and how to extend them).

Specifically, you learned how to:

- Install a basic OpenLDAP implementation
- Configure Alfresco to authenticate against LDAP, including "chaining" LDAP with Alfresco authentication
- Configure LDAP synchronization
- Install and configure a popular open source SSO solution from JA-SIG called CAS
- Establish SSO between Alfresco and two of Tomcat's sample servlets
- Create users and groups with the Alfresco API
- Understand the out of the box permissions
- Define a custom permission group or role, which you then leveraged to refactor how the SomeCo Web Enable/Disable links work

I am always surprised at how often people will save security considerations until the end of the project when they are inevitably short on time. Hopefully, this chapter has shown you that with a little planning, configuration, and some code here and there, you can integrate Alfresco into the rest of the security infrastructure in your company.

API Reference and Examples

This section is not a reprint of the Javadoc for every existing Alfresco class. Instead, it focuses on just enough to get you pointed in the right direction. This critical subset of the reference material includes:

- An index of Alfresco's "public services" classes. These are the interfaces you should be writing against when using the Foundation API.

- A set of Lucene query syntax examples. It's hard to do anything without a Lucene query—this section gives you the basic syntax.

- A comprehensive listing of JavaScript root objects and a JavaScript API reference. Ultimately, the Alfresco JavaScript API is implemented in Java, so the JavaScript API is already documented in the Javadoc. But JavaScript is such an integral part of web scripts, and the framework is becoming so popular, that it seemed a good idea to reprint the Javadoc here to make it easily scannable and update it with minor edits to fill in some missing details.

- A set of basic code snippets by function, and by API. These snippets show you how to perform a basic task with each of the major APIs: Java-based Foundation API, JavaScript API, and Web Services.

Foundation API Public Services

When working with the Alfresco Foundation API, you should use Alfresco's services interfaces as much as possible, rather than the implementation classes. The definitive resource for these classes is the Javadoc, the source code, and the test classes that often accompany each of the services. The goal of this section is to make you aware of the "public" services that are available and provide a cross-reference between the service's interface, the implementation class, the test class (if one's available), and the Spring Bean ID.

ActionService

Description	Get, create, and execute rule actions.
Interface	`org.alfresco.service.cmr.action.ActionService`
Implementation Class	`org.alfresco.repo.action.ActionServiceImpl`
JUnit Test Class	`org.alfresco.repo.action.ActionServiceImplTest`
Spring Bean ID	`ActionService`

ActivityService (3.0 Labs)

Description	Used to post activities and retrieve feeds of activities scoped to a particular site or across all sites. See `SiteService`.
Interface	`org.alfresco.repo.activities.ActivityService`
Implementation Class	`org.alfresco.repo.activities.ActivityServiceImpl`
JUnit Test Class	`org.alfresco.repo.activities.ActivityServiceImplTest`
Spring Bean ID	`ActionService`

AttributeService

Description	Gets and sets global, arbitrary attributes. Note: This is not what you would use to get the attributes (more correctly, "properties") of a node. Use the NodeService for that. Alfresco uses this service to store things such as a table of locked objects. But you could use it to store settings for your own needs as well.
Interface	`org.alfresco.service.cmr.attributes.AttributeService`
Implementation Class	`org.alfresco.repo.attributes.AttributeServiceImpl`
JUnit Test Class	`org.alfresco.repo.attributes.AttributeServiceTest`
Spring Bean ID	`AttributeService`

AuditService

Description	Public service used to write (and list) audit entries for a node. Unlike the lower-level auditing functionality, which is configured by adding annotations to service classes, this service is meant to be called by higher-level classes such as actions.
Interface	`org.alfresco.service.cmr.audit.AuditService`
Implementation Class	`org.alfresco.repo.audit.AuditServiceImpl`
JUnit Test Class	`org.alfresco.repo.audit.AuditServiceTest`
Spring Bean ID	`AuditService`

AuthenticationService

Description	Service used to authenticate with the repository. Includes methods for authenticating as guest, getting, validating and invalidating tickets, and getting the current username.
Interface	`org.alfresco.service.cmr.security.AuthenticationService`
Implementation Class	`org.alfresco.repo.security.authentication.AuthenticationServiceImpl`
JUnit Test Class	`org.alfresco.repo.security.authentication.AuthenticationTest`
Spring Bean ID	`AuthenticationService`

AuthorityService

Description	Service used to find authorities, check for the presence of an authority, and find the authorities that contain a particular authority (where an authority might be a user or a group). This service is not used to create new users, however. That's done with the `PersonService` and the `AuthenticationService`. See Chapter 9.
Interface	`org.alfresco.service.cmr.security.AuthorityService`
Implementation Class	`org.alfresco.repo.security.authority.AuthorityServiceImpl`
JUnit Test Class	`org.alfresco.repo.security.authority.AuthorityServiceTest`
Spring Bean ID	`AuthorityService`

AVMService

Description	Used for working with AVM stores. Its equivalent on the Document Management side of Alfresco is NodeService. The AVMService is used to manage nodes (including adding and removing aspects, and setting properties), stores, and branches.
Interface	`org.alfresco.service.cmr.avm.AVMService`
Implementation Class	`org.alfresco.repo.avm.AVMServiceImpl`
JUnit Test Class	`org.alfresco.repo.avm.AVMServiceTest`
Spring Bean ID	`AVMService`

AVMLockingService

Description	Service used to add and remove locks to and from nodes in the AVM store.
Interface	`org.alfresco.service.cmr.avm.locking.AVMLockingService`
Implementation Class	`org.alfresco.repo.avm.locking.AVMLockingServiceImpl`
JUnit Test Class	`org.alfresco.repo.avm.locking.AVMLockingServiceTest`
Spring Bean ID	`AVMLockingService`

AVMSyncService

Description	Service used for differentiating and merging of two branches, directories, or stores.
Interface	`org.alfresco.service.cmr.avmsync.AVMSyncService`
Implementation Class	`org.alfresco.repo.avm.AVMSyncServiceImpl`
JUnit Test Class	N/A
Spring Bean ID	`AVMSyncService`

CategoryService

Description	Service used to manage categories. This service is not used to categorize content. That is handled by setting a property on the node using the NodeService.
Interface	`org.alfresco.service.cmr.search.CategoryService`
Implementation Class	`org.alfresco.repo.search.impl.lucene.LuceneCategoryServiceImpl`
JUnit Test Class	N/A
Spring Bean ID	`CategoryService`

CheckOutCheckInService

Description	Used to check out, check in, or cancel the check out of a particular node.
Interface	`org.alfresco.service.cmr.coci.CheckOutCheckInService`
Implementation Class	`org.alfresco.repo.coci.CheckOutCheckInServiceImpl`
JUnit Test Class	`org.alfresco.repo.coci.CheckOutCheckInServiceImplTest`
Spring Bean ID	`CheckOutCheckInService`

ConfigurableService

Description	The `ConfigurableService` makes a node "configurable" by applying the configurable aspect. Out of the box, this is used to make person nodes configurable. The configuration is used to persist the user's preferences.
Interface	`org.alfresco.repo.configuration.ConfigurableService`
Implementation Class	`org.alfresco.repo.configuration.ConfigurableServiceImpl`
JUnit Test Class	`org.alfresco.repo.configuration.ConfigurableServiceImplTest`
Spring Bean ID	`ConfigurableService`

ContentUsageService (3.0 Labs)

Description	Service used to get and set a quota for disk usage for a particular user.
Interface	`org.alfresco.service.cmr.usage.ContentUsageService`
Implementation Class	`org.alfresco.repo.usage.ContentUsageImpl`
JUnit Test Class	N/A
Spring Bean ID	`ContentUsageService`

ContentService

Description	Service used for reading and writing content from and to a node.
Interface	`org.alfresco.service.cmr.repository.ContentService`
Implementation Class	`org.alfresco.repo.content.RoutingContentService`
JUnit Test Class	`org.alfresco.repo.content.RoutingContentServiceTest`
Spring Bean ID	`ContentService`

CopyService

Description	Service used for copying nodes. It is up to you to rename the new node if duplicate child names are not allowed by the containing association. See also `FileFolderService`.
Interface	`org.alfresco.service.cmr.repository.CopyService`
Implementation Class	`org.alfresco.repo.copy.CopyServiceImpl`
JUnit Test Class	`org.alfresco.repo.copy.CopyServiceImplTest`
Spring Bean ID	`CopyService`

CrossRepositoryCopyService

Description	Service used to copy nodes from one repository implementation to another (for example, copying from the DM store to the WCM or AVM store).
Interface	`org.alfresco.service.cmr.repository.` `CrossRepositoryCopyService`
Implementation Class	`org.alfresco.repo.copy.CrossRepositoryCopyServiceImpl`
JUnit Test Class	N/A
Spring Bean ID	`CrossRepositoryCopyService`

DeploymentService

Description	Service for initiating deployments.
Interface	`org.alfresco.service.cmr.avm.deploy.DeploymentService`
Implementation Class	`org.alfresco.repo.deploy.DeploymentServiceImpl`
JUnit Test Class	`org.alfresco.repo.deploy.FSDeploymentTest`
Spring Bean ID	`DeploymentService`

DescriptorService

Description	Service used to retrieve (but not set) metadata about the Alfresco installation. The metadata is limited to the schema that was present when it was installed, and information about the currently installed license file (issuer, expiration date, and so on).
Interface	`org.alfresco.service.descriptor.DescriptorService`
Implementation Class	`org.alfresco.repo.descriptor.DescriptorServiceImpl`
JUnit Test Class	`org.alfresco.repo.descriptor.DescriptorServiceTest`
Spring Bean ID	`DescriptorService`

DictionaryService

Description	Used to query the deployed content model. The service can get the list of types, aspects, properties, and associations deployed in the repository. It can also be used to check whether a type is a subtype of another.
Interface	`org.alfresco.service.cmr.dictionary.DictionaryService`
Implementation Class	`org.alfresco.repo.dictionary.DictionaryComponent`
JUnit Test Class	N/A
Spring Bean ID	`DictionaryService`

EditionService

Description	Service used to create and manage versions of a multilingual container, which are called "Editions".
Interface	`org.alfresco.service.cmr.ml.EditionService`
Implementation Class	`org.alfresco.repo.model.ml.EditionServiceImpl`
JUnit Test Class	N/A
Spring Bean ID	`EditionService`

EmailService

Description	This service, not to be confused with the `MailService`, is used for processing inbound email messages sent to the SMTP listener.
Interface	`org.alfresco.service.cmr.email.EmailService`
Implementation Class	`org.alfresco.email.server.EmailServiceImpl`
JUnit Test Class	N/A
Spring Bean ID	`EmailService`

ExporterService

Description	Service used to export a view of the repository.
Interface	`org.alfresco.service.cmr.view.ExporterService`
Implementation Class	`org.alfresco.repo.exporter.ExporterComponent`
JUnit Test Class	`org.alfresco.repo.exporter.ExporterComponentTest`
Spring Bean ID	`ExporterService`

FileFolderService

Description	Service for copying, creating, deleting, and searching files and folders.
Interface	`org.alfresco.service.cmr.model.FileFolderService`
Implementation Class	`org.alfresco.repo.model.filefolder.FileFolderServiceImpl`
JUnit Test Class	`org.alfresco.repo.model.filefolder.FileFolderServiceImplTest`
Spring Bean ID	`FileFolderService`

ImporterService

Description	Service used to import files and metadata into the repository. The service expects a ZIP file that follows the ACP format. See "ACP Files" in Appendix C.
Interface	`org.alfresco.service.cmr.view.ImporterService`
Implementation Class	`org.alfresco.repo.importer.ImporterComponent`
JUnit Test Class	`org.alfresco.repo.importer.ImporterComponentTest`
Spring Bean ID	`ImporterService`

LinkValidationService

Description	Used as part of Alfresco's WCM functionality, this service performs link checks on objects in the AVM store. It can also be used to retrieve a list of the objects that another object depends on.
Interface	`org.alfresco.linkvalidation.LinkValidationService`
Implementation Class	`org.alfresco.linkvalidation.LinkValidationServiceImpl`
JUnit Test Class	N/A
Spring Bean ID	`LinkValidationService`

LockService

Description	Service used to lock or unlock a node or collection of nodes. Can also be used to find out nodes that are locked across the entire store.
Interface	`org.alfresco.service.cmr.lock.LockService`
Implementation Class	`org.alfresco.repo.lock.LockServiceImpl`
JUnit Test Class	`org.alfresco.repo.lock.LockServiceImplTest`
Spring Bean ID	`LockService`

MailService

Description	Used to send outgoing SMTP messages.
Interface	`org.springframework.mail.javamail.JavaMailSender`
Implementation Class	`org.springframework.mail.javamail.JavaMailSenderImpl`
JUnit Test Class	N/A
Spring Bean ID	`MailService`

MimetypeService

Description	Service used to work with mimetypes such as getting the mimetype for a particular extension (or vice-versa) and for guessing a mimetype based on a file name. The service also includes an `isText()` method, which returns true if the format is plain text.
Interface	`org.alfresco.service.cmr.repository.MimetypeService`
Implementation Class	`org.alfresco.repo.content.MimetypeMap`
JUnit Test Class	`org.alfresco.repo.content.MimetypeMapTest`
Spring Bean ID	`MimetypeService`

ModuleService

Description	Service used to determine the list of currently deployed modules.
Interface	`org.alfresco.service.cmr.module.ModuleService`
Implementation Class	`org.alfresco.repo.module.ModuleServiceImpl`
JUnit Test Class	N/A
Spring Bean ID	`ModuleService`

MultilingualContentService

Description	Service used to declare that a node is a translation of another. The service can also be used to find translations for a given node, and test whether or not a given node is a translation.
Interface	`org.alfresco.service.cmr.ml.MultilingualContentService`
Implementation Class	`org.alfresco.repo.model.ml.MultilingualContentServiceImpl`
JUnit Test Class	`org.alfresco.repo.model.ml.tools.MultilingualContentServiceImplTest`
Spring Bean ID	`MultilingualContentService`

NamespaceService

Description	Service for registering and unregistering namespaces.
Interface	`org.alfresco.service.namespace.NamespaceService`
Implementation Class	`org.alfresco.repo.dictionary.DictionaryNamespaceComponent`
JUnit Test Class	N/A
Spring Bean ID	`NamespaceService`

NodeService

Description	Service for doing just about anything you could ever want to with a node, including creating and deleting nodes, checking a node for the presence of an aspect, getting and setting a node's properties, and getting a node's associations.
Interface	`org.alfresco.service.cmr.repository.NodeService`
Implementation Class	`org.alfresco.repo.version.NodeServiceImpl` `org.alfresco.repo.avm.AVMNodeService` (see AVMNodeService)
JUnit Test Class	`org.alfresco.repo.version.NodeServiceImplTest`
Spring Bean ID	`NodeService`

OwnableService

Description	Service used to determine the owner of an object and take ownership of that object.
Interface	`org.alfresco.service.cmr.security.OwnableService`
Implementation Class	`org.alfresco.repo.ownable.impl.OwnableServiceImpl`
JUnit Test Class	`org.alfresco.repo.ownable.impl.OwnableServiceTest`
Spring Bean ID	`OwnableService`

PermissionService

Description	Service used for getting and setting the permissions on a node.
Interface	`org.alfresco.service.cmr.security.PermissionService` `org.alfresco.repo.security.permissions.PermissionServiceSPI`
Implementation Class	`org.alfresco.repo.security.permissions.impl.PermissionServiceImpl`

JUnit Test Class	`org.alfresco.repo.security.permissions.impl.` `PermissionServiceTest`
Spring Bean ID	`PermissionService`

PersonService

Description	Service used to manage person objects in the repository. Everyone has a person object, even if their authentication credentials are managed by some other source.
Interface	`org.alfresco.service.cmr.security.PersonService`
Implementation Class	`org.alfresco.repo.security.person.PersonServiceImpl`
JUnit Test Class	`org.alfresco.repo.security.person.PersonTest`
Spring Bean ID	`PersonService`

RegistryService

Description	Service used to manage system-wide metadata. For example, after an AMP is installed, its configuration data is stored using the `RegistryService`.
Interface	`org.alfresco.repo.admin.registry.RegistryService`
Implementation Class	`org.alfresco.repo.admin.registry.RegistryServiceImpl`
JUnit Test Class	`org.alfresco.repo.admin.registry.` `RegistryServiceImplTest`
Spring Bean ID	`RegistryService`

RepoAdminService (3.0 Labs)

Description	Service used to do things such as reloading a message bundle or hot-deploying a content model without requiring a restart of the repository.
Interface	`org.alfresco.service.cmr.admin.RepoAdminService`
Implementation Class	`org.alfresco.repo.admin.RepoAdminServiceImpl`
JUnit Test Class	`org.alfresco.repo.admin.RepoAdminServiceImplTest`
Spring Bean ID	`RepoAdminService`

RepositoryExporterService

Description	Service used to export the repository as an ACP file.
Interface	`org.alfresco.service.cmr.view.RepositoryExporterService`
Implementation Class	`org.alfresco.repo.exporter.RepositoryExporterComponent`
JUnit Test Class	`org.alfresco.repo.exporter.RepositoryExporterComponentTest`
Spring Bean ID	`repositoryExporterComponent`

RuleService

Description	Service for retrieving, enabling, and disabling the rules on a node.
Interface	`org.alfresco.service.cmr.rule.RuleService`
Implementation Class	`org.alfresco.repo.rule.RuleServiceImpl`
JUnit Test Class	`org.alfresco.repo.rule.RuleServiceImplTest`
Spring Bean ID	`RuleService`

SearchService

Description	Service used for searching the repository.
Interface	`org.alfresco.service.cmr.search.SearchService`
Implementation Class	`org.alfresco.repo.search.SearcherComponent`
JUnit Test Class	`org.alfresco.repo.search.SearcherComponentTest`
Spring Bean ID	`SearchService`

ScriptService

Description	Service for executing JavaScript stored in the repository, on the classpath, or passed in as a String.
Interface	`org.alfresco.service.cmr.repository.ScriptService`
Implementation Class	`org.alfresco.repo.processor.ScriptServiceImpl`
JUnit Test Class	N/A
Spring Bean ID	`ScriptService`

SiteService (3.0 Labs)

Description	Service for creating and manipulating Alfresco Share sites.
Interface	`org.alfresco.repo.site.SiteService`
Implementation Class	`org.alfresco.repo.site.SiteServiceImpl`
JUnit Test Class	`org.alfresco.repo.site.SiteServiceImplTest`
Spring Bean ID	`SiteService`

TaggingService (3.0 Labs)

Description	Service for creating tags, assigning tags to nodes, and finding nodes based on a given tag.
Interface	`org.alfresco.service.cmr.tagging.TaggingService`
Implementation Class	`org.alfresco.repo.tagging.TaggingServiceImpl`
JUnit Test Class	`org.alfresco.repo.tagging.TaggingServiceImplTest`
Spring Bean ID	`TaggingService`

TemplateService

Description	Service for executing templates using a template rendering engine. FreeMarker is the default template rendering engine.
Interface	`org.alfresco.service.cmr.repository.TemplateService`
Implementation Class	`org.alfresco.repo.processor.TemplateServiceImpl`
JUnit Test Class	N/A
Spring Bean ID	`TemplateService`

ThumbnailService (3.0 Labs)

Description	Used to create, retrieve, and update thumbnails for the content property of a node.
Interface	`org.alfresco.service.cmr.thumbnail.ThumbnailService`
Implementation Class	`org.alfresco.repo.thumbnail.ThumbnailServiceImpl`
JUnit Test Class	N/A
Spring Bean ID	`ThumbnailService`

TransactionService

Description	Service for getting access to a user transaction.
Interface	`org.alfresco.service.transaction.TransactionService`
Implementation Class	`org.alfresco.repo.transaction.TransactionServiceImpl`
JUnit Test Class	`org.alfresco.repo.transaction.TransactionServiceImpl`
Spring Bean ID	`TransactionService`

VersionService

Description	Service for creating and reverting to versions of a node.
Interface	`org.alfresco.service.cmr.version.VersionService`
Implementation Class	`org.alfresco.repo.version.VersionServiceImpl`
JUnit Test Class	`org.alfresco.repo.version.VersionServiceImplTest`
Spring Bean ID	`VersionService`

WorkflowService

Description	Service for working with workflows and workflow definitions. Includes methods for deploying definitions, starting workflows, and signaling nodes.
Interface	`org.alfresco.service.cmr.workflow.WorkflowService`
Implementation Class	`org.alfresco.repo.workflow.WorkflowServiceImpl`
JUnit Test Class	`org.alfresco.repo.workflow.WorkflowServiceImplTest`
Spring Bean ID	`WorkflowService`

Lucene Queries

Lucene queries are part of everyday life when working with Alfresco. The syntax can take some time to get used to, and that is where this section can help. Let's start with the basics.

Suppose the repository has three test files in it as shown in the following table:

File	Folder	Description	Full Text
sample-a.pdf	**SomeCo|Marketing|Whitepapers**	This is a wonderful Whitepaper entitled, "Sample A", which you should really read when you have time to absorb it.	This is a sample Whitepaper named "Sample Whitepaper A".
sample-b.pdf	**SomeCo|Marketing|Whitepapers**	This is an advanced paper, which you should read after absorbing the earlier material.	This is a sample Whitepaper named "Sample Whitepaper B".
class-roster.txt	**SomeCo|Operations**	Class roster for the internal training, "How to write an effective whitepaper".	Writing an Effective Whitepaper: Ray Abby Julian Loren Meurice Debra

Basic Lucene Syntax

Given the set of test documents, let's use the search box in the Node Browser to run some sample searches against the repository to demonstrate basic Lucene search syntax.

`roster`

This search returns no results because by default, when using the Node Browser's search field, only the full text is searched and although the name and description of `class-roster.txt` includes "roster", the document content does not contain the string.

`sample whitepaper`

This search returns all three documents because this query is effectively the same as "sample OR whitepaper".

`sample AND whitepaper`

This search returns only `sample-a.pdf` and `sample-b.pdf`. This is the same as using the plus ("+") operator as in `+sample +whitepaper`. The plus operator requires a term to be in a document for it to be included in the search results.

`-sample whitepaper`

This search returns only the class roster. The minus ("-") operator specifies that results must not include the word "sample".

```
M?urice
```

```
Ab*
```

```
Lauren~
```

Each of these searches successfully returns the class roster. The question mark ("?") is a single character replacement. The asterisk ("*") is a wildcard. The tilde ("~") denotes a fuzzy search—it finds words that are similar. In this case, it matched "Lauren" to "Loren".

```
sample effective whitepaper
```

```
sample^10 effective whitepaper
```

Compare these two searches. They both return the sample PDFs and the class roster. In the first search, `class-roster.txt` shows up at the top of the result list. In the second search, the caret ("^") character has been used to "boost" or increase the weight of the term, "sample", by a factor of 10. That gives the PDFs more weight. So for the second search, the two PDFs move to the top of the search results.

Property Search

So far you've searched the full text of the sample documents, but what if you wanted to search against a specific property? To do that, use the at ("@") symbol followed by the namepsace and property name, and then the search phrase.

```
@cm\:description:read
```

This search returns both sample PDFs because both contain the word `read` in their description fields.

```
@cm\:description:(whitepaper -sample)
```

This search shows a combination of a field-based search with the minus operator to return only the documents that have `whitepaper`, but not `sample` in their description property. In this case, the search returns only `class-roster.txt`.

```
 @sc\:isActive:true
```

Searches for custom properties work as well. This one returns documents where the SomeCo `isActive` property is set to true.

Proximity Search

If you need to find documents where two words appear within certain proximity of each other, you can use a proximity search.

```
@cm\:description:"wonderful absorb"~12
```

This search returns only `sample-a.pdf`. Of course, in our limited sample set it is the only document that contains those two words in its description property. If you need convincing, increase the proximity number and you'll see that the document gets removed from the result list. Note that the proximity number is supposed to be the number of words that separate the two terms, but it is not precise.

Range Search

Properties can also be searched by range.

```
@cm\:created:[2008-07-01T00:00:00 TO 2008-07-22T00:00:00]
```

returns the sample PDFs, but not the class roster. This is because at least for this particular sample set, the class roster was created on July 24, 2008.

```
@cm\:created:[2008-07-01T00:00:00 TO 2008-07-24T00:00:00]
```
```
@cm\:created:{2008-07-01T00:00:00 TO 2008-07-24T00:00:00}
```

Compare these two search strings. The difference is that one uses square brackets ("[]") and the other uses curly braces ("{}"). The square brackets indicate an inclusive search, while the curly braces indicate an exclusive search. The inclusive search returns the class roster, created on July 24th, but the exclusive search does not because the end date of the date range matches the creation date.

```
@cm\:name:([clam TO dog])
```

Range searches work on strings as well. This search returns `class-roster.txt`, but neither of the sample Whitepapers.

Field Search

Certain pieces of metadata about the objects stored in Alfresco are indexed into Lucene fields such as TYPE, ASPECT, PARENT, TEXT, and so on. Lucene queries can be executed specifically against these fields.

TYPE and ASPECT

The TYPE and ASPECT fields return objects, where the object type or an applied aspect matches the fully-qualified QName provided in the search.

```
TYPE:"{http://www.someco.com/model/content/1.0}whitepaper"
```
```
TYPE:"sc:whitepaper"
```

These searches are equivalent. They return all `sc:whitepaper` objects. Note that a search against `sc:doc` will also include these documents because, as defined in the content model, `sc:whitepaper` inherits from `sc:doc`. If you want only instances of `sc:doc` but not a child type, you could use the minus ("-") operator to exclude instances of those types.

```
ASPECT:"{http://www.someco.com/model/content/1.0}webable"
```

```
ASPECT:"sc:webable"
```

These searches, also equivalent, return any object with the `sc:webable` aspect applied.

ID

The ID field contains the node's node reference.

```
ID:"workspace://SpacesStore/3f2831e1-4db9-11dd-83c8-a5bb8dda71b3"
```

For example, this search returns a node with a `node-uuid` property set to `3f2831e1-4db9-11dd-83c8-a5bb8dda71b3`, which resides in the `SpacesStore`.

PARENT

The PARENT field refers to the node reference of the parent node of the object.

```
PARENT:"workspace://SpacesStore/0da35100-4c59-11dd-9b6d-ed6cfed7fcb0"
```

This search returns the contents of the folder identified by the specified node reference.

PATH

The PATH field is the path to the node from the store root. Note that each node in the expression is the QName of the node, which may or may not match the value of the name property. The out of the box example of this is `Company Home`, which is the value of that node's name property. But the QName of the node is "{`http://www.alfresco.org/model/application/1.0`}`company_home`" (note the lowercase and the underscore).

```
PATH:"/app:company_home/cm:SomeCo/cm:Marketing/cm:Whitepapers
```

This search returns the specific `Whitepapers` folder.

```
PATH:"/app:company_home/cm:SomeCo/cm:Marketing/cm:Whitepapers/*"
```

```
PATH:"/app:company_home/cm:SomeCo/*/cm:Whitepapers/*"
```

These searches show the use of wildcards in the path. The first search returns all child nodes of the Whitepapers node. The second search returns the children of all nodes named `Whitepapers`, which are children of some other node under `SomeCo`. For example, if there were an `Operations` folder that also had a `Whitepapers` folder, the search results would include those objects as well.

QNAME

The QNAME field stores the QName of the object.

`QNAME:"cm:Whitepapers"`

This search would return all of the nodes with the matching QName. In the previous example where you had a `Whitepapers` folder under both `Marketing` and `Operations`, you would get two nodes back.

TEXT

The TEXT field contains the full text of all of the `d:content` properties on the object. To put it more simply, this field allows you to do a full-text search of the object.

`TEXT:"sample"`

This search returns any objects with the word `sample` in the text.

Category

Category searches use the PATH field, but you construct a path using the classification hierarchy. Suppose that `sample-a.pdf` is classified under "Languages/German", and `sample-b.pdf` is classified under "Languages/German/Swiss-German". Now consider the following two searches:

`PATH:"/cm:categoryRoot/cm:generalclassifiable/cm:Languages/cm:German/*"`

`PATH:"/cm:categoryRoot/cm:generalclassifiable/cm:Languages/cm:German//*"`

The first search will return `sample-a.pdf` because it is classified as "German" and the "Swiss-German" category. `sample-b.pdf` won't be returned because `sample-b.pdf` is under a subcategory, "Swiss-German". The second search uses double slashes ("//") at the end to denote that matches should include "German" as well as anything classified under a subcategory. It returns both documents and the "Swiss-German" subcategory.

So the category searches, as shown above, will return both objects that have been categorized ("members") and also the category nodes. If what you want are only documents and not categories, you can use "member" as follows:

`PATH:"/cm:categoryRoot/cm:generalclassifiable/cm:Languages/cm:German/member"`

`PATH:"/cm:categoryRoot/cm:generalclassifiable/cm:Languages/cm:German//member"`

The first search would return only `sample-a.pdf`, while the second search would return `sample-a.pdf` and `sample-b.pdf`.

Using Saved Searches as Examples

If you have trouble in getting a query right, try creating it through the Advanced Search page in the web client. When it works the way you want, save the search. Then, use the node browser to look at the XML that defines the saved search to see how Alfresco built the query. You can then use that query in your own code.

For example, if you saved the search performed in the previous example, the XML for the saved search would look as follows:

```
<?xml version="1.0" encoding="UTF-8"?>
<search>
  <text><![CDATA[]]></text>
  <mode>0</mode>
  <categories>
      <category>/cm:categoryRoot/cm:generalclassifiable
      /cm:Languages/cm:German//*</category>
  </categories>
  <attributes/>
  <ranges/>
  <fixed-values/>
  <query><![CDATA[( PATH:"/cm:categoryRoot/
   cm:generalclassifiable/cm:Languages/cm:German//*" ) AND
   ((TYPE:"{http://www.alfresco.org/model/content/1.0}content"
   TYPE:"{http://www.alfresco.org/model/content/1.0}folder" ))
    ]]></query>
</search>
```

Public saved searches are stored in the Data Dictionary under "Saved Searches".

 Another handy way to debug queries is to update `log4j.properties` to enable debugging for the query parser. That will allow you to see the query produced by the query parser. The log4j logger for the query parser is:

```
org.alfresco.repo.search.impl.lucene.
LuceneQueryParser=DEBUG
```

JavaScript

As you learned in examples throughout the book, JavaScript is used in several different places across the Alfresco platform, particularly as one option for controller logic in web scripts. This section starts with a listing of the out of the box root JavaScript objects available to all scripts (except where noted), and then provides details for the rest of the JavaScript API.

Root Objects

The root objects available to your scripts are either utility objects or entry points into different areas of the JavaScript API. This section lists the root objects available and notes where further APIs exist. API details are provided in the next section, "JavaScript API".

Root Object	Description
`actions`	Entry point into the Actions API. Used to retrieve the list of actions configured in the repository or as a factory to retrieve an instance of an action.
`args`	Available when the script is run as a web script controller. Contains the arguments passed to the script.
`avm`	Entry point into the AVM API. Used to retrieve a list of all AVM stores, to search for a store based on ID, or to search for a specific node.
`cache`	Available when the script is run as a web script controller. The cache object is used to dynamically modify the cache settings for a web script.
`classification`	Entry point into the Classification API. Used to get and create root categories, or to get all category nodes for a classification.
`companyhome`	`ScriptNode` representing the Company Home folder.
`crossRepoCopy`	Utility object for copying nodes between the DM and AVM store (and vice-versa).
`document`	`ScriptNode` representing the document against which the script is running, if applicable. See `space`.
`logger`	Utility object for logging messages to the console.
`model`	Available when the script is run as a web script controller. The associative array used to pass data to the view.
`people`	Entry point into the People API, which is used to work with people and groups.
`person`	`ScriptNode` representing the current user executing the script.
`script`	`ScriptNode` representing the script being executed.
`search`	Entry point into the Search API, which can be used to execute Lucene searches, XPath searches, saved searches, and searches based on node reference.
`session`	Used to retrieve the ticket for the current user executing the script.
`space`	`ScriptNode` representing the space against which the script is running. See `document`. Note that `space` is available even when the script is running in the context of a document. In that case, the space returned is the enclosing folder.

Root Object	Description
status	Available when the script is run as a web script controller. Used to set the response code, error message, and redirect flag.
userhome	ScriptNode representing the home space of the current user executing the script.
utils	A generic utility object with commonly used functions.
workflow	Available in Labs only, this is the entry point into the Workflow API. It is used to get tasks, workflow definitions, and workflow instances. It can also be used to create workflow packages.

JavaScript API

The classes that implement the JavaScript root objects are in org.alfresco.repo. jscript. Much of the information in the tables within this section has been taken directly from the Alfresco Javadoc comments for the classes in that package.

 In this section, method names are listed as they appear in the underlying Java class. For getters and setters, this means the "get" or "set" is shown even though it is typically dropped in JavaScript. For example, document.tags and document.getTags() are equivalent.

General

This section lists general utility classes or classes that are used across multiple APIs, such as ScriptNode.

Association

Function	Description	Return value
getAssociationRef()	Gets the AssociationRef object for this association.	AssociationRef
getSource()	Gets the source ScriptNode of the association.	ScriptNode containing the source node.
getTarget()	Gets the target ScriptNode of the association.	ScriptNode containing the target node.
getType()	Gets the type of the association.	String containing the QName of the association type.

ChildAssociation

Function	Description	Return value
getChild()	Gets the child node on the target end of this association.	ScriptNode containing the child.
getChildAssociationRef()	Gets the AssociationRef object for this association.	AssociationRef
getName()	Gets the name of the association.	String containing the QName of the association.
getParent()	Gets the parent node.	ScriptNode containing the parent.
getType()	Gets the type of the association.	String containing the QName of the association type.
isPrimary()	Determines whether or not this is the primary association for this node.	True if this is the primary association, otherwise false.

ScriptNode

Function	Description	Return value
addAspect(String type) addAspect(String type, ScriptableObject props)	Adds an aspect to the node.	True if the aspect was added successfully, false if an error occurred.
addNode (ScriptNode node)	Adds an existing node as a child of this node.	Void
addTag(String tag) (3.0 Labs)	Adds the specified tag to the node.	Void
getAspects()	Gets the aspects applied to the node.	ScriptableObject (an Array) of QNames.
getAspectsSet() (3.0 Labs)	Gets the aspects applied to the node.	Set of QNames.
getAssociations() (3.0 Labs)	Gets the target associations for a node.	Associative array of target associations.
getAssocs()	Gets the target associations for a node.	Associative array of target associations.
cancelCheckout()	Cancels the check-out of a working copy document.	ScriptNode representing the original object that was checked out.

Function	Description	Return value

`checkin()`
 	
`checkin(String history)`
 	
`checkin(String history, boolean majorVersion)`
	Checks in a working copy document.	`ScriptNode` representing the original object that was checked out.

`checkout()`
 	
`checkout(ScriptNode destination)`
	Performs a check-out of this document into the current parent space or, alternatively, the specified destination folder.	`ScriptNode` representing the working copy Node for the checked out document.

`getChildAssociations()` (3.0 Labs)	Gets the child associations for a node.	Associative array of child associations.
`getChildAssocs()`	Gets the child associations for a node.	Associative array of child associations.
`getChildByNamePath (String path)` (2.2 Enterprise)	Returns the node at the specified `cm:name`-based path by walking the children of this node.	`ScriptNode` of the matching child.
`getChildren()`	Gets the child nodes for a node.	`ScriptableObject` of `ScriptNodes` representing each child.
`getChildrenByXPath (String xpath)`	Searches the children of this node with the supplied XPath expression.	Array of matching nodes.
`getContent()`	Gets the content property of this node as a string.	String containing the node content.
`getCrossRepository CopyHelper()`	Brings in use the cross repository copy object to copy nodes between the DM and AVM repositories.	`CrossRepositoryCopy` object.

`copy(ScriptNode destination)`
 	
`copy(ScriptNode destination, boolean deepCopy)`
	Copies this node to a new parent destination. Note that children of the source node are not copied unless the `deepCopy` flag is used.	`ScriptNode` representing the newly copied node, or null if the copy fails.

`createAssociation (ScriptNode target, String assocType)`	Creates an association between this node and the specified target node.	Void

Function	Description	Return value
`createFile(String name)`	Creates a new File (cm:content) node as a child of this node. Once created the file should have content set using the content property.	ScriptNode representing the new node, or null if the creation fails.
`createFolder(String name)`	Creates a new folder (cm:folder) node as a child of this node.	ScriptNode representing the new node, or null if the creation fails.

`createNode(String QName, String QNameType)`
`createNode(String QName, String QNameType, ScriptableObject properties)`
`createNode(String QName, String QNameType, ScriptableObject properties, String QnameAssocName)`
`createNode(String name, String type, Object properties, String assocType, String assocName)` (3.0 Labs)
`createNode(String QName, String QNameType, String QNameAssocName)`
	Creates a new Node of the specified type as a child of this node.	ScriptNode representing the new node, or null if the creation fails.

`createThumbnail(String thumbnailName)` (3.0 Labs) `createThumbnail(String thumbnailName, boolean async)` (3.0 Labs)	Creates a thumbnail for the content property of the node.	ScriptThumbnail representing the new thumbnail.
`getDisplayPath()`	Gets the human-readable path to the node.	String containing the path.
`getDownloadUrl()`	For a content document, this method returns the download URL to the content for the default content property.	String containing the URL.
`hasAspect(String QNameAspect)`	Checks for the presence of the specified aspect.	True if the aspect has been applied, otherwise returns false.

Function	Description	Return value
`hasPermission(String permission)`	Checks to see if the current user has the specified permission on this node.	True if the user has permission, otherwise returns false.
`getIcon16()` `getIcon32()`	Returns the small or large icon for the node.	String containing the URL for the image.
`getId()`	Returns the UUID for the node.	String containing the ID.
`inheritsPermissions()`	Checks to see whether or not this node inherits its permissions from a parent.	True if the inherit permission flag is turned on, otherwise returns false.
`getIsCategory()`	Checks whether or not the node is a category.	True if the node is a category, otherwise it returns false.
`getIsContainer()`	Checks whether or not the node is a folder.	True if the node is a folder, otherwise it returns false.
`getIsDocument()`	Checks whether or not this node is of type `cm:content`.	True for `cm:content` or its children, otherwise it returns false.
`getIsLinkToContainer()`	Checks whether or not this node is a link to a folder.	True if the node is a folder link, otherwise returns false.
`getIsLinkToDocument()`	Checks whether or not this node is a link to a document.	True if the node is a document link, otherwise returns false.
`getIsLocked()`	Checks whether or not this node is locked.	True if the node is locked, otherwise returns false.
`getIsTagScope()`	Checks whether or not this node is a tag scope.	True if it is, false if it is not.
`getMimetype()`	Gets the mimetype for the node.	String containing the mimetype.
`move(ScriptNode destination)`	Moves this Node to a new parent destination.	True if the move succeeds, and false if it fails.
`getName()`	Gets the `cm:name` property of the node.	String containing the value of the `cm:name` property.
`getNodeRef()`	Gets the node reference for the node.	String containing the node's node reference.
`getOwner()`	Gets the owner of the node.	String containing the owner of the node.
`getParent()`	Gets the node reference for the node's parent.	`ScriptNode` containing the parent's node reference.

Function	Description	Return value
`getPermissions()`	Retrieves the permissions for the node.	Array of permissions applied to this Node. Strings returned are of the format [ALLOWED|DENIED];[USERNAME|GROUPNAME];PERMISSION for example: ALLOWED;kevinr;Consumer so can be easily tokenized on the ";" character.
`getPrimaryParentAssoc()`	Gets the primary parent association for this node.	`ChildAssociationRef` representing the parent association.

`processTemplate(String template)`
 	
`processTemplate (ScriptNode template)`
 	
`processTemplate(String template, ScriptableObject args)`
 	
`processTemplate (ScriptNode template, ScriptableObject args)`
	Processes the specified FreeMarker template against this node.	String containing the output of the FreeMarker template.

`getProperties()`	Gets all properties for the node.	An Associative Array of QNames and values.
`getQnamePath()`	Gets the QName-based path for this node.	A String representing the path.
`getQnameType()`	Gets the QName type for this node.	A String representing the QName type.
`getSourceAssociations()` (3.0 Labs)	Gets the source associations for this node.	Map of source associations.
`getSourceAssocs()` (3.0 Labs)	Gets the source associations for this node.	Map of source associations.
`getStoreId()` (3.0 Labs)	Gets the store ID for this node.	String representing the store ID.
`getStoreType()` (3.0 Labs)	Gets the store type for this node.	String representing the store type.
`getTags()` (3.0 Labs)	Gets the list of tags applied to this node.	String array containing the tags.

Function	Description	Return value
`getThumbnail(String thumbnailName)` (3.0 Labs)	Gets the thumbnail for this node given a thumbnail name.	`ScriptThumbnail` object containing the thumbnail.
`getThumbnails()`	Gets all thumbnails for this node.	Array of `ScriptThumbnail` objects.
`remove()`	Deletes the node.	Returns true if the deletion was successful, false if it wasn't.
`removeAspect(String QNameType)`	Removes the specified aspect from the node.	Returns true if the removal was successful, false if it wasn't.
`removeAssociation (ScriptNode target, String QNameAssocType)`	Removes an association between this node and the specified target node.	Void
`removeNode(ScriptNode node)`	Removes an existing child node of this node.	Void
`removePermission(String permission)` `removePermission(String permission, String authority)`	Removes permission for ALL users from this node or from the specified authority.	Void
`removeTag(String tag)`	Removes the specified tag from this node.	Void
`save()`	Saves the property changes to this node.	Void
`setContent(String content)`	Sets the content of this node to the value of the provided String.	Void
`setInheritsPermissions (boolean inherit)`	Sets whether this node should inherit permissions from the parent node.	Void
`setIsTagScope(boolean tagScope)` (3.0 Labs)	Sets whether or not this node is a tag scope.	Void
`setMimetype(String mimetype)`	Sets the mimetype for the content attached to this node.	Void
`setName(String name)`	Sets the `cm:name` property of this node.	Void
`setOwner(String userId)`	Sets the owner of the node.	Void

Function	Description	Return value

`setPermission(String permission)`
 	
`setPermission (String permission, String authority)`
	Sets the permission for all users of this node or for the specified authority.	Void

`specializeType(String type)`	Specializes the type of the node.	True if successful, otherwise false.
`getSize()`	Gets the size of the content that is attached to the node.	The size, in bytes, of the content.
`takeOwnership()`	Takes ownership of the node.	Void

`transformDocument (String mimetype)`
 	
`transformDocument (String mimetype, ScriptNode destination)`
	Transforms a document to a new document mimetype format. A copy of the document is made and the extension changed to match the new mimetype, then the transformation is applied.	`ScriptNode` representing the newly transformed content.

`transformImage(String mimetype)`
 	
`transformImage(String mimetype, String options)`
 	
`transformImage(String mimetype, String options, ScriptNode destination)`
 	
`transformImage(String mimetype, ScriptNode destination)`
	Transforms an image to a new image format. A copy of the image document is made and the extension changed to match the new mimetype, then the transformation is applied.	`ScriptNode` representing the newly transformed image.

`getType()`	Gets the content type of this node.	String containing the content type.
`getUrl()`	Gets either the content stream URL or, for folders, the browse details URL for this node.	String containing the URL.
`getWebdavUrl()`	Gets the WebDAV URL for this node.	String containing the URL.

ScriptUtils

Function	Description	Return value
`getNodeFromString (String nodeRefString)`	Retrieves a `ScriptNode` based on the string representation of its node reference.	`ScriptNode` representing the desired node.
`pad(String string, int length)`	Pads a string with zeros ("0") to the desired length.	Padded String.
`toBoolean(String booleanString)` (3.0 Labs)	Converts a String to a boolean.	Boolean value.

Root object: cache

Function	Description	Return value
`getIsPublic()`	Determines if the web script can have its response placed in a public cache.	True if the content is public, false if it is not.
`getMustRevalidate()`	Determines whether or not the cache should re-validate to make sure it is picking up the latest version of the web script response.	True if cache should revalidate, false if it does not have to revalidate.
`getNeverCache()`	Determines if the web script response should never be cached.	True if the response should never be cached, false if it is OK to cache.
`setIsPublic(boolean isPublic)`	Sets the `isPublic` flag.	Void
`setMustRevalidate(boolean mustRevalidate)`	Sets the `mustRevalidate` flag.	Void
`setNeverCache(boolean neverCache)`	Sets the `neverCache` flag.	Void

Root object: crossRepoCopy

Function	Description	Return value
`copy(ScriptNode src, ScriptNode dest, String name)`	Performs a copy of a source node to the specified parent destination node. The name will be applied to the destination node copy. Inter-store copy operations between Workspace and AVM and visa-versa are supported.	`ScriptNode` of the copied node if successful, otherwise null.

Root object: logger

Function	Description	Return value
isLoggingEnabled()	Determines whether or not logging is enabled.	True if logging is enabled, false if it is not.
log(String message)	Writes a message to the log.	Void

Root object: status

Function	Description	Return value
getCode()	Gets the status code for the web script's response.	Code as an int.
setCode(int code) setCode(int code, String message) (3.0 Labs)	Sets the status code for the web script's response.	Void
getCodeDescription()	Gets the description of the status code.	String representing the status code description.
getCodeName()	Gets the short name of the status code.	String representing the short name of the status code.
getException()	Gets the exception that's been set on this status object.	Throwable representing the exception.
getLocation()	Gets the location.	String representing the location.
setLocation(String location)	Sets the location.	Void
getMessage()	Gets the web script status message.	String representing the status message.
setMessage(String message)	Sets the web script status message.	Void
getRedirect()	Gets the redirect flag.	Boolean representing the redirect flag.
setRedirect(boolean redirect)	Sets the redirect flag.	Void
setException(Throwable exception)	Sets the exception.	Void

Actions API

Root object: actions

Function	Description	Return value
`create(String actionName)`	Creates a reference to an Action	`ScriptAction` object representing the action.
`getRegistered()`	Gets the registered list of actions.	An Array of registered actions.

ScriptAction

Function	Description	Return value
`execute(ScriptNode nodeRef)`	Executes the script.	Void
`getName()`	Gets the name of the action.	String representing the name of the action.
`getParameters()`	Gets the parameters for the action.	`ScriptableObject` (a Map) of the action parameters.

AVM API

The AVM API is used for working with objects in the AVM store, which is currently only used by Alfresco's WCM functionality:

Root object: avm

Function	Description	Return value
`assetUrl(String avmPath)` `assetUrl(String storeId, String assetPath)`	Gets the preview URL for the given `avmPath`.	String containing the URL.
`getModifiedItems (String storeId, String username, String webapp)`	Gets the list of modified items for the specified user sandbox for a specific webapp as compared against the staging store in the store specified by the store ID.	List of AVMNodes.
`lookupNode(String path)`	Return an AVM Node for the fully qualified path.	AVMNode of the matching node.
`lookupStore(String store)`	Returns an AVM store object for the specified store name	`AVMScriptStore` of the matching store.

Function	Description	Return value
`lookupStoreRoot(String store)`	Returns an AVM Node representing the public store root folder.	AVMNode of the root folder.
`stagingStore(String storeId)`	Gets the staging store name for the given store ID.	String containing the name.
`getStores()`	Gets a list of AVM stores in the repository.	`ScriptableObject` containing the list of stores.
`userSandboxStore (String storeId, String username)`	Gets the Sandbox Store name for the given store ID and username.	String containing the name.
`getWebappsFolderPath()`	Gets the folder path to the webapps folder.	String containing the path.
`websiteStagingUrl (String storeId)`	Gets the preview URL for the web site managed in the store represented by the store ID.	String containing the URL.
`websiteUserSandboxUrl (String storeId, Stri ng username)`	Gets the preview URL for the user sandbox for the store and username specified.	String containing the URL.

AVMNode (extends ScriptNode)

Function	Description	Return value
`copy (String destination)` `copy (ScriptNode destination)`	Copies this node into a new parent destination.	`ScriptNode` representing the copy of this node.
`getAspects() (2.2)` `getAspectsSet() (3.0)`	Gets the list of aspects applied to this node.	List of `QNames`.
`getName()`	Gets the name property of the node.	String representing the name.
`hasLockAccess()`	Determines whether or not the current user can make a change to the node either because the node is not locked or the node is locked and the user is the lock owner or a Content Manager.	True if the user can make a change, false if they cannot.
`isDirectory()`	Determines whether or not this node is a directory.	True if it is a directory, false if it is not.
`isFile()`	Determines whether or not this node is a file.	True if it is a file, false if it is not.
`getIsLocked()`	Determines whether or not this node is locked.	True if it is locked, false if it is not.

Function	Description	Return value
`isLockOwner()`	Determines if this node is locked and the current user is the lock owner.	True if the node is locked and the user is the lock owner, otherwise false.

`move(String destination)`
 	
 `move(ScriptNode destination)`
	Moves this node to the specified destination.	True if the move is successful, false if it is not.

`getParentPath()`	Gets the path to this node's parent.	String representing the path.
`getPath()` (3.0 Labs)	Gets the full AVM path to this node.	String representing the path.
`rename(String name)`	Renames this node to the new name specified.	True if the rename is successful, false if it is not.
`getType()`	Gets the `Qname` type of the node.	String representing the type.
`getVersion()`	Gets the version of the node.	Version number of the node as an integer.

AVMScriptStore

Function	Description	Return value
`getCreatedDate()`	Gets the store's creation date.	Date the store was created.
`getCreator()`	Gets the user who created the store.	String representing the store creator.
`getId()`	Gets the store's ID.	String representing the store ID.
`lookupNode(String path)`	Looks up a node in the store; the path is assumed to be related to the webapps folder root. Therefore a valid path would be **|ROOT/WEB-INF|lib|web.xml**.	`AVMNode` matching the path specified
`getName()`	Gets the store's name.	String representing the name of the store.
`lookupRoot()`	Gets the store's root node.	`AVMNode` representing the root node.
`luceneSearch(String query)`	Executes a Lucene query against this store and returns the results.	`ScriptableObject` containing the search results. See Chapter 8 for information concerning the limitations of search in the AVM store.

Classification API

The Classification API is used for working with categories.

Root node: classification

Function	Description	Return value
getAllClassification Aspects()	Gets all the aspects that define this classification.	String array containing a list of aspect names.
createRootCategory(String aspect, String name)	Creates a root category for this classification.	Void
getAllCategoryNodes (String aspect)	Gets all category nodes for this classification.	ScriptableObject containing a list of the category nodes.
getCategoryUsage(String aspect, int maxCount) (3.0 Labs)	Gets categories with the most number of objects. The number of categories returned is specified in maxCount.	ScriptableObject containing the top categories.
getRootCategories (String aspect)	Gets all root categories for this classification.	ScriptableObject containing the root categories.

CategoryNode (extends ScriptNode)

Function	Description	Return value
getCategoryMembers()	Gets all of the members of a category.	An array of ScriptNodes.
createSubcategory(String name)	Creates a new subcategory.	CategoryNode representing the new subcategory.
getImmediateCategoryMembers()	Gets the immediate members of a category.	Array of ScriptNodes.
getImmediateMembersAnd SubCategories()	Gets the immediate members and subcategories.	Array of ScriptNodes.
getImmediateSubCategories()	Gets the immediate subcategories.	Array of CategoryNodes.
getMembersAndSubCategories()	Gets the members and subcategories for this category.	Array of ScriptNodes.
removeCategory()	Removes this category.	Void
getSubCategories()	Gets the subcategories for this category.	Array of CategoryNodes.

People API

The People API is for working with people and groups:

Root node: people

Function	Description	Return value
addAuthority(ScriptNode parentGroup, ScriptNode authority)	Adds an authority (a user or group) to a group container as a new child.	Void
createGroup(String groupName) createGroup(ScriptNode parentGroup, String groupName)	Creates a new root-level group (or a subgroup if a parent is specified) with the specified unique name (do not use the "GROUP_" prefix).	ScriptNode representing the new group if it was successful, otherwise null.
createPerson(boolean createUserAccount, boolean setAccountEnabled) (3.0 Labs)	Creates a person with a generated username.	ScriptNode containing the person object if it was successfully created.
deleteGroup(ScriptNode group)	Deletes the specified group.	Void
deletePerson(String username) (3.0 Labs)	Deletes the specified person object.	Void
enablePerson(String username) (3.0 Labs)	Enables the specified user account.	Void
getContainedAuthorities (ScriptNode container, AuthorityType type, boolean recurse) (3.0 Labs)	Gets the authorities this authority contains, optionally recursing into subauthorities.	Array of Objects representing the contained authorities.
getContainerGroups(Script Node person)	Gets the groups that contain the specified authority.	ScriptableObject (a JavaScript Array) containing the list of groups.
getGroup(String groupName)	Gets the group specified.	ScriptNode representing the specified group.
getMembers(ScriptNode group) getMembers(ScriptNode group, boolean recurse)	Gets the people that belong to the specified group and, optionally, any sub-groups of the specified group.	ScriptableObject (a JavaScript Array) containing the list of people.
getPeople(String filter) (3.0 Labs)	Gets all the people in the repository, optionally filtered by a query string.	ScriptableObject representing the collection of people.

Function	Description	Return value
getPerson(String username)	Gets the person given the specified username.	ScriptNode representing the specified user or null if the user does not exist.
removeAuthority(ScriptNode parentGroup, ScriptNode authority)	Removes a person or group from the specified group.	Void

Presence API (3.0 Labs)

The Presence API can be used to determine whether or not someone is online according to their preferred presence provider:

presence

Function	Description	Return value
getDetails(ScriptNode person)	Gets the presence provider and presence user name of the person specified.	String of the format [presence provider]|[presence username].
hasPresence (ScriptNode person)	Determines whether or not the person specified is configured with a presence provider.	True if the person is configured for presence, otherwise false.

Search API

The Search API is for executing queries, including saved searches:

search

Function	Description	Return value
findNode(String nodeRef) findNode (ScriptNode nodeRef) findNode(String referenceType, String[] reference) (3.0 Labs)	Finds a single Node by the Node reference. 3.0 version adds the ability to pass in a reference type and string as follows: • The "Node" reference type resolves to a node via its Node Reference: {store_type}|{store_id}|{node_id} • The "Path" reference type resolves to a node via its display path: {store_type}|{store_id}|{path} • The "AVM Path" reference type resolves to a node via its AVM display path: {store_id}/{path} • The QName reference type resolves to a node via its child qname path: {store_type}/{store_id}/{child_qname_path}	ScriptNode if found or null if failed to find.

Function	Description	Return value
`luceneSearch (String searchString)` `luceneSearch (String store, String search)` (3.0 Labs) `luceneSearch (String search, String sortColumn, boolean asc)` (3.0 Labs) `luceneSearch (String store, String search, String sortColumn, boolean asc)` (3.0 Labs)	Executes a Lucene search.	JavaScript array of Node results from the search — can be empty, but not null.

`savedSearch (String nodeRef)`
 	
`savedSearch (ScriptNode nodeRef)`
	Executes a saved Lucene search.	JavaScript array of Node results from the search — can be empty, but not null.

`xpathSearch (String search)` `xpathSearch (String store, String search)` (3.0 Labs)	Executes an XPath search.	JavaScript array of Node results from the search — can be empty, but not null.

API Examples

Step-by-step examples for working with the various Alfresco APIs are provided throughout the book. But the examples are limited in scope to the specific requirement at hand. This section shows how to perform the same functional task (for example, "Create an object") using the three major APIs: Foundation, JavaScript, and Web Services.

Create a Node

These examples show how to create a new node in the repository.

Foundation

```
ChildAssociationRef association =    nodeService.
createNode(companyHome,
    ContentModel.ASSOC_CONTAINS,
    QName.createQName(NamespaceService.CONTENT_MODEL_PREFIX,
    name),
    ContentModel.TYPE_CONTENT,
    contentProps);
```

JavaScript

```
var newNode = space.createNode(nodeName, contentType);
```

Web Services

```
// Construct CML statement to create content node
CMLCreate createDoc = new CMLCreate("ref1", docParent, null, null,
null, Constants.createQNameString(SomeCoModel.NAMESPACE_SOMECO_
CONTENT_MODEL, getContentType()), contentProps);
// Construct CML Block
CML cml = new CML();
cml.setCreate(new CMLCreate[] {createDoc});
// Execute CML Block
UpdateResult[] results = WebServiceFactory.getRepositoryService().
update(cml);
```

Perform a Search

These examples show how to execute a Lucene search.

Foundation

```
StoreRef storeRef = new StoreRef(StoreRef.PROTOCOL_WORKSPACE,
"SpacesStore");
ResultSet resultSet = searchService.query(storeRef, SearchService.
LANGUAGE_LUCENE, queryString);
```

JavaScript

```
var queryResults = search.luceneSearch(queryString);
```

Web Services

```
Query query = new Query(Constants.QUERY_LANG_LUCENE, queryString );
QueryResult queryResult = getRepositoryService().query(getStoreRef(),
query, false);
```

Persist Content

These examples show how to write content to a node.

Foundation

```
ContentWriter writer = contentService.getWriter(content, ContentModel.
PROP_CONTENT, true);
writer.setMimetype(MimetypeMap.MIMETYPE_TEXT_PLAIN);
writer.setEncoding("UTF-8");
String text = "The quick brown fox jumps over the lazy dog";
writer.putContent(text);
```

JavaScript

```
var newDoc = targetFolder.createFile(filename);
newDoc.properties.content.write(content);
newDoc.properties.content.mimetype = mimetype;
newDoc.save();
```

Web Services

```
ContentServiceSoapBindingStub contentService = WebServiceFactory.
getContentService();
ContentFormat contentFormat = new ContentFormat("text/plain", "UTF-
8");
String docText = "This is a sample " + getContentType() + " document
called " + getContentName();
Content docContentRef = contentService.write(docRef, Constants.PROP_
CONTENT, docText.getBytes(), contentFormat);
```

Add an Aspect

These examples show how to add an aspect to a node.

Foundation

```
nodeService.addAspect(nodeRef, aspectQName, props);
```

JavaScript

```
document.addAspect(aspectQName, props);
```

Web Services

```
CMLAddAspect addWebableAspectToDoc = new CMLAddAspect(Constants.creat
eQNameString(SomeCoModel.NAMESPACE_SOMECO_CONTENT_MODEL, SomeCoModel.
ASPECT_SC_WEBABLE), null, null, "ref1");
// Construct CML Block
CML cml = new CML();
cml.setUpdate(new CMLUpdate[] {updateDoc});
cml.setAddAspect(new CMLAddAspect[] {addWebableAspectToDoc});
// Execute CML Block
UpdateResult[] results = WebServiceFactory.getRepositoryService().
update(cml);
```

Set a Property

These examples set a single-value property on a node.

Foundation

```
nodeService.setProperty(nodeRef, propertyQName, value);
```

JavaScript

```
document.properties["sc:published"] = new Date();
document.save();
```

Web Services

```
// Create a reference to the doc to be updated
Store storeRef = new Store(Constants.WORKSPACE_STORE, "SpacesStore");
Reference doc = new Reference(storeRef, this.targetUuid, null);

// Create an array of NamedValue objects with the props to set
NamedValue nameValue = Utils.createNamedValue(Constants.PROP_NAME,
this.contentName);
NamedValue[] contentProps = new NamedValue[] {nameValue};

// Construct CML statement to update node
CMLUpdate updateDoc = new CMLUpdate(contentProps, new Predicate(new
Reference[] {doc}, storeRef, null), null);

// Construct CML Block
CML cml = new CML();
cml.setUpdate(new CMLUpdate[] {updateDoc});

// Execute CML Block
UpdateResult[] results = WebServiceFactory.getRepositoryService().
update(cml);
```

Set Permissions

These examples grant the custom `PortalPublisher` permission created in Chapter 9 to the `Publisher` group for a specific node.

Foundation

```
permissionService.setPermission(nodeRef, "GROUP_Publisher",
"PortalPublisher", true);
```

JavaScript

```
document.setPermission("PortalPublisher", "GROUP_Publisher")
```

Web Services

```
Store storeRef = new Store(Constants.WORKSPACE_STORE, "SpacesStore");
Reference doc = new Reference(storeRef, this.targetUuid, null);
ACE ace = new ACE("GROUP_Publisher", "PortalPublisher", AccessStatus.
acepted);
WebServiceFactory.getAccessControlService().addACEs(new Predicate(new
Reference[] {doc}, storeRef, null), new ACE[] {ace});
```

Start a Workflow

These examples start the out of the box "adhoc" workflow, assign it to `tuser1` and give it a description. In 2.2 Enterprise, there is no workflow API for JavaScript for Web Services. To work around that, the code simply executes the `start-workflow` action.

Foundation

```
Map<QName, Serializable> workflowParameters = new HashMap<QName,Seria
lizable>();
workflowParameters.put(QName.createQName("bpm", "assignee"),
"tuser1");
workflowParameters.put(QName.createQName("bpm", "description"),
"Started from Foundation");
workflowService.startWorkflow("jbpm$wf:adhoc", workflowParameters);
```

JavaScript

```
var workflow = actions.create("start-workflow");
workflow.parameters.workflowName = "jbpm$wf:adhoc";
workflow.parameters["bpm:workflowDescription"] = "Workflow from
JavaScript";
workflow.parameters["bpm:assignee"] = "tuser1";
workflow.execute(document);
```

Web Services

```
Store storeRef = new Store(Constants.WORKSPACE_STORE, "SpacesStore");
Reference doc = new Reference(storeRef, this.targetUuid, null);
NamedValue workflowValue = Utils.createNamedValue("workflowName",
this.workflow);
NamedValue descriptionValue = Utils.createNamedValue("bpm:
workflowDescription", "Submitted from web service");
NamedValue assigneeValue = Utils.createNamedValue("bpm:assignee",
this.assignee);
NamedValue[] actionArguments = new NamedValue[] {workflowValue,
descriptionValue, assigneeValue};

Action startWorkflowAction = new Action(null, this.targetUuid, "start-
workflow", null, null, actionArguments, null, null, null);

WebServiceFactory.getActionService().executeActions(new
Predicate(new Reference[] {doc}, storeRef, null), new Action[]
{startWorkflowAction});
```

B
Alfresco Configuration Reference

Alfresco has a lot of configuration files. Sometimes, it helps to know how the out of the box configuration is set up. Maybe you want to invoke an action, or perhaps you'd like to do something in the web client or the content model. You can search through the XML configuration files and the source code, but you might want to start here to save a little bit of time. This section includes:

- A list of out of the box actions by Spring Bean ID with a cross-reference to their handler bean, if one exists
- A breakdown of the web client configuration elements defined in Alfresco's various web client configuration XML files
- A list of all UI action groups, including where in the web client those menus appear
- A list of the out of the box metadata extractors
- A list of the out of the box transformers
- A graphical view of the Alfresco Content Model, broken down by namespace

Actions

This section catalogues the out of the box actions, including the action name, executer class, and handler class (if it has one). For more information on Actions, see Chapter 4.

Actions Available in both Enterprise and Labs

These actions are available in both Alfresco editions:

Action Name (Bean ID)	Action Executer Class Handler Class (if present)
add-features	org.alfresco.repo.action.executer. AddFeaturesActionExecuter
	org.alfresco.web.bean.actions.handlers. AddFeaturesHandler
avm-deploy-website	org.alfresco.repo.avm.actions. AVMDeployWebsiteAction
avm-link-validation	org.alfresco.linkvalidation.LinkValidationAction
avm-revert-list	org.alfresco.repo.avm.actions.AVMRevertListAction
avm-revert-store	org.alfresco.repo.avm.actions. AVMRevertStoreAction
avm-revert-to-version	org.alfresco.repo.avm.actions. AVMRevertToVersionAction
avm-undo-list	org.alfresco.repo.avm.actions. AVMUndoSandboxListAction
check-in	org.alfresco.repo.action.executer. CheckInActionExecuter
	org.alfresco.web.bean.actions.handlers. CheckInHandler
check-out	org.alfresco.repo.action.executer. CheckOutActionExecuter
	org.alfresco.web.bean.actions.handlers. CheckOutHandler
composite-action	org.alfresco.repo.action.executer. CompositeActionExecuter
copy-to-web-project	org.alfresco.repo.action.executer. CopyToWebProjectActionExecuter
	org.alfresco.web.bean.actions.handlers. CopyToWebProjectHandler
copy	org.alfresco.repo.action.executer. CopyActionExecuter
	org.alfresco.web.bean.actions.handlers. CopyHandler
count-children	org.alfresco.repo.action.executer. CountChildrenActionExecuter

Action Name (Bean ID)	Action Executer Class / Handler Class (if present)
counter	`org.alfresco.repo.action.executer.` `CounterIncrementActionExecuter`
create-version	`org.alfresco.repo.action.executer.` `CreateVersionActionExecuter`
execute-all-rules	`org.alfresco.repo.action.executer.` `ExecuteAllRulesActionExecuter`
export	`org.alfresco.repo.action.executer.` `ExporterActionExecuter`
extract-metadata	`org.alfresco.repo.action.executer.` `ContentMetadataExtracter`
import	`org.alfresco.repo.action.executer.` `ImporterActionExecuter`
	`org.alfresco.web.bean.actions.handlers.` `ImportHandler`
link-category	`org.alfresco.repo.action.executer.` `LinkCategoryActionExecuter`
	`org.alfresco.web.bean.actions.handlers.` `LinkCategoryHandler`
mail	`org.alfresco.repo.action.executer.` `MailActionExecuter`
	`org.alfresco.web.bean.actions.handlers.` `MailHandler`
move	`org.alfresco.repo.action.executer.` `MoveActionExecuter`
	`org.alfresco.web.bean.actions.handlers.` `MoveHandler`
remove-features	`org.alfresco.repo.action.executer.` `RemoveFeaturesActionExecuter`
	`org.alfresco.web.bean.actions.handlers.` `RemoveFeaturesHandler`
repository-export	`org.alfresco.repo.action.executer.` `RepositoryExporterActionExecuter`
script	`org.alfresco.repo.action.executer.` `ScriptActionExecuter`
	`org.alfresco.web.bean.actions.handlers.` `ScriptHandler`
set-property-value	`org.alfresco.repo.action.executer.` `SetPropertyValueActionExecuter`

Action Name (Bean ID)	Action Executer Class / Handler Class (if present)
simple-avm-promote	org.alfresco.repo.avm.actions. SimpleAVMPromoteAction
simple-avm-submit	org.alfresco.repo.avm.actions. SimpleAVMSubmitAction
simple-workflow	org.alfresco.repo.action.executer. SimpleWorkflowActionExecuter
	org.alfresco.web.bean.actions.handlers. SimpleWorkflowHandler
specialise-type	org.alfresco.repo.action.executer. SpecialiseTypeActionExecuter
	org.alfresco.web.bean.actions.handlers. SpecialiseTypeHandler
start-avm-workflow	org.alfresco.repo.avm.actions. StartAVMWorkflowAction
start-workflow	org.alfresco.repo.workflow. StartWorkflowActionExecuter
transform	org.alfresco.repo.action.executer. TransformActionExecuter
	org.alfresco.web.bean.actions.handlers. TransformHandler
transform-image	org.alfresco.repo.action.executer. ImageTransformActionExecuter
	org.alfresco.web.bean.actions.handlers. TransformImageHandler

Actions Available in Labs Only

These actions are only available in the Labs edition:

Action Name (Bean ID)	Action Executer Class
blog-post	org.alfresco.repo.action.executer.BlogAction
create-thumbnail	org.alfresco.repo.thumbnail. CreateThumbnailActionExecuter
update-tagscope	org.alfresco.repo.tagging. UpdateTagScopesActionExecuter
update-thumbnail	org.alfresco.repo.thumbnail. UpdateThumbnailActionExecuter

Web Client Config Elements

The web client is configured using an XML format proprietary to Alfresco. At a high level, there are two types of configuration elements in the XML. The first type uses an evaluator for condition-specific configuration. The second includes unconditional configuration elements. This section contains one table for each type of configuration element. The tables include what they do and where they can be found out of the box.

Conditional Configuration Elements

This table lists elements that are conditional. Conditional elements use one of the three evaluators: node-type, aspect-name, or string-compare. For example, the out of the box Languages configuration element is shown here:

```
<config evaluator="string-compare" condition="Languages">
    <!-- the list of available language files -->
    <languages>
        <language locale="en_US">English</language>
    </languages>
</config>
```

The following table lists conditional configuration elements:

Evaluator	Condition	What it does	Where it is defined
node-type	[node type]	Configuration for nodes matching a specific node type. Typically used for property sheets, but can be used for any conditional configuration based on node type.	`web-client-config-properties.xml`
aspect-name	[aspect name]	Configuration for nodes that have a matching aspect applied. Typically used for property sheets, but can be used for any conditional configuration based on aspect name.	`web-client-config-properties.xml`
string-compare	Server	Commented out by default; specifies host name and port when using Alfresco behind a proxy.	`web-client-config.xml`
string-compare	Languages	Lists the languages in the login drop-down.	`web-client-config.xml`
string-compare	Views	View selections available in the web client ("list", "details", and "icons")	`web-client-config.xml`

Evaluator	Condition	What it does	Where it is defined
string-compare	Node Event Listeners	Lists JSF-managed beans that the `BrowseBean` should notify on changes.	`web-client-config.xml`
string-compare	Command Servlet	Lists the available servlet command processors.	`web-client-config.xml`
string-compare	Advanced Search	Configures types, folders, aspects, and properties listed on the advanced search page.	`web-client-config.xml`
string-compare	Dashboards	Dashboard layouts and dashlets shown on **My Alfresco**.	`web-client-config.xml`
string-compare	Sidebar	Lists available sidebar plug-ins ("Navigator", "Shelf", and "Open Search").	`web-client-config.xml`
string-compare	Space Wizards	Lists the folder types that show up when you use the Advanced Space Wizard.	`web-client-config.xml`
string-compare	Action Wizards	Lists the types, aspects, and transformers to show in drop-downs when configuring a rule action. Also used to configure condition handler and action handler classes.	`web-client-config.xml`
string-compare	`cm:folder` icons	Lists the icon images to show as choices when a user creates a folder.	`web-client-config.xml`
string-compare	`fm:forums` icons	Specifies the high-level "forums" icon.	`web-client-config.xml`
string-compare	`fm:forum` icons	Specifies the "forum" icon.	`web-client-config.xml`
string-compare	`fm:topic` icons	Specifies the icons related to different post types.	`web-client-config.xml`

Unconditional Configuration Elements

Some web client config elements do not use an evaluator. They are just children of `alfresco-config/config`. For example, this is the start of the out of the box configuration element for wcm:

```
<alfresco-config>
    <config>
        <wcm>
            <workflows>
                wcmwf:submit,scwf:noApprovalSubmit
            </workflows>
    ...
```

The following table shows the unconditional web client configuration elements:

Configuration Element	What it does	Where it is defined
client	Controls various client settings such as the error page, the login page, the number of items you see in certain lists, the default location the user sees on login, and the from email address.	web-client-config.xml
navigation	Configures navigational overrides based on node-type, aspect-name, or other evaluators.	web-client-config-navigation.xml
wizards	Defines multi-step dialogs, or wizards. See Chapter 5.	web-client-config-wizards.xml
dialogs	Defines dialog icon, JSP, and managed beans.	web-client-config-dialogs.xml
actions	Defines UI Actions and action groups. See "Action Groups" in this Appendix.	Various
wcm	Defines the workflows available from within a web project, default view size, XForms widgets, link checking polling frequency, and deployment progress polling frequency.	web-client-config-wcm.xml

Action Groups

Action groups are collections of UI Actions into a menu. You can extend action groups with your own actions. For information on how to do that, see Chapter 5.

Core Web Client Action Groups

These action groups are used in the core web client and are defined in web-client-config-actions.xml:

Action Group ID	Description
add_content_menu	Menu for uploading content
browse_actions_menu	List of UI Actions under **More Actions**
browse_create_menu	List of UI Actions that appears when clicking **Create**
doc_details_actions	List of UI Actions when viewing the details of a document
document_browse	List of UI Actions shown when viewing the document in a list
document_browse_menu	List of UI Actions shown in the **More Actions** menu for a document when the document appears in a list

Action Group ID	Description
file_link_details_actions	List of UI Actions that is shown when viewing the details of a file link
multilingual_details_actions	List of UI Actions that appears when viewing the details of multilingual content
rules_actions_menu	List of UI Actions that is available when managing the rules for a space
space_browse	List of UI Actions shown when viewing the space in a list
space_browse_menu	List of UI Actions shown in the **More Actions** menu for a space when the space appears in a list
space_details_actions	List of UI Actions that is available when looking at the details of a space
spacelink_details_actions	List of UI Actions that is shown when viewing the details of a space link

Forums-Related UI Action Groups

These action groups are related to the discussion threads or forums that can be attached to a piece of content. These action groups are defined in web-client-config-forum-actions.xml.

Action Group ID	Description
forum_actions	List of UI Actions adjacent to an individual topic in the list of topics
forum_actions_menu	List of UI Actions shown in the **More Actions** menu when viewing a list of topics
forum_create_menu	List of UI Actions shown in the **Create** menu when viewing a list of topics
forum_details_actions	List of UI Actions shown when viewing the details of a forum
forums_actions	List of UI Actions shown adjacent to a forum within a forum space
forums_actions_menu	List of UI Actions shown for the **More Actions** menu when viewing a forum space
forums_create_menu	List of UI Actions shown on the **Create** menu when browsing a forum space
forums_details_actions	List of UI Actions shown when viewing the details of a forum space (as opposed to a forum on a specific object)
topic_actions	List of UI Actions adjacent to an individual post when viewing a list of posts
topic_actions_menu	List of UI Actions shown in the **More Actions** menu when viewing a list of posts

Action Group ID	Description
topic_create_menu	List of UI Actions shown in the **Create** menu when viewing a list of posts
topic_details_actions	List of UI Actions available when viewing the details of a post

Workflow-Related Action Groups

The advanced workflow user interface in the web client has its own action configuration, which is defined in `web-client-config-workflow-actions.xml`:

Action Group ID	Description
add_package_item_actions	UI Actions for working with items in a workflow package. The name describes what types of actions are available in each action group.
dashlet_completed_actions	UI Actions for working with completed tasks.
dashlet_pooled_actions	UI Actions that appear in the **Pooled To Do** dashlet for managing pooled workflow tasks.
dashlet_todo_actions	UI Actions that appear in the **To Do** dashlet for managing workflow tasks.
edit_and_delete_wcm_package_item_actions	UI Actions for working with items in a workflow package. The name describes what types of actions are available in each action group.
edit_and_remove_package_item_actions	See above.
edit_and_remove_wcm_package_item_actions	See above.
edit_package_item_actions	See above.
edit_wcm_package_item_actions	See above.
read_package_item_actions	See above.
read_wcm_package_item_actions	See above.
remove_package_item_actions	See above.
remove_wcm_package_item_actions	See above.
review_wcm_package_item_actions	See above.
start_package_item_actions	See above.

WCM-Related Action Groups

Web projects have their own action groups specific to Alfresco's WCM functionality. These actions are defined in `web-client-config-wcm-actions.xml`:

Action Group ID	Description
`avm_create_menu`	UI Actions shown in the **Create** menu when browsing a web site
`avm_deleted_modified`	UI Actions shown adjacent to each deleted web asset in the modified items list
`avm_file_browse`	UI Actions shown adjacent to each web asset in a list when browsing a web site
`avm_file_details`	UI Actions shown when viewing the details of a file
`avm_file_modified`	UI Actions shown adjacent to each modified item in the modified items list
`avm_folder_browse`	UI Actions shown adjacent to each folder in a list when browsing a web site
`avm_folder_details`	UI Actions shown when viewing the details of a folder
`avm_folder_modified`	UI Actions shown adjacent to each modified folder in the modified items list
`avm_more_menu`	UI Actions shown in the **More Actions** menu in a sandbox
`broken_file_actions`	UI Actions shown adjacent to files containing broken links
`broken_form_actions`	UI Actions for files created with web forms that contain broken links
`browse_website_menu`	UI Actions shown in the **Actions** menu when browsing a web project folder
`website_details_actions`	UI Actions shown when viewing the details of a web project folder

Metadata Extractors

Metadata extractors (Chapter 4) are used to inspect a piece of content when it is uploaded to the repository and extract data. The data is then stored in properties on the content's node.

Metadata extractors are defined in `content-services-context.xml`. The following table lists the out of the box metadata extractors, and shows what gets extracted and how it is mapped to the node properties:

Bean ID	Class	Property Map
extracter. PDFBox	org.alfresco.repo. content.metadata. PdfBoxMetadataExtracter	author=cm:author title=cm:title subject=cm:description created=cm:created
extracter. Office	org.alfresco.repo. content.metadata. OfficeMetadataExtracter	author=cm:author title=cm:title subject=cm:description createDateTime=cm:created lastSaveDateTime=cm: modified
extracter. Mail	org.alfresco.repo. content.metadata. MailMetadataExtracter	sentDate=cm:sentdate originator=cm: originator, cm:author addressee=cm:addressee addressees=cm:addressees subjectLine=cm: subjectline, cm: description
extracter. Html	org.alfresco.repo. content.metadata. HtmlMetadataExtracter	author=cm:author title=cm:title description=cm: description
extracter. MP3	org.alfresco.repo.content. metadata.MP3MetadataExtracter	songTitle=music: songTitle, cm:title albumTitle=music: albumTitle artist=music:artist, cm:author description=cm: description comment=music:comment yearReleased=music: yearReleased trackNumber=music: trackNumber genre=music:genre composer=music:composer lyrics=music:lyrics

Bean ID	Class	Property Map
extracter. OpenDocument	org.alfresco.repo. content.metadata. OpenDocumentMetadataExtracter	creationDate=cm:created creator=cm:author date= description= generator= initialCreator= keyword= language= printDate= printedBy= subject=cm:description title=cm:title
extracter. OpenOffice	org.alfresco.repo. content.metadata. OpenOfficeMetadataExtracter	author=cm:author title=cm:title description=cm: description

Transformers

The out of the box transformers are defined in content-services-context.xml. Transformers are used to transform one MIME type to another. Transformers that have a plain text target are also used by the full-text indexer. More information on transformers can be found in Chapter 4.

Bean ID	Class	From	To
transformer. PdfBox	org.alfresco.repo. content.transform. PdfBoxContentTransformer	**application|pdf**	**text|plain**
transformer. PdfBox. TextToPdf	org.alfresco.repo. content.transform. TextToPdfContentTransformer	**text|plain**	**application| pdf**
transformer. Poi	org.alfresco.repo. content.transform. PoiHssfContentTransformer	**application| vnd.excel**	**text|plain**
transformer. TextMining	org.alfresco.repo. content.transform. TextMiningContentTransformer	**application| msword**	**text|plain**

Bean ID	Class	From	To
transformer. HtmlParser	org.alfresco.repo. content.transform. HtmlParserContentTransformer	**text	html**	**text	plain**
transformer. OpenOffice	org.alfresco.repo. content.transform. OpenOfficeContentTransformer	Handles any conversion OpenOffice knows how to do unless the target is XHTML or Word Perfect	
transformer. complex. OpenOffice. PdfBox	org.alfresco.repo. content.transform. PdfBoxContentTransformer	**application	pdf**	**text	plain**
transformer. OutlookMsg	org.alfresco.repo. content.transform. MailContentTransformer	**message	rfc822**	**text	plain**
transformer. ImageMagick	org.alfresco.repo. content.transform.magick. ImageMagickContentTransformer	Handles any type ImageMagick knows how to handle	

Graphical View of the Alfresco Content Model

Sometimes it is helpful to be able to trace the inheritance of types in a model, or identify how objects are related to each other through associations. The definitive reference for this type of information is the set of *Model.xml files distributed with the Alfresco web application. This section shows the content of those files graphically, with one diagram for each model file.

The diagram syntax is essentially UML. The following image shows the `bpm:task` from the `bpmModel.xml` file:

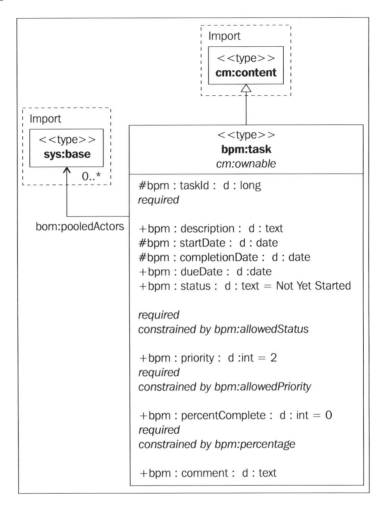

These notes will help you read the diagram:

- The **<<type>>** indicates that this is a type rather than an aspect.
- The type has one mandatory aspect, **cm:ownable**, shown in italics just below the type name.
- The type has several properties. Properties that begin with a hash (**taskId**, for example) are protected. Properties that begin with a plus (**bpm:description**, for example) are public.

- The **bpm:status** property has a default value of **Not Yet Started**, and it is a mandatory property and has a constraint on its values.

- Two imported types are shown. The **cm:content** type is the parent type as indicated by the line with a triangle. The **sys:base** type is the target of an association called **bpm:pooledActors**. In this case, there can be zero or many instances of **sys:base** associated with a **bpm:task**.

System Model

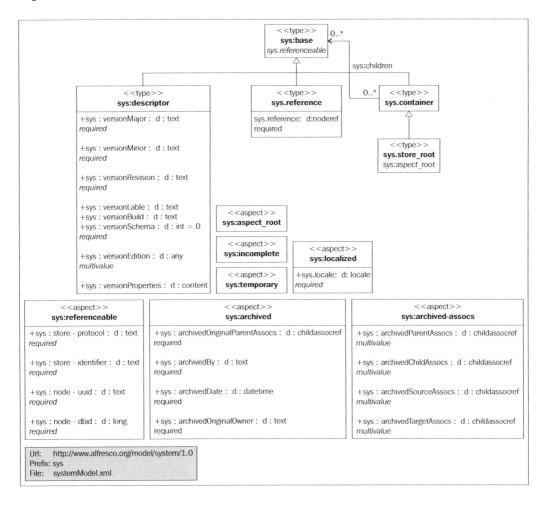

User Model

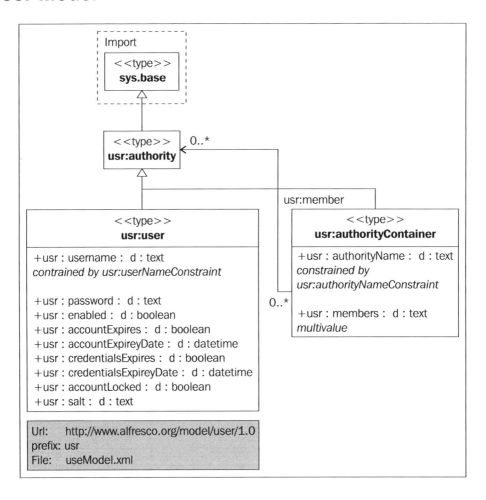

Content Model

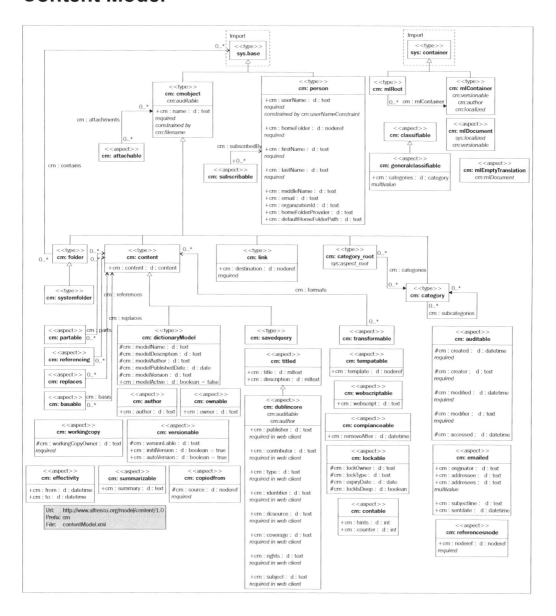

App Model

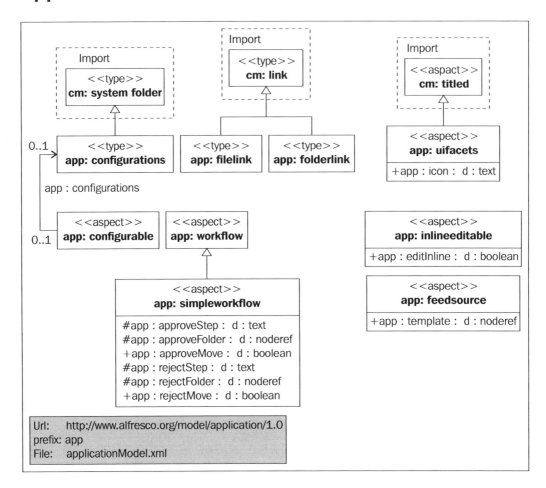

BPM Model

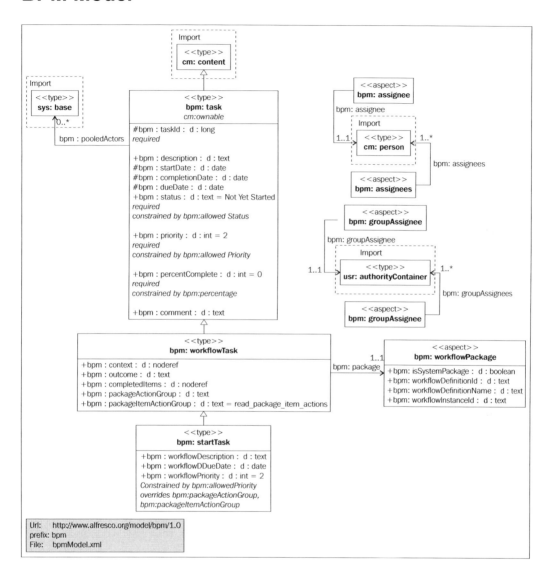

Workflow Model

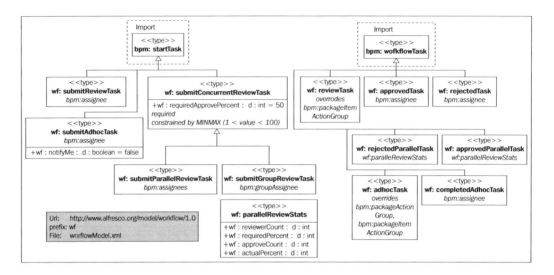

WCM Model

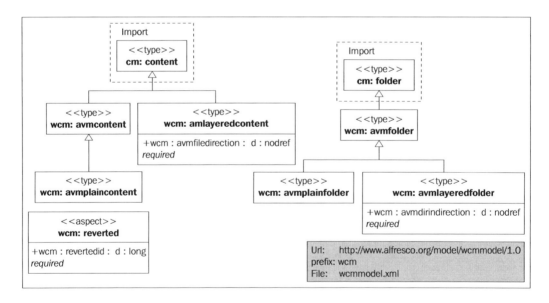

WCM App Model

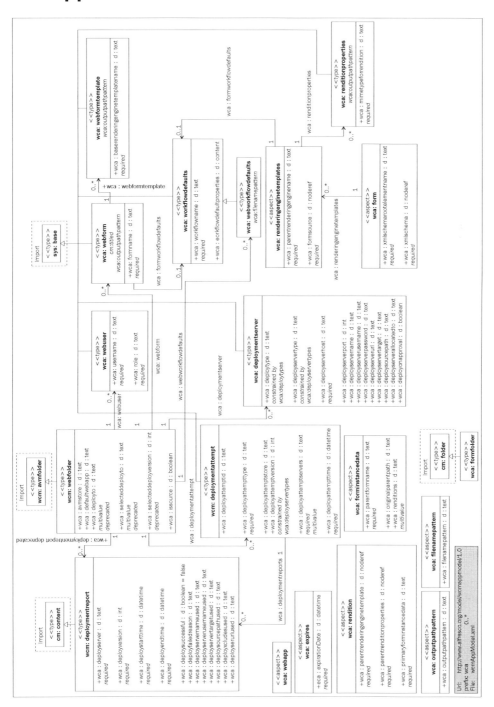

WCM Workflow Model

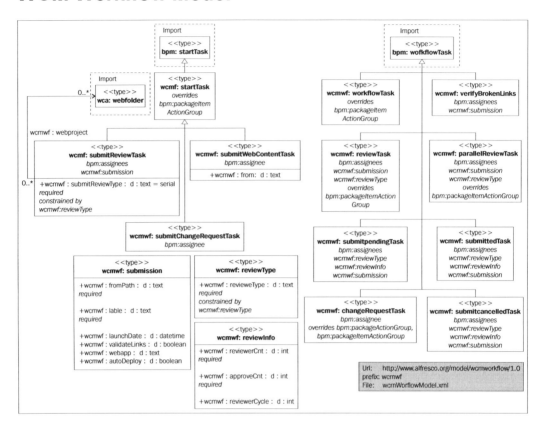

Index

D

data
  handling 259
data, handling
  file upload, using in multipart
      form 261, 262
  form-based Hello World,
      implementing 259, 260
data, retrieving
  debugging 232
  error handling code 238, 239
  facts 232, 233
  file system, using 234
  optional argument, specifying 238
  repository and file system, choosing
      between 235
  URL, choosing 234
  web script, creating 226-231
  web script, organizing 233
  web script, overriding 233
  web script, using 225
  Whitepaper rating, retrieving 235-237
deployment methods, jBPM GPD
  location 295
  mimetype setting 295
  redloy flag 295
  Spring 294
  using 294
DM and WCM
  diffrerences between 343, 344
Document Management. *See* **DM, Alfresco**
DM, Alfresco
  about 8, 342
  examples 8
  functionalities 9
  implementing 7, 10

E

editions, Alfresco
  differences 30
  Enterprise edition 30
  Labs edition 29
error handling code, data
  naming conventions 240

extension mechanism, Alfresco
  about 38
  file types, creating 38
  framework files 39
  standard Java web application files 38
externalized label
  configuring 85
  locales, creating 86

F

field search, Lucene Queries
  category 475
  ID 474
  PARENT 474
  PATH 474
  QNAME 475
  saved searches, using as example 476
  TEXT 475
  TYPE and ASPECT 473
File System Receiver. *See* **FSR**
framework files, extension mechanism
  Alfresco code modification, avoiding 46
  Alfresco configuration files 43
  Alfresco configuration files, example 44, 45
  Alfresco configuration files, overriding 43
  Alfresco configuration modification,
      avoiding 46
  JSF configuration files 41
  solution specific files 45, 46
  spring configuration files 39
  spring configuration files, example 39-41
  spring configuration files, overriding 39
FSR 377
FSR, content
  multiple FSR hosts, running 377
  multiple FSR targets, running 377
functionalities, WCM
  deployment 343
  preview 342
  sandboxes 342
  snapshots and rollback 343
  virtualization 342
  web forms 342
  workflow 342

G

general utility classes, JavaScript API
  association 478
  cache 486
  ChildAssociation 479
  crossRepoCopy 486
  listing 478
  logger 487
  ScriptNode 479-485
  ScriptUtils 486
  status 487
graphical view, Alfresco content model
  App Model 518
  BPM Model 519
  Content Model 517
  System Model 515
  User Model 516
  WCM App Model 521
  WCM Model 520
  WCM Workflow Model 522

H

Hello World process definitions,
    process definitions
  creating, steps 284, 285
  nodes 284
Hello World web script, web script
    framework
  implementing, steps 217, 218

I

init method, logic
  using 121
interface, logic 122

J

Java-Backed web script
  writing 241
Java-Backed web script, writing
  Java, using for controller logic 247
  JavaScript, using for controller logic 247
  steps 242-246
  testing 247

  web script bean ID, using 247
Java Process Definition Language. *See* **jPDL**
JavaScript
  JavaScript API 478
  root objects 477
JavaScript API, JavaScript
  action API 488
  AVM API 488
  Classification API 491
  general utility classes, listing 478
  People API 492
  Presence API 493
  Search API 493
JavaScript content
  batch manipulation 88
  document, saving 87
  root objects 87
  writing, to content property 88
JavaServer Faces. *See* **JSF**
Java simple behavior
  creating 118-121
  writting 118
  writting, requirements 118
Java Web services content
  Content Manipulation Language (CML) 90
  Content Manipulation Language (CML),
    executing 91
  creating 88, 89
  SomeCoDataCreator class, running 92
  steps, overviewing 88
  stores 89
  workspaces 89
jBPM engine 283
jBPM GPD
  dependencies, deploying 294
  deployment methods, using 294
  node types 293
  process definitions, versioning 293, 294
  processes, creating 287
  processes, deploying 287
  processes, implementing 288-292
  token 292
  using 286, 287
jBPM Graphical Process Designer. *See*
    jBPM GPD
jPDL 283

Thank you for buying
Alfresco Developer Guide

Packt Open Source Project Royalties

When we sell a book written on an Open Source project, we pay a royalty directly to that project. Therefore by purchasing Alfresco Developer Guide, Packt will have given some of the money received to the Alfresco Team.

In the long term, we see ourselves and you—customers and readers of our books—as part of the Open Source ecosystem, providing sustainable revenue for the projects we publish on. Our aim at Packt is to establish publishing royalties as an essential part of the service and support a business model that sustains Open Source.

If you're working with an Open Source project that you would like us to publish on, and subsequently pay royalties to, please get in touch with us.

Writing for Packt

We welcome all inquiries from people who are interested in authoring. Book proposals should be sent to author@packtpub.com. If your book idea is still at an early stage and you would like to discuss it first before writing a formal book proposal, contact us; one of our commissioning editors will get in touch with you.

We're not just looking for published authors; if you have strong technical skills but no writing experience, our experienced editors can help you develop a writing career, or simply get some additional reward for your expertise.

About Packt Publishing

Packt, pronounced 'packed', published its first book "Mastering phpMyAdmin for Effective MySQL Management" in April 2004 and subsequently continued to specialize in publishing highly focused books on specific technologies and solutions.

Our books and publications share the experiences of your fellow IT professionals in adapting and customizing today's systems, applications, and frameworks. Our solution-based books give you the knowledge and power to customize the software and technologies you're using to get the job done. Packt books are more specific and less general than the IT books you have seen in the past. Our unique business model allows us to bring you more focused information, giving you more of what you need to know, and less of what you don't.

Packt is a modern, yet unique publishing company, which focuses on producing quality, cutting-edge books for communities of developers, administrators, and newbies alike. For more information, please visit our website: www.PacktPub.com.

Alfresco Enterprise Content Management Implementation

ISBN: 978-1-904811-11-4   Paperback: 350 pages

How to Install, use, and customize this powerful, free, Open Source Java-based Enterprise CMS

1. Manage your business documents: version control, library services, content organization, and search

2. Workflows and business rules: move and manipulate content automatically when events occur

3. Maintain, extend, and customize Alfresco: backups and other admin tasks, customizing and extending the content model, creating your own look and feel

Liferay Portal Enterprise Intranets

ISBN: 978-1-847192-72-1   Paperback: 336 pages

A practical guide to building a complete corporate intranet with Liferay

1. Install, set up, and use a corporate intranet with Liferay—a complete guide

2. Discussions, document management, collaboration, blogs, and more

3. Clear, step-by-step instructions, practical examples, and straightforward explanation

Mastering OpenLDAP

ISBN: 978-1-847191-02-1   Paperback: 400 pages

Install, Configure, Build, and Integrate Secure Directory Services with OpenLDAP server in a networked environment

1. Up-to-date with the latest OpenLDAP release

2. Installing and configuring the OpenLDAP server

3. Synchronizing multiple OpenLDAP servers over the network

4. Creating custom LDAP schemas to model your own information

Business Process Management with JBoss jBPM

ISBN: 978-1-847192-36-3   Paperback: 300 pages

Develop business process models for implementation in a business process management system.

1. Map your business processes in an efficient, standards-friendly way

2. Use the jBPM toolset to work with business process maps, create a customizable user interface for users to interact with the process, collect process execution data, and integrate with existing systems.

3. Set up business rules, assign tasks, work with process variables, automate activities and decisions.

Please check **www.PacktPub.com** for information on our titles

17805226R00296

Made in the USA
Lexington, KY
28 September 2012